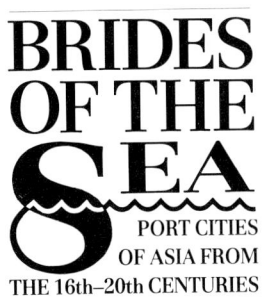

BRIDES OF THE SEA

PORT CITIES OF ASIA FROM THE 16th–20th CENTURIES

Trade and tribute: the Dutch East India Company (VOC) as Queen of the East, with the nations of Asia offering her their goods. Title page from Francois Valentijn *Oud en Nieuw Oost Indien* Dordrecht, 1724-26.
Courtesy of Mitchell Library, State Library of New South Wales.

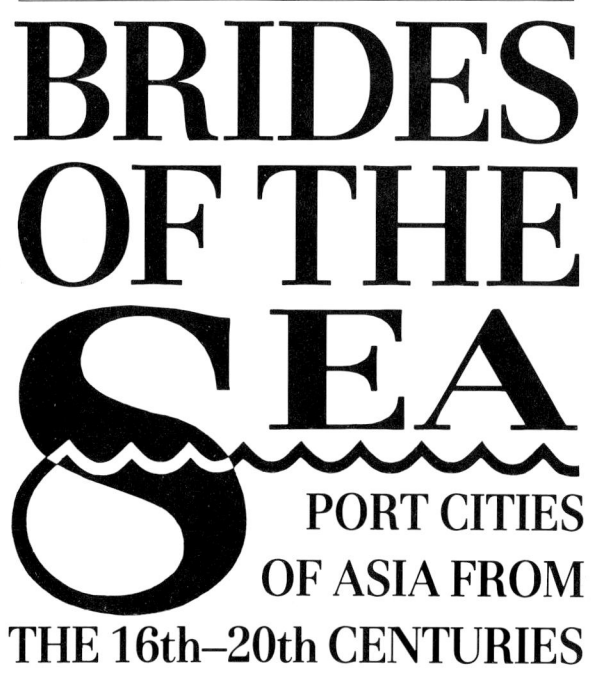

BRIDES OF THE SEA

PORT CITIES OF ASIA FROM THE 16th–20th CENTURIES

Edited by
Frank Broeze

UNIVERSITY OF HAWAII PRESS
HONOLULU

© Frank Broeze 1989

All Rights Reserved

Published in North America by
University of Hawaii Press
2840 Kolowalu Street
Honolulu, Hawaii 96822

Simultaneously Published in Australia by
New South Wales University Press
PO Box 1 Kensington NSW Australia 2033

Printed in Singapore

Library of Congress Cataloguing-in-Publication Data

Brides of the sea: port cities of Asia from the 16th to the 20th
centuries / edited by Frank Broeze.
    p. cm.
    Includes index.
    ISBN 0 8248 1266 2 : $32.00.
    1. Harbors — Asia, Southeastern — History. 2. Harbors — South Asia
  — History. I. Broeze, Frank.
HE559.A75B75 1989
387.1'0954 — dc20   89-4891
                                          CIP

Contents

Preface to the Series vii
Illustrations viii
Tables x
Figures xi
Maps xii
Contributors xiii
Acknowledgements xvi

Introduction: Brides of the Sea 1
   Frank Broeze

1 Studying the Asian port city 29
   Peter Reeves, Frank Broeze and Kenneth McPherson

2 The organisation of production in the pre-colonial Southeast Asian port city 54
   Anthony Reid

3 European port-settlements in the Coromandel commercial system 1650-1740 75
   S. Arasaratnam

4	Eastern emporium and company town: trade and society in eighteenth-century Makassar *Heather Sutherland*	97
5	The transformation of a semi-colonial port city: Shanghai, 1843-1941 *Robert Y. Eng*	129
6	Colombo: gateway and oceanic hub of shipping *K. Dharmasena*	152
7	The two faces of the port city: Colombo in modern times *Michael Roberts*	173
8	Maritime perspectives on ports and port systems: the case of East Africa *B. S. Hoyle*	188
9	Port cities in a national system of ports and cities: a geographical analysis of India in the twentieth century *Atiya Habeeb Kidwai*	207
10	On the evolution of the port city *Rhoads Murphey*	223
	Index	247

Preface to the Series

Sponsored by the Asian Studies Association of Australia, *Comparative Studies in Asian History and Society* is a new publishing venture designed to meet the peculiar imperatives of academic discourse on this continent.

For many years, the Association has published three regional monograph series for South, Southeast and East Asia. Serving as a spatial capstone to the regional series, *Comparative Studies* ranges across the whole of Asia, reaching as far as East Africa and the Western Pacific. Chronologically, there are no limits. Reflecting the composition of Australia's Asia specialists, however, we expect that most volumes will deal with modern history or contemporary problems. Thematically, we intend to produce a series which is strongly comparative. Supervised by a guest editor, each volume will be well integrated and broadly thematic, encouraging discourse across the regional boundaries.

Although format will vary with topic, most volumes will include an extended analytical essay by the editors, substantive chapters by specialists, and a survey of the literature in each field. We hope that each volume will become both benchmark of existing scholarly study and guide to future research.

Alfred W. McCoy and M. N. Pearson
General Editors
Kensington, New South Wales
January 1989

Illustrations

1	The Dutch East India Company as Queen of the East	frontispiece
2	The exotic world of the maritime era	5
3	Mocha, the main focus of international trade around the Red Sea	7
4	The Dutch Factory in Surat, West India	15
5	Javanese inhabitants of Banten (Bantam), west Java	25
6	A Chinese junk	31
7	A street scene in Goa, western India	33
8	A 'Tupas' or 'Mardijker' of Batavia (Jakarta), and his wife	36
9	Javanese and Malay vessels	38
10	The Governor's house in the castle of Batavia	41
11	The family of a 'Moorish pedlar' of Batavia	43
12	Banten, c. 1630	46
13	A depiction of the city of Aceh, north Sumatra	56
14	View of eighteenth-century Melaka, Malaysia	58-59
15	The castle of Ambon, eastern Indonesia, in 1607	62
16	Nutmeg-weighing at Nera in Banda, eastern Indonesia	66
17	Direct trade in a bay in Borneo	68
18	The markets at Banten	70
19	Portuguese aboard a ship off the Malabar Coast	78
20	Paleacat (Pulicat), Coromandel Coast, a Dutch trading base	81
21	View of the Coromandel Coast	84

22	Fort St George and Madras, 1709	88
23	Hugli, Calcutta	89
24	Tuticorin, a pearl-trading post in South India	95
25	Ternate, one of the former major Sultanates of eastern Indonesia	101
26	'An Ambonese soldier', eastern Indonesia	103
27	Somba Opu Fort, Makassar, eastern Indonesia	105
28	Kampung Melayu, Makassar, c. 1840	110
29	A Javanese trader of Batavia, c. 1680	116
30	Amboina (Ambon), the mestizo port town of eastern Indonesia	125
31	View of Macau from the harbour	131
32	The Matzou Chinese temple of Macau	140
33	Jaffna, the northern port of Sri Lanka	166
34	Kandy, the inland capital of Sri Lanka	180
35	Ayutthaya, the Thai capital	224
36	View of Manila in the surrounding landscape	226
37	The fishmarket of Batavia	229
38	'Prau of the Sultan of Batchian', eastern Indonesia	231
39	Two complementary views of Batavia	233
40	Meimbun, Sulu Island, southern Philippines	239
41	Dobbo (Aru) 'in the Trading Season'	244

Tables

2.1	Comparison of the rice needs of workers in various cities	63
5.1	Shanghai's share of total foreign trade of China, 1870-1930	132
5.2	Population of Shanghai, 1855-1930	149
6.1	Tonnage of shipping using Galle and Colombo, 1855-79	156
6.2	Tonnage of shipping using Colombo, and value of Sri Lanka's trade, 1858-82	158
6.3	Distribution of tonnage of shipping using Sri Lanka ports among the major trade routes, 1860-69	160
6.4	World ranking of ports, 1910	167
6.5	The oil trade of Colombo and Aden, 1924-32	168
6.6	Percentage of shipping that entered and cleared at Colombo with working cargo, 1914-39	170
8.1	Container traffic at major East African seaports, 1975-83	204
9.1	Variability of ranks of major ports in India, 1920-80	213
9.2	Percentage share of cargo handled by major ports in India, 1915-20 to 1981-85	214
9.3	Port workers, total workers and transport workers in the major port cities of India, 1961-86	216
9.4	Sectoral distribution of workers in the primate port cities, 1872-1981	217
9.5	Industrial structure of the primate port cities of India, 1901, 1971	218
9.6	Percentage distribution of tertiary workers in the primate port cities of India, 1961, 1971	219

Figures

5.1	Value of total Shanghai trade, 1872-1928	132
5.2	Total shipping tonnage entering and clearing Shanghai, 1873-1928	133
5.3	Total shipping tonnage entering and clearing Shanghai, by nationality of registration, 1873-1928	138
5.4	Share of shipping tonnage in and out of Shanghai, by nationality of registration, 1871-1930	138
5.5	Population of Shanghai, 1865-1930	145
5.6	Production capacity of Shanghai silk filatures, 1887-1933	145
5.7	Production capacity of Shanghai cotton mills, 1890-1935	146
8.1	Some elements in port geography	190

Maps

1	Port cities of Asia and the Asian Seas	2
2	Jeddah, c. 1980	10
3	The Arabian/Persian Gulf	20
4	Yokohama during its brief phase as a semi-colonial city, 1870	47
5	Maritime Southeast Asia, c. 1600	49
6	The Coromandel Coast, c. 1700	76
7	Makassar and its trading world, c. 1750	99
8	Makassar: Fort Rotterdam and environs, seventeenth century	112
9	Shanghai and maritime China	134
10	Semi-colonial Shanghai, 1843-1941	135
11	Colombo and the steam shipping of the Indian Ocean	153
12	The transport network of Sri Lanka, 1814-1913	163
13	The seaports of East Africa, 1500, 1850 and 1980	194
14	The port of Mombasa, Kenya	201
15	The port of Dar es Salaam, Tanganyika	203
16	The ports of India, twentieth century	211
17	Major ports and chief commercially productive areas in East Asia, 1600-1940	235

Contributors

S. Arasaratnam   Professor of History at the University of New England, Armidale. His research and publications are on the maritime and commercial history of Coromandel and the Bay of Bengal in the seventeenth and eighteenth centuries. He has worked in archival sources in London, The Hague, Madras, Colombo, Singapore and Kuala Lumpur and has travelled widely in the region about which he writes.

Frank Broeze   Associate Professor in History, University of Western Australia. Research interests in many aspects of maritime affairs, including the history of port cities, overseas trade, merchant shipping, seafaring and 'maritime ideology'. Formerly editor of *The Great Circle*. Recent publications include 'Markets' in M. Aveling and A. Atkinson (eds) *Australians 1838* Sydney, 1987; 'Engineering and Empire: The Making of the Modern Indian Ocean Ports' in Satish Chandra (ed.) *The Indian Ocean. Explorations in History, Commerce & Politics* New Delhi, 1987 (with Peter Reeves and Kenneth McPherson); *A Merchant's Perspective: Jacobus Boelen's Visit to Hawaii in 1828* Honolulu, 1988; and 'Robert Brooks (1790-1882)' in R. T. Appleyard and C. B. Schedvin (eds) *Australian Financiers* Melbourne, 1988.

K. Dharmasena Professor and head of the Department of Economics, University of Kelaniya, Sri Lanka. Published works include his doctoral thesis, 'The Port of Colombo 1860-1939' and a number of articles on maritime affairs, most in international journals. He serves on the Editorial Board of *International Journal of Maritime History* (Norwegian School of Economics and Memorial University of Canada). He has written the *Status Report on the Teaching and Research in Economics in Sri Lanka* for UNESCO, Bangkok.

Robert Y. Eng Associate Professor of History at the University of Redlands, California, USA. He is the author of *Economic Imperialism in China: Silk Production and Exports, 1861-1932* Berkeley 1986 and numerous articles on the socio-economic history of Qing and Republican China and the demographic history of Tokugawa Japan.

B. S. Hoyle Reader in Geography at the University of Southampton, England. His research interests focus on tropical development and transport geography, especially seaports, and his numerous publications include a major study, *The Seaports of East Africa*.

Atiya Habeeb Kidwai Associate Professor, Centre for the Study of Regional Development, Jawaharlal Nehru University, New Delhi. She has degrees in Geography, Regional Planning and Social Sciences. Her current research focuses on themes related to the history of urbanisation in colonial India.

Kenneth McPherson Post-doctoral Humboldt Fellow at the University of Heidelberg. He is currently director of the Centre for Indian Ocean Regional Studies at Curtin University and is working with Frank Broeze and Peter Reeves on Indian Ocean maritime history projects.

Rhoads Murphey Professor of History and Asian Studies at the University of Michigan. President of the Association for Asian Studies. His teaching, research and publications have been characterised by a multidisciplinary approach. He has taught at the universities of Washington, Pennsylvania, Cambridge, Tokyo, Sichuan, and the National Taiwan University. His many publications include *An Introduction to Geography* New York 1961, 4th edn 1978, *The Fading of the Maoist Vision* New York 1980 and several which immediately and closely relate to the port city concept. The two most important ones for creating academic interest in the role of port cities and providing the stimulus for further research and thought, including that which has found its way into this volume, are *Shanghai: Key to Modern China* Cambridge, Mass. 1953 and 'Traditionalism and Colonialism: Changing Urban Roles in Asia' *Journal of Asian Studies* 29 1969, pp. 67-84. Others which should be noted are *The Treaty Ports and China's Modernization* Ann Arbor 1970, *China Meets the West: The Treaty Ports* New York 1975 and *The Outsiders: Westerners in India and China* Ann Arbor 1977.

Peter Reeves Deputy Vice-Chancellor (Arts, Education and Social Sciences), Curtin University, Perth. His research interests are in India and the Indian Ocean. He is currently working with Frank Broeze and Kenneth McPherson on trade and shipping in the Indian Ocean and on a study of the maritime world of the Indian Ocean since 1815. He has also research under way on the effects of modernisation on the traditional fishing industry of India.

Anthony Reid Senior Fellow in Southeast Asian History at the Research School of Pacific Studies, Australian National University. He is the author of *Southeast Asia in the Age of Commerce I The Lands below the winds* (1988); *The Blood of the People: Revolution and the end of traditional rule in northern Sumatra* (1979); *The Indonesian National Revolution* (1974); and *The Contest for North Sumatra* (1969).

Michael Roberts Reader in the Department of Anthropology, University of Adelaide. He has taught history at Peradeniya University, Sri Lanka. He has published two books on nationalism in Sri Lanka and one entitled *Caste Conflict and Elite Formation*. He is director of the Ceylon Studies Seminar and editor of *Modern Ceylon Studies* and *Social Analysis*.

Heather Sutherland Professor of Non-Western History at the Free University, Amsterdam. She worked at the University of Malaysia from 1972 to 1974. Her research interests concentrate on the social history of Malaysia and Indonesia, from the eighteenth to the twentieth centuries.

Acknowledgements

Several people have contributed to the lengthy process of making this book. The editor, and the general editors, wish to thank Douglas Howie, managing director of the New South Wales University Press, for his patience, helpfulness, and enthusiasm. Venetia Nelson was a diligent and efficient copy editor; we thank her for her efforts. This volume is in a sense two books—a text written by many hands; and a visual essay of etchings, maps and figures. We thank the contributors of the various essays, especially Rhoads Murphey who pioneered studies in the field and contributed a valuable overview for this volume. Viv Forbes at the University of Western Australia drew most of the fine maps which illustrate this volume. The etchings which comprise an autonomous visual essay were selected by Dr Adrian Vickers of the University of New South Wales. Drawing upon his expertise on European representations of Asia, Dr Vickers has constructed a lively and informative graphic essay showing Western images of the East from the sixteenth to the nineteenth centuries.

Frank Broeze

Introduction:
Brides of the Sea

My responsibility and my concern are twofold—for the dynamic growth of a flourishing modern city and for the preservation of the religious, social and environmental attributes of our ancient, Islamic, Arab Jeddah, 'Bride of the Red Sea'.

It is not enough to plan, organise and monitor the development of a major city. The quality of life and of the place itself are central to the scheme of things. I am reminded of Ibn Khaldun, six centuries ago: 'The purpose of cities is to provide a place to build and to give shelter. One must keep out what is harmful and bring in what is useful ... The craft of architecture is the first and oldest craft of sedentary civilisation.'

It is a ceaseless challenge ... to cope with the tremendous pressures of rapid growth, and the improvement, beautification and renewal of the city.

Few phrases could so effectively evoke the notions of continuity despite dramatic change, of the blending rather than the succession of the traditional and the modern, of the integration of the religious and the secular, of the inner idea and the outer physical and visual world, than these words. They were written in 1980 by the man who perhaps more than any other through his location, career and vision, embodies the human element in the Asian port city standing at the crossroads of modernisation: Mohamed Said Farsi, architect by profession and as mayor of Jeddah presiding over and responsible for what has probably been one of the most dramatic and large-scale transformations of any port city in Asia (or the world for that matter). Presented in striking

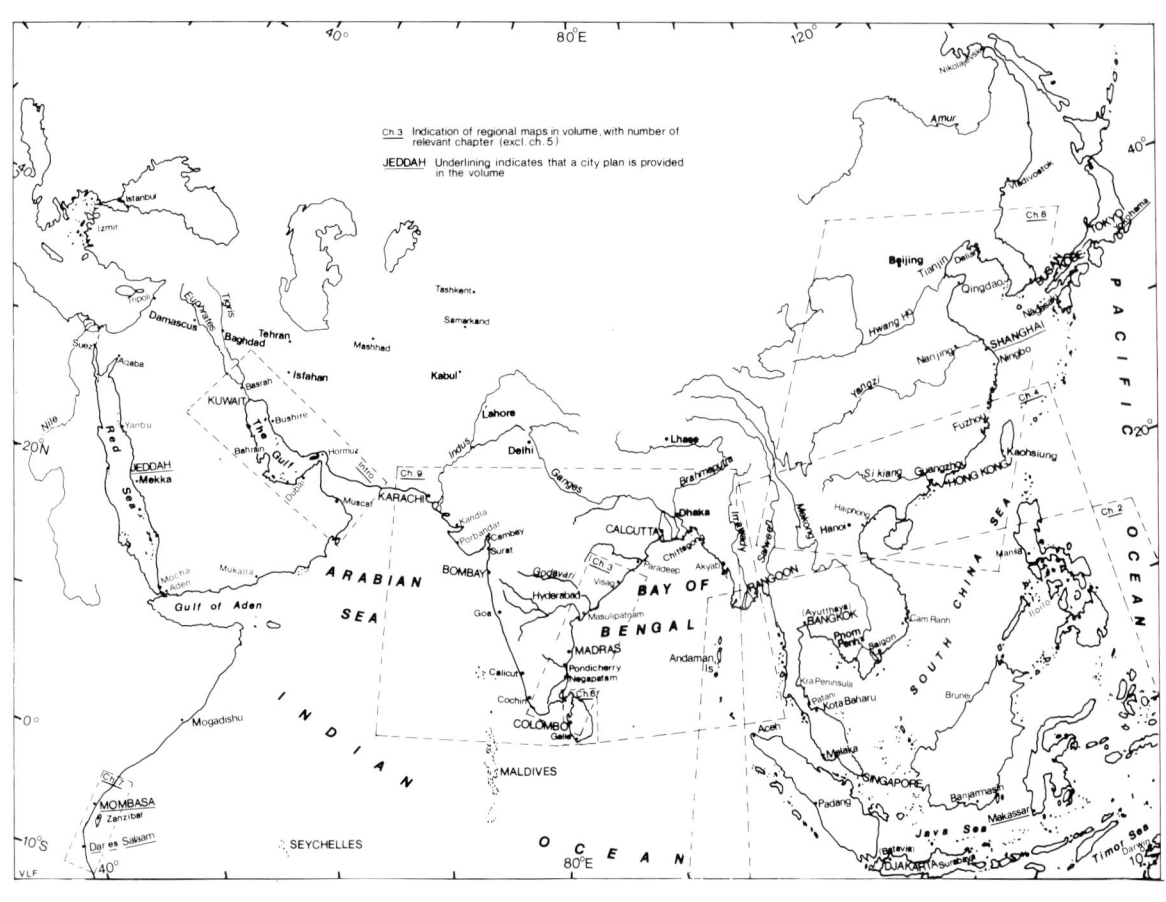

Map 1 Port cities of Asia and the Asian Seas

juxtaposition with a double-page photograph of the new hajj passenger terminal at Jeddah's International Airport, stunningly designed in the shape of a Beduin tent camp, Farsi's words introduce a magnificent and sensitive book, which as a textual and visual portrait of and a tribute to 'the city of Jeddah—Jeddah old, and Jeddah new'—is the visual counterpart and elaboration of his deep concerns and his economic and ideological objectives.[1]

Many might immediately object that they could not possibly regard Jeddah, risen phoenix-like out of the oil wealth of Saudi Arabia,[2] as representative for Asia as a whole. Indeed, 'Asia' to many historians and others is no more than a geographical term devoid of generic meaning. They would argue that the obvious divergence in the historical experiences and civilisations of—to use modern, strategic parlance—Northeast, Southeast, South and Southwest Asia in many ways transcends whatever cohesive explanatory power lies in the inanimate Asian land mass with its adjacent islands and archipelagoes. From the maritime perspective, at first sight there appear to be even starker contrasts between, for example, the seaborne character of the Malay world and the vast land-based tributary empires which for much of the historical period dominated China and India. In consequence, the nature and role of overseas trade, political economy and ideology have differed greatly from region to region, and from time to time. While all of this is largely incontestable, the fact remains that over the last two millennia, and probably longer, the littoral of much of Asia (and, connected to it, the Swahili coast of East Africa) did show a similarity of experience and development which make it stand out against, for example, West Africa or the Americas. Continuously nurtured by myriads of small fishing communities, a network of regional and, in due course, oceanic communications evolved which, through the requirements as well as the rewards of overseas shipping, trade and passenger traffic led to the formation and growth of littoral settlements. These settlements, in the beginnings often seasonal only, in the course of time grew into port towns and larger, more fully developed port cities.[3] Linked together by long-distance searoutes and centrally located entrepots in a string of closely related regional systems stretching from East Asia around the continent and across the Indian Ocean to East Africa (to which sea space a new generic name, such as 'the Asian Seas', might well be given), these port cities through their maritime functions did have much more in common than their hinterlands or the political entities, in which they were located, could ever have.

Thus I should venture to suggest that one can in the essence of Jeddah's history and experiences discern many elements, influences and trends, which, far from being idiosyncratic and relating only to its specific historical and locational conditions, are of a much more general nature. As such they constitute the locally flavoured manifestation of broad developments shared by many if not all of its sister port cities around Asia's littoral. Many of Jeddah's historical moments as a port city can be found to lie equally at the heart of their collective experiences during the last five centuries, perhaps even the last two millennia or more. Two quite different examples may immediately suggest the range of such social and material highlights: the long-time dominance enjoyed by her commercial elite and the demolition of her city walls for the express purpose of obtaining the building material for her modern harbour.

Indeed, if one accepts the functional model proposed in Chapter 1 of this volume by Reeves, McPherson and Broeze, viz. that port cities through their very existence and functioning as true 'brides of the sea' link together their respective hinterlands and forelands in dynamic unions giving birth to urban communities of a very special character and atmosphere, then it is possible to see how such historical similarities resulted from their very nature as port cities. Jeddah like her sister port cities served as the focal arena for economic, social and cultural interactions spanning the full range of human endeavour and experience on three levels of ascending order: between the primate port city and its subordinated hinterland containing both countryside with its villages, towns and markets, and regional sea space spanned by shipping links with minor ports; between the various regional sub-systems of Asia; and, finally between Asia as a whole and the outside world. Thus port cities encapsulate in their evolution and transformation—and, at times, their decline or even total destruction—the historical vicissitudes of maritime Asia, which in themselves are a rough yardstick and, in many ways, an effective paradigm of the relative position of Asia in the world. Hence it is not surprising that authors such as Murphey, Basu and King have seen Asia's port cities above all as the gateways through which European power and influence, economic dominance and technological modernisation (to which could be added diseases and health care)[4] flowed from overseas to the furthest corners of the continent and as primate cities controlling their hinterlands and acting as vital lynchpins in the development of the world economic system.[5]

What must be stressed here, however, is that these exchange functions of Asia's 'port cities', at both gateways and entrepots, were not a phenomenon exclusive to the colonial period, created and sustained by European expansion and penetration into Asia. If defined in broader than eurocentric and 'colonial-specific' terms, they clearly are not limited in space and time but of a universal character and applicability. Jeddah herself had strong roots predating Muslim times already in A.D. 648 when its historical rise began as caliph Othman designated it as the port for Mekka.[6] Ever since that moment Jeddah was the uncontested premier port of the Hejaz, the Muslim Holy Land, and as such the gateway through which millions of hajis passed—as well as unknown quantities of trade goods. This commercial dimension made it during the hajj season one of the most remarkable meeting and market places of Asia, dominating the Red Sea as well as knotting together overseas links with Egypt, Africa, South and Southeast Asia.

Yet, it would be foolish to deny that no difference existed in the roles and, for that matter, the internal evolution of colonial port cities under western control and those which nominally or also factually remained outside the power of the colonisers. Prime examples of the latter are, of course, found in Japan,

The exotic world of the maritime era: the parade of rulers, inhabitants, cultures and natural produce of the East and West Indies was to the Europeans a true paradise of trade and opportunity. From Hendrik Nieuhof *Joan Nieuhofs Gedenkwaerdighe Zee-en Lant-reize door de voornaemste Landschappen van West en Oostindien* Amsterdam, 1682.
Courtesy of Mitchell Library, State Library of New South Wales.

which during the centuries preceding its rapid modernisation associated with the Meiji Restoration effectively closed all its harbours, except Nagasaki, to foreigners.[7] Here was only the ephemeral hint of a 'semi-colonial' experience equal to that of China—in our context perhaps best symbolised by the British trading house Jardine Matheson & Co., as they had done in Shanghai, purchasing Lot No. 1 in the first land sales at Yokohama[8]—before indigenous political and economic power took control over their destiny. Nevertheless, and to some extent just because of the very active way in which Japanese overseas trade and maritime enterprise developed, Japanese port cities functioned very much like colonial Bombay or Batavia in acting as the conduit, and often also location, for the modernisation and secularisation of the country. Thailand provides a quite different scenario: no colonial power was established there, but Western economic influence was as extensive as in many other areas of Southeast Asia. The careful manoeuvring of the Thai government between Britain and France—the meeting zone of whose expanding empires Thailand had unwittingly become—can explain the relatively strong impact made by 'non-imperialist' Scandinavians; yet, through Bangkok they were westernisers as all other Europeans. By contrast to Japanese port cities however, Bangkok had already experienced, and inevitably passed on to its hinterland, strong influences from Chinese trade, merchants and the immigrants who came in their wake. Basra (Iraq) and Jeddah (Hejaz) in Southwest Asia for a long time also experienced little direct influence from western sources, but certainly were not immune against forces—material, social, cultural as well as ideological—from the Asian port cities and regions with which they maintained regular contacts.[9] In fact, in the long run these Asian linkages and influences may well turn out to have been of greater impact and more lasting duration than those associated with Western expansion.

What indeed now can be perceived with more clarity than even as little as a decade ago is that the 'era of Vasco da Gama', the ages of the Portuguese, the East India Companies, Western colonialism and imperialism, however incisive they at one time may have appeared to be, did not make Asia undergo a metamorphosis in which it was altered irrecognisably and permanently according to Europe's image. Just as the political overlordship of Europe ultimately proved to be ephemeral, just so the inner forces of Asia, albeit influenced in many ways by ever more intensive material, social and ideological interactions with the Western world (including in due course also the United States and the Soviet Union), have thrown off their shackles and reassumed their once-lost prominence and vigour. At the same time and more than just symbolically, since World War II Asia has gradually assumed the mantle of maritime leadership of the world. It is now the leading continent in terms of shipbuilding and shipping and the value and volume of its seaborne trade. In 1985 the value of transpacific trade surpassed that carried across the Atlantic Ocean. Asian ports and port cities are leaders in cargo throughput, industrialisation, modernisation and productivity. While Asian merchant fleets are now largely crewed and officered by their own nationals, Asian seafarers

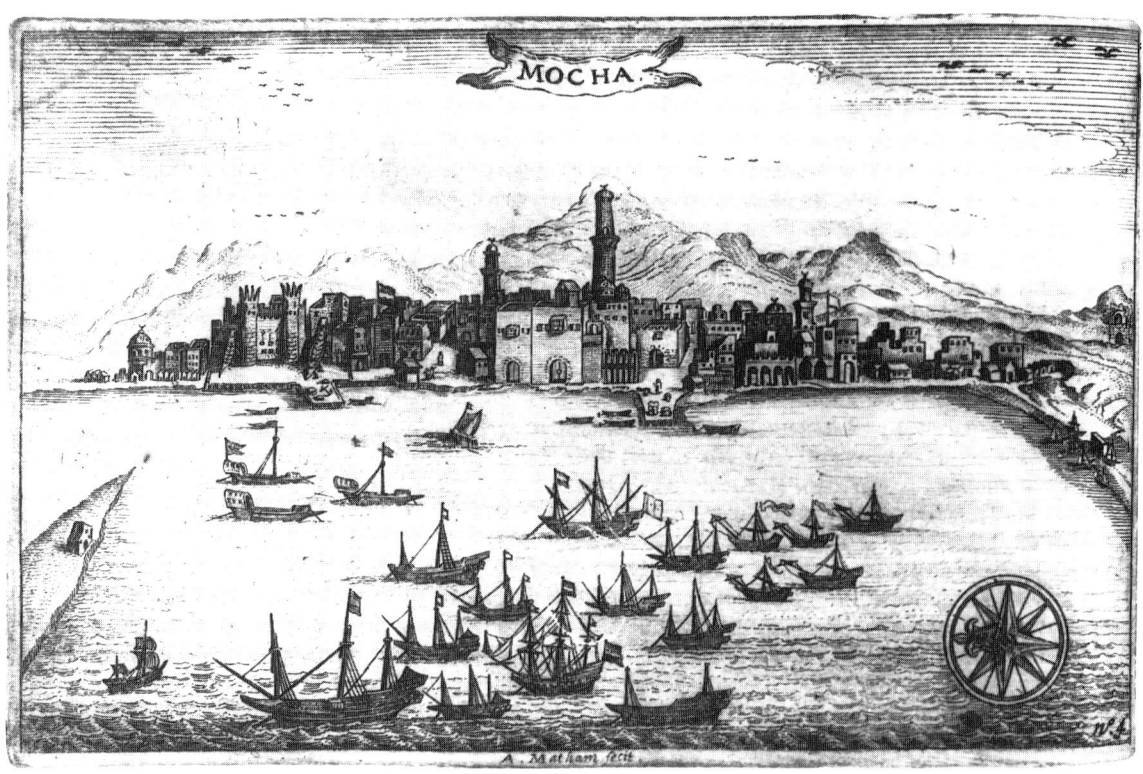

Mocha: the main focus of international trade around the Red Sea and a port in which Europeans had to compete as just one of many trading groups, as shown by the variety of vessels in the harbour. Mocha is here distinguished by its fort and commanding minaret.
From Isaak Commelin *Begin ende Voortgangh van de Vereenighde Nederlandtsche Geoctroyeerde Oost-Indische Compagnie Amsterdam, 1646. Courtesy of Mitchell Library, State Library of New South Wales.*

(especially from the Philippines, Korea and India) find employment under virtually every flag flown on the seven seas.

This current maritime pre-eminence is matched by the rapidly growing insights (through a range of techniques including maritime archaeology and replica voyages as well as more critical and imaginative analysis of documentary, pictorial, oral and other sources) into the true extent and significance of Asia's historical maritime trade links and travelling. These advances cover not only the distant eras which witnessed the dawn of seagoing navigation and the rise of regional seafaring and maritime systems but also the whole of the 'Vasco da Gama period' of European (or, more cautiously, supposedly European) dominance.[10] It is now clear that, if one adopts the really long-term perspective — spanning, say, the last two millennia — Asia and not Europe is the leading maritime continent of the world. It is incontestable that coastal and regional seafaring originated independently in several distinct regional sub-systems such as the Gulf, the Bay of Bengal, the Malay world, and the seas of East Asia. Long before Europeans crossed the Atlantic Ocean or Indian Ocean, indigenous seafarers in the latter region established regular shipping communications between distant maritime centres, carrying significant quantities of trade goods and passengers and profoundly influencing the societies and civilisations they linked together. Whether one uses Curtin's paradigm of trade diasporas, considers the peopling of Madagascar or the Swahili coast, or analyses the dynamic spread of Islam, all approaches lead to the realisation that Asia was the cradle of maritime enterprise, which by the time of the arrival in Asian waters of European explorers, traders and 'pirates' had evolved in a remarkably dense, elaborate and sophisticated network of seaborne interactions. Already by that time these interactions profoundly affected much of the hinterland of the ports and port cities from which the merchants, seamen and — to a much lesser extent — admirals and fighting sailors of Asia ventured outwards.[11]

It was within this existing, but by no means inflexible, framework of Asian shipping, commerce and port cities that the Europeans had to find their place; only in the rarest of locations and circumstances (as, e.g., the Moluccas) could they totally suppress and supplant indigenous powers and entrepreneurs. At the other end of the scale, in East Asian and Arab waters they had to accept conditions imposed upon them by local rulers; more usually, a symbiosis, not always clearly defined or stable yet often productive and quasi-permanent, existed. The indigenous role in and contribution to these arrangements has only recently begun to be thoroughly appreciated. Moreover, it is now also clear that outside the European sphere of operations extensive native shipping, trade and movement of passengers continued. The marked eurocentricity of both sources and literature makes it frustratingly difficult to glean more than incidental and qualitative flashes of such traffic and interactions, but even such fleeting impressions can leave no doubt about the extent of these links and their economic and social significance. Names such as Deshima, Canton, Surat and Mocha are symbols of either European subordination to local exclusivity or Europeans being forced to work within the traditional maritime political economy of Asia, in which in principle naval force was not allowed to interfere with the peaceful enterprise of all commercial contenders.[12]

This dramatic resurgence of maritime Asia in all its various elements[13] has profound implications for our understanding of the overall history of the continent and its relations with the outside world. It would not be too much to state that it constitutes an historiographical and ideological revolution which poses as many exciting and exacting challenges to historians of Asia as the development of Jeddah posed to her mayor. Historians have not been slow in responding and the process of revision is well under way and steadily gaining such momentum and impetus that it has now probably reached the stage of self-sustained growth. It is the purpose of this volume to add to this rising tide and at the same time, by taking the port city as its central theme, to show how that concept can be used to assist in opening up new avenues of approach. Of equal importance and stimulus is, I believe, that the port city concept, developed out of and given substance and meaning through influences from all social sciences, lends itself effectively for the development of truly multidisciplinary directions, i.e. research programmes where theoretical insights from geography, economics, anthropology, sociology, etc. are integrally amalgamated with the more empirical findings from the many and varied more purely historical sciences (such as economic, social, imperial, maritime or technological history).

The organisation of *Brides of the Sea* has been shaped accordingly. First is a theoretical and conceptualising essay, 'Studying the Asian port city', by Reeves, McPherson and the editor. Then follows a series of eight case studies drawn from both a variety of geographical locations and a chronological sequence of historical junctures: one deals with the traditional (i.e., pre-European) period; two with that of the East India Companies; and another five relate to the modern, post-1800, era (several of their authors, however, do not hesitate to look far back over their shoulders). Written by representatives from different social sciences and locations, they vary in approach and perspective. Four authors (Reid, Arasaratnam, Kidwai and Hoyle) discuss evolving port systems, while four others (Sutherland, Dharmasena, Eng and Roberts) concentrate on the individual port city. There are further contrasts in method and emphasis, but despite their divergent nature these chapters, in their collectivity and historicity, demonstrate the creative potential of the port city concept. At the same time they dramatically illustrate the extent to which altered perceptions of maritime Asia and a focusing on Asia's port cities as nodal points of economic organisation and social change can lead to historical reappraisals. The final reflections, 'On the Evolution of the Port City', by Rhoads Murphey, survey what gains have been made in the recent historiography and, with an impressive agenda for comparative and network studies, indicate just how much of a challenge still lies ahead.

In Chapter 1, then, Reeves and associates proffer a very specific conceptualisation of the port city as a dynamic functional model to be, in principle, universally applied. They draw on a wide and cross-disciplinary range of studies

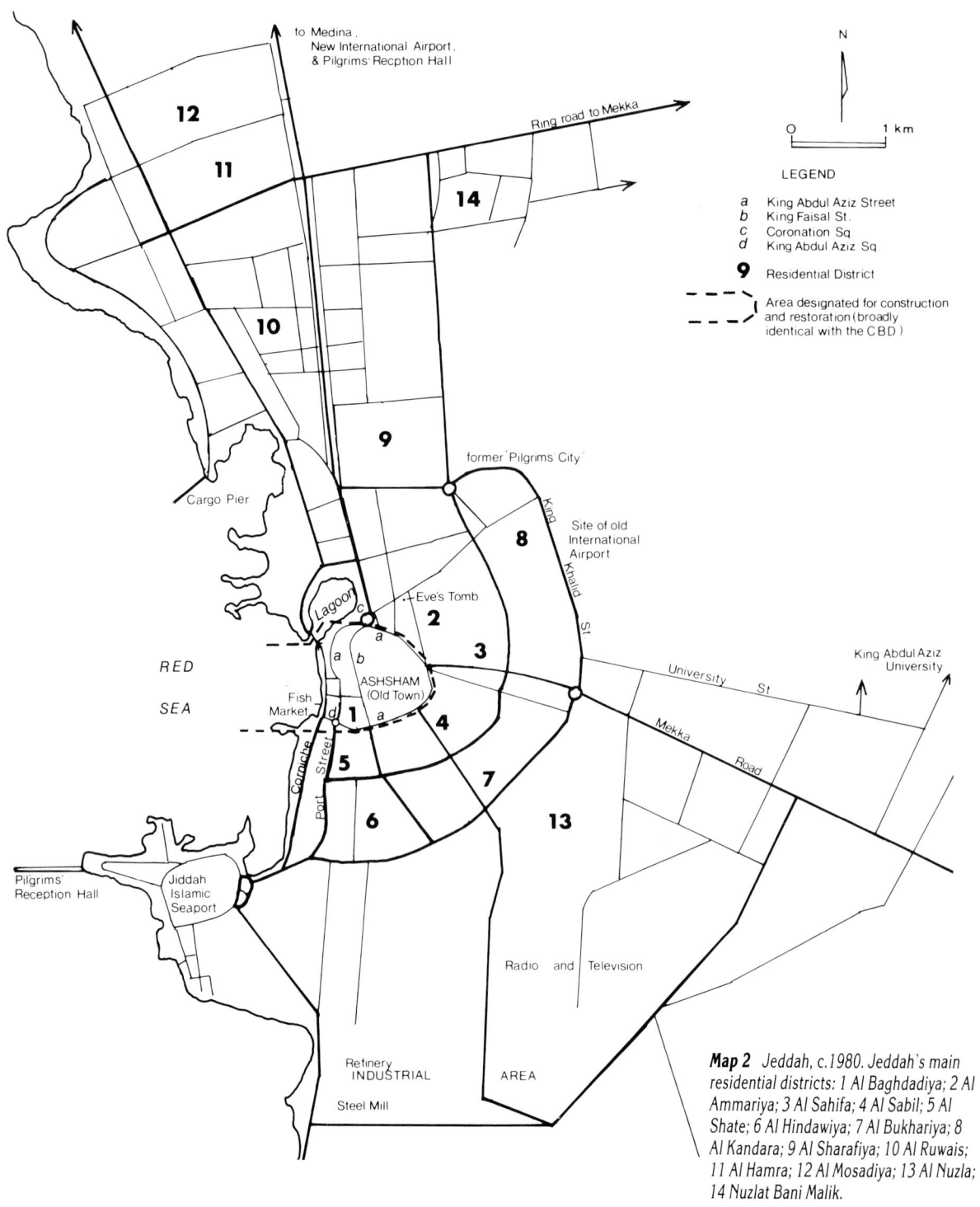

Map 2 Jeddah, c.1980. Jeddah's main residential districts: 1 Al Baghdadiya; 2 Al Ammariya; 3 Al Sahifa; 4 Al Sabil; 5 Al Shate; 6 Al Hindawiya; 7 Al Bukhariya; 8 Al Kandara; 9 Al Sharafiya; 10 Al Ruwais; 11 Al Hamra; 12 Al Mosadiya; 13 Al Nuzla; 14 Nuzlat Bani Malik.

in order to illustrate the immediate benefits to be gained from, in particular, urban and historical geography on the one hand, and transport economics and location theory on the other. Fundamental to their definition of the port city is the notion that the specific nature and classification of a city depends on the essential character of its economy and, in particular, on the major products or services it exports to external markets. A port city, then, is a city whose main economic base for its non-local market is its port, i.e. the area where goods and/or passengers are physically transferred between two modes of transport, of which at least one is maritime (transfer from ship to ship can of course also occur and, in the case of pure entrepots, may assume overwhelming importance).

Around the physical heart of the port city the authors construct a series of conceptually concentric circles representing the economic, social, cultural and political life of the human community constituting its population; all of this is firmly set within the port city's spatial and architectural configuration and appearance. The essence of the model is twofold: the all-embracing and integratory perspective that is adopted in tracing the influence of the port and the close connections that are postulated between the economic base of the port city and its social, cultural and political superstructure. Only in this way, it is argued, can both the inner functioning and the organic evolution of the port city be understood. (Sutherland's Makassar, later in this volume, will be an eloquent case in point.) These insights, in turn, are the indispensable basis for an understanding of the port city's external role and influence. Conversely, as Dharmasena and Hoyle specifically demonstrate with regard to Colombo and the East African port system, external 'foreland' or maritime influences can often be decisive in shaping not just the physical existence but also the overall life of port cities.

Indeed, it is impossible to isolate the port city from its double hinterland/foreland matrix; it is within the twin contexts of these interlocking relationships, too, that one must look for the dynamics to help explain the rise and fall of individual ports as well as the relationships (hierarchical, rival or otherwise) between ports. What must be recognised, of course, is that urban communities can move into and out of a port city classification, as their overall size and complexity on the one hand and the *relative* importance of the port sector of their economy on the other can wax and wane. These themes will, in fact, be specifically discussed in Kidwai's chapter on the port cities of India; here it may be emphasised that the purpose of the clearer definition of the port city concept is not to develop a categorisation to be applied for its own sake (is Tokyo, Bombay, Bahrain, etc. a port city, or not?), but to stress the necessity of a functional method (to 'put ports back into port cities') for a better understanding of the internal functioning and external influence of port cities.

The series of chronologically arranged case studies is opened with Anthony Reid's analysis of the organisation of production in the traditional, pre-European, port city of Southeast Asia (Chapter 2). In the first instance, this involves the identification of the particular type of urban settlement 'containing' the most important ports of Southeast Asia during the sixteenth century, when international (at first exclusively Asian, then also Western) shipping had grown to be of greater importance than at any earlier stage. It is clear that the political culture of Southeast Asia decisively influenced the economic and social life of its cities (as well as their historiographical record), as the royal courts were given central place of prominence. But even if the commercial activities of middle and lower groups remained largely outside the scope of chroniclers and other image-makers, evidence about the industrial activity and the social organisation of the labour market of these pre-colonial port cities is unambiguous in its demonstration of the importance of external maritime influences and, in consequence, of that of overseas shipping, trade and passenger traffic (which, of course, often included involuntary movement of people as slaves, debtors, prisoners of war or castaways). There is insufficient quantitative documentation to make substantive observations rather than mere assertions about the relative importance of the port sectors of these cities, or about their economic position within the regional system they served, in parts of which they were still overshadowed by the 'classical' Asian administrative and tribute-dependent inland cities. Yet it does not seem too bold to conclude that they occupied nodal positions which through their commercial and industrial functions economically but also socially played a pivotal role in the region.[14] Moreover, even if local rulers recruited most of their labour force from their surroundings and their control over foreign merchants and their communities remained strong, the port cities demonstrated such a mixture—perhaps coexistence would be a better term—of ethnic groups that it would certainly merit further analysis and consideration, whether it would not be possible to apply concepts such as trade diasporas or mercantile colonisation, even if it was shown that many non-indigenous residents of these port cities were not permanent immigrants.

At the same time, if one considers broader phenomena such as the diffusion of Islam or Hinduism, the impact of Chinese overseas trade or the responses to shifting demands for Southeast Asian produce (rice, for example, or spices) or slaves, it can be argued that the classical Southeast Asian port city could certainly function as the gateway for external ideas, cultural trends and economic (and probably also significant technological) influences well before the arrival of the Europeans. Reid, for example, stresses the 'remarkable ... openness to technical innovation' of the rulers of late sixteenth century Makassar—an important factor in the rise of the city to the regional hegemony which provides the basis for Sutherland's chapter later on in this volume. In Makassar, as in Arasaratnam's Coromandel, these policies were largely carried out by mobilising the human resources of the local population and through diffusion of ideas and knowledge gained through the port from abroad. Elsewhere, new initiatives more often involved the immigration of foreigners who, as was the case with the Chinese in Thailand, in the course of time could exercise a profound influence on local economic, cultural and even political affairs.

Arasaratnam's Chapter 3 deals with the regional port system of Coromandel during the critical years when the European East India Companies (notably those from Holland, England and France) established their settlements on that coast. It is a vivid illustration of both the new perspectives with which the European presence is nowadays viewed by historians and the process of competition for shipping, trade and primacy between ports in a relatively clearly defined regional system. Salient points are the aggressive and even in their historical setting 'modern' rivalry between Company and native port towns; the symbiosis that, nevertheless, often existed between Western and indigenous entrepreneurs; and, in particular, Arasaratnam's insistence that one should not take the ultimate 'success' of the European creations in their maturity for granted in analysing the dynamics and vicissitudes of their infancy. He argues convincingly that one should be careful in accepting standard explanations for the triumph of Madras over its neighbouring rivals, as a close reading of their records reveals both numerous ambiguities and much greater fluctuations of fortune than has previously been assumed.

Arasaratnam's essentially historical approach implicitly constitutes an eloquent application of a geographical port system model as outlined later in Hoyle's chapter, with a keen appreciation for the importance of and the influences exerted by maritime as well as inland transport and transfer systems. But he also provides the essential linkages between the full internal (economic-social-political) structure of the port cities and the role they could externally play in their region. Ultimately, San Thome as the gateway of the Nawab of the Carnatic may not have been able to survive, but during the late seventeenth and early eighteenth century it certainly mobilised an impressive array of indigenous entrepreneurs and resources in its attempt to thwart the rise of Madras. In this, as in his explanation of the success of the English in the latter port over their European rivals in Paleacat and Pondichery, Arasaratnam convincingly demonstrates the necessity of such historical weaving together of European and Indian as well as external and internal dynamics.

Despite, but perhaps also in response to, all methodological advances of recent years and, in particular, the rise of structuralism and functionalism and the insemination of 'history' with social science theory, the biography has remained a vital ingredient of the historian's *repertoire;* this is as true in urban and maritime history as it is in political, economic or any other of the historical sciences. Evocative works, like Geoffrey Moorhouse's *Calcutta* or Gillian Tindall's *City of Gold,* on Bombay, are without equal in giving the reader the feeling of immediate contact with, indeed immediate involvement in and almost instinctive understanding of the individual—I am inclined to write 'personal'— life and appearance of the cities they describe and depict. Moreover, even without explicitly providing the structural and conceptual framework their subjects require, Moorhouse and Tindall implicitly adopt the port city notion and in consequence infuse their descriptive imagery with such numerous and rich maritime and commercial elements that it is easy to accept the legitimacy of the impressionistic painting besides, and to a certain extent even as the necessary emotional counterpart to, the social-scientific analysis.

Thus, as Chapter 4, by Sutherland on eighteenth-century Makassar (as well as Chapters 5 and 7 by Eng and Roberts on 'semi-colonial' (1843-1941) Shanghai and nineteenth- and twentieth-century Colombo respectively) is designed to show, in the final analysis the individual experience is the building block of collective awareness and stochastic generalisations, just as individual case studies are still the stuff of which good theory is made. Only within the specific confines of each port city can the interacting influence of internal and external dynamics be observed, analysed, explained and assessed. Only on the basis of numerous such case studies can deductively general patterns be distilled which, in turn, can be matched and, ultimately, integrated with the inductive reasoning based on an approach from theoretical or other structuralist bases.

As Sutherland puts it, eighteenth-century Makassar was a 'hybrid town, created by the forcible grafting of a Dutch outpost upon an Indonesian port'. It never was or became a port of intercontinental significance, but from the beginning of its existence as a port, predating the arrival of the Dutch in the East Indies by several centuries, it was a vital nodal point in the trading systems of Southeast Asia and also the wider context of the trade between that region and both South and Northeast Asia. As was so often the case, the very opportunities possible within these indigenous systems induced first local rulers to build up a port city along the model proposed by Reid; subsequently, and inevitably, the very success of 'Malay'—or perhaps even 'Asian'—Makassar provoked the jealousy of the dominant European power in the region, in this case the Dutch East India Company (VOC), into a policy designed to subordinate such an independent and—often potentially rather than in reality—dangerous rival to Company power. The substance and essence of Makassar's challenge was its shipping and trade; the tragic irony of its bloody conquest by the Dutch was the latter's dependence on locally established entrepreneurs, labourers and others, for the subsequent functioning of the place as a port of significance. Moreover, much of Makassar's maritime economy continued to exist and flourish outside the orbits of Dutch power and commercial interests; a striking example of the entrepreneurship of its shipowners was their shifting vessels and resources from trades which were prohibited by the Dutch into the trepang fishery on the northern Australian coast.[16]

Sutherland's chapter falls into three closely intertwined parts: a brief overview of the external forces and circumstances which gave Makassar its unique position, the administrative policies of the VOC, and a detailed and empathetic analysis—in, I believe, the best traditions of the city biography—of its domestic life. Roughly following the port city model with its concentric circles, she successfully integrates the power-political, economic, social/ethnic, cultural and, especially also, morphological elements of this port city which 'despite its formally segmented organisation ... was much more than the sum of its parts'. It was this inner vitality, the result of the creative and synergic interaction between its various ethnic groups, social classes and political and economic

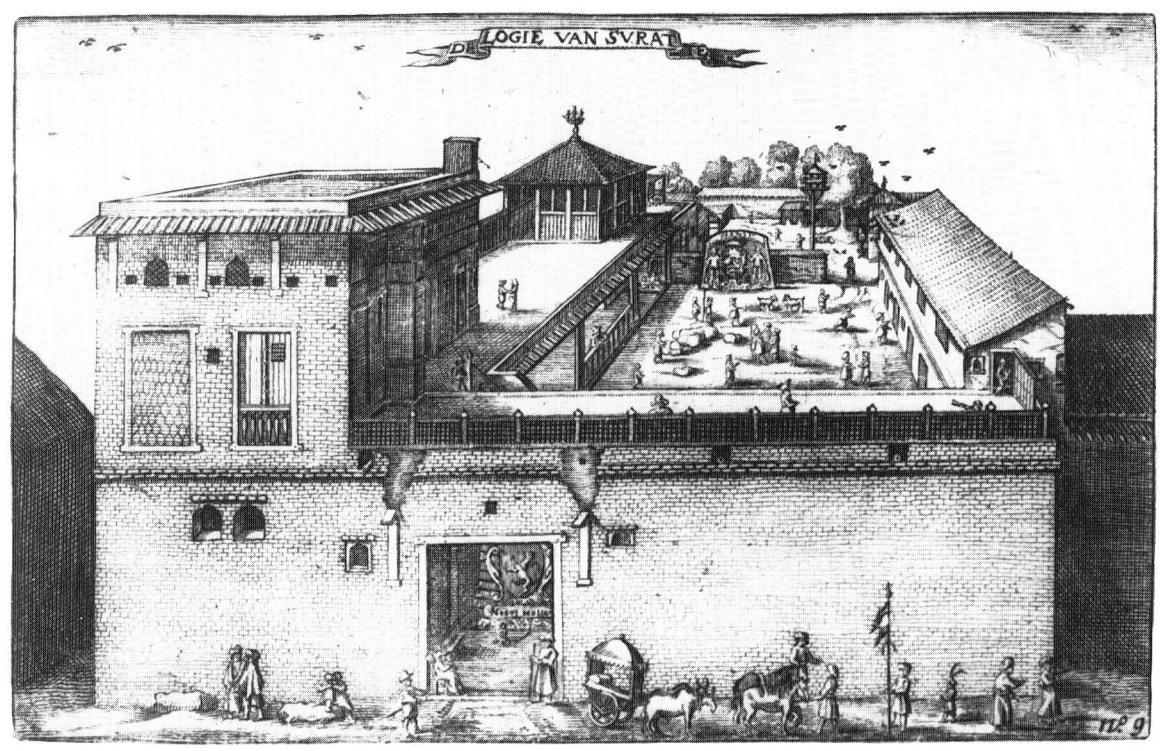

The Dutch Factory in Surat, West India: in the cosmopolitan contexts of port cities Europeans had to establish their 'factories' or 'lodges' as community bases for competition with traders of other nations. This perspective of such a 'lodge' shows the variety of types of traders with whom the Dutch had to interact in the Indian context, and conveys how the Dutch were asserting their importance through architecture.
From Isaak Commelin *Begin ende Voortgangh van de Vereenighde Nederlandtsche Geoctroyeerde Oost-Indische Compagnie* Amsterdam, 1646. Courtesy of Mitchell Library, State Library of New South Wales.

functionaries, which allowed Makassar to realise 'both its own identity and its contribution to the region'.

'Hybrid' Makassar finds a striking counterpart in 'semi-colonial' Shanghai, the subject of Eng's Chapter 5. In many ways—not in the least through Murphey's classic study of the city which was responsible for integrating the urban dimension into the history of Western expansion and the development of the world economic system[17]—Shanghai is the epitome of that titanic encounter between the dynamics of West and East of which the glib phrase 'irresistible force meeting unmovable object' is such a totally deceptive description. Risen from an already thriving Chinese port on a branch of the Yangzi (Yangtze) Kiang to being one of the very largest metropolises of the world, its historical role as one of the main power houses of China's modernisation did, of course, not stop in 1941. Indeed, despite problems such as congestion, housing shortages, lack of services, the impact of the Great Proletarian Revolution and other political struggles, its economic primacy remains unchallenged; the uncertainty about Hong Kong's future is only likely to add to its role. The strength of Shanghai was less its accessibility to Western shipping (which from the beginning has had to be artificially maintained and improved) than its superb location at the crossroads of the inland, coastal, regional and intercontinental maritime transportation networks. It may indeed be suggested that the sheer geographical span and economic extent of Shanghai's junk shipping and trade before the arrival of the Europeans make it perhaps a more powerful paradigm of that continuity of maritime Asia than any other port city could be.

Basing his account on the incontestable superiority of Shanghai's strategic location, Eng first discusses the measures needed to enable its port and port facilities to handle the tremendous throughput of shipping and trade, which its opening as a treaty port after the First Opium War occasioned. He then successively deals with ways in which the port influenced the transformation of Shanghai into the transport, trading and industrial centre of imperial and nationalist China. The entrepreneurial and financial influence of foreigners is duly noted, but set against the active response and participation of Chinese, without whom it is doubtful Shanghai could have functioned at all. Eng is also careful to stress, as Arasaratnam did for the seventeenth-century Coromandel coast, that one should not take the standard explanation of the inexorable rise of Shanghai for granted. In this complex process there were many negative and destructive factors even if, ultimately, the sheer economic momentum generated by the spectacular growth of Shanghai's overseas trade, the employment created in and around the port and also the strong transition towards port industrialisation created an irresistible forward push which by the 1930s had made Shanghai 'world-famed as being the largest city in China as well as the leading international metropolis of the world. Inevitable meeting place of world travellers, the habitat of people of 40 different nationalities, of the Orient yet Occidental ...'.[18] While the social dimensions of Shanghai largely fall outside the scope of Eng's chapter, and still remain on the agenda, I may recall here the phrase with which Farsi evoked the essence of Jeddah:

Islamic yet modern ... and which carried in it the fundamental ability of Asia's port cities to reconcile, even to integrate, what seemingly are contradictory tendencies. It is so often assumed that Japan, which had learned her lessons on European imperialism and economic development so well, was the Asian power which, because of its particular traditions, social values and aptitudes, was best capable of harnessing extraneous influences to achieve its national purposes. It may be more correct to stress that she was merely the first to do so. Research in the rise of Japan's maritime industries has become a growth industry; unfortunately, her ports and port cities have not yet gained any significant attention in (at least English language) literature.[19]

Dharmasena's explanation of the rise of Colombo (Chapter 6) to seventh ranking (in 1910) amongst the world's ports illustrates strikingly the usefulness of a macroeconomic and transport-geographical approach, as the dynamics of its growth were a unique blend of the 'hinterland gateway' and the 'oceanic port of call' functions. Viewing ports as nodal points in international and intercontinental trade and shipping networks, he can thus relate individual port development, with its comprehensive implications, to shifts in economic production and consumption on the one hand and maritime technology (in the form of the introduction and diffusion of the ocean-going steamships and the opening of the Suez Canal) on the other. Comparisons with Bombay and Singapore help to specify Colombo's position as 'hub' of the Indian Ocean. Of particular interest in Dharmasena's account is the relationship between Sri Lanka's two main overseas ports during the period, Colombo and Galle. Initially they were quite distinct in their roles, as the former catered for the island's import and export trades which were almost exclusively carried on sailing ships and the latter, because of its oceanic location and bay topography as a 'natural harbour', attracted the mail steamers en route from Suez or Bombay to the ports of eastern India, Singapore, China and Australia. But the 'natural' quality of harbours is only relative to the current state of shipping technology and traffic;[20] with the growth of steamers' numbers and dimensions Galle became cramped and dangerous. Ironically, Colombo was equally unsuitable for modern steamers, so that the two ports became rivals in adversity, i.e. rivals for the location of the modern port which had to be built in order to connect the plantations of Sri Lanka with the outside world and thus firmly articulate the island to the world economy. Once the contest had thus been sharply defined, the vested interests of Colombo and the capital's superior communications with its plantations hinterland easily won the day. Now Colombo became the receptacle of all functions associated with and derived from its uncontested twin roles as both Sri Lanka's gateway and the Indian Ocean's main refuelling station. As a result it showed a truly remarkable growth. But it also meant that, once Colombo's oceanic advantages were eroded by further technological change, its regional pre-eminence was equally affected. (In recent years containerisation has, once again, turned the wheel and propelled Colombo to the top of its regional hierarchy.)[21] How these external dynamics influenced and helped shape the social, cultural and political life of Colombo's fast-growing urban population, remains outside the scope of Dharmasena's chapter. Some elements, however, of such an investigation are contained in the following chapter on Colombo by Michael Roberts.

In contrast to Eng's primarily economic and quantitative analysis of the life of maritime Shanghai, Michael Roberts' study of Colombo during the imperial period of British control over Sri Lanka as well as after independence focuses on some of the social and superstructural effects caused by Colombo's rise to pre-eminence, as explained in Dharmasena's previous chapter. Crucially, British power was not directly established as the result of the destruction of an indigenous polity (although native resistance still had to be taken into account) but rested on their conquest of the island from the Dutch who, in their turn, had wrested the island from the Portuguese, the original Western predators. In consequence, the ethnic composition of Colombo, its traditional gateway and colonial capital of Sri Lanka, was in some respects even more complex than that of other otherwise comparable cities in colonial Asia. Moreover, the island itself was ethnically split between the Sinhalese majority, largely concentrated in the southwest close to Colombo and long-established Tamils in the north, to which dichotomy as a result of the nineteenth-century development of the island's plantation economy was added another contingent of Tamils which, however, in economic occupation, social organisation and ideological outlook was markedly different. The perspective adopted by Roberts is to complement the work of Dharmasena and his predecessors[22] by taking the nineteenth-twentieth-century regional role of Colombo for granted, and, instead, to illuminate the other, often neglected, face of the port city: its relationship with its hinterland and immediate surroundings. Using a concept not unlike Pearson's 'littoral society',[23] i.e. that community of people who are significantly influenced by the maritime forces radiating from the port, he explores two major aspects of that relationship. Both are determined by the unique nature of Sri Lankan society in which Colombo was embedded, yet add considerably to our understanding of more general trends inherent in the rise and decline of the port city as an historical phenomenon.

The relationship between British Colombo and its hinterland was at first characterised by the need to counter a hostility which was mostly latent but sometimes erupted into violent rebellion and which until deep into the nineteenth century continued the necessity of maintaining a fort as well as an open green to protect the city against insurrection. Although Colombo to a certain extent reflected the ethnic heterogeneity of the island, it had increasingly become a different and in several respects alien element in it. Interestingly, and here general insights may well be gained from Roberts' arguments, in the twentieth century and especially since Sinhalese-dominated Independence the relative position of hinterland and primate city appear to have been reversed, at least politically and socially.[24] (It may be added here that it is difficult to see signs for a diminution of Colombo's economic hegemony, even if attempts are being made to develop Trincomalee into an overseas port of some magnitude; Colombo's recent rise to prominence in the still fluid network of container shipping in the Indian Ocean and its ambitions to even serve as hub to south and east Indian ports in combination with the development of free-trade zone industrialisation leave little doubt about its ability and determination to stay on top.)[25] As Roberts sees it, the island—or more accurately, the Sinhalese southwest—has commenced to 're-invade' the city, which first became the stage for a revival of Sinhalese power and cultural traditions, and then was set to lose its function as the seat of government to the old Sinhalese lowland capital of Kotte (now renamed Sri Jayawardenapura).

Two further aspects of the recent experiences of Colombo, not elaborated in Roberts' account, may be stressed here. First, that the economic development of Colombo is now firmly embedded in the physical entity, as well as the ideology, of a Greater Colombo so that the Sri Lankan capital now experiences the same generalisation of economic and social diversification with its concomitant disappearance of port city characteristics as observed in Habeeb's discussion of Calcutta and Bombay. Second, that, as Reeves and associates argue in Chapter 1, there are dynamic tensions within the mature port city and even more in the relationship between the port city and the polity in which it is located, which can lead to such a physical stripping of functions; Calcutta and Karachi have both been subjected to such loss of overall political power. Hoyle will discuss the theme later on from a geographer's perspective, specifically with regard to Tanzania's Dar es Salaam. Historically and conversely, in those countries, such as Iraq, Malaysia, China, or Saudi Arabia, where no direct colonial regime was established, the retention of the seat of political power in inland cities (Baghdad, Kuala Lumpur, Beijing, Riyadh) often represented at least partly the result of conscious policies of indigenous rulers to, literally, keep foreigners (as well as modernising and potentially radical middle classes!) at bay.

The second element of Colombo's experience emphasised by Roberts is the impact of British rule and hegemony on the social life of Colombo and its spatial organisation. Here he brings together details on leisure time activities of the British and their being imitated by aspiring Ceylonese who in neo-marxist terminology would no doubt be described as 'compradors'—indigenous entrepreneurs and others willing to throw in their lot with that of their European masters in the hope of personal social and economic improvement and at the expense of the long-term development and political aspirations of their own people. These themes are well established in imperial history,[26] but Roberts graphically carries his description of the life of British expatriates and the local anglophile elite in Colombo into their clubs and games, suburbs and gardens, their homes and furniture as well as the other material trappings with which they attempted to maintain or create a material identity as Britishers. He does not discuss the 'high culture' and ideology of the pseudo-British Colombians nor the social life of the indigenous lower classes, of whom so many found their employment in and around the port, but his ideas and images may well stimulate fuller social analyses elsewhere.

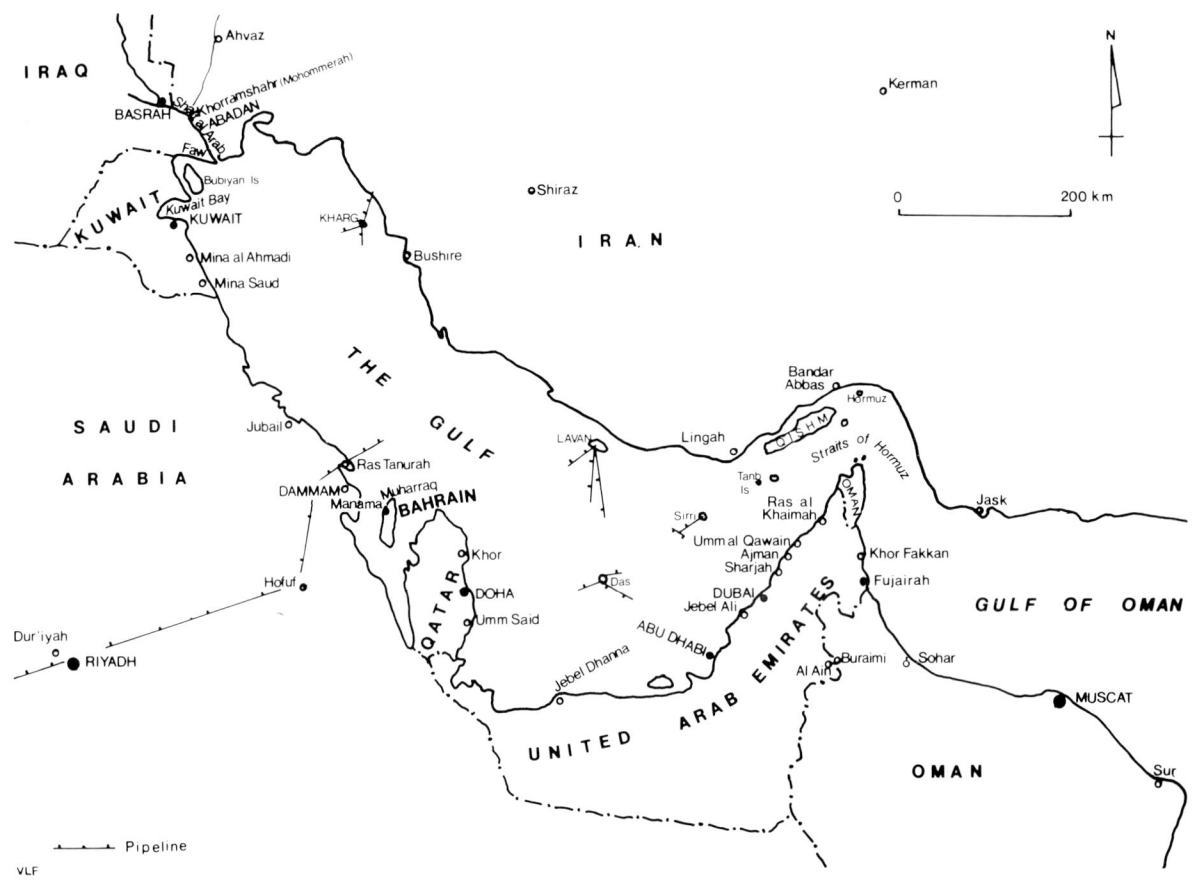

Map 3 The Arabian/Persian Gulf

Port systems are the subject of the next, and last, two historical chapters, but with that virtually all similarity ends. Vastly different methods underlie the respective analyses of Hoyle and Kidwai. In many ways Hoyle's approach resembles that of Dharmasena. But while the latter in his study of Colombo was concerned with that port's twin function as the gateway to a relatively small and compact island economy, where no room or opportunity existed for a system of ports to develop over time, and as the hub of the Indian Ocean, Hoyle's Chapter 8 addresses itself to the historical evolution of such a 'seaport system', a series of ports in complex competitive and subordinative relationships. Using East Africa with its particular interior and littoral configuration as his main example, Hoyle shows how the continuous dynamics of external forces led to significant shifts in the geographical layout of trade routes and, in consequence, port hierarchies and individual port city fortunes. Amongst the most important of these forces he counts 'maritime influences', above all technological changes spilling over from the most advanced area of the world's oceans. The introduction of steam navigation and, most recently, the container revolution have had the most profound effects on ports and port hierarchies.

Hoyle's definition of the port hierarchy concept and his insistence on its historical importance are most valuable, as it can equally well be applied to all regional systems of Asia, including Japan, Southeast Asia, India and the Gulf,[27] as to East Africa. In fact, through his largely comparative approach he does provide many references which are directly concerned with port cities in Asia and their development under modern competitive circumstances. Historically, moreover, as has been argued earlier, the Benadir and Swahili coasts for at least a thousand years were integral parts of the western Indian Ocean sub-system, locked into the maritime economies of Western India and the Arabian world, and as such constituted the southwestern facade of 'the Asian Seas'. Their particular experience, in consequence, also provides useful insights into the development of ports and port cities in those adjacent and related regions.[28] Arasaratnam's study of the rivalry of Coromandel's ports in the late seventeenth and early eighteenth centuries (Chapter 3) may be recalled here as, written from a historical rather than geographical perspective, it demonstrated the usefulness and applicability of the port system approach to the specific historical question of the complex relationship between European and indigenous entrepreneurs and the port cities through which their trade and shipping was channelled.

In order to gauge the wider implications of Hoyle's argument it must be stressed that European imperialism and the arrival of the steamship and railway dramatically affected the ports of East Africa as well as their hinterlands, which not only came under white colonial rule but were also turned into plantation economies for the world market. One of the most telling port transformations during this period of British expansion was that of Mombasa where the dhow harbour with its associated old city was rapidly pushed aside and overshadowed by Kilindini Harbour with its modern transport and servicing facilities, and embryonic industrialisation.[29] Immediately behind it arose Mombasa's new

Central Business District, from which Western economic control over its trade and hinterland was exercised. In their clear physical separation and dynamic impact on the urban morphology of their port city, the two harbours of Mombasa are perhaps extreme examples; nevertheless they are perfectly indicative of the dualism between European and indigenous shipping which since the early nineteenth century has characterised well-nigh all Asian ports, whether it concerned those of India with their native bunders, Southeast Asia and China with designated harbours and anchorages for prahus and junks, the Gulf, Jeddah, or Aden, where the physical distance between Steamer Point and Ma'alla (some six kilometres) was but a fraction of the economic and cultural chasm it represented.[30]

Another general problem raised by Hoyle which also affects many modern ports is that of congestion and dramatic contests for the use of scarce urban land space; well-known in present-day Sydney,[31] it tends to affect all ports whose morphology, shaped during the heyday of a previous technology, is tightly fitted into surrounding industrial and residential areas. Political independence since the 1950s has not fundamentally altered the dependence of East Africa on outside forces and influences. Indeed, as Hoyle argues, the recent containerisation revolution—the impact of which has affected all corners of the globe[32]—influences its seaports and internal transport systems as profoundly as the steam power revolution did some one hundred years previously. Moreover, container services now also link East Africa directly with the United States, the Far East and the Soviet Union, thus creating through their gateway terminals new economic relationships which, in turn, will have significant consequences for the port cities and national economies involved.

Hoyle's concept of port hierarchy and his analysis of the dynamics of port rivalry are taken further in the broad sweep of Atiya Kidwai's overview of the port cities of India during the full century 1880-1980, which period straddles the heyday of British imperialism and the first one and a half generations of independence (Chapter 9). She develops a multi-pronged statistical method, based on both the port and urban hierarchies of India as defined by their rankings in terms of cargo throughput and population, in order to test the port city concept as defined by Reeves, McPherson and Broeze.[33] She correlates the port and urban rankings of India's ten major ports as well as the changes over time in their ranking. Further statistics establish the extent of the dominance of the ports over their respective hinterlands, the development of their economy in terms of secondary and tertiary industry, and the extent to which this process was influenced by their port functions. Two major points arise out of this broadly conceived and imaginative analysis. First, historically, the confirmation of the role of Calcutta, Madras, Bombay and Karachi as primate port cities during the colonial period. All four port cities experienced tremendous growth and diversification in the process through which they gradually attracted port and other functions from minor rivals or prevented them from assuming or initiating new roles. Interestingly, the degree of dominance of the major four within their regional port system could differ quite significantly (only Karachi approximated total control, while the construction of Cochin after World War I led to increased rivalry in South India).[34] Similarly, while in the long term the association between port expansion and population growth was overwhelmingly positive, in the short term significant fluctuations did occur. After Independence, two important qualifications to this overall pattern need to be observed. First, there is the significant rise of new ports of initially intermediate but subsequently primary importance in terms of their throughput and ranking—but *not* in urban growth, industrialisation or indeed the development of a diversified urban society. Kidwai does not discuss the social and cultural development of these new ports, such as Marmagao and Paradeep, but their primary function as exportation points of bulk commodities such as iron ore or coal (they often are little more than single commodity 'jetty ports') rather than as general ports makes such superstructural diversification highly unlikely.

The second major conclusion to arise from Kidwai's analysis is that India's general cargo ports (Bombay, Calcutta, Madras and, to a lesser extent, Cochin) after Independence have continued to show vigorous port development and diversification—but the latter, significantly, on increasingly autonomous lines. Kidwai's indicators suggest strongly that the pattern of their industrialisation and tertiarisation (to which one might well add their social and cultural superstructure) is not any more dominated or even significantly influenced by their port function but closely resembles that of India's other large urban conglomerates—thus demonstrating the validity of the proposition that port cities can lose their specific character and turn into general, economically diversified and broadly based, cities.

Besides the continued rapid pace of urbanisation and urban diversification, one must also stress the importance of the recent shrinking of maritime transport in both its share of and physical centrality in international trade and, even more so, passenger traffic in reducing employment opportunities which ports directly and indirectly generate. Dynamic factors are (besides vast improvements in port cargo-handling productivity) especially the spectacular development of air and road traffic as well as the communications revolution which has strongly diminished the need for central physical commodity markets and the location of commercial/financial decision-making in port cities. In consequence, the geographical links between the conduct of international trade and its ancillaries, such as finance and insurance, and the physical movement of the commodities imported and exported have been loosened dramatically. This shrinking of maritime and port employment may well be a secular phenomenon which will, it seems inevitably, lead to the disappearance of the port city as it has historically existed as a type of city for some two thousand years or so. Instead, we may, on the one hand, see the growth of metropoles and general cities possessing still significant but not dominant port sectors (and free trade production zones) with examples like Tokyo, Shanghai, Guangzhou, Calcutta, Karachi, Basra or Kuwait joining London, New York, Sydney and others from the non-Asian part of the world; and, on the other, increasingly specialised loading or discharging terminals or 'jetty ports' such as Kharg Island or Mina al Ahmadi for oil; Paradeep and Marmagao for iron ore; Aqaba for rock phosphate (and temporarily the re-export overseas of Iraqi oil brought down by convoys of road tankers).

Kidwai's chapter, through the specific task the author set herself in testing specific concepts and definitions of the port city, provides a fitting finale to the varied range of historical case studies contained in this volume. At the same time, in closing the conceptual circle and stressing the need and suggesting directions for further research, it sets the scene for the final contribution, Rhoads Murphey's reflective essay 'On the Evolution of the Port City'. Returning to the field to which in so many ways he himself built the gateway some thirty-five years ago, Murphey ranges broadly over both the concept of the 'port city' and its place in the history and historiography of Asia. He acknowledges that there is no geographical or, for that matter, temporal limitation: the very functions of the port city, the very influence it as a result inevitably exercises, make it pivotal to the understanding of international economic and cultural exchanges. At the same time Murphey insists, it is not sufficient to merely analyse the seaside elements and forces of port cities; as the once 'pitifully poor harbours' of both Calcutta and Shanghai show, landward factors can often be of equal or even greater importance. Reviewing the 'state of the art' as it now stands, Murphey accentuates both the colossal powers of change contained in port cities, the places where maritime trade hooks into terrestrial systems, and the strong continuity they at the same time exhibit. It is more than a personal homecoming for him to quote the *China Weekly Review* of 4 December 1926: 'Shanghai would have been a great city had there never been a foreigner in the place. It would continue to be a great city even if the foreigners should vacate their modern buildings and go home.' One can only agree with Murphey's call—reinforcing that of Kidwai in the previous chapter—for further micro-level and comparative studies. Only then can the dialectic between continuity and change be fully developed and that complex relationship between Asia and the waters surrounding it, of which this volume may symbolise the essentials, be better understood.

This volume can have no ambition to or pretence of being comprehensive in any meaning of the term in its overview of the evolution of the port cities of Asia from the sixteenth to the twentieth centuries. Arising, in the first instance, out of the proceedings of a multi-disciplinary conference on Indian Ocean studies (in which ports and port cities *a priori* figure more largely than they usually do in the continental context of Asian studies),[35] its geographical span alone falls far short of fully covering the fascinating patchwork of Asia's many and diverse maritime regions and port systems. In particular, it is regretted that no case study of a continuously non-colonised port city (such as Kobe, Busan, Bangkok or Jeddah) or region can be included. Its main function, therefore, is to signpost new approaches and directions, and to suggest the value of insights based on both the functional (rather than more limited cultural/ historical) conceptualisation of the 'port city' and the use of this concept as a dynamic model and as an investigative and analytical tool. This does not,

The human elements of the port city: Javanese inhabitants of Banten (Bantam), West Java, including a Chinese porcelain trader (right), as seen by the first Dutch expedition to the Indies.
From Cornelis de Houtman *Verhael van de Reyse by de Hollandtsche Schepen gedaen naer Oost Indien* Middleburgh, 1597.
Courtesy of Mitchell Library, State Library of New South Wales.

of course, imply that one can or should approach the study of Asian history and society only or even mainly through port cities or overseas trade and passenger traffic; that would be like squeezing the proverbial camel through a needle's eye and expecting the animal to reappear unscathed after this distressing and distorting experience!

But it would be appropriate to liken the port city model to a prism through which the general history of Asia is uniquely refracted to reveal new elements, dynamic forces and relationships. (These, moreover, can lend themselves to comparisons with the evolution of other world regions, including not just those which also for some time stood under Western imperial control but also others like the independent Americas, Australia and even pre-global Europe itself.) Within the Asian context, its creative and imaginative implementation may stress the powers of historical continuity, in terms of location, economic and social organisation, as well as cultural ideology. Here we may return to Farsi's concerns about the renewal of old Jeddah and my conviction that the current rise of maritime Asia constitutes a return to old traditions as well as a positive response to the challenges of economic expansion and modernisation. It also signifies the overcoming of the Asian/European dualism which characterised the most recent centuries. Port cities, probably more than any other urban or man-made environment, embodied that dualism between indigenous and extraneous cultures. Now they have firmly joined capital cities and other centres of political power in the quest for the reassertion of national and local ideologies and the revitalisation of those cultural, artistic and in particular architectural traditions which are seen as the visual and material expression of such deeply felt concerns. Even if such renewal schemes (prominent examples besides Jeddah include Singapore, Tianjin, Rangoon, Zanzibar, as well as Sydney and Fremantle!)[36] on occasion owe much to a desire to attract the tourist dollar, one should not lose sight of the fact that amongst the financial and material aspects of national and international tourism there are strong cultural and philosophical concerns about the material and spiritual heritage of one's own and other societies. Although some might argue that these concerns because of their mercenary nature are suspect, in the final analysis they are no less real, valuable or valid than those of social elites and policy- or image-makers such as historians and other social scientists. Whatever the source of their inspiration, most port city restoration and renewal projects emphasise the cultural importance of port cities, and hence, the necessity of further research into their origins and growth. A more profound understanding of their functioning and pivotal historical role is not only of intrinsic importance but can only assist social scientists in their vital responsibility of communicating their views and findings to the community at large.

Notes

1. James Buchan (text), Khalid Khidr & John French (photographs), *Jeddah. Old and New* London, 1980
2. The city's population swelled from a mere 20 000 to 30 000 by the end of World War II to some 1 500 000 forty years later
3. K. N. Chaudhuri *Trade and Civilization in the Indian Ocean* Cambridge, 1985, chs. 1-5
4. Cf. Daniel R. Headrick *The Tools of Empire* New York/Oxford, 1981, ch. 3
5. R. Murphey 'Traditionalism and Colonialism: Changing Urban Roles in Asia', *Journal of Asian Studies* 29, 1969, pp. 67-84; D. K. Basu 'Introduction' in D. K. Basu (ed.) *The Rise and Growth of Port Cities in Asia* (conference proceedings, Santa Cruz, Calif., 1979); Anthony D. King 'Colonial Cities: Global Pivots of Change' in Robert Ross & Gerard J. Telkamp (eds.) *Colonial Cities. Essays on Urbanism in a Colonial Context* Dordrecht/Boston/Lancaster, 1985, pp. 7-32
6. Richard H. Sanger *The Arabian Peninsula* Ithaca, NY, 1954, p. 4
7. Even through this only narrowly opened window considerable, albeit mainly cultural, influence flowed from the Netherlands, the only Western nation allowed to trade with Japan. On the development and significance of the *Rangaku*, or 'Dutch Learning', in Japan, see C. R. Boxer *Jan Compagnie in Japan* The Hague, 1936
8. M. Keswick (ed.) *The Thistle and the Jade* London, 1982
9. Port city studies for the Middle East have, for obvious reasons, been concentrated on places like Aden and Kuwait, but see the articles 'Basra' and 'Djudda' in *The Encyclopedia of Islam* 2nd edn, vol. 1, 1960, pp. 1117-20, and vol. 2, 1965, pp. 571-73.
10. From the plethora of references to newly uncovered archaeological evidence one may select Jeremy Green 'The Maritime Archaeology of Shipwrecks of the Indian Ocean Five Years On', which paper also contains references to wrecksites in Thai and Chinese waters (conference paper, Second International Conference on Indian Ocean Studies [henceforth ICIOS II], Perth, December 1984, vol. E: *Maritime Studies: Shipping, Trade and Port Cities*); S. R. Rao 'Underwater Archaeological Expeditions in India' (ibid.); Paolo Biagi, Wolfgang Torke, Maurizio Tosi & Hans-Peter Uerpmann 'Qurum: A Case Study of Coastal Archaeology in Northern Oman' *World Archaeology* 16, 1984, pp. 43-61; Jean Deloche 'Études sur la circulation en Inde. IV; Notes sur les sites de quelques ports anciens du pays tamoul' *Bulletin de l'École Francaise d'Extrême-Orient* 74, 1985, pp. 141-82; W. J. Jobling & R. V. H. Morgan 'The Port of Aqaba, Revisited' *The Great Circle* 8, 1986, pp. 96-103; and Southeast Asian Ministers of Education Organisation, Project in Archaeology and Fine Arts (SPAFA) *Final Report, Consultative Workshop on Research on Maritime Shipping and Trade Networks in Southeast Asia, Cisarua, November 1984* 2 vols, Bangkok, 1986. For a conceptual definition of maritime archaeology see Graeme Henderson *Maritime Archaeology in Australia* Nedlands, W.A, 1986, ch. 2. Significant replica voyages include Tim Severin's passage in an (India-built) Arab dhow from Muscat to Canton (1979), that of the prahu *Sarimanok* navigated by Bill McGrath from Bali to Madagascar (1985), and the Pacific crossing of the Japanese *wasen Shinyetsu Maru* from Awaji to Vancouver (1985-86). A comprehensive history of Asian shipping in pre-modern times remains to be written, for which the building stones are indicated in Sean McGrail *The Ship* vol. 1: *Rafts, Boats and Ships* London, 1981, with bibliography. Classics remain works such as J. Hornell *Water Transport* rep. Newton Abbott, 1970; G. F. Hourani *Arab Seafaring* Princeton 1957; R. Mookerji *Indian Shipping* Bombay, 1912; and also R. Furata & Y. Hirai *A Short History of Japanese Merchant Shipping* Tokyo, 1967
11. Ph.D. Curtin *Cross-Cultural Trade in World History* Cambridge, 1984, esp. chs. 1 and 5-6, and Chaudhuri *Trade and Civilization* ch. 2
12. See Curtin's and Chaudhuri's works cited in the previous note, and, among many other titles, J. Feenstra Kuiper *Japan en de buitenwereld in de achttiende eeuw* The Hague, 1921; L. Dermigny *La Chine et l'Occident au XVIIIe siècle* 4 vols, Paris, 1964; M.A.P. Meilink-Roelofsz (ed.) *De V.O.C. in Azië* Bussum, 1976; Ashin Das Gupta *Indian Merchants and the Decline of Surat c. 1700-1750* Wiesbaden, 1979; Blair B. Kling & M. N. Pearson (eds.) *The Age of Partnership: Europeans in Asia before Domination* Honolulu, 1979; S. Arasaratnam *Merchants, Companies and Commerce on the Coromandel Coast 1650-1740* New Delhi, 1986; and Ashin Das Gupta & M. N. Pearson (eds.) *India and the Indian Ocean 1500-1800* Calcutta, 1987
13. On the aspect of merchant shipping see Frank Broeze 'From Imperialism to Independence: The Decline and Re-emergence of Asian Shipping' *The Great Circle* 9, 1987, pp. 73-95
14. Cf. Kenneth R. Hall *Maritime Trade and State Development in Early Southeast Asia* Sydney/London/Honolulu, 1985
15. G. Moorhouse *Calcutta* London, 1971; Gillian Tindall *City of Gold. The Biography of Bombay* London, 1982.

A particularly fascinating form of the genre is that in which urban biography is blended with personal autobiography as, e.g., in George L. Peet *Rickshaw Reporter* Singapore/Selangor, 1985, on Singapore; Sir Reader Bullard *The Camels Must Go: An Autobiography* London, 1961, chs. 5 and 11 (on Jeddah); or Violet Dickson *Forty years in Kuwait* London, 1971

16 C. C. MacKnight *The Voyage to Marege'. Macassan Trepangers in Northern Australia* Melbourne, 1976
17 R. Murphey *Shanghai—Key to Modern China* Cambridge, Mass., 1953
18 Nippon Yusen Kaisha *Glimpses of the East 1939-40* Tokyo, 1939, p. 115
19 An interesting article is Hiromi Masuda 'Japan's Industrial Development Policy and the Construction of the Nobiru Port: The Case Study of a Failure' *The Developing Economies* Tokyo, vol. 3, Sept. 1980, pp. 333-63
20 Frank Broeze, Peter Reeves & Kenneth McPherson 'Imperial Ports and the Modern World Economy: The Case of the Indian Ocean' *Journal of Transport History* 7, 1986, pp. 1-20
21 K. Dharmasena 'Bombay and Colombo 1948-1984: A Study in Port Development with Special Reference to Containerisation' *The Great Circle* 9, 1987, pp. 119-33
22 K. Dharmasena *The Port of Colombo 1860-1939* Colombo, 1980; C. R. de Silva *Ceylon under British Occupation* 2 vols, Colombo, 1962; E. F. C. Lodewyk *The Modern History of Ceylon* London, 1966; and 'Zeylanicus' *Ceylon between Orient and Occident* London, 1970
23 M. N. Pearson 'Littoral Society. The Case for the Coast' *The Great Circle* 7, 1985, p. 1
24 In this context an especially relevant case study of a specific occupational group is K. Dharmasena 'The Port and Dock Workers of Colombo 1860-1960' *The Great Circle* 7, 1985, pp. 100-115
25 K. Dharmasena 'Colombo, The Port of Asia' and M. H. Gunaratne 'Future Prospects for the Port of Colombo' *Economic Review* (published by the People's Bank, Colombo), 12, 5, August 1986, pp. 4-16 and 17-23
26 For much informative material on one particular port city see C. M. Turnbull *A History of Singapore 1819-1975* Singapore, 1975; and Song Ong Siang *One Hundred Years of the Chinese in Singapore* rep. Singapore, 1967
27 The large number of independent states in the Gulf and their strong interest in port industrialisation as a means of diversifying their oil-based economies has in recent years made port rivalry there assume extraordinary significance; a fascinating attempt to regulate and co-ordinate at least the liner shipping sector was the formation in 1976 of the United Arab Shipping Company, registered at Kuwait but jointly owned by the governments of Kuwait, Saudi Arabia, Iraq, Bahrain and Qatar. In this context one should see Fatimah H. Y. Al-Abdul-Razzak *Marine Resources of Kuwait* Kuwait/London, 1984
28 For recent contributions on the subject of the Swahili civilisation see several chapters in Jeffrey C. Stone (ed.) *Africa and the Sea* Aberdeen, 1985, viz. Gill Shepherd 'Trading Lineages in Historical Perspective', J. Knappert 'East Africa and the Indian Ocean', A. A. Mazrui 'Towards abolishing the Red Sea and re-Africanizing the Arabian Peninsula', and J. de V. Allen 'Habash, Habshi, Sidi, Sayyid'
29 H. J. de Blij *Mombasa: An African City* Evanston, Ill., 1968
30 On Aden see R. J. Gavin *Aden under British Rule, 1839-1967* London, 1975, *passim;* a comparable but Arab-centred account, unfortunately, is not available.
31 P. D. Proudfoot 'Changing Patterns of Maritime Activity in Central Sydney' *The Great Circle* 8, 1986, pp. 33-53
32 See, e.g., H. L. Beth et al. *25 Years of World Shipping* London, 1984, ch. 2
33 As set out in its original version: 'Port Cities: The Conceptual Problems', conference paper, Australian Historical Association, Sydney 1982
34 On Cochin see Sir Robert Bristow *Cochin Saga* 2nd ed, Cochin, 1967, and K. G. Kumar 'The Voyage of the Port of Cochin' *Business India* 26 August-8 September 1985, pp. 126-33
35 ICIOS II, section E: *Maritime Studies: Shipping, Trade and Port Cities* Perth, 1984. An international meeting of experts, held during ICIOS I (Perth, 1979) at the invitation of UNESCO, identified port cities as the central element of a future research programme devoted to intercultural relationships across the Indian Ocean. A further meeting was held at Zanzibar in February 1983, but as yet no tangible results have emanated from these initiatives
36 See, e.g., SPAFA *Historical and Archaeological Sites and Monuments of Southeast Asia* Bangkok, 1986, pp. 397-436 (Singapore); *Far Eastern Economic Review* 31 July 1986, pp. 18-21 (Tianjin) and 57-59 (Rangoon), and Maryann Bowen 'Architectural Conservation in Tanzania with Case Studies on Zanzibar Old Stone Town and Kilwa Kivinje' ICIOS II, vol. E: *Maritime Studies*

CHAPTER

Peter Reeves, Frank Broeze and Kenneth McPherson

Studying the Asian port city

The 'port city', and indeed the 'colonial' and the 'Asian' port city, is now familiar in both the general and the scholarly literature. It is a term which evokes a clear image without being conceptually well developed in the studies that we have. Most of these studies deal with ports rather than port cities; and they are concerned with aspects of the physical development or operation of a port or a series of ports.[1] Other studies discuss the city as a whole but, in doing so, relegate the port to a completely subordinate position so that the so-called 'port city' is robbed of its maritime character and becomes little more than a city that happens to be on a shoreline.[2] The result: we either have studies of ports with no reference to the cities to which they relate; or we have studies which discuss port cities as if there were no specific maritime functions that could influence the spatial and social evolution of the city.

It is clear, therefore, that while 'ports' and 'cities' are both well-enough understood and written about, the term 'port city' does not have the same degree of specific meaning. The conjoining of the two terms brings no modification of either which would allow an effective concept of 'port city' to emerge. Such a conceptualisation can only come, we maintain, if proper consideration is given to the role which ports play in determining the structure and functioning of port cities. We see a need, in other words, to put ports back into port cities!

One reason why there has been no development of this kind is that the dominant forms of 'Western' urban theory provide little or no basis for such an approach.[3]

The nineteenth century literature on urban sociology, which has provided the conceptual basis for almost all discussion of cities and the processes of urbanisation, was overwhelmingly concerned with socio-political structures in the city and the socio-political relationships that developed within urbanised groups; with 'urban culture and personality' as Michael Peter Smith has called it.[4] The economic character of cities was certainly recognised and the importance of trade in the origins of cities was stressed. Max Weber, indeed, saw trade as the 'decisive' influence;[5] and Henri Pirenne would not define an urban settlement as a city if it did not operate on the basis of long-distance trade.[6] Richard Fox has argued, in fact, that mercantile cities 'have been given special weight in the development of ideas about the nature of urbanism'.[7]

That, however, is precisely the difficulty: it was *urbanism*—the social-political operation of the city—rather than *economic functioning* to which the urban theorists paid attention.[8] Perhaps because the unprecedented rate of urbanisation in Europe and the United States in the later nineteenth century brought the problematic aspects of city life to the fore,[9] urban theorists concentrated their attention on the social structure of the city and the nature of the socio-political relationships that developed within it. Tönnies, and following him, Weber, focused most sharply on the extent to which urbanisation denoted a shift from the 'traditional' community with values derived from strong, affective, attachments (*'Gemeinschaft'*) to the 'modern', purposive, contract-based society (*'Gesellschaft'*). It was a shift which they detected in the cities of which they were themselves citizens and which they sought to understand from the study of the historical development of classical and medieval cities in Europe.[10]

This work was brought to its most sophisticated level by Max Weber. It is embodied in his final series of lectures, which were published posthumously as the *General Economic History*.[11] But it has its fullest expression in the essay *Die Stadt* which was incorporated into his major systematic work, *Wirtschaft und Gesellschaft (Economy and Society)*, which was also published posthumously. *Die Stadt* was later published in English translation as *The City*.[12] American urban sociologists, particularly of the Chicago school, developed a similar concern for socio-political structure and relationships and for urban culture both through empirical research in the burgeoning cities of the United States and through the development of theory. Such a concern is best typified by the writings of Robert E. Park and his associates; especially Louis Wirth whose mature article 'Urbanism as a way of life' marks perhaps its high point.[13]

Chinese junk: the mainstay of large-scale shipping between East Asia and the rest of the world.
From Theodore de Bry *Tertia Pars Indiae Orientalis* Frankfurt, 1601.
Courtesy of Mitchell Library, State Library of New South Wales.

Later, there was the anthropological development of these ideas by Robert Redfield in the 'rural-urban continuum model' which, while influential, has not gone uncriticised for its effects on comparative urban studies.[14]

More recently there have been signs that theoretical attention might be directed to the influence of particular economic functions on cities. Richard Fox's typology of 'primary urban types' which seeks to relate cities to urban economy and state power, for example, locates mercantile, administrative and industrial cities within that typology.[15] But the fact remains that earlier theory left much of that area vacant. The result was that the study of particular types of cities—as opposed to the study of city life as a phenomenon in itself—became the concern of other disciplines, most notably geography, and through that influence much of this kind of urban study became concerned with spatial, morphological and infrastructural aspects.[16] The consequent disjuncture between social theory and functional analysis has made it difficult to develop the kind of analysis that is needed for an understanding of port cities.

If we turn to the recent literature on the Asian port city we will see what has been possible and where the difficulties lie.

The seminal articles are those of the geographer Rhoads Murphey: the initial themes were spelt out in his article 'Urbanisation in Asia' published in 1966 and then considerably elaborated in his 1969 article 'Traditionalism and Colonialism: Changing Urban Roles in Asia'.[17] His lead has been picked up most effectively perhaps by Susan Lewandowski who published a series of articles on Madras in the mid to late 1970s; in these she directly employs the 'colonial port city' terminology as a basis for the discussion of the growth of Madras city and the development of relations within it.[18] In the mid 1970s the term also became the basis for a wide-ranging conference, at the University of California, Santa Cruz, at which an international gathering of scholars (including Murphey and Lewandowski) discussed 'The rise and growth of the colonial port cities in Asia'. The conference proceedings, including abstracts of the papers given and the verbatim record of discussion, appeared in 1979 under the editorship of Dilip Kumar Basu.[19]

The analytical thrust of Murphey's work, which can be seen as a development from his earlier very fine study of Shanghai and his work on Calcutta,[20] is directed at what he regarded as the historically pivotal role of the ports which were founded and/or developed by the European colonisers in Asia. These colonial port cities became the transformers of Asia, the 'beachheads of an exogenous system, planted by Westerners in a variety of Asian contexts, peripheral but nevertheless revolutionary'[21]; they became the centres in which Asia and the West confronted each other and from which Western institutions and values moved out to reorient the traditional states and societies of Asia. It is this theme which many of the participants at the Santa Cruz conference took up.

Port city life: A street scene in Goa, Western India. Here Portuguese as foreigners were integrated into the mestizo cultural life of the port city. In Goa they became the local ruling class, and were brokers and buyers in the slave trade. Both aspects of their role are illustrated here.
From Theodore de Bry *Tertia Pars Indiae Orientalis* Frankfurt, 1601.
Courtesy of Mitchell Library, State Library of New South Wales.

The published proceedings show that the main preoccupation of the discussions at the conference was with the part which the port cities studied played in the development of colonial control in Asia—in different regions and over quite a long time-span.

What has come from this 'colonial port cities' literature is an important set of ideas, and a range of examples, relating to the effects that colonial port cities have had on their respective hinterlands. But what was said of the port cities themselves?

Murphey, as he did with his Shanghai and Calcutta work earlier, deals very fully and effectively with the important question of the site and location of the colonial port cities and their consequent difficulties. He makes it clear in his approach that the importance and effectiveness of the colonial port cities derives from their position, and their functions, as ports: it is because they are ports, and because they operated as the main entry/exit points for the burgeoning, European-dominated trade of these states, that the colonial port cities acquired their importance in the colonial states' economies and hence in their social and political development. He shows how they became the largest cities in each state and how, in the larger states like India or Indonesia, colonial port cities came to occupy the top position in the state's urban hierarchy. Economically the port cities were pre-eminent throughout the nineteenth century and into the twentieth century, controlling (and often creating) trade, industry, finance (banking, insurance, capital markets) and transport networks of a modern kind, and exercising a dominant role over their agrarian hinterlands.

Lewandowski's focus on one city enables her to bring out in very sharp detail the developing morphology of Madras and its relation to the economic standing and activity of the city; this is particularly well done in the article in which she contrasts the colonial port city (Madras) with the ceremonial city (Madurai).[22] In this she demonstrates how the city expanded beyond the Fort and the early residential areas of 'Black Town' and 'White Town' to incorporate settlements built up by the East India Company (e.g., to accommodate weavers brought to the settlement to supply the Company's needs), and villages some of which were acquired from local rulers and others simply absorbed by the spread of the urban area. And she points to the significance of the shift of harbour facilities from the beachfront before the Fort to a new position further to the north. Moreover, in this discussion she always keeps in front of her the way in which the Indian merchant groups, through their work as intermediaries, acted to make settlements possible for agents and importers, on the one hand, and to exercise control over the population in the Indian areas of the town, on the other. In analysing this situation she follows the lead of Murphey. But she also draws on the theoretical work on the colonial city of Horvath, McGee and Balandier,[23] using this material to understand in particular the nature of the power relations within the city, especially those between colonisers and colonised. As a result she has given us a close and detailed insight into the internal dynamics of the colonial city which backs up Murphey's wider survey.

The writers and speakers at the Santa Cruz conference—who were asked to centre their work on three main themes: 'city-hinterland relationships, morphogenesis, and the interactions between indigenous and foreign elites'[24]— provide a further range of studies which, like Lewandowski's, extend our understanding of the 'colonial' role of the colonial port cities. The papers add considerably to our understanding, in particular, of mercantile groups and intergroup relations in colonial port cities; the morphology of the cities in relation to social developments within them; and the ways in which institutional and ideological development, which are important aspects of the Murphey picture, were stimulated.

What, in the final analysis, has this literature said about these centres as *port* cities? Or about the port as one of the dynamic forces of social change? In almost all the articles and papers comprising this colonial port city literature the port—apart from questions of its site and location and the general questions of the trade which passes through it—remains a shadowy appendage of the city. The ports have been taken for granted: it appears to be thought sufficient to have discussed trade, or commercial activity, to have discussed the port. The implicit view seems to be that the port's functions associated with commercial activity are uncomplicated, that they have no special features that require comment. The result is that the analyses concentrate on the overall structure of the city: merchants are seen within the 'colonial' power structure of the city as a whole (i.e. rulers/ruled, colonisers/colonised); or in relation to their own particular social groups (e.g., as caste or community leaders); but almost never in their directly commercial roles or in their commercial context. The discussions, although ostensibly of 'colonial port cities', in fact dealt with 'colonial cities' or 'Asian cities', in which the port and the port functions, if considered at all, were taken as a derivative of commercial activity and simply 'tacked on'.

It is not that the problem was not recognised. At the Santa Cruz conference there were two extended debates which worked around the questions, 'Why the *port* city?', 'What is the *port* city?'.[25] These discussions produced some valuable suggestions about the structure and historical role of the colonial port cities, (especially their extractive functions vis-à-vis their hinterlands) and some helpful pointers to the phases of development of colonial port cities in Asia. But the discussions did not produce any resolution of the basic problems raised. Basu, in his editorial introduction to the conference volume, underlined this: no commonly accepted definition was reached over the conference, he wrote,[26] but 'by the end of the conference some sort of complex consensus emerged as to the employment of the phrase "colonial port city in Asia" as a meaningful ideal-type that deserved further exploration and study'.[27]

In a recent collection of essays on *Colonial Cities*—'global pivots of change' as the position paper by Robert King sees them—there is a recognition by the editors, Robert Ross and Gerard Telkamp, that the requirement of colonisation 'demanded many unequivocally urban functions' and that 'pre-eminent amongst these was of course the need for a port'.[28] In due course,

The international culture of port cities: a 'Tupas' or 'Mardijker' of Batavia (Jakarta), Indonesia, and his wife. The Mardijkers were free traders of South Asian origin who filled important intermediary roles as a group of trading middlemen with a unique ethnic identity, furthered by their use of Portuguese as a lingua franca. From Hendrick Nieuhof Joan Nieuhofs Gedenkwaerdighe Zee-en Lant-reize door de voornaemste Landschappen van West en Oostindien *Amsterdam, 1682. Courtesy of Mitchell Library, State Library of New South Wales.*

the editors argue, these port settlements acquired ancillary functions while other cities sprang up as government garrison and/or industrial centres. In the following stage a small number of ever larger cities without any distinctive economic or functional base evolved. But, although the initial centrality of the port and port cities is certainly recognised, the process whereby 'the great port cities have so often become the megalopolises of the modern world...'[29] remains unexplored. The functioning of the port and its influence on the city is allowed to silently fade away with its metropolitanisation; no attempt is made to give social and cultural dimensions to the port and its encapsulating city as a single urban phenomenon.

This lack of conceptual detail in the introduction to *Colonial Cities* is more than compensated for by the series of historical case studies which follow, covering Asia, Africa, Latin America and the Caribbean. The variety of approaches adopted and the variety of urban situations discussed is particularly stimulating. What is significant, moreover, is that most chapters concern port cities and several offer valuable case studies and novel methodological approaches and insights.

Several chapters deal with places in Asia which were designed to become or did become major port cities. The one which failed most patently, Dutch Zeelandia in Taiwan, is the subject of a comprehensive chapter by J. L. Oosterhoff in which external forces and internal development are neatly interrelated. L. Blussé's discussion of the health problems of Batavia highlights a structural flaw almost inevitably inherent in the location of tropical port cities under Western control. X. Guillaume's brief account of the growth of Saigon-Cholon contains several other elements revealing the incompatibility of local climate and European life-style; more important for our purposes here is his observation that Saigon failed to grow into a port city of significance, as its port was unable to compete with the superior facilities of Singapore and Hong Kong and thus rise from its modest status as a regional port in the Southeast/East Asian port system to the apex of its hierarchy. Guillaume also gives illuminating details of the economic diversification of Saigon (less so of its Chinese satellite Cholon), but the links between internal evolution and external failure remain sketchy. Two essays on British Indian port cities contain several novel and interesting historical elements, but fall squarely within the traditional mould of general urban history. Dick Kooiman's 'Bombay: From Fishing Village to Colonial Port City (1662-1947)' is not really the systematic analysis of maritime-induced urban growth that its title would suggest. But it uses dialectic juxtapositions as a means to focus Bombay's experiences as a microcosm of western India. Peter Marshall's 'Eighteenth Century Calcutta' firmly reassesses the impact of this British implant in Bengal on the indigenous regional economy in which it was embedded (and considers it to have been but slight); but it is largely silent on the economic, social and spatial development of Calcutta itself. To a certain extent Marshall's contribution is quite representative of *Colonial Cities* as a whole: although it offers much new material, valuable insights and reassessments and some highly innovative perspectives, it does

*In the maritime world of Asia technological advantages revolved around shipping. Observation and description of types of ships, such as this example from the record of the first Dutch voyage to the Indies, was an investment. Shown are different Javanese and Malay vessels.
From* Cornelis de Houtman Verhael van de Reyse by de Hollandtsche Schepen gedaen naer Oost Indien *Middelburgh, 1597.
Courtesy of Mitchell Library, State Library of New South Wales.*

not confront either the specific and distinct identity of the port city or the implications of the use of the term.

In case it should be thought that this uncertainty about the concept of the 'port city' is especially an Asian problem, it is instructive to look at another symposium volume. This is the proceedings volume from a conference held in 1966 in Delaware on US 'seaport cities'.[30] The purpose of the conference was to investigate the growth of the major seaport cities—New York, Boston, Baltimore and Philadelphia—in the period 1790-1825 and to assess their impact on the economic growth of the US. Two salient points stand out in the analyses provided: first, the historical importance of the overseas merchants and their role as shipowners, bankers, and initiators of new business ventures; and, second, the function of the port cities as the 'centres for the introduction and diffusion of new industries'.[31] There is also in the collection an insistence on macroeconomic factors and the necessity to employ location theory for an understanding of both the regional hegemony of the four cities and their mutual relationships.[32] But very little was said about spatial and social factors, and in the collectivity of the papers and discussions these approaches were largely lost. One participant was moved to voice his uneasiness in the most telling words:

some of the speakers have talked about cities, some have talked about seaports, and others have talked about seaport cities. I believe that we need to examine more closely which of the problems and questions that have been raised are uniquely city problems, which are seaport problems, and which are seaport city problems.[33]

If the 'port city' exists as a type, and if the concept is to be used as a dynamic historical and functional model, the main economic base must be its port. Indeed, the port must become the central dynamic force and organising principle of the port city, and not remain a 'hidden function',[34] a mere appendage.

Advances have recently been made in the construction of theoretical frameworks for both the external and internal development of ports. Hoyle and Rimmer, in their studies on ports in East Africa and Australasia, have firmly established the concept of port hierarchy.[35] Drawing on the pioneering articles of the American geographer Guido Weigend,[36] they offer valuable insights into the crucial twin working spheres of each port, their forelands and hinterlands. The historical development of the physical port facilities has been critically analysed by James Bird,[37] and his six-stage 'Anyport' model has found widespread acceptance. In a recent article we have ourselves surveyed the construction of the modern ports in the Indian Ocean, developments which altered port hierarchies in the region and created the functional heart of the port cities.[38]

But, however useful the focus on the ports and port facilities may be, their relation to the overall evolution of the city must take account of economic, social and political dimensions. What is necessary, therefore, in order to properly understand the nature, functioning and significance of port cities, is a dynamic multi-disciplinary synthesis of port and city. The starting point must be that, in Stoianovich's words, the port creates in the urban community that surrounds it a 'distinctive form of environment',[39] a milieu that derives its uniqueness from the physical and economic dominance of the port.

Although not fully sustained in his excellent study of Hobart, Robert Solomon's insistence on the importance of 'Hobart's port development as an integral part and a prerequisite of total urban growth'[40] may well be taken as the specific formulation of this approach. At a vital point in his analysis he says:

Throughout the nineteenth and into the twentieth century the port continued to be a major section of inner Hobart, both of its fabric and its function. Its function of exchange was absolutely basic to the capital's increasingly normal role as a "trading town", and the warehouses backing the wharves formed the link between production of the land and commerce of the sea.[41]

In the following chapter, however, Solomon does not make the links which he postulated as being essential. He lays out in detail the evolution of the port, and he provides splendid detail on every aspect of the social and urban development of the city. But, in the end, he fails to translate the port into social terms. His book is, as its subtitle suggests, a study of an evolution of a capital city, but it misses the possibility of being a study of a port city. How the latter could have proceeded is suggested by Barrie Dyster's exploratory analysis of Hobart's north Tasmanian rival, Launceston, during the apogee of its historical importance.[42]

A much more satisfactory—indeed, in many ways, exemplary—study is K. Dharmasena's recent *The Port of Colombo 1860-1939*.[43] (From this work Dharmasena has developed chapter 6 of the present volume.) It deals with the rise of the port of Colombo after the construction of its new harbour, and the impact this had on the city of Colombo as a whole. Dharmasena has studied the geographical literature (Bird and Hoyle figure largely in his bibliography) and as a result his analysis has become an effective multi-disciplinary account. He gives a thorough review of both the seaborne and inland transport networks that focused on Colombo and, by 1910, made it the third largest port of the British Empire and the seventh of the world. Dharmasena demonstrates that Colombo's port fulfilled a double function as both the import-export gateway of Ceylon and the main coaling station of the Indian Ocean through which virtually all shipping to and from the Far East and Australasia passed.

The building and functioning of the port is recounted economically and lucidly. The circular causation of growing trade and shipping tonnages is matched by a discussion of port administration and the application of political power by the main users of the port to ensure it fulfilled their needs. The spatial development of port and dockland is traced in detail, as are the labour and social implications of their growth. In particular this meant the importation

The Governor's house in the castle of Batavia (Jakarta), Indonesia. Port cities which served as capitals or headquarters of trade empires, as did Batavia, depended on the creation of strong infrastructures and of symbols of strength and organisation. This depiction of the Governor's house shows how the hierarchy of a port city worked by separating the various ethnic groups and by the exertion of direct power over those groups.
From Hendrik Nieuhof *Joan Nieuhofs Gedenkwaerdighe Zee-en Lant-reize door de voornaemste Landschappen van West en Oostindien* Amsterdam, 1682.
Courtesy of Mitchell Library, State Library of New South Wales.

of massive groups of Tamils from India as construction and dock workers.[44] Dharmasena, however, includes other occupational groups and professions that were boosted by the port, its industries and services, and the people they employed.

In his last two chapters, Dharmasena deals with the twin problems of housing and public health. Through a judicious and creative use of both statistical and qualitative material (the latter mainly from official inquiries) he is able to reconstruct the material living conditions of those who inhabited the crowded dockland district, especially the Pettah ward. He also offers comparative figures with Paris, London and New York. Indeed, throughout he is conscious of the need to provide an international framework for his study, in order to both present a comprehensive explanation of growth and be able to evaluate the relative position and condition of Colombo.

Dharmasena, an economist, falls short of providing a full urban history. As he acknowledges himself, there is no account of the political, cultural or religious life of Colombo. But in the tightness of his organisation, the integration of macro- and micro-economic elements, and the structural approach to his subject, he has certainly created the groundwork for a comprehensive study of this particular colonial port city and provided a model that should find widespread emulation for Asia and elsewhere.

Such port city studies must take their start at the places where goods and passengers are transferred between ship and shore—which is, after all, the ultimate rationale of the port—and in consecutive stages include all aspects of urban economic, social, cultural and spatial development that are generated, dominated or significantly influenced by the port. This *functional and historically dynamic* 'port sector', finally, must be integrated into the specific identity of the port city and its people: location and morphology; economic functioning and performance; social structure and cultural character; political economy and culture.

It is obvious that a static statistical approach will not be sufficient. In order to understand the functional links that emanate from the port—shipowning, shipbuilding and repair, providoring and stevedoring, trading, finance, inland transport facilities, security services, communication industries, import and export industries—one must have a qualitative and historical as well as quantitative insight into the specific circumstances of the origins, growth and circumstances of each individual enterprise and sector. Both macroeconomic studies, like that of Chiu on Hong Kong or Lobe's more general *Metropolen der Meere*,[45] and histories of pivotal companies, firms and individuals are indispensable for such a dynamic synthesis. Of particular importance are business histories of port-based firms, such as shipping companies and agencies, mercantile and insurance enterprises, banks or construction companies, all of which may reveal the intimate functional, financial and entrepreneurial links which are at the core of the inner dynamism of the port city in its organic evolution.[46]

This cannot be achieved without a complete breakdown of aggregate

Studying the Asian port city

The family of the 'Moorish pedlar' of Batavia (Jakarta), Indonesia. Arab or Muslim traders constituted one of the most important ethnic groups linking Southeast Asia and China with Western Asia and ultimately Europe.
From Hendrik Nieuhof *Joan Nieuhofs Gedenkwaerdighe Zee-en Lant-reize door de voornaemste Landschappen van West en Oostindien* Amsterdam, 1682.
Courtesy of Mitchell Library, State Library of New South Wales.

quantitative data so that we can learn about the nature of individual firms and their relationship to the port and its maritime industries. Thus the transport sector of a port city will contain both elements and firms that are specifically related to its port (e.g. tugs, ferries, lighters, inland water, road and rail traffic to link the port with its hinterland), and others that are generated by the sheer size of its population (e.g. rickshaws, taxis, and public transport systems). Often it is also difficult to distinguish sharply between a 'port function' or a 'general function'. A road network can serve both the port sector and the general urban population, while merchant bankers and corporate trading banks may change over time from being primarily related to the needs of overseas commerce to serving as general financial and investment institutions. The same applies to industries that originated through the port, as the textile mills of Bombay, but in due course can assume a much more independent role and position.

Even more complex problems arise, when one considers the social, cultural and political connections within the port city. How much does the demographic and ethnic evolution of Bombay reflect its port city function? How much of the Chinese presence and influence in Singapore is due to its port? These general questions can be matched with very specific ones. Nowadays all major urban centres have universities, and it would be foolish to insist that the tertiary institutions of Calcutta, Singapore, Colombo or Kuwait were founded as a direct result of their being port cities rather than fully developed urban centres. Yet on closer examination it may well be found that their establishment and development, their curriculum, and regional and even national roles and significance were to a certain extent shaped by factors that can immediately be related to the sphere of influence of the port and the people connected with it. To cite two European cases: the University of Hamburg was not founded until after World War I because of the determined opposition from Hamburg's commercial and financial elite. Yet, paradoxically, it grew out of a colonial institute that itself constituted a striking example of how the cultural horizons of Hamburg were widened by its global shipping links. The influence of the University of Glasgow on the development of the city's and Scotland's marine engineering (including the building of many dredgers for Asian ports!) in the nineteenth century is equally well documented. It is no coincidence that Kobe boasts a University of Commerce (as did Rotterdam whose institute was later 'generalised' into the Erasmus University), or that geographers at the University of Southampton are greatly interested in port city development. The University of Sydney's Challis Chairs in History and English were founded by bequests from John Henry Challis, a partner of the city's leading mercantile house, Flower Salting & Co.

Other aspects of the cultural dynamism of port cities are illuminated in *Die Hafenstadt. Eine maritime Kulturgeschichte* by the East German ethnologist and historian Wolfgang Rudolph.[47] In this book Rudolph devoted particular attention to the rise of museums and zoological gardens as well as the many maritime/overseas influences on the folk life and popular culture in port cities. With these themes he identified important elements of what, specifying

Stoianovich's 'distinctive form of environment', constitutes the port city's maritime milieu.

Problems also exist in disentangling the influence of the port and the political power that is associated with it. It is no more than a statement of historical fact to observe that all European settlements across the oceans, whether in Asia, Australia, Africa or the Americas, emanated from ports. This is true for new creations as well as existing indigenous port cities that were 'taken over' by the European invaders. Bombay, Calcutta, Colombo, Singapore, or Sydney functionally served very comparable purposes as, for example, Boston or Buenos Aires; comparisons with the endogenous port cities of Japan after the Meiji restoration would be highly interesting. Because of the early predominance of trading and migration concerns, political power was also vested in those centres. This could, of course, later be shifted, in order to overcome acute problems of shortage of physical space (as when the Philippine government relocated to Quezon City), but more usually was accomplished to prevent the economic hegemony of the port city from stifling the interests of the remainder of its political entity or to provide a balance between the various regional interests of a much larger polity (e.g. the foundation of New Delhi, Islamabad or Canberra); a particularly interesting example with many significant features, even if it geographically only involved a small shift, is the move discussed in Chapter 7 of this volume of the Sri Lankan government from Colombo to Sri Jayawardenapura. However diverse in their historical and political setting, all such relocations can be related to what might be termed the 'overdevelopment' of the port city in its maturity. By contrast, in many other cases considerable power—sometimes national, sometimes regional—remained vested in the port city: one may think here of Rangoon, Bangkok and Jakarta but, on the provincial level, also of Bombay, Madras, Ujung Pandang or Fremantle/Perth. Even so, it is clear that in the course of time, political life becomes increasingly separate from functional beginnings.

It can thus be seen that it will not be an easy task to identify individual aspects of the physical, economic, social, cultural and political life of a port city that can be fully or mainly attributed to the stimulus of the port. What is needed is a conceptual framework in which the urban community that comprises the port city is seen as a dynamic organism whose development is predominantly influenced by its port. And being dynamic, there will be changes in this port city character. Some settlements can exist for a considerable time before they can be classified as 'port cities'. It is also possible for an urban community to outgrow or transcend its 'port city' character—as has happened in Bombay, Calcutta, Jakarta, Manila and Sydney, all of which have developed into general cities.[48] But such a shift can occur also through the withering of the port sector—as in the virtual death of the inner-city dock areas of many European port cities through the recent growth of bulk shipping and containerisation. Difficult as this analysis, therefore, will be, it is only through an understanding of the fundamental functioning and comprehensive internal structure of the port city that its external role and significance can be assessed and, in turn, understood.

The port city as a thin line between the sea and the hinterland. Banten (Bantam), West Java, Indonesia, c. 1630, a West Javanese royal capital and port city, with its prominent Javanese-style mosque. Courtesy of the Bibliothèque Nationale, Paris, Catres et Plans.

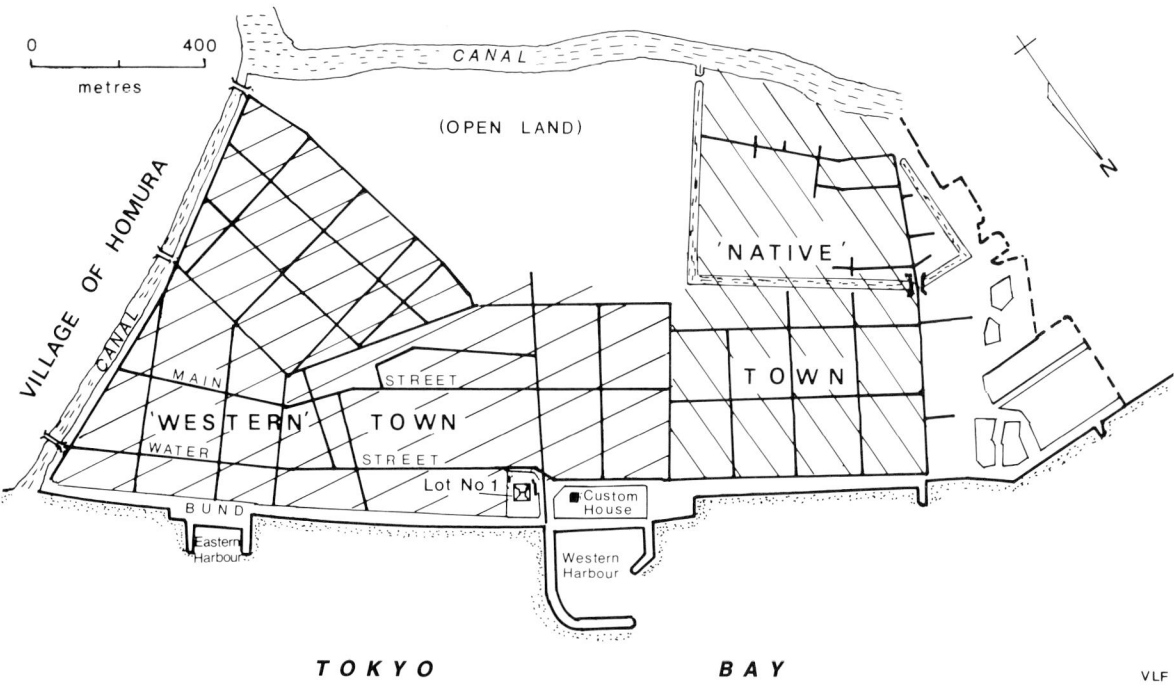

Map 4 Yokohama during its brief phase as a 'semi-colonial city', 1870. At the first land sales, in 1860, the leading British firm, Jardine Matheson & Co, as they had done in Shanghai, purchased Lot No.1, right on the Bund and closest to the Custom House.

Port cities are the interface between land and seas; but are they the only vehicle through which that relationship can be studied? Michael Pearson has suggestively argued that maritime historians should consider the broader concept of 'littoral society' — a community extending inwards from the coast with porous frontiers acting as filters through which the salt of the sea is gradually replaced by the silt of the land.[49] A particular application of this idea can be seen in Roberts' chapter on Colombo, where the author discusses the interaction between that port city and the surrounding southwestern lowlands of Sri Lanka.

By emphasising the need to identify the specific maritime character of the people inhabiting the littoral, Pearson is able to include all seas-related behaviour in this concept. This is extremely valuable and should form the basis for serious maritime history. But it does group together many communities whose socio-economic structure and role are very different. Perhaps it is here that port cities can also play a role—as a means of understanding the evolution of the littoral society surrounding them? (Or conversely, as Roberts suggests, for understanding how, in the course of time the port city is gradually 'invaded' by its surroundings and consequently assumes a much less 'distinctive form of environment'?) Connections of importance easily come to mind: those implied in the port hierarchy concept; hinterland politics; and the recruitment of seafarers, dockers and other port industry workers. Thus 'littoral society' and 'port city' might be seen as concentric but distinct concepts. The former may have great value as an analytical tool for the maritime history of Asia; the latter would seem to be indispensable as an explanatory vehicle for the history of the region. Asia's 'imperial age' cannot be understood—any more than can earlier periods in its long and complex history—without a comprehensive analysis of its port cities.

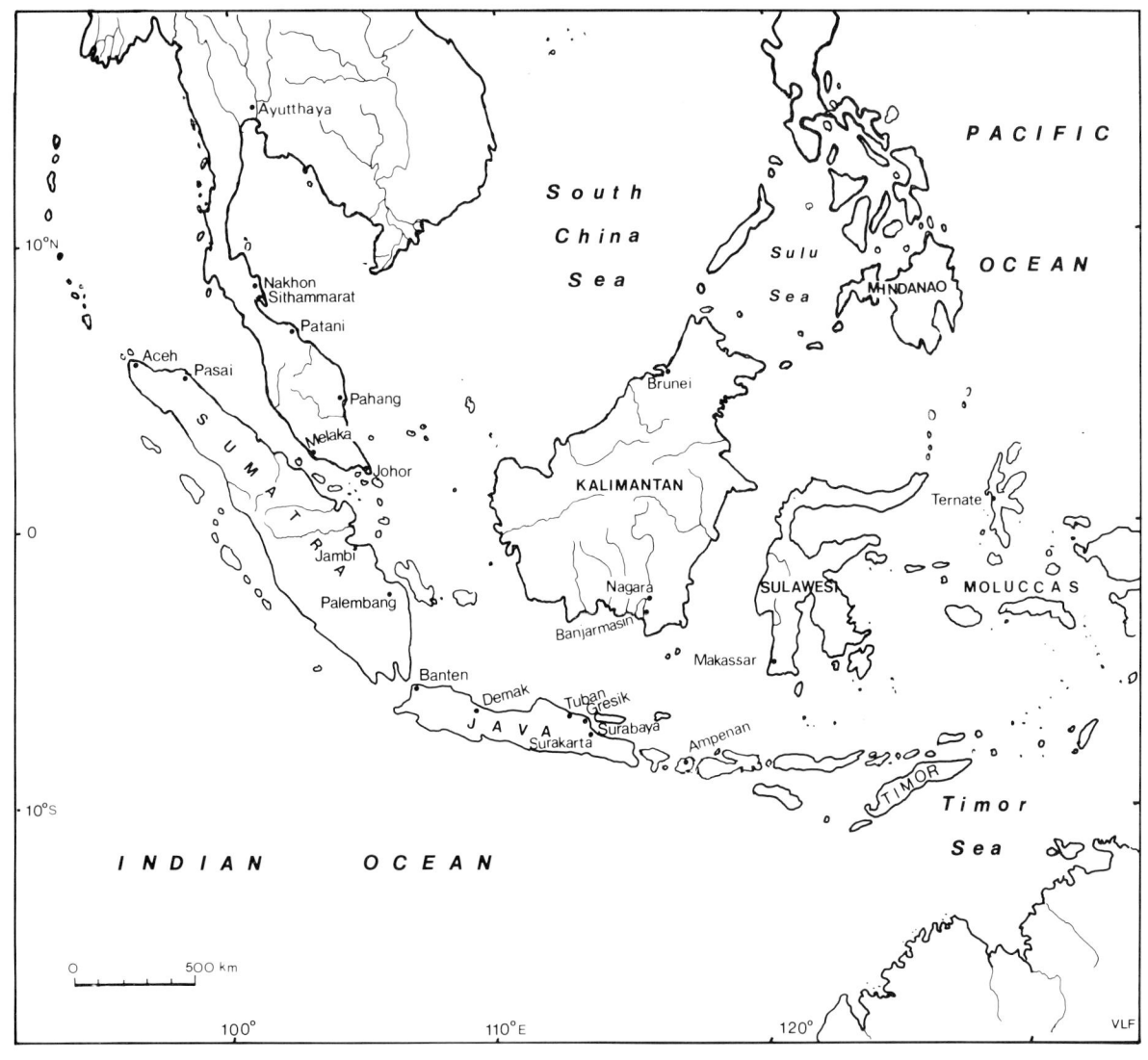

Map 5 *Maritime Southeast Asia, c.1600*

Notes

1. See, e.g., G. Jackson *The History and Archaeology of Ports* Tadworth, 1983; W.R.S. Sharpe, *The Port of Bombay* Bombay, [1930]; A. Haider *History of Karachi* Karachi, 1974; or J. Bird *Seaport Gateways of Australia* London, 1968
2. Cf. the review article by Frank Broeze, 'Port Cities. The Search for an Identity' *Journal of Urban History* II, 1985, pp.209-225, dealing with works on Glasgow, Liverpool, Hamburg and Colombo
3. Al McCoy makes a similar point in his detailed study of a Philippine port city, 'A Queen Dies Slowly: The Rise and Decline of Iloilo City', in A. McCoy & E.C. de Jesus, (ed.) *Philippine Social History. Global Trade and Local Transformations* Manila and Sydney, 1982, p.298 and fn. 2. A comparable concern is expressed in T.G. McGee's critical essays in his *The Urbanisation Process in the Third World: Explorations in Search of a Theory* London, 1971, reprint 1975, esp. ch. 1, 'The Urbanization Process: Western Theory and Third World Reality'
4. Michael Peter Smith *The City and Social Theory* Oxford, 1980, p.vii. Cf. Don Martindale's 'Notes on a Social-Psychological Theory of the City', in his preface to Max Weber *The City*, trans. and ed. D. Martindale & G. Neuwirth, New York, 1966, pp.30-42
5. Max Weber *General Economic History*, trans. F.H. Knight, New York, 1961, p.239: 'It is characteristic that in antiquity there was no city of importance which lay more than a day's journey from the sea; only those places flourished which for political or geographical reasons possessed exceptional opportunities for trade. Consequently Sombart is essentially incorrect in asserting that ground rent is the mother of the city and of commerce. The facts stand in the reverse order; settlement in the city is occasioned by the possibility and the intention of employing the rents in trade, and the decisive influence of trade in the founding of cities stands out.' Cf. *The City* pp.66-70 for the economic definition of the city
6. H. Pirenne *Medieval Cities. Their Origins and the Revival of Trade*, first pub. Princeton, 1925; references here to a new revised translation by F.D. Halsey, pub. by Princeton 1946 and reprinted by Doubleday in paperback, n.d. See pp.39-53 'City Origins', and pp.55-74 'The Revival of Commerce'. Martindale discusses this view in his preface to *The City*, pp.49-50. Lewis Mumford is critical of it in *The City in History. Its Origins, Its Transformations and Its Prospects* Penguin, 1966, p.293
7. Richard Fox *Urban Anthropology. Cities in Their Cultural Settings* Englewood Cliffs, NJ, 1977, p.93
8. It is interesting to note, in this present context, what is almost Weber's last mention of economic functioning in *The City*: 'There is no intention here of advancing the further casuistic distinction required by a purely economic theory of the city. Moreover, it hardly needs to be mentioned that actual cities nearly always represent mixed types. Thus, if cities are to be classified at all, it must be in terms of their prevailing economic component, p.70. It should also be underlined here that Weber, of all theorists, was conscious of the economic effects of social organisation: his *Protestant Ethic and the Spirit of Capitalism* is proof of that. Note also Reinhard Bendix's pointer to the subtlety of Weber's analysis of these matters: *Max Weber, An Intellectual Portrait* London, 1966, p.74, n.47
9. Don Martindale provides a framework for this interpretation in his preface to *The City*, esp. pp.12-17
10. F. Tönnies *Gemeinschaft und Gesellschaft* began as his doctoral dissertation in 1881 and was published in 1887; it had its definitive edition in 1912 (a significant date given that this was in the middle of Weber's period of writing *Wirtschaft und Gesellschaft* and, specifically, *The City*); see J. Freund, 'German Sociology in the Time of Max Weber', in T. Bottomore & R. Nisbet (eds.) *A History of Sociological Analysis* London, 1978, p.152; see also his discussion of Tönnies' concepts, pp.153-57. Weber acknowledges his connection with Tönnies in *The Theory of Social and Economic Organisation*, trans. A.M. Henderson & T. Parsons, New York, 1964, p.88; *The Theory* is the first part of *Wirtschaft und Gesellschaft*. Bendix *Max Weber* p.476, n. 8, makes the important point that while Weber adopted the distinction he opposed the reification that was implicit in Tönnies' concept; for this reason Weber spoke of 'Vergemeinschaftung' and 'Vergesellschaftung'—the 'coming into existence' of community and society. There is a further useful treatment of Tönnies in W.J. Cahnman 'Hobbes, Toennies and Vico: starting points in sociology' in B. Rhea, (ed.) *The Future of the Sociological Classics* London, Boston and Sydney, 1981, esp. pp.19-22
11. *General Economic History*, trans. F.H. Knight, New York, 1961. The German edition was prepared in 1923. The book was reconstituted from his lecture series 'Outlines of Universal Social and Economic History' at the University of Munich in 1919-20; preface by German editors, pp. xvii-xviii
12. *The City* was written between 1911 and 1913 during the period when Weber, now financially independent, was able to devote himself to the writing of *Wirtschaft und Gesellschaft (WuG)*; Bendix *Max Weber* p.72, n.42. It

was published posthumously in 1921 and later incorporated into *WuG*—it formed pp.514-601 in vol.II; Bendix, p.ix. Bendix gives an overview of the ideas in pp.70-79. One further point of Weber's analysis should be noted; this was his conclusion, given his premises as to the essential character of city life, that cities of the 'Occidental' kind could not exist in 'the Orient'; see *General Economic History* p.234: 'The citizen in the quality of membership in a class is always the citizen of a particular city, and the city in this sense, has existed only in the western world, or elsewhere, as in the early period in Mesopotamia, only in an incipient stage'; p.235-36: 'It is true that outside the western world there were cities in the sense of a fortified point and the seat of political and hierarchical administration. But outside the occident there have been cities in the sense of a unitary community ... That cities have not existed outside the occident in the sense of a political community is a fact calling for explanation. That the reason was economic in character is very doubtful. As little is it the specific "Germanic spirit" which produced the unity, for in China and India there were unitary groups much more cohesive than those of the occident, and yet the particular union in cities is not found there.' Cf. *The City* pp.99-100: 'The magical barriers to Oriental civic development'

13   Martindale in his preface to *The City*, pp. 16-30, gives an excellent overview of developments up to Park/Wirth. G. Sjoberg, 'Theory and Research in Urban Sociology', in P.M. Hauser & L.F. Schnore (ed.) *The Study of Urbanization* New York, 1965, pp.156-89 brings that through to the 1960s. The key writings were R.E. Park, E.V. Burgess & R.D. McKenzie *The City* Chicago, 1925, which incorporated Park's seminar paper, 'Suggestions for the investigation of human behaviour in the urban environment'; and Louis Wirth 'Urbanism as a Way of Life' *American Journal of Sociology* XLIV, 1938, pp.1-24. Note that Wirth prepared the bibliography for Park et al. *The City*. Wirth was reprinted in P.K. Hatt & A.J. Reiss (eds.) *Cities and Societies* New York, 1957, pp.46-63

14   Robert Redfield *The Folk Culture of Yucatan* Chicago, 1941; R. Redfield & Milton Singer 'The Cultural Role of Cities' *Economic Development and Cultural Change* III, 1954, pp.53-73; R. Redfield *Peasant Society and Culture* Chicago, 1961. McGee *The Urbanization Process and the Third World* ch.2, 'The Rural-Urban Continuum Debate: The Pre-Industrial City and Rural-Urban Migration', is a good critique of the debate with a full bibliography to the late 1960s; this was first published in *Pacific Viewpoint* V, 2, September 1964. For a more sympathetic anthropological summary see Fox *Urban Anthropology*, pp.9-12

15   Fox *Urban Anthropology* pp.32-38. It is interesting to note that Fox includes among his examples Japanese port cities from the fourteenth to the sixteenth centuries, drawing on Takeo Yazaki *Social Change and the City in Japan: From Earliest Times through the Industrial Revolution* 1968

16   Among these may be noted: R.S. MacElwee *Port Development* New York, 1925; A.J. Sargent *Seaports and Hinterlands* London, 1938; F.W. Morgan *Ports and Harbours* London, 1952; rev. edn J. Bird, 1958; L.E. Klimm 'Man's ports and harbours' in W.L. Thomas (eds.) *Man's Role in Changing the Face of the Earth* Chicago, 1956; G.G. Weigend, 'Some elements in port geography' *Geographical Review*, XLVIII, April 1958, pp.185-200; J. Bird *The Major Seaports of the United Kingdom* London, 1963 and *Seaports and Seaport Terminals* London, 1971; B.S. Hoyle *The Seaports of East Africa* Nairobi, 1967 and B.S. Hoyle & D. Hilling (eds.) *Seaport Development in Tropical Africa* London, 1970. On the more technical side: R.S. MacElwee *Ports and Terminal Facilities* New York, 2nd. edn, 1926; F.M. DuPlat Taylor *Design Construction and Maintenance of Docks, Wharves and Piers* London, 3rd. edn, 1949; and H.F. Cormick *Dock and Harbour Engineering* 4 vols, London, 1958-62. A recent example from the viewpoint of urban planning is Josef W. Konvitz *Cities and the Sea. Port City Planning in Early Modern Europe* Baltimore and London, 1978 which, despite its strong European focus, does have some interesting ideas about port cities, maritime culture and approaches to the development of ports

17   R. Murphey, 'Urbanisation in Asia' *Ekistics*, 21, 122, pp.8-17; reprinted in G. Breese (ed.) *The City in Newly-Developing Countries: Readings in Urbanism and Urbanisation* Englewood Cliffs, NJ, 1966, pp.58-75; 'Traditionalism and Colonialism: Changing Urban Roles in Asia' *Journal of Asian Studies* 29, 1969, pp.67-84

18   S. Lewandowski, 'Urban Growth and Municipal Development in the Colonial City of Madras, 1860-1900' *Journal of Asian Studies* 34, 1975, pp.342-60; 'Merchants, Temples and Power in the Colonial Port City of Madras', abstract of paper in Dilip K. Basu (ed.) *The Rise and Growth of the Port Cities in Asia* Santa Cruz: Centre of South Pacific Studies, University of California, Santa Cruz, 1979, pp.82-87; see also pp.102-4; 'Urban Planning in the Asian Port City: Madras, an Overview, 1920-1970' *South Asia*, n.s., 2, 1 & 2, 1979, pp.30-45; 'Changing Form and Function in the Ceremonial and Colonial Port City in India: an Historical Analysis of Madurai and Madras' in K.N. Chaudhuri & C.J. Dewey (eds) *Economy and Society* Delhi, 1979, pp.299-329; see also her *Migration and Ethnicity in Urban India. Kerala Migrants in the City of Madras, 1870-1970* Delhi, 1980, esp. ch.2, 'The colonial city of Madras and its migrants, 1870-1920'. Also interesting is Robert Frykenberg 'The Socio-Political Morphology of Madras: An Historical Interpretation' *Indo-British Review* XI, 2, 1985, pp.5-37

19 Basu *Port Cities in Asia*
20 R. Murphey *Shanghai: The Key to Modern China* Cambridge, Mass., 1953; and 'The City in the Swamp: Aspects of the Site and Early Growth of Calcutta' *The Geographical Journal* 130, 1964, pp.241-56
21 Murphey 'Traditionalism and Colonialism' p.83
22 Lewandowski 'Changing Form and Function'
23 G. Balandier 'The Colonial Situation: A Theoretical Approach' in I. Wallerstein *Social Change: The Colonial Situation* New York, 1966; T.G. McGee *The Southeast Asian City* London, 1967; and R.J. Horvath 'In Search of a Theory of Urbanisation: the Colonial City' *East Lakes Geographer* 5, 1969, pp.60-82
24 Basu 'Introduction' *Port Cities in Asia* p.xvi
25 *Ibid*, pp.77-79 and 238-48
26 *Ibid*, p.xxiv
27 *Ibid*, p.xvi
28 Robert Ross & Gerard J. Telkamp (eds) *Colonial Cities. Essays on Urbanism in a Colonial Context* Dordrecht/Boston/Lancaster, 1985, p.1
29 *Ibid* p.2
30 D.T. Gilchrist (ed.) *The Growth of the Seaport Cities 1790-1825* Charlottesville, 1967
31 *Ibid*. p.92
32 *Ibid*. p.83-91
33 *Ibid*. p.196 (the speaker was James P. Baughman)
34 J. Bird *Seaports and Seaport Terminals* London, 1971, p.144
35 B.S. Hoyle *The Seaports of East Africa: a Geographical Study*; B.S. Hoyle & D. Hilling (eds) *Seaports and Tropical Development in Africa* cited above, note 16; P.J. Rimmer 'The Search for Spatial Regularities in the Development of Australian Seaports 1861-1961/2' in B.S. Hoyle (ed.) *Transport and Development* London, 1973
36 See 'Some Elements in the Study of Port Geography' *The Geographical Review* 48, 1958, cited above, note 16; also 'Ports: Their Hinterlands and Forelands' *The Geographical Review* 42, 1952, pp.660-72; 'The Problem of the Hinterland and Foreland as Illustrated by the Port of Hamburg' *Economic Geography* 32, 1956, pp.1-16
37 J. Bird *The Major Seaports of the United Kingdom* and *Seaports and Seaport Terminals* cited above, note 16; also *Seaport Gateways of Australia* London, 1968. For an East German response see H. Obenaus & J. Salenski *Geographie des Seeverkehrs* Berlin, GDR, 1979
38 Frank Broeze, Peter Reeves & Kenneth McPherson 'Imperial Ports and the Modern World Economy: The Case of the Indian Ocean' *Journal of Transport History* 7, 1986, pp.1-20
39 T. Stoianovich *French Historical Method. The Annales Paradigm* Ithaca/London, 1976, p.86
40 R.J. Solomon *Urbanisation: The Evolution of an Australian Capital City* Sydney, 1976
41 *Ibid*. p.363
42 Barrie Dyster 'The Port of Launceston before 1851' *The Great Circle* 3, 1981, pp.103-124
43 K. Dharmasena *The Port of Colombo 1860-1939* Colombo, 1980
44 Since then elaborated in his article 'The Port and Dock Workers of Colombo 1860-1960' *The Great Circle* 7, 1985, pp.100-115
45 T.N. Chiu *The Port of Hong Kong* Hong Kong, 1973; Karl Löbe *Metropolen der Meere* Düsseldorf, 1979. A general history with a keen eye for the maritime/economic base is C.M. Turnbull *A History of Singapore 1819-1975* Singapore, 1975. Generally on port city industrialisation see B.S. Hoyle & D.A. Pinder (eds.) *Cityport Industrialization and Regional Development* Oxford, 1981; and B.S. Hoyle & D. Hilling (eds.) *Seaport Systems and Spatial Change: Technology, Industry and Development Strategies* Chichester, 1984. An incisive critique of the People's Republic of China's port-based 'Special Economic Zones' development can be found in *South* October 1985, pp.75-150; *see also* Y.C. Jao & C.K. Leung, (eds.) *China's Special Economic Zones: Policies, Problems and Prospects* New York, 1986.
46 Among the many individual and collective business histories one should see G.C. Allen & A. Donnithorne *Western Enterprise in Far Eastern Economic Development* London, 1954; F.R. Harris *Jamsetji Nusserwanji Tata* 2nd edn, Bombay, 1958; H. Baudet (ed.) *Trade World and World Trade* Rotterdam, 1963; G.D. Khanolkar *Walchand Hirachand* Bombay, 1969; C. Drage *Taikoo* London, 1970; A. Coates, *Whampoa. Ships on the Dry* Hong Kong, 1980; M. Keswick (ed.) *The Thistle and the Jade* Hong Kong, 1982; Stanley Chapman *The Rise of Merchant Banking* (London, 1984), esp. pp.140-44 on James Finlay & Co; and Stephanie Jones *Two Centuries of Overseas Trading. The Origins and Growth of the Inchcape Group* London, 1986

In the European context it is significant to note the strong developmental and diversifying impact of active liner shipping; this is most clearly understood and pursued by the leaders of shipping companies in ports like Bremen and Amsterdam, which geographically are at a fundamental disadvantage compared to their main rivals such as Hamburg and Rotterdam. See, for example, A. Petzet's biography *Heinrich Wiegand* (one of the major figures in the history of the Norddeutscher Lloyd and Bremen industralisation; Bremen 1932), p.189 (Petzet was Wiegand's son-in-law and largely used autobiographical material); or the memoirs of a prominent member of the Amsterdam business world, D.A. Delprat *De Reeder Schrijft Zijn Journaal* The Hague, 1983, pp.293-94. How even in Hamburg, ultimately much rested on the active intervention and personal connections of the maritime and business elite of the city appears most strongly from Elsabea Rohrmann's biography *Max von Schinckel* Hamburg, 1971, which could well serve as a prototype for similar biographical studies elsewhere; importantly, for our understanding of the comprehensive functioning of the port city, she does not restrict herself to Von Schinckel's economic activities, but also devotes attention to his social, cultural and political roles. How these were rooted in his personal and family life can be gleaned from his *Lebenserinnerungen* Hamburg, 1929.

These business and individual studies of course should not be seen as valuable only for an understanding of modern or European enterprise; see, for example, Song Ong Siang *Chinese in Singapore, passim*; Yusof A. Talib 'Les Hadramis et le monde malais' *Archipel* 7, 1974, pp.41-68; Calvin H. Allen Jr 'The Indian Merchant Community of Masqat' *Bulletin of the School of Oriental and African Studies* 44, 1981, pp.39-53; Asiya Siddiqi, 'The Business World of Jamsetjee Jeejeebhoy' *Indian Economic and Social History Review* 19, 1982, pp.301-324; Blair B. Kling *Partner in Empire: Dwarkenath Tagore and the Age of Enterprise in Eastern India* Berkeley, 1986; and Rajat Ray 'Chinese Financiers and Chetti Bankers in Southern Waters' *Itinerario* II, 1987, 1, pp.209-234

Other valuable publications, which all too often are regarded as merely ephemeral, include annuals produced by steamship companies (such as Nippon Yusen Kaisha's *Glimpses of the East*), tourist and business directories (such as the just reprinted *All About Shanghai* intr. by H.J. Lethbridge, Hong Kong, 1984), or compilations like A. Macmillan *Seaports of India and Ceylon* London, 1928

47 Wolfgang Rudolph *Die Hafenstadt. Eine maritime Kulturgeschichte* Oldenburg/Munich/Hamburg, 1980
48 Cf. James E. Vance, Jr *This Scene of Man. The Role and Structure of the City in the Geography of Western Civilization* New York, 1977, pp.20-21 on the metropolitanisation of the one-time port cities of San Francisco, New York and Montreal.
49 M.N. Pearson 'Littoral Society: The Case for the Coast' *The Great Circle* 7, 1985, pp.1-8

Further reading

Basu, Dilip K. (ed.) *The Rise and Growth of Port Cities in Asia* Santa Cruz 1979. An important collection with both abstracts and notes of discussion at a pioneering conference. Publication of the full text of the conference papers (*Colonial Port Cities in Asia*) was foreseen for 1988.

Broeze, F., P. Reeves and K. McPherson 'Imperial Ports and the Modern World Economy: the Case of the Indian Ocean' *Journal of Transport History* 7, 1986, pp. 1-20. Important as an overview of the processes involved in the physical development of ports.

Dharmasena, K. *The Port of Colombo, 1860-1939* Colombo 1980. Perhaps the best study of a single South Asian port that we have so far.

Hoyle, B.S. and D. Hilling (eds) *Seaport Systems and Spatial Change: Technology, Industry and Development Strategies* Chichester 1984. Contains significant work on the geographical dimensions of port development.

McCoy, A. ' "A Queen Dies Slowly": the rise and decline of Iloilo City' in A. McCoy and E.C. de Jesus (eds) *Philippine Social History, Global Trade and Local Transformations* Manila and Sydney, 1982. A strongly developed study of the political, economic and social dynamics of change in a colonial port city.

Murphey, R. 'Traditionalism and Colonialism: Changing Urban Roles in Asia' *Journal of Asian Studies* 29, 1969, pp.67-84. A seminal article on the effects of European colonialism on port cities in Asia.

Anthony Reid

CHAPTER

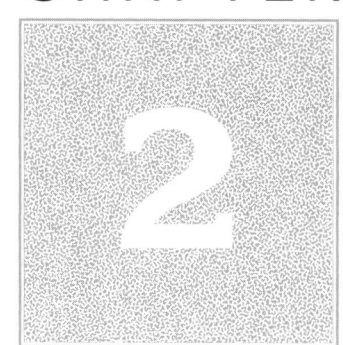

The organisation of production in the pre-colonial Southeast Asian port city

Much of the writing on Asian port cities in recent years, including the present volume, has been devoted to understanding the functioning and role of European colonial port cities—'beachheads of an exogenous system ... peripheral but nevertheless revolutionary'.[1] These colonial ports in Asia were indeed revolutionary, chiefly because they became in the nineteenth and twentieth centuries the channel through which the industrial revolution and finance capitalism began to transform Asia. They first undermined and finally overwhelmed the older cities which had always been at the centre of Asian life. To understand how and to what extent they did so, it is necessary to understand how the traditional Asian port city functioned, and how it related to the political and cultural life of its surroundings. One of the neglected aspects of this prominence of the port city in Southeast Asia is the extent of industrial activity carried on in them which, in producing for both local and overseas markets, significantly added to commercial and maritime entrepot functions. The purpose of this chapter is to discuss the organisation of this production.

In Southeast Asia, that meeting place of oceans and waterways, by contrast to most other regions of Asia where inland cities held the supremacy, the port city was a much more dominant element, as maritime trade had always been prominent. Indeed, international shipping was never more central in the economic life of Southeast Asia than in the period of this study, the sixteenth and seventeenth centuries, which happen to be relatively well documented. Nevertheless, the port city of the 'exogenous beachhead' type was almost unknown until introduced by Europeans. Then, it borrowed not so much from Asian precedents but from the longstanding tradition of Phoenician, Greek and Venetian trading colonies in the Mediterranean and German ones in northern Europe which stood politically independent from their surroundings. In Southeast Asia traders from other parts of the region, China, India or Arabia, did not set up politically separate or autonomous 'Javanese' or 'Chinese' cities, even in trading ports where their communities formed a virtual majority. Even if such communities enjoyed a large degree of internal self-government, local rulers always retained ultimate power. Moreover, local patterns of state-forming appear to have been sufficiently flexible to integrate the elite of each foreign community. In consequence, the syncretic urban cultures which resulted from this incorporation did not cease to extend themselves to a significant dependent hinterland. A sharp distinction between 'port city' and 'administrative city' cannot therefore be made in Southeast Asia until the colonial era. Southeast Asian languages did not normally distinguish the concepts of state and city. States were defined in terms of their urban centres, which in most cases were also ports. Nakhon Sithammarat (Ligor) was not a port of Siam, or Pahang a port of Melaka; rather these were seen as city-states (*negeri*) with their own kings (*raja*) who were tributary to other kings in Siam (Ayutthaya) or Melaka.

Southeast Asia is permeated by water. Even those capitals far inland (very few in our period), like Pegu or Ava (in modern Burma), Pnompenh (Cambodia), or Ayutthaya (Siam), were great river ports accessible to large vessels. In the island world the important states of the period were all (with the partial exception of central Java) centred in port cities—Pasai, Melaka, Aceh, Palembang, Patani, Brunei, Manila, Makassar, Ternate, Banten, Demak, Grisek/Surabaya.

Despite the pre-eminence of maritime relations, the published literature sheds little light on the economic functions of indigenous Southeast Asian cities. In part this is a function of the sources. Royal inscriptions and chronicles are primarily concerned to show the all-pervading role of the court as the centre of the city, and there have been no sources remotely comparable to the Geniza documents of Cairo to reflect the economic activities of the middle and lower classes. The sources which do exist, however, notably the reports of foreign (especially Dutch) traders, have not been used as they might to fill in the gaps. Part of the reason for this is the academic preoccupation with establishing the 'uniqueness' of the independent, economically dynamic European port city. In emphasising the dichotomy between East and West, scholars from Weber to Braudel have encouraged a stereotype of the 'traditional' Asian city as 'enormous, parasitic, soft and luxurious'.[2] While we now know enough about Japanese and Middle Eastern cities to make such a broad dichotomy untenable, Southeast Asian historians cannot be said to have shaken it off. In two stimulating recent monographs, Wolters and O'Connor have given new life to the old assumption that the market had a small place in the Southeast Asian city.[3]

The other city of life in the port city: beggars shown in front of a depiction of the city of Aceh, north Sumatra, Indonesia.
From Isaak Commelin Begin ende Voortgangh van de Vereenighde Nederlandtsche Geoctroyeerde Oost-Indische Compagnie *Amsterdam, 1646. Courtesy of Mitchell Library, State Library of New South Wales.*

As I have argued elsewhere,[4] Southeast Asian cities of the sixteenth and seventeenth centuries were relatively large in relation to the total population of the region. The capitals of Siam (Ayutthaya), Aceh, Melaka, Banten or Makassar at their peak certainly contained more than 10 percent of the populations they ruled over—a bigger percentage than inhabited the cities of pre-industrial Europe, although still smaller than the 15 percent of contemporary India. Most of these cities were not 'parasitic' in the sense that they drew their livelihood from a subject rural population by tribute. On the contrary, the bulk of the food supply of Pasai and Melaka around 1500, and of Aceh, Patani, Pahang and Banten around 1600, was obtained by purchase in the international market. About thirty rice junks a year supplied Melaka from Siam, about twenty from Pegu and another fifty to sixty from Java,[5] providing a total of perhaps 5000 tonnes or enough to feed almost 50 000 citizens from these long-distance imports alone. Patani, Pahang and Brunei were supplied from Siam and Cambodia, while Central Java was the source of rice for urban centres such as Banten, Jambi, Palembang and Banjarmasin.

Not only rice was imported by these large cities, but most other essentials as well. Banten for example obtained its dried fish from Banjarmasin, its palm-sugar and salt from Javanese ports controlled by Mataram (much of the salt subsequently re-exported to Sumatra), its coconuts and coconut oil from Balambangan, its honey from as far afield as Timor and Palembang.[6] Aceh, which obtained most of its rice from Pegu, Bengal, Arakan and Sumatran ports, welcomed in just two months of 1642 twelve Javanese junks laden with 'salt, sugar, peas, beans and other goods'.[7]

The needs of these urban populations, not only for foodstuffs but also for clothing (imported on a massive scale from India) and other consumer goods, were paid for in cash on the international market. How did the cities earn the wherewithal to do so? The answer lies only to a small extent in the role of tribute from a subject population. Most of these cities prospered not by exporting royal goods delivered as tribute from the hinterland, but by re-exporting trade goods already brought in from elsewhere by sea. Melaka at its height around 1500 was perhaps an extreme case as one of the world's leading entrepot ports of the time, with total trade estimated by Tomé Pires at about 2.4 million cruzados, of which only a few exports originated in its own territories.[8] After Melaka's fall in 1511, this lucrative intermediate trade between India, China and the 'spice islands' during the next century or so was divided between a number of ports such as Patani, Johor, Banten and Aceh. The 'value added' to goods in this kind of trade was very high. Goods bought in Melaka for one cruzado could be sold in the Moluccas for cloves which would fetch ten or more cruzados on return to Melaka. The ruling elite of these cities took their percentage of the profits of this trade through obligatory gifts and port duties, but also benefited directly as financiers of much of the trade.

In addition, port cities such as Aceh, Banten, Patani and Banjarmasin were the point of international sale for pepper produced in extensive areas subject to their authority. As rulers frequently controlled the terms on which such

Melaka, Malaysia, in the fifteenth century one of the world's greatest trading cities. As a quiet eighteenth-century Dutch outpost Melaka here shows many of the features of the European-ruled port city: the dominating fort, dwellings outside it and warehouses in between the two.

From Francois Valentijn Oud en Nieuw Oost Indien *Dordrecht, 1724-26. Courtesy of Mitchell Library, State Library of New South Wales.*

produce was sold, forcing foreign buyers and domestic sellers to deal through the ruler or his agent, large fortunes were made through handling such goods. The Acehnese Governor (*Panglima*) of Periaman, for example, left an inheritance which included 4000 Spanish dollars at his death in 1662, derived from his percentage of the pepper being exported from this minor Acehnese port alone.[9] The Acehnese ruler, reckoned by Van Leur to control a quarter to a third of the pepper passing through his capital,[10] was incomparably richer. Whether and on what forms these rulers actively entered the market, must remain a question for future research.

Entrepot and export trade of this type required some labour input from the port cities involved. Goods had to be loaded and unloaded in the port, carried to warehouses and to the market where they were sold. The warehouses of the king and the merchants had to be built, as did fortifications and public buildings. Obviously, a sizeable labour force was required for these tasks. But the larger port cities did not only contain large numbers of unskilled workers, as they unquestionably were centres of production as well as redistribution. There was a tradition in Southeast Asia for craftsmen to reside in specialised rural villages, the location of which was determined either by proximity to raw materials, like the iron-working villages of Turawan in Minangkabau, Karimata in West Borneo and Banggai in eastern Sulawesi, or by the poverty of the soil which forced people into non-agricultural specialisation, like the boat-builders and cloth-weavers of the Bira Peninsula in South Sulawesi. Nevertheless, the concentration of wealthy consumers in the big cities, the demand of the royal court itself for specialised manufactures and the convenience of these entrepot centres for export, ensured that major manufacturing activities would also concentrate in the suburbs of these cities. Perhaps the best-known example of this urban production is the fine ceramic ware produced in northern Thai cities for export throughout Southeast Asia in the thirteenth to fifteenth centuries. The main kilns have been located just outside the walls of Sukhothai, the most important Thai capital of the period and Si Satchanalai (Suwankhulok), another city about fifty kilometres to its north.[11] Everyday essentials like tools and utensils were also produced in the cities.

Of Aceh in 1599, John Davis noted, 'Off mechanical Artesmen, they have gold-smithes, Gun-founders, Ship-wrights, Taylors, Weavers, Hatters, Pot-makers and Aquavitae stillers ..., Cutlers and Smiths'.[12] Of Ayutthaya in the 1630s, Schouten wrote that 'The Siammers, who live in Towns and populous places are either Courtiers, Officers, Merchants, Watermen, Fishermen, Tradesmen or Artificers, each one containing himself in his vocation'[13] while Van Vliet confirmed that the townspeople 'earn their living by trade, court services, navigating ... fishery and industries and handicraft by making of ingeniously worked gold and silver objects'.[14] Grisek, one of Java's leading port cities before it was absorbed into nearby Surabaya around 1600, developed a major bronze industry, exporting gongs and gamelan sets to the whole archipelago.[15] Even though Java produced little copper of its own, these Grisek gongs were produced at a substantially cheaper price than the 'Chinese'-styled gongs made in Patani, another major city and port of the period.[16] In 1857, when the industry was rapidly declining as a result of competition from cheaper European ironwork, 230 copper and bronze workers were still employed in Surabaya which was 'far less important' even at that time than Grisek.[17]

Aceh was also an importer of most raw materials, tin coming from Perak and copper and lead from the Siamese port of Tenasserim, yet it, too, was able to export (or perhaps re-export from Java) manufactured 'copper basins' to Bengal in the 1630s.[18] Along with Sungai Puar in West Sumatra, Grisek in Java and Nagara in Borneo, Aceh remained one of the major exporters of finished bronze and copper articles—betel-sets, water-vessels, basins and vases—into the nineteenth century.[19] Another Southeast Asian manufacture exported to distant consumers was the Javanese *kris*. Iron had to be imported to Java to make them, but Tomé Pires nevertheless assures us that krises and swords were made relatively cheaply there and were much appreciated as trade goods in Bengal.[20]

Just as in rural areas there were specialised villages occupied almost exclusively with pottery, ironwork, boatbuilding, stoneware or whatever, so in the great cities specialist settlements clustered around the suburbs. When Symes passed the ancient Burmese capital of Pagan on his journey up the Irrawaddy in 1795, he noticed one whole street full of lacquer shops and another 'occupied by blacksmiths' shops, furnished with bill-hooks, spike-nails, adzes, etc'.[21] Later, as he approached the bustling new capital of Amerapura, the villages became much more closely packed together and 'each ... was for the most part inhabited with one particular class of people, professing some separate trade, or following some peculiar occupation'.[22] In nineteenth century Surabaya (as presumably for centuries before) each manufacture had its own *kampung* or quarter—copperworkers in Kranggan, ivory and bone workers in Bubuttan, leatherworkers and shoemakers in Tukangan, furniture-makers in Tambak-gringsing, *songket*-weavers in Ampel, *pelangi* (scarf) dyers in Kemayoran, and so forth.[23]

Southeast Asia's cities certainly were production centres and so were its port cities. When we turn to an examination of how their production was organised and paid for, however, we must sift the small amount of evidence with considerable care to find clues. The first and clearest point that can be made is that free wage labour was expensive and hard to find, especially among the indigenous population. When the Dutch in Aceh were desperate for labour to construct their warehouse in 1642, they could obtain only Chinese carpenters, at what they regarded as an exorbitant rate, and captive 'black Portuguese' as labourers. Even these were controlled by royal officials and were not always available. Deprived of their services, the Dutch factor went one day to the *kuala* (river-mouth, i.e. the port) to look for labour but found only workers who were 'old and clapped-out, and also at such high prices that I returned empty-handed'.[24] Similarly, the English needing rowers to get their vessel up the Jambi river in 1615 could find only Chinese and these at the exorbitant price of a shilling a day plus food.[25] This is about the same labour cost that Crawfurd

The castle of Ambon, eastern Indonesia, in 1607, the first Dutch base in the Indies. Originally taken from the Portuguese, this fort was the Dutch gateway to the spice trade of Maluka (Moluccas).
From Isaak Commelin Begin ende Voortgangh van de Vereenighde Nederlandtsche Geoctroyeerde Oost-Indische Compagnie *Amsterdam, 1646. Courtesy of Mitchell Library, State Library of New South Wales.*

found outrageously high in Bangkok as late as in 1822.[26]

Table 2.1 demonstrates just how expensive it was for Europeans to engage indigenous or Chinese workers in sixteenth- and seventeenth-century Southeast Asia. To calculate the real cost of urban labour, the daily wage paid by foreigners in various cities is also expressed in terms of the amount of rice this sum would buy in the same city.[27] The measure of rice is the *gantang*, equivalent to c. 3.1 kg of rice, or about five times the daily needs of an adult worker.

TABLE 2.1
Comparison of the rice needs of workers in various cities

Location	Daily Wage	Rice equivalent in *gantangs*	Number of daily needs covered
Ayutthaya, 1655	1 *fuang* (Thai labourer)	8	40
Martaban, 1512	1 *viss* (caulker)	130	650
	.05 *viss* (labourer)	6.5	32.5
Melaka, 1520	(craftsman)	4	20
	(slave labourer)	0.54	2.7
Aceh, 1642	1.5 *mas* (Chinese carpenter)	4.5	22.5
	0.75 *mas* (slave labourer)	2.2	11
	1 *mas* (Acehnese thatcher)	3	15
Jambi, 1615	12 pence (Chinese)	3	15
Banten, 1596	1000 *cash* (slaves)	3	15
Manila, 1590	1 *real* (Chinese)	12	60

In this list, the Portuguese wage rates in Melaka are exceptional in constituting payments to 'slaves' of the Portuguese themselves, though the same source notes that rope-makers (paid the equivalent of two *gantang* rice a day) were not paid when not working 'as they belong to Indian merchants'.[28] All other workers, whether Chinese or hired slaves, received at least ten times a subsistence wage and frequently many times this amount. Why, even at such high wages, was it very difficult to find indigenous labour?

The answer is that there was no free wage market in the Southeast Asian city, except in so far as it was provided by Chinese immigrants and traders— 'hard workers and very greedy for money'.[29] Labour, especially manual labour, was associated in these cities with servitude and anybody who could afford to do so bought or hired a slave to do it for him. In Banten, 'the Javans are generally exceeding proud; although extreme poor, by reason that no one amongst a hundreth of them will work'.[30] In Melaka, 'all is chivalry with them and this goes to such an extent that you will not find a native Malay, however poor he be, who will lift on his back his own things or those of another, however much he be paid for it; all their work is done by slaves'.[31] In Aceh, 'they send their slaves for what they want and the poorer sort, who do not have a slave of their own, will yet hire one to carry a *mas* worth of rice for them, though not a hundred paces from their own homes, scorning to do it themselves'.[32] In Makassar, Speelman thought that the object of the saving of the 'ordinary man' was to accumulate a sum 'which will eventually serve to buy a male or female slave in order to be free from labour themselves'.[33]

The high cost of labour, therefore, was not a free wage but in most cases the cost of hiring slaves from the king or some wealthy citizen. Speaking of Siam and Aceh in particular, Ibn Muhammad Ibrahim noted, 'It is their custom to rent slaves. They pay the slave a sum of money, which he gives to his master and then they use the slave that day for whatever work they wish'.[34] The Malay law code, first written in the cosmopolitan city of Melaka, provides for various situations which may arise when slaves are hired (*di-upah*) or borrowed (*di-pinjam*), but there is no mention in it of wages.[35]

There was a similar absence of 'free wage labour' in the sexual marketplace, though port cities had their own means of filling the demands of visiting male traders. Freelance prostitution for a fee is never mentioned by travellers. The basic pattern was a temporary marriage, with a negotiated payment analogous to the bride price required in all Southeast Asian marriages. As described by a Dutch captain in Patani, foreigners upon arrival in the port were able to choose from women who came and presented themselves,

provided they agree what he shall pay for certain months. Once they agree about the money (which does not amount to much for so great a convenience), she comes to his house and serves him by day as his maidservant and by night as his wedded wife. He is then not able to consort with other women or he will be in grave trouble with his wife, while she is similarly wholly forbidden to converse with other men, but the marriage lasts as long as he keeps his residence there, in good peace and unity. When he wants to depart ... she may look for another man as she wishes, in all propriety, without scandal.[36]

Because Southeast Asian women played a dominant part in retailing, such contract wives were doubly valued by traders to help them sell their goods.[37]

Prostitution was less common, but was reported more frequently as the seventeenth century progressed, perhaps because European and Chinese traders who were increasingly numerous were accustomed to shorter port visits and required more immediate gratification. But the prostitutes reported in Brunei in the 1570s, Patani in 1602, Ayutthaya in the 1680s, and Rangoon in the 1790s were all slaves.[38] In most cases they belonged to the king or some high court official to whom the bulk of their earnings returned. As late as the nineteenth century Balinese and Malay rajas reportedly put their female slaves regularly to work as prostitutes. In Ampenan, the port of the flourishing kingdom of Lombok in the 1840s, such slave prostitutes were expected to give half their earnings to their royal owners.[39]

It would be a mistake to imagine that everybody in these cities was either a slave-owning aristocrat or a slave, even if that is the picture given by some sources.[40] There was, however, enough servile labour to create a social model in which labour itself was seen as servile. In sharp contrast to our own value system, to labour for wages was considered even more demeaning than to labour for one's legitimate master. The king, in particular, demanded the unpaid services of all his subjects, or at least of all who were not in a position to send or pay another to work for them.

At times of war or crisis the whole population could be mobilised for royal purposes, either directly or through the great men of the realm who had their own subjects and bondsmen. Some were more completely dependent on the king. In Siam for example, the *phrai luang* category which comprised the bulk of the population owed the king a half or a third of their time. War captives (*chaloei*) were bonded more fully and in practice it was often these who must have carried out the more onerous tasks of construction and other labour for the king in the city.[41] In Aceh the major forts and other royal building projects in the city seem to have been erected by royal slaves (*hamba raja*) captured in Aceh's many wars. 'The king uses them to cut wood, dig stone from the quarries, make mortar and build.' These royal slaves were spared from being a burden on the royal purse for upkeep by having half their days free to seek their own livelihood.[42] Non-Muslim captives, 'black Portuguese' and Chinese, were especially prominent in the servile labour force, even after they had been forcibly converted to Islam. Forty Portuguese were captured in 1635, for example, when their ship was wrecked near Aceh and forty-two Chinese when two Chinese junks from Batavia were captured by royal galleys off the Malayan coast. Three years later 150 Portuguese (mostly of Asian or Eurasian blood) were captured, enslaved and converted to Islam.[43] It was this labour force, used normally on royal construction projects, which the Dutch were attempting to hire in 1642, but the captives were closely controlled by one of the most powerful eunuchs of the court and a few of them were made available only after lengthy negotiations.[44]

Craftsmen with some particular skill were especially in demand by the wealthy courts. Even if they were frequently well treated and even honoured for their talents, they were not so much paid for their service as bonded to the king or a powerful official, so that their labour was essentially an unpaid obligation. As Crawfurd complained of Bangkok as late as 1822:

Every mechanic of skill is immediately seized upon, and becomes the retainer of the King, or of some courtier, or other man in authority, who employs him for life on some useless service of vanity or ostentation. It is accordingly a matter of difficulty for a private individual, or a stranger, to obtain the services even of the most homely mechanic and the few that can be procured are usually natives of China, or Cochin-China.[45]

Sultan Iskandar Muda of Aceh reputedly retained 300 goldsmiths in his palace compound, 'besides diverse sorts of other artisans'.[46]

The urban culture of Makassar in the late sixteenth and early seventeenth centuries was remarkable for both its openness to technical innovations and its concern to record them in writing. From the Makassar chronicles we learn a good deal about not only the point at which various new techniques were adopted, but also the way production for the court appears to have been organised. Under King Tunipalangga (1548-86) bricks, gunpowder, large cannons and various other items were first manufactured in Makassar, probably through learning from Malay and Portuguese traders. The same king is recorded as creating a number of officials called *tumakkajannangngang* (from the

From production to exchange: nutmeg weighing and trading at Nera in Banda, eastern Indonesia, as seen by the second Dutch voyage to the Indies.
From Isaak Commelin Begin ende Voortgangh van de Vereenighde Nederlandtsche Geoctroyeerde Oost-Indische Compagnie *Amsterdam, 1646. Courtesy of Mitchell Library, State Library of New South Wales.*

Makassarese root *jannang*, supervisor, cf. Malay *jenang*) to supervise each of a series of crafts—'blacksmiths, goldsmiths, house-builders, boat-builders, blowpipe-makers, copper-workers, grinders, turners, ropemakers'.[47] The subsequent king, Tunijallo (1556-90) added arrowmakers to the list of craftsmen supervised by their own *Tumakkajannangngang*, but also created a yet higher office of *Anrong guru tumakkajannangngang*. This office, always held by a high court official and relative of the king, was evidently intended to coordinate all of the *Tumakkajannangngang* and to convey to them royal commands and requirements. *Tumakkajannangngang* has been glossed as 'guild-master',[48] but this is misleading since it suggests a degree of contractual autonomy within the political structure of the city. Rather these were officials to superintend the obligations of craftsmen to provide services for the court as their form of tribute or corvee, presumably to the exclusion of other types of service.[49] It is probably significant that the chronicle also credits Tunipalangga with being the first king to impose heavy corvee (*masarro pa'ngarana*) on his people.[50]

Part of the key to Makassar's remarkable commercial and military success was its ability to build institutions like these which exploited the talents of its subjects without crushing their initiative. In a position very much resembling that of their colleagues in China, craftsmen elsewhere had to provide a similar form of service to the king, which frequently may have been on a more arbitrary basis. In 1643-44, for example, 'gamelan-makers and smiths' were suddenly pressed into service to try to make a giant cannon for Sultan Agung in Mataram.[51] Nagara, which had been the royal capital of Banjarmasin before its Islamisation in the sixteenth century, remained thereafter as a town almost entirely devoted to metalwork. The few hundred craftsmen of Nagara probably profited from the relative autonomy they enjoyed once the court moved downriver. By the nineteenth century they were manufacturing guns, knives, gongs and betel-sets which they carried for sale at markets throughout the Indonesian archipelago. Nevertheless they were still required to produce implements for the sultan free of charge whenever he required it, the ruler providing only the raw material for the work.[52] It is easy to believe that the origins of this remarkable community of craftsmen lay primarily in service to the Banjarmasin court, although its capacity eventually far outgrew the needs of that court. A similar pattern may have occurred at export centres such as Grisek, Surabaya, Surakarta (for bronze items), Tuban (gold) and perhaps even the Minangkabau manufacturing villages.

In addition to production under a labour obligation to the king, there was also production of a servile kind for the great merchant-aristocrats of the city. In Banten in 1596, for example, the Dutch noted that female slaves of the important men 'sit in the *pasar*, and sell all wares to obtain a little money ... Others sit at home and weave, others spin, so that all are busy supporting themselves and their lord'.[53] Aceh of the late seventeenth century was another city where royal power was held in check by the merchant oligarchs and there too most productive activities—fishing, farming, gold-mining and gold-working,

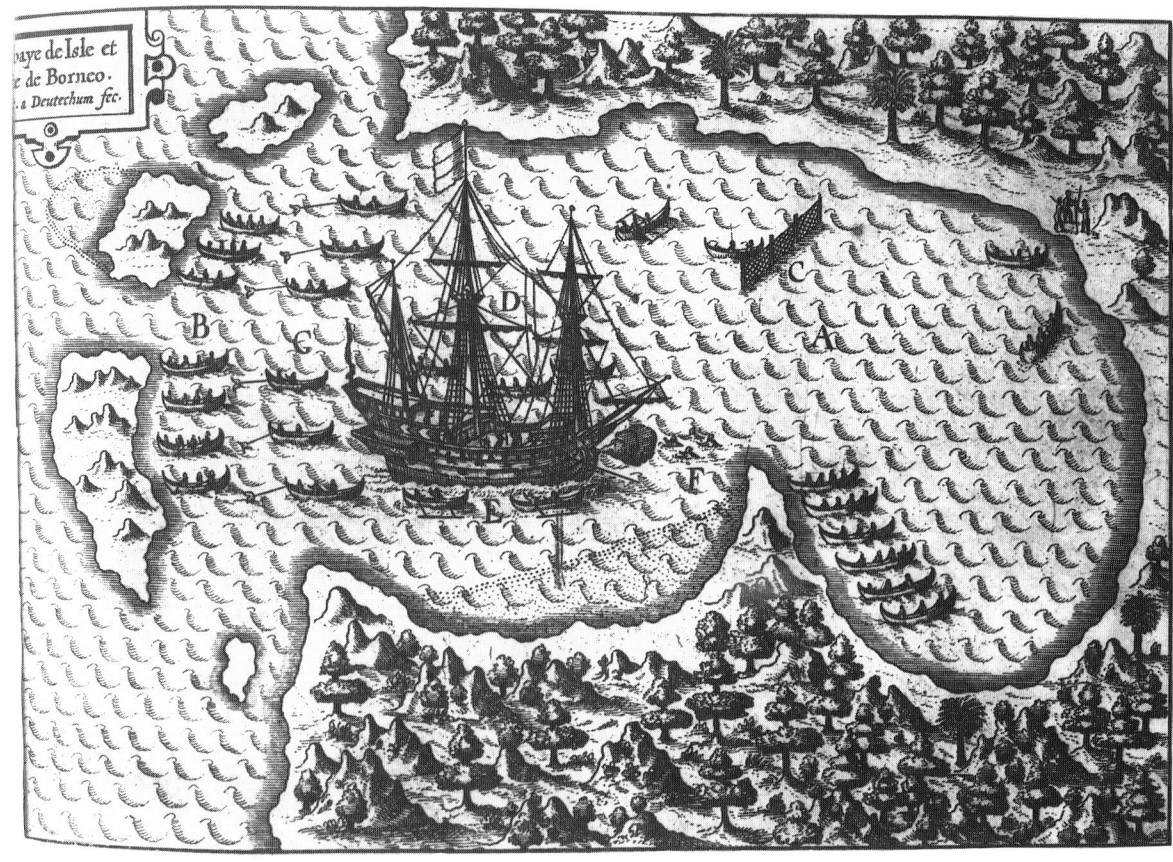

Bypassing the port city: direct trade in a bay in Borneo.
From Isaak Commelin *Begin ende Voortgangh van de Vereenighde Nederlandtsche Geoctroyeerde Oost-Indische Compagnie* Amsterdam, 1646. Courtesy of Mitchell Library, State Library of New South Wales.

trade and construction—were performed by their slaves or dependents. Even so, as Dampier reported, 'there is nothing of rigour used by the Master to his Slave, except it be the very meanest, such as do all sorts of servile work: but those who can turn their hands to anything besides Drudgery, live well enough by their industry. Nay, they are encouraged by their Masters who often lend them Money to begin some trade or business withall'.[54]

In Melaka before the Portuguese conquest of 1511, as in seventeenth-century Patani, it appears to have been Javanese slaves or dependents who performed much of the productive work. Duarte Barbosa, who can have known the Javanese only in Melaka, described them as 'very clever at cabinet-making. Other trades which they follow are the making of arquebuses and all other kinds of firearms ... They are also very cunning locksmiths and they make weapons of every kind'.[55] Albuquerque, the conqueror of Melaka, was so impressed with the Javanese craftsmen he found there that he shipped out sixty Javanese carpenters of the dockyard, 'very handy workmen', to help repair Portuguese ships in India. The carpenters never reached India, but mutinied and took their Portuguese vessel to Pasai where they were also very welcome.[56] Most of the Melaka Javanese appear to have been bought to the city by wealthy Javanese merchants who had settled in Melaka and wielded great influence there. The wealthiest of them, who bore the title Utama Diraja (Port. Ultimuti Raja), was alleged to control as many as 8000 Javanese 'slaves' in the settlement of Upeh, just across the Melaka river from the city centre.[57]

As I have sought to explain elsewhere,[58] the most important element in what Europeans perceived as 'slavery' in Southeast Asia was debt and the assumption that indebtedness entailed an obligation to work without pay for the patron or master. As we can see from Dampier's observation of Aceh above, masters frequently advanced money to their 'slaves' to enable them to work more profitably. Indeed this may often have been the essence of the bondage relationship. Except with the most menial captives, masters were expected to provide credit and protection and bondsmen to provide labour or any other form of service on demand.

One very important effect of this type of relationship was to inhibit craftsmen from developing into small capitalists themselves. In the Southeast Asian context craftsmen could rise to comfort and security only by acquiring a powerful patron/creditor, such as the king himself. Their position was never sufficiently secure to enable them to accumulate wealth independently. Thus Dampier noted in the city of Mindanao that gold and silversmiths would 'make anything that you desire, but they have no shop furnished with ware ready made for sale'.[59] And even two centuries later, in Surabaya of the 1850s, craftsmen would refrain from working until they had received an order accompanied by an advance, which would establish a relationship of patronage and protection if only of a temporary kind. 'When the workman has no further debt, he considered the relationship broken and will not work again until he feels a need again to expose himself to new debts.'[60]

Our tentative conclusion, then, is that in Southeast Asian port cities

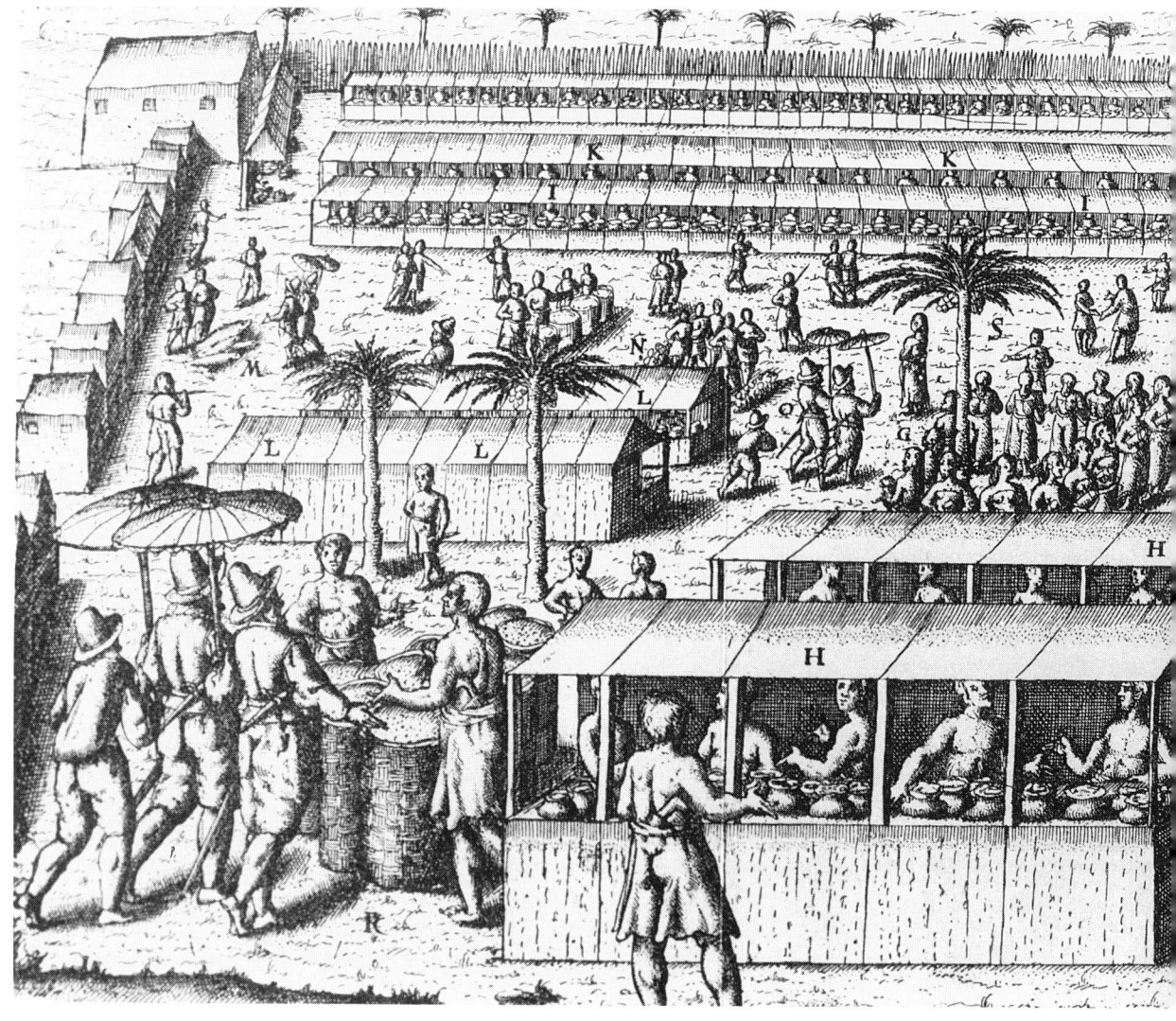

The diversity of skills and goods. The markets of Banten (Bantam), West Java, Indonesia, the centre of social and economic life.
Legend:
a. Women fruit sellers
b. Sellers of 'sugar and honey in pots'
c. Sellers of beans
d. Sellers of bamboo
e. 'The place where they sell krisses, sabres, spears and bussen'
f. Selling cloth for men
g. Selling cloth for women
h. 'Indicates booths where all kinds of spices and drugs are sold'
i. 'The booths where Bengalis and Gujeratis sell all kinds of ironwork and small manufactures'
k. 'The Chinese booths'
l. 'The meat stalls'
m. The fish market
n. 'The fruit market'
o. The vegetable market
p. The pepper market
q. The ayun and leek market
r. The rice market
s. 'The place where the merchants and adventurers walk'
t. The jewellers' stalls
v. The poultry market
From G. P. Rouffaer and J. W. IJzerman (ed.) De eerste schipvaart der Nederlanders naar Oost-Indië onder Cornelis de Houtman 1595-1597 The Hague, 1915.

production was primarily a matter of obligation. Where the king was in a strong and monopolistic position most artisans and productive workers were dependent on him. In many urban situations, on the other hand, wealth and power was spread sufficiently widely among an oligarchy of merchant-nobles to allow some movement on the part of capable workers, including working for others than their master for part of their time. By working for a wider than just the local market—result of the extensive development of maritime trade in the region—and apparently being able to retain a share of the profits made, they could thus hope for economic, and perhaps, social betterment. Even so, by contrast to other parts of the world, the opportunity for skilled craftsmen to develop into independent entrepreneurs or capitalists appears to have been low.

Notes

1. Rhoads Murphey 'Traditionalism and Colonialism: Changing Urban Roles in Asia' *Journal of Asian Studies* 29, 1969, p.83
2. Fernand Braudel *Capital and Material Life 1400-1800* London, 1968, p.4
3. O.W. Wolters *History, Culture and Region in Southeast Asian Perspectives* Singapore, 1982, p.37; R. O'Connor *A Theory of Indigenous Southeast Asian Urbanism* Singapore, 1983, p.117
4. Anthony Reid 'The Structure of Cities in Southeast Asia, Fifteenth to Seventeenth Centuries' *Journal of Southeast Asian Studies* 11, 1980, pp.235-50
5. Tomé Pires *The Suma Oriental of Tome Pires* [1515], trans. & ed. by A. Cortesao, London 1944, pp. 98, 107 and 268-69; Rui de Araujo 'Letter from Melaka, 5 February 1510' in Arthur de Sa (ed.) *Documentacão para a Historia das Missoes do Padroado Portugues do Oriente: Insulindia* 1 (*1506-1549*) Lisbon, 1954, p.28
6. Willem Lodewycksz, 'D'eerste Boeck: Historie van Indien Waer inne Verhaelt is de avontueren die de Hollandtsche Schepen bejeghent zyn' in G.P. Rouffaer & J.W. IJzerman (ed.) *De eerste Schipvaart der Nederlanders naar Oost-Indië onder Cornelis de Houtman 1595-1597* The Hague, 1915, pp. 110 and 119
7. Algemeen Rijksarchief (The Hague), Koloniaal Archief [henceforth KA] 1051 bis (VOC 1143), Pieter Willemsz 'Atchins daghregister' 26 September-22 November 1642, fol. 524.
8. Pires *Suma Oriental* pp.213-14
9. W.J.A. de Leeuw *Het Painansch Contract* Amsterdam, 1926, p.36
10. J.C. van Leur 'On Early Asian Trade', trans. by J.S. Holmes and A. van Marle, in J.C. van Leur *Indonesian Trade and Society* The Hague, 1955, p.134
11. Charles N. Spinks *The Ceramic Wares of Siam* red. edn. Bangkok, 1971, pp.14-15 and 27-40
12. John Davis 'The Voyage of Captaine John Davis to the Easterne India, Pilot in a Dutch Ship; written by himselfe' in A.H. Markham (ed.) *The Voyages and Works of John Davis the Navigator* London, 1880, p.151.
13. Joost Schouten 'A Description of the Government, Might, Religion, Customes, Traffick and other remarkable Affairs in the Kingdom of Siam' [written in 1636], trans. by R. Manley, in F. Caron and J. Schouten *A True Description of the Mighty Kingdoms of Japan and Siam* London, 1671, p.147
14. Jeremias van Vliet 'Description of the Kingdom of Siam' [written in 1636], trans. by L.W. van Ravenswaay *Journal of the Siam Society* 7, 1910, p.91
15. KA 1059 bis (VOC 1157), A. de Vlamingh van Outshoorn 'Journal of Daghregister gehouden geduijrent sijn aenwijs in Aitchien' [1644], fol. 609v; Antonio Galvão *A Treatise on the Moluccas (c.1544), probably the preliminary version of Antonio Galvao's lost Historia das Moluccas* trans. by Hubert Jacobs SJ Rome, 1971, p.111
16. G.P. Rouffaer *De voornaemste industrieën der inlandsche bevolking van Java en Madoera* The Hague, 1904, p.99
17. J. Hageman 'Verslag omtrent de nijverheid te Soerabaja' *Tijdschrift voor Nijverheid en Landbouw in Nederlandsch Indië* 6, 1860, p.143
18. KA 1031 (VOC 1119), Jacob Compostel 'Origineel daghregister van de voyagie, handel en rescontre met t schip d'Revengie naer Atchin' [1636], fols. 1200 and 1217
19. Augustin de Beaulieu 'Memoires du Voyage aux Indes-Orientales du General Beaulieu, dresses par luy-mesme' in M. Thévenot (ed.) *Relations de divers voyages curieux* Paris, 1666, p.99; J.E. Jasper & M. Pirngadie, *De inlandsche kunstnijverheid in Nederlandsch Indie* vol. 5, The Hague, 1930, pp.7-8 and 99-100
20. Pires *Suma Oriental* pp.93-179
21. M. Symes *An Account of an Embassy to the Kingdom of Ava in the year 1795* 2 vols, Edinburgh, 1827, vol. 1, p.309
22. *Ibid.* vol.2, p.10
23. J.E. Jasper 'Inlandsche methoden van hoorn-, been-, schildpad-, schelp- en paarlemoer-bewerking' *Tijdschrift van het Bataviaasch Genootschap* 1904, p.1; J. Hageman 'Aanteekeniugen nopens de industrie, handel en nijverheid van Soerabaja' *Tijdschrift voor Nijverheid en Landbouw in Nederlandsch Indië* 5, 1859, p.141
24. Willemsz 'Atchins daghregister' fol. 509v
25. F.C. Danvers & W. Foster (eds.) *Letters Received by the East India Company from its Servants in the East* 6 vols, London, 1896-1905, vol. 3 pp.166 and 201
26. John Crawfurd *Journal of an Embassy from the Governor-General of India to the Courts of Siam and Cochin China* London, 1828, p.453
27. G. Smith, The Dutch East India Company in the Kingdom of Ayutthaya, 1604-1624, PhD thesis, Northern Illinois

University, Ann Arbor, 1974, p.316; G. Bouchon 'Les premiers voyages portugaises à Pasai et à Pégou, 1512-1520' *Archipel* 18, 1979, pp.142-43; Pierre-Yves Manguin 'Manpower and Labour Categories in Early Sixteenth Century Malacca' in Anthony Reid (ed.) *Slavery, Bondage and Dependency in Southeast Asia* St. Lucia, 1983, pp.212-13; Willemsz 'Atchins daghregister' fols. 508-520; Danvers & Foster *Letters* vol.3, p.201; Lodewycksz 'D'eerste Boeck' p.129; Bishop Salazar 'The Chinese and the Parian at Manila' [24 June 1590], trans. in Emma H. Blair & James A. Robertson *The Philippine Islands, 1493-1595* 55 vols, Cleveland, 1903-1909, vol.7, p.229

28   Manguin 'Manpower and Labour Categories' p.213
29   Salazar 'The Chinese and the Parian at Manila' p.229
30   Edmund Scott 'An exact discourse of the Subtitles, Fashions, Policies, Religion and Ceremonies of the East Indians . . .' [1606] in Sir William Foster, (ed.) *The Voyage of Sir Henry Middleton to the Moluccas* London, 1943, pp.170-71
31   João de Barros *Da Asia, 4 Decada* [1563] (9 vols., Lisbon, 1777, rep. 1973), vol.2, part ii, p.24
32   William Dampier *Voyages and Discoveries* [1699], ed. by C Wilkinson, London, 1931, p.94
33   Cornelis Speelman 'Notitie dienend voor eenen korten tijd en tot nader last van de Hooge Regering op Batavia voor den ondercoopman Jan van Oppijnen' [1670], typescript copy held in the Koninklijk Instituut voor Taal-, Land-, en Volkenkunde, Leiden (Netherlands)
34   Ibn Muhammad Ibrahim *The Ship of Sulaiman* [1688], trans. from the Persian by J. O'Kane, London, 1972, pp.177-78
35   *Undang-undang Melaka: The Laws of Malacca* ed. by Liaw Yock Fang, The Hague, 1976, pp.88-93 and 162-63.
36   J. van Neck 'Journal' [1604], in H.A. van Foreest & A. de Booy (eds.) *De Vierde Schipvaart der Nederlanders noor Oost-Indië* 2 vols, The Hague, 1980-1981, vol.1, p.225
37   A. Hamilton, *A New Account of the East Indies* Edinburgh, 1727, rep. London, 1930, p.28; Chou Ta Kuan *Mémoires sur les coutumes du Cambodge de Tchou Ta-Kovan* [1297], trans. by P. Pelliot, Paris, 1951, p.27; William Dampier *A New Voyage Round the World* London, 1697, rep. 1927, p.268
38   John Carroll (ed.) 'Berunai in the *Boxer Codex*', *Journal of the Malaysian Branch of the Royal Asiatic Society* 1, 55, ii, 1982, p.414; Van Neck 'Journaal' p.225; Symes *Embassy to Ava* vol.1, pp.252-53
39   H. Zollinger 'The Island of Lombok' *Journal of the Indian Archipelago and Eastern Asia* vol.5, 1851, p.335
40   Dampier *Voyages and Discoveries* p.98
41   B. Terwiel 'Bondage and Slavery in Early Nineteenth Century Siam' in Anthony Reid (ed.) *Slavery, Bondage & Dependency in Southeast Asia* St. Lucia, 1983, pp.113-37
42   Beaulieu 'Memoires du voyage', p.108
43   Compostel 'Origineel daghregister' fol.1200; Takeshi Ito, The World of the Adat Aceh: A Historical Study of the Sultanate of Aceh, PhD thesis, ANU, Canberra, 1984, pp.404-411
44   Willemsz 'Atchins daghregister' fols.510-25
45   Crawfurd *Journal of an Embassy* p.322
46   Beaulieu 'Mémoires du Voyage' p.100
47   G.J. Wolhoff & Abdurrahim (eds.) *Sejarah Goa* Makassar, n.d. p.25
48   *Ibid.* p.50
49   A. Ligtvoet 'Transcriptie van het dagboek der vorsten van Gowa en Tells, met vertaling en aanteekeningen' *Bijdragen tot de Taal-, Land-, en Volkenkunde van Nederlandsch Indië* IV, iv, 1880, pp.98-99; A.A. Cense *Makassaars-Nederlands Woordenboek* The Hague, 1979, p.175
50   *Sejarah Goa* p.30
51   Babad ing Sangkala *Modern Javanese Historical Tradition: A Study of an Original Kartasura Chronicle and Related Materials* [1730], trans. by M.C. Ricklefs, London, 1978, pp.44-45
52   Denys Lombard 'Regard nouveau sur les "pirates Malais", lère moitié du XIXe siecle', *Archipel* 18, 1979, pp.231-49; Wolfgang Marschall 'Metallurgie und frühe Besiedlungsgeschichte Indonesiens' in W. Frohlich (ed.) *Beiträge zur Völkerkunde Südostasiens und Ozeaniens* Cologne, 1968, pp.137-39; J.J. Ras *Hikajat Bandjar: A Study in Malay Historiography* The Hague, 1960, p.626
53   Lodewycksz 'D'eerste Boeck' p.129
54   Dampier *Voyages and Discoveries* p.98
55   Duarte Barbosa *The Book of Duarte Barbosa. An Account of the Countries Bordering on the Indian Ocean and their Inhabitants* [1518], trans. by M. Longwarth Dames, London, 1918, pp.177 and 193
56   Braz de Albuquerque *The Commentaries of the Afonso Dalboquerque* [1557] trans. by W. De Gray Birch, 4

vols, London, 1875-1884, vol.3, p.168
57 Giovanni da Empoli 'Letter to Lionardo his Father' [1514], in A. Bausani (ed.) *Lettera di Giovanni da Empoli* Rome, 1970, pp.139-40; Barros *Da Asia* vol.2, part ii, p.52
58 Anthony Reid (ed.) *Slavery, Bondage and Dependency in Southeast Asia* St Lucia 1983
59 Dampier *A New Voyage* p.227
60 Hageman 'Aanteekeningen' p.142

Further reading

Blusse, Leonard *Strange Company: Chinese settlers, mestizo women and the Dutch in VOC Batavia* Dordrecht 1986. Fascinating social history of seventeenth-century Batavia, with much incidental information on Chinese and Javanese social organisation of the period.

Meilink-Roelofsz, M.A.P. *Asian Trade and European Influence in the Indonesian Archipelago between 1500 and about 1630* The Hague 1962. Copious detail on the trade and organisation of Malay Melaka and Javanese Banten in particular.

Reid, Anthony (ed.) *Slavery, Bondage and Dependency in Southeast Asia* St Lucia Qld 1983. First steps to understanding the labour systems of pre-colonial Southeast Asia.

Southeast Asia in the Age of Commerce vol. 1 *The Lands below the Winds* New Haven 1988. An attempt to establish a Southeast Asian pattern of social organisation and production.

Schrieke, B. *Indonesian Sociological Studies* 2 vols, The Hague 1955. Translations of pioneering Dutch work of the 1930s, still very valuable on Javanese trade and society in the period 1300-1650.

Thomaz, Luis Filipe *De Malaca a Pegu. Viagens de um feitor Portugues (1512-1515)* Lisbon 1966. Fascinating data on Southeast Asian shipping methods around 1500, based on Portuguese participation. More accessible is the same author's article in *Archipel* 18, 1979, pp.105-25.

CHAPTER

S. Arasaratnam

European port settlements in the Coromandel commercial system 1650-1740

There is an assumption, both implicit and explicit, in much of our current historiography on the beginnings of European commercial enterprise in India of a natural and almost inevitable growth of European settlements on the Indian coast from tiny beginnings to vast sprawling metropolises of trade and investment.[1] By the use of hindsight, it is easy to see these small early settlements growing into busy ports, attracting European and neighbouring Indian enterprise and becoming nodal points from which the English and the French launched their thrust into the interior. There is a shade of truth in this picture, of course, but the real story of the fortunes of these ports and their relationships with the older Indian ports is far more complex and governed by a number of factors that illustrate the dynamism and flux in the Indian maritime world of that time.

These developments can, perhaps, be best observed in the port system of the Coromandel during the first century or so of permanent European settlements. This region had long traditions of seaborne trade and involvement with markets along the Indian coast, across the Bay of Bengal and further afield in both Southeast and Southwest Asia. As a result of this maritime activity a number of rival Indian ports grew up which, in a manner akin to that described by Hoyle for East Africa during the pre-European era, coexisted side by side

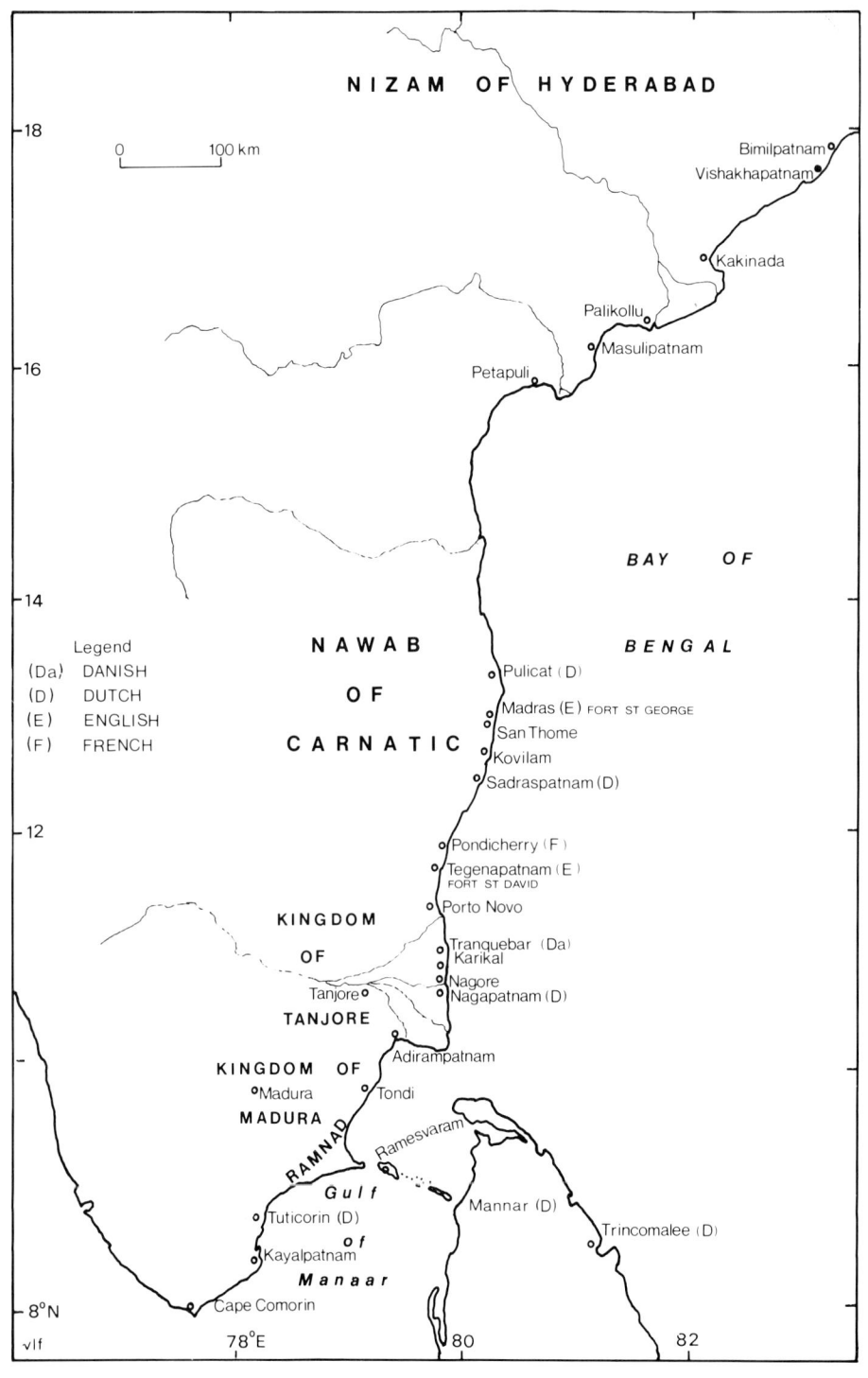

Map 6
The Coromandel coast, c.1700

in mild competition over their largely not contested hinterlands. With the possible exception of Masulipatnam with its specific Muslim connections with the Gulf region, very little hierarchical differences could be observed between the twenty-odd ports which from Tondi in the south to Bimilipatnam in the north cluttered the coast. The arrival of the Portuguese occasioned no perceptible change, but this was not the case when the English, Dutch and French East India Companies deliberately went 'outside' the system and established new, European ports.

The European ports, as they were founded and developed in the seventeenth century, had three props on which their growth was founded. First and basic to their survival as well as the *raison d'être* of their establishment, was their role as centres of the European trade of the Companies which founded them. The trading activity in this sector was geared to the annual fleets that came into and left these ports conducting business in imports from Europe and exports thence. The rate of growth of this sector of activity depended on the financial health of the Companies and the support they derived from the metropolis. Thus in the seventeenth century, the Dutch East India Company was the steadiest performer, its European demand being pitched at a continuous high level, and there was brisk activity in the Indian settlements to satisfy this demand.[2] The English East India Company was less steady in the support it derived from home and thus its investment in the Indian settlements registered ups and downs. After 1660, however, its affairs were put on a more sound financial footing and its trade in Coromandel showed a steady increase till the last decade of the seventeenth century. This gave its Coromandel ports a base for growth.[3] The French East India Company was plagued with financial problems right from its inception and its European trade was sporadic and fitful. This was reflected in its chief Coromandel port of Pondichery, which thus lacked a sound base of French European trade on which to grow, right up to the 1720s. When, after that, the European demand was steady and well supported, it grew like the other European ports of the coast.

A second prop of activity was the entry of the Companies into inter-Asian trade from the base of these ports. This was a much more problematic activity and depended on a number of factors for its success. Besides being backed by resources and shipping, it needed much more intricate managerial expertise and a sound knowledge of markets, geography and political environment. The Dutch were the most proficient in securing this expertise, in Coromandel as elsewhere, and their ports became centres from which they drove an active Asian trade. The English were more handicapped by resource problems and the Company itself did not emerge as a major participant in the Asian trade of Coromandel. In fact, after the 1670s the Company reduced its trade commitments within Asia and passed over the rights to its servants and then to licensed freetraders.[4] The French were even more handicapped in this respect and did not develop these operations till the eighteenth century.

The third prop was the ability of these ports to attract Asian shipping and merchant enterprise. This is a much more complex subject and its history passes

The European entrée into Indian trade: Portuguese aboard a ship off the Malabar Coast, western India, making use of Indian navigational skills and labour.
From Theodore de Bry Tertia Pars Indiae Orientalis *Frankfurt, 1601.*
Courtesy of Mitchell Library, State Library of New South Wales.

through several stages which will be explored in detail later. The point to be made here is that the potential for the growth of this sector was there, given the possibilities in interaction between the European trade of the Companies and the trade of Asian merchants. It depended on the policies followed by individual companies, their resources and the extent of their operations. A company such as the Dutch East India Company, though vast and extensive in its own operations, managed a closed economy in its ports and stifled the growth of a non-Company sector. Others, such as the English, the French and the Danes, permitted free trade and even encouraged Asian shipping in their ports within certain limits. Their ports therefore developed along different lines from those of the Dutch.

A brief sketch of the growth of each of the major European ports will enable us to identify the special features characteristic of these ports. The English were given a plot of ground in the coastal village of Chennapatnam in 1639 which they were allowed to fortify with the construction of Fort St George in 1641. It was by all accounts an abandoned fishing village and thus, starting from a zero base, its initial growth was spectacular. The very fact of its becoming the centre of Company shipping and investment, establishing a large export and import trade between Coromandel and Europe, enabled the port to take off as an important place of trade along the coast. Up till the 1660s, when the Company did not have a sound financial base, this European trade was uneven and this was reflected in the fortunes of Madras. After this period, however, the demand from Europe was steadily increasing and this was reflected in the growth of the port and the settlement. The nature of growth was conditioned by the demands of this dominant sector of Madras' trade. A sizeable Company bureaucracy and a small military force was the English core of the settlement. A growing Indian satellite group ranging from coolie labouring classes in the port and the godowns to clerical hands and security personnel was soon present. Another element that migrated to Madras was a class of merchant brokers who were wholesale buyers and sellers to the Company.

Madras was rather slow in developing as a centre of English trade within the Asian maritime world. When it did develop, it attempted to lock into the traditional trade ties of Coromandel with Southeast Asia and in the coastal trade. The Company's attempts in this direction were not very successful and after 1665 it abandoned much of this trade to its servants who were somewhat more successful. This part of the trade of Madras grew towards the end of the century and the senior servants of the Company were making good fortunes out of it. There is little evidence of Madras attracting to itself the trade of Indian and other Asian merchants till the end of the seventeenth century. The English did not have an import trade in commodities that could be utilised in Asian trade, nor were they buyers of these commodities which this trade embraced. So, after an initial period of modest growth, Madras' commerce and shipping with other Asian ports remained more or less stagnant till the last decade of the seventeenth century.

The other English settlement of Fort St David, ceded and fortified in 1690, was of a different nature. It was in the vicinity of an active trading outlet, provided by the mouth of the Gadilam river whose estuaries kept shifting their course. The ground where the English were allowed to put up a small fort was a mile to the south of the old port of Devanampatnam which had declined for some years. It was a few yards to the north of Cuddalore, an equally old port but still in a flourishing state. Here there was some trade in the English part of the port generated by English investment in textiles in the hinterland villages. Besides this there was no other trade, while the port of Cuddalore, controlled by the Maratha ruler of Jinji and then the Mughals, continued as the major outlet of Indian trade.

The two major Dutch ports on the coast were Paleacat and Nagapatnam. Paleacat was an old Indian port at the mouth of an inlet and inland lake in which the Dutch had been ceded some substantial ground to build a fort and other accommodation. Outside the area covered by the Dutch fort there was a loading place that continued to be used by Indian shipping. Through the massive strength of the Dutch Company's export and import trade, Paleacat expanded in the middle decades of the seventeenth century. This growth was caused by both elements in the Dutch Company's trade, namely the trade to Europe and the trade within Asia. The trade to Europe was a major component of the Company's trade from Coromandel and, for a greater part of the seventeenth century, by far the largest in volume among all the Companies. This itself made Paleacat the home of the large East Indiamen of the Company's fleet, making regular visits to supply the Company's establishment and to carry away the assembled goods. The second aspect of the Company's trade, the trade within Asia, was no less important and tied Paleacat into a number of major trading ports of the Indian Ocean through the Company's scheduled sailings. This aspect of the trade not only expanded Paleacat's traditional role as a centre of export in the Coromandel coast. It also considerably augmented its importing capacity, as the Dutch linked Paleacat directly with Southeast Asian and East Asian markets, some of which they succeeded in controlling exclusively.

The growth of Paleacat was therefore totally determined by the institutional trade of the Company. Private European trade, which as seen above was a growing factor in the English ports, was totally absent. Indian trade was admitted in so far as it contributed to Company trade and any competition with Company trade was stifled with increasingly stringent regulations. The Dutch attempted, as the English did not, to regulate Indian shipping in and out of Paleacat by passes which directed ports where they could sail to and those which they had to avoid and even commodities they could carry. Consequently, from very early on the Dutch port of Paleacat lost its free character and became one which Indian shipping avoided if it could. It tended to move away from the vicinity of Paleacat northwards and southwards to ports where it could operate with greater freedom. The 'black' town outside the Fort did not grow, as it did in Madras, by attracting Indian entrepreneurs, except those who were attached to the trade of the Company. Wealthy merchants and shippers, far

European port settlements in the Coromandel commercial system

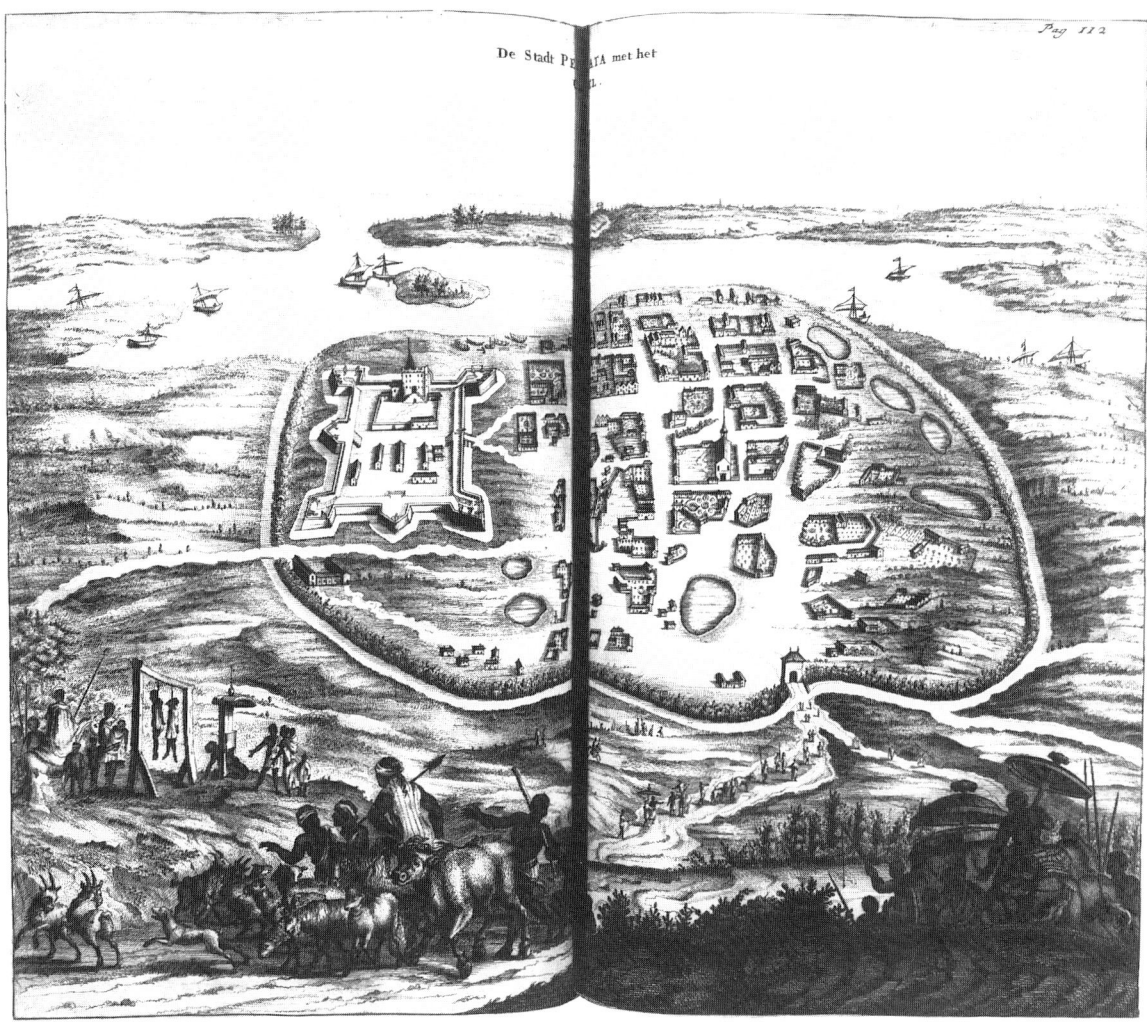

Paleacat, Coromandel Coast, eastern India: Dutch trading base and Indian capital. While this illustration of the city itself draws attention to the Dutch fort and church, the illustrations in the foreground focus on Indian 'despotism', law and lifestyles. The city is shown as a magnet drawing from the surrounding countryside and linking sea and hinterland.
From Hendrik Nieuhof *Joan Nieuhofs Gedenkwaerdighe Zee-en Lant-reize door de voornaemste Landschappen van West en Oostindien* Amsterdam, 1682.
Courtesy of Mitchell Library, State Library of New South Wales.

from being attracted to that port, found themselves avoiding it. The fortunes of Paleacat thus ebbed and flowed with the trade of the Dutch Company.

Another factor also worked to Dutch disadvantage in Paleacat. The grant of the port did not contain the same fiscal freedom which the English had in Madras. The sea and land customs on goods that passed to and from Paleacat were shared in equal proportions between the Dutch Company and the Golconda state (later the Mughal Empire).[5] Golconda and Mughal customs authorities participated in customs collection of the port and the Dutch had no freedom to manipulate fiscal policy in the interests of their trade as the English had in Madras. More importantly, the hinterland of Paleacat was subject to greater incidence of road taxes and tolls than most other ports because of historic rights of taxation accruing to a variety of authorities. This particularly affected the import trade of the Dutch. Merchants would bid less for spices and minerals in Paleacat than in other Coromandel ports because of the higher road taxes they were subject to on their way to inland markets.[6] These factors combined to operate against a continuing growth of this port in the latter part of the seventeenth century.

Nagapatnam was the other major port of the Dutch in Coromandel. They secured this from the Portuguese in 1658 by conquest and thus exercised rights bordering on sovereignty in the port. Nagapatnam had been an important port of the Bay of Bengal and coastal trades for centuries. Its conquest by the Portuguese had not affected these commercial and maritime links, but when it passed into Dutch hands its position changed considerably. Indian trade from Nagapatnam to Melaka and Aceh competed directly with Dutch trade to Southeast Asia, and Dutch policy was not to permit such competition in places controlled by them. The passes policy was operated to divert Indians from the lucrative textile trade to Melaka and over a long period Indian shipping began to move away from its traditional home port in Nagapatnam to neighbouring ports. The trade of Nagapatnam too, like that of Paleacat, was grounded firmly on the Company's trade of which there was some growth in the last decade of the seventeenth century as the Dutch shifted their textile investments southwards to Tanjore and Madura. In Nagapatnam the Dutch had more rights than they had in Paleacat and were able to impose controls on Indian shipping domiciled in that port. Consequently by the end of the century, Nagapatnam lost its role in the Bay of Bengal trade of the Indians.

When the French were allowed to settle in Pondichery in 1672, it was a port with a reasonable volume of traffic, mainly across the Bay of Bengal and along the coast. French investments for Europe assisted in the growth of Pondichery, but the uncertain finances and organisation of the French Company made such investments very unsteady till the 1720s. Consequently, in its initial phase, Pondichery did not grow as a centre of French trade as the other European ports had done. This very denial of continuing French investment enabled it to grow as a centre of Indian trade under French protection. This protection was of immense value and very timely in the 1680s in the trade to Southeast Asia. Indian shipping resorted to Pondichery and was encouraged and fostered by French policy. In this way the growth of Pondichery had a continuity the other European ports did not have. When the French Company was better organised to participate more steadily in eastern trade, it had a double base of Indian and Franco-Indian enterprise on which to build. The Franco-Indian partnership, to a degree not prevalent in the other European settlements, drew to Pondichery some of the wealthy entrepreneurial groups among Coromandel merchants.

It will be seen from this that, with the exception of Pondichery, in the second half of the seventeenth century European ports of Coromandel grew with the trade of the Companies as their base. It is important for an understanding of their nature to examine their relationship, if any, to neighbouring older Indian ports and how their growth affected these ports. The European ports were growing in a context of expanding trade in the Indian Ocean and there is no evidence of these ports drawing trade away from the older ports in the first phase. On the contrary, there was a great reliance on major Coromandel ports such as Masulipatnam, Sadraspatnam, Porto Novo, Cuddalore and Karikal. This reliance took several forms. The first and most important was for the drawing of textiles for the European market for which the European ports themselves were an inadequate base. Every Company had to retain its factors and purchasers in these and other ports which were still the major collecting points for textiles for export. However much they tried, neither the English at Madras nor the Dutch at Paleacat were able to develop their ports as their chief centres for the collection of textiles till the end of the seventeenth century. Secondly, these Indian ports provided better markets for the sale of imports. The established distribution networks for imported goods into inland markets were located here. Thirdly, the bullion markets of the coast were located in these ports or in their hinterland and it was here that the best prices could be got for the silver and gold brought in by the Companies. Lastly, provisioning of ships was done more conveniently and at better cost in some of these ports.

In this way, far from drawing trade away from the older Coromandel ports, the rise of European ports contributed to the expansion of trade in almost all of these ports. Masulipatnam and Porto Novo were two excellent examples of this. In both these places, all the Companies had factories manned by a number of their servants. Company shipping, based on their home port in Coromandel, frequented these ports. The two ports proved major sources for investment in textiles and proved central points from which to tap the producing villages in the hinterland. As old ports, they had well-developed communications links with a very deep hinterland, a feature which the newer European settlements had to develop over time. Furthermore, it was noted that large-scale transactions, both of import and export, could be made here, and there were merchants here with substantial regional and interregional links across the maritime world.

By the 1680s, the European ports, with the exception of Pondichery, had achieved optimum growth as far as the trade to Europe was concerned; from then on we should distinguish specific factors affecting the fortunes of individual

*A view of the Coromandel Coast, eastern India. The fort here is a tenuous outpost in an otherwise 'wild' setting.
From Hendrik Nieuhof Joan Nieuhofs Gedenkwaerdighe Zee-en Lant-rieze door de voornaemste Landschappen van West en Oostindien Amsterdam, 1682.
Courtesy of Mitchell Library, State Library of New South Wales.*

ports. From now the relationship of a port to its hinterland and to the trading region both in a narrow and a broad circle of contacts became the key to its further growth, stagnation or even decline. Beginning as alien intrusions on the landscape of maritime Asia, they now had to merge into that landscape if they were to survive. This integration was being attempted in a context of maximum competition in overseas trade and increasing difficulties that had been put in the way of maritime trade both by the actions of the Dutch and by regional problems in many trade centres. In this context it is interesting to see how each power and each port faced up to the challenges that arose.

There were some factors that operated in favour of the growth of European ports. Security was one important factor. The extent of security offered depended on the military capability of each power, and all European powers at the turn of the seventeenth century were strengthening their defences and fortifying themselves. Madras was among the earliest ports to benefit from this. During the Mughal wars against Golconda and Bijapur (1683-89) and the Mughal-Maratha wars (1690-1702), Madras increased its population and offered security of property to merchant groups. This factor operated to a lesser degree in Fort St David, as the environs of the fort were much smaller and the degree of protection less. Pondichery also grew in similar fashion, attracting merchants and artisans fleeing Mughal attack on Jinji and the Maratha raids in the countryside looking for plunder. The search for security did not benefit the Dutch in Paleacat as the port and the town were in such a geographical location as not to afford expansion. Besides, as noted above, the Dutch did not have complete legal and fiscal jurisdiction over the whole of Paleacat.

The disturbed hinterland benefited some of the European ports in another way. While in the earlier period, hinterland political powers were strong enough to keep the Europeans within the limits of the concessions they had been granted, this now became difficult and the opportunity was there for the European powers, if they chose, to break out of their bounds, abuse their concessions and push into the hinterland. This could be done with or without the acquiescence of hinterland powers. Rivals in conflict thought they could secure European support in the form of arms and ammunition, bullion or shipping by adding to concessions they already had. In this way, for example, the Maratha ruler of Jinji sought to secure English support by giving them a piece of ground near the port of Cuddalore to build a fort. It was through this process that most European ports were able to expand their jurisdiction by the addition of neighbouring villages granted to them in exchange for a loan or gift of ammunition or a promise of annual payment. Thus Madras more than doubled in its area from 1690 to 1730. Likewise Pondichery secured four additional villages by 1734. The growth that is recorded in the early eighteenth century of these ports is more due to the acquisition of neighbouring villages than through a drift of population towards them.

Population statistics are sometimes quoted in support of the thesis that the security afforded by the European ports caused a continuous migration to them from the neighbourhood. This is not supported by a close look at the evidence of any one of these ports. There was certainly a movement of merchants and labouring castes in the early stages of the growth of these ports. But this movement stopped once a certain point had been reached and the ports showed no capacity to grow further. After this there was an occasional spurt of migration caused by some immediate crisis, such as war, a pillaging attack or famine. But when this ceased, there would be a drift back. It is significant that in none of the ports was there immigration of weavers. It was only in 1736 that Madras was able to settle its first colony of weavers in a suburb in Chindadrepettah. About the same time there was some movement of weavers towards Pondichery.

On the contrary, there is evidence that merchant communities rejected enticements to shift to English ports from neighbouring Indian-controlled ports. The best example of this comes from Madras and San Thome. San Thome (Mylapore), four miles south of Madras, had been captured from the Portuguese by the king of Golconda in 1664 and had passed under Mughal rule in 1687. At the Golconda conquest of the port, the English had urged the king to destroy the fort and township, which he had done partially. The English were thereafter suspicious of any signs of the growth of San Thome as detrimental to the trade of Madras. San Thome did grow, however, under the encouragement of Golconda district governors and revenue farmers. With the decline of the northern port of Masulipatnam after the Mughal conquest, some of the merchants and shipowners moved to San Thome. Among these were a group the English called Pathans, who were probably Perso-Afghans who had dominated the westward trade of Masulipatnam for decades. Their move to San Thome in the 1690s led to a dramatic growth in the shipping and overseas trade of this port and the English began to show signs of concern.[7]

A number of measures were put in train to entice the 'Pathans' to Madras to trade under the English flag. The governors entered into negotiations with the heads of their community to effect a wholesale migration. This had to be done carefully without offending the Fausdar of San Thome and his master the Nawab of Carnatic. Some customs concessions were offered to Pathans, though again the English had to be cautious not to be seen to discriminate against older merchants. The period within which duty was to be paid on goods unloaded was extended from one to three months. A system of drawback on goods re-exported was arranged.[8] None of these had the desired effect and in 1729 the Madras government confessed that the Pathans were not trading in Madras but in San Thome.

Similar efforts were made to attract shipowners to the other English settlement of Fort St David. Soon after its foundation, there were encouraging signs when a prominent Chulia merchant, Makdum Nina of Porto Novo, brought his family to settle under English protection.[9] This was of course caused by the Maratha wars and in particular the Maratha attack on Porto Novo. But this appears to have been a temporary solution and there was no drift of merchants to Fort St David. Now and then there were negotiations between merchant heads and English officers but nothing came of them. There was nothing in Fort St David to attract the merchants and when English trade here declined they lost all interest in moving to that port.

In the case of Dutch ports, the movement, for reasons already noted, was away from them. Indian merchants moved away from Paleacat, leaving it a shell of its former activity by the end of the seventeenth century. During the period that they held Sadraspatnam on lease, they drove away its Indian merchants through restrictive policies on sales of imports. The most remarkable movement was from Nagapatnam to Nagore. Nagore, four miles to the north of Nagapatnam, had always been a minor satellite port of this larger entrepot. Now, after fifty years of Dutch rule, merchants left it for Nagore which, in the eighteenth century, became the home of a large merchant fleet. The Tanjore administration nurtured this growth with fiscal concessions.[10] The two cases of Paleacat and Nagapatnam show the dwindling and dispersal of commercial activity from European ports.

Not even in the eighteenth century, when there is undisputed evidence of decline in Indian mercantile activity, can it be assumed that the European ports were centres of growth and therefore of attraction to their maritime neighbours. This is seen from a close look at Madras in the first three decades of the eighteenth century, a port which is often held up as an exemplar of growth in a declining environment. There were certainly some factors that told in the direction of commercial strength. The export trade of the Company was a steadying factor in the port's commerce. Its imports were picking up during this period: woollens were selling in the Mughal armies of the Deccan; metals and coral had a good market. Madras was always a good supplier of silver and gold to the region. One major growth was the trade in grain for which Madras soon became an import market for the central Carnatic region. The ample storage and godown facilities, many wholesale merchants, the extensive anchorage out in the open and the growing demand of the Madras population made it an attractive calling point for the grain barges of north Coromandel.

In all these respects the trade of Madras grew, sometimes at the expense of neighbouring ports. Madras had throughout the seventeenth century imported foodgrains for its consumption from the Carnatic hinterland by land. The decline in productivity and the devastation of the wars had made the region a deficit area for foodgrains. Now Madras became a point of import by sea from north and south Coromandel and from Bengal, not only for its own consumption but also for an extensive hinterland. Port facilities were widened to handle these shipments. Import duties on grain of 5 percent made up a large proportion of the customs revenue of the port, during some years the single major item in customs returns.[11]

Apart from grain, trade was generally depressed in Madras in the first decade of the eighteenth century. The trade consisted of voyages by Company servants, individually or in partnership with Indians of the port, shipping of Indian merchants who were prominent in supplying the Company and that of free merchants, English, Portuguese and Armenians, who had made Madras their home. English free merchants were prominent in the trade westwards, to Malabar, Surat and West Asia. Indians tended to concentrate on the trade

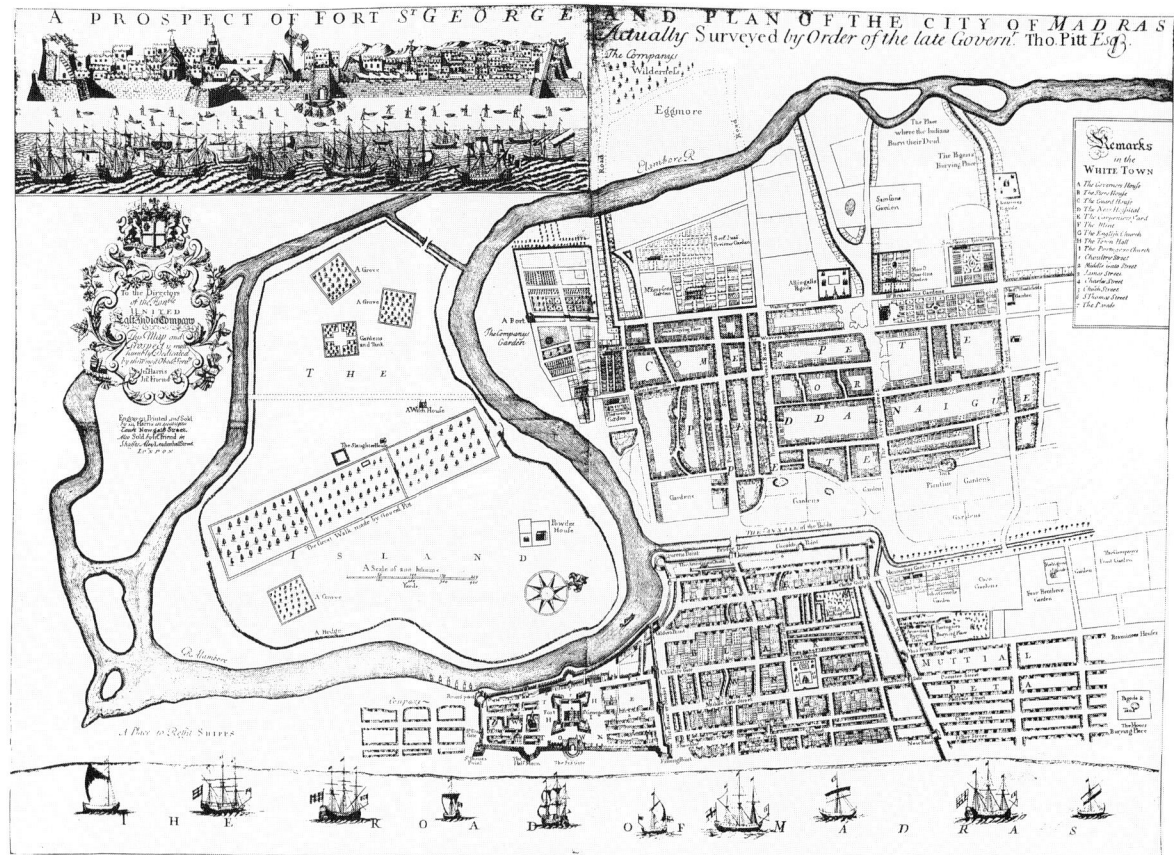

Fort St George and Madras, eastern India, 1709. The major British port city of the Coromandel Coast, surveyed, organised and controlled.
From H. D. Love Vestiges of Old Madras *Madras, 1713, repr. 1968.*

eastwards to mainland and island Southeast Asia and along the coast up to Bengal, and Company servants and Armenians traded everywhere. The trade to Manila and to China were growth points of Madras trade in the early decades of the eighteenth century. Records of private shipping of Madras, which unfortunately are not continuous, show a large proportion of ships calling in Madras as being Indian-owned, both Hindu and Muslim. Some of these were owned by persons domiciled in Madras, many were not. Most of the Muslim-owned vessels seem to be from other Coromandel ports.[12]

After 1710, the bottom had fallen out of the trade to West Asia. This was attributed to political problems in Jeddah. Thereafter Madras merchants could barely subsist in this trade and there came a time when it was not returning the cost of investment. The Madras government was so concerned at the effect of this on liquidity that it imposed regulations on voyages to West Asia. It intervened to prohibit private ventures to Mocha on the grounds that they were damaging the Company's trade there and would not provide sufficient returns to investors.[13] Likewise, in the 1870s Madras was losing the trade to Bengal. It had been a profitable sector of the private trade of Company servants and English free merchants. Some of the Bengal imports of rice, edible oils, sugar and muslins to Coromandel had been channelled through Madras. Coromandel textiles and indigo were shipped from Madras to Calcutta for transshipment to Southeast Asia and China. But now Madras lost out on both the import and export trade. Muslim shippers from San Thome and Porto Novo were importing Bengal goods through these ports. Even Bengal ships which sailed to Coromandel were buying their goods not at Madras but at San Thome, Porto Novo and other ports.[14]

There was a degree of commercial rivalry between the two English settlements on the Bay of Bengal, Madras and Calcutta. Up to the first decade of the eighteenth century, Madras Company servants had benefited from the expanding Calcutta trade. Now it appears that the Calcutta servants had decided to keep for themselves the benefits of this trade and imposed a number of commission charges on Madras merchants. The Madras Company servants complained bitterly to the directors that even Indian merchants from neighbouring ports were able to trade on better terms in Bengal than they could and unsuccessfully sought their intervention.[15] Before the outbreak of the War of Austrian Succession (1744), Madras trade presented a depressing picture, with the Company servants complaining bitterly about loss of trade to a number of regions and unfair competition from other settlements, and from Armenians and Muslims.

It is even more remarkable that Madras felt the competition from the Carnatic Nawab's port of San Thome. The spectacular growth of this port in the first decades of the eighteenth century runs counter to the general drift of declining trade in Coromandel. This should be also juxtaposed with the stagnation and even decline during many years of this period of the trade of Madras. The growth of San Thome can partly be explained in the context of the decline of ports of north Coromandel which were troubled by a disturbed hinterland.

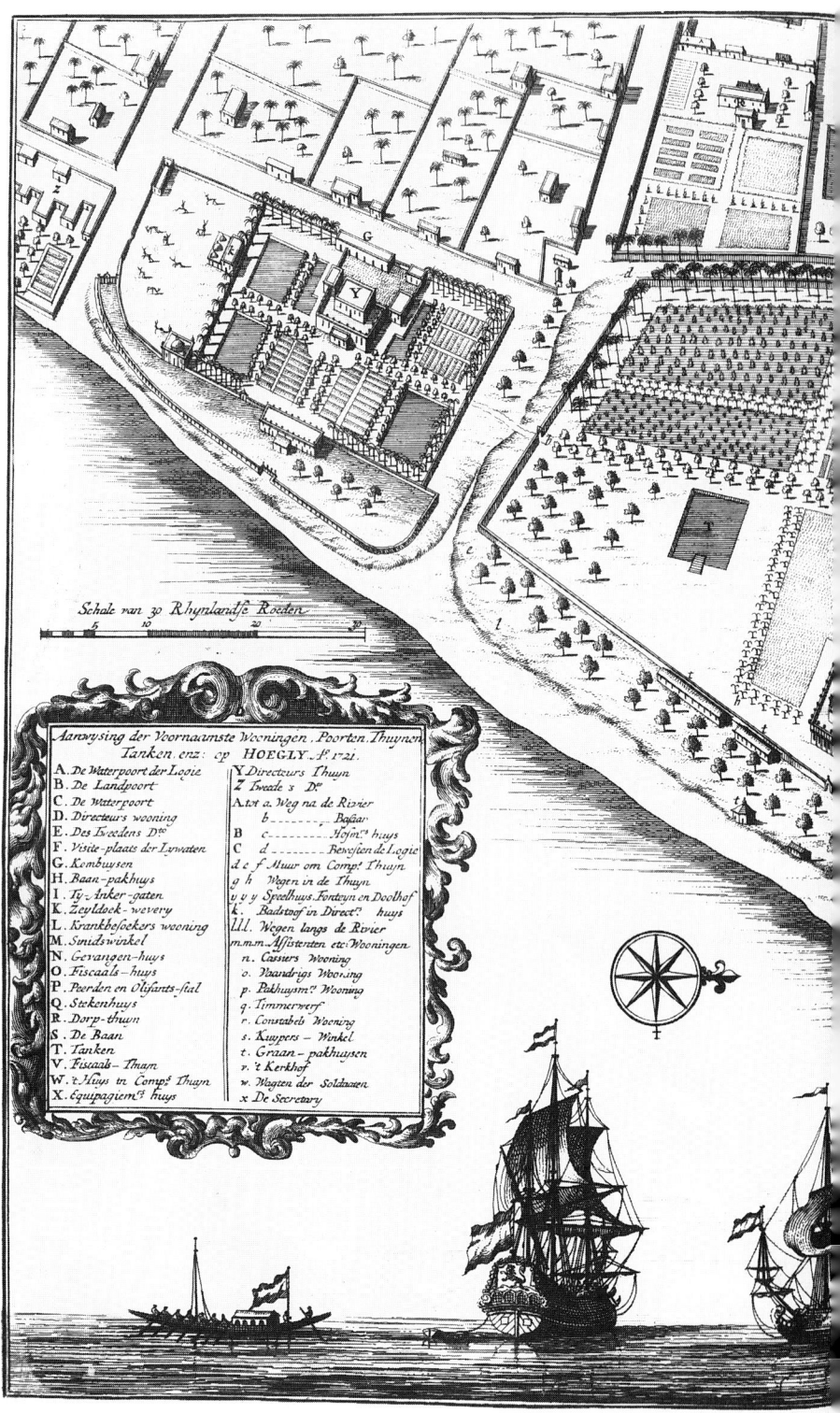

*The rising competitor of the Coromandel Coast: Hugli (near Calcutta), eastern India.
From* Francois Valentijn Oud en Nieuw Oost Indien Dordrecht, *1724-26.
Courtesy of Mitchell Library, State Library of New South Wales.*

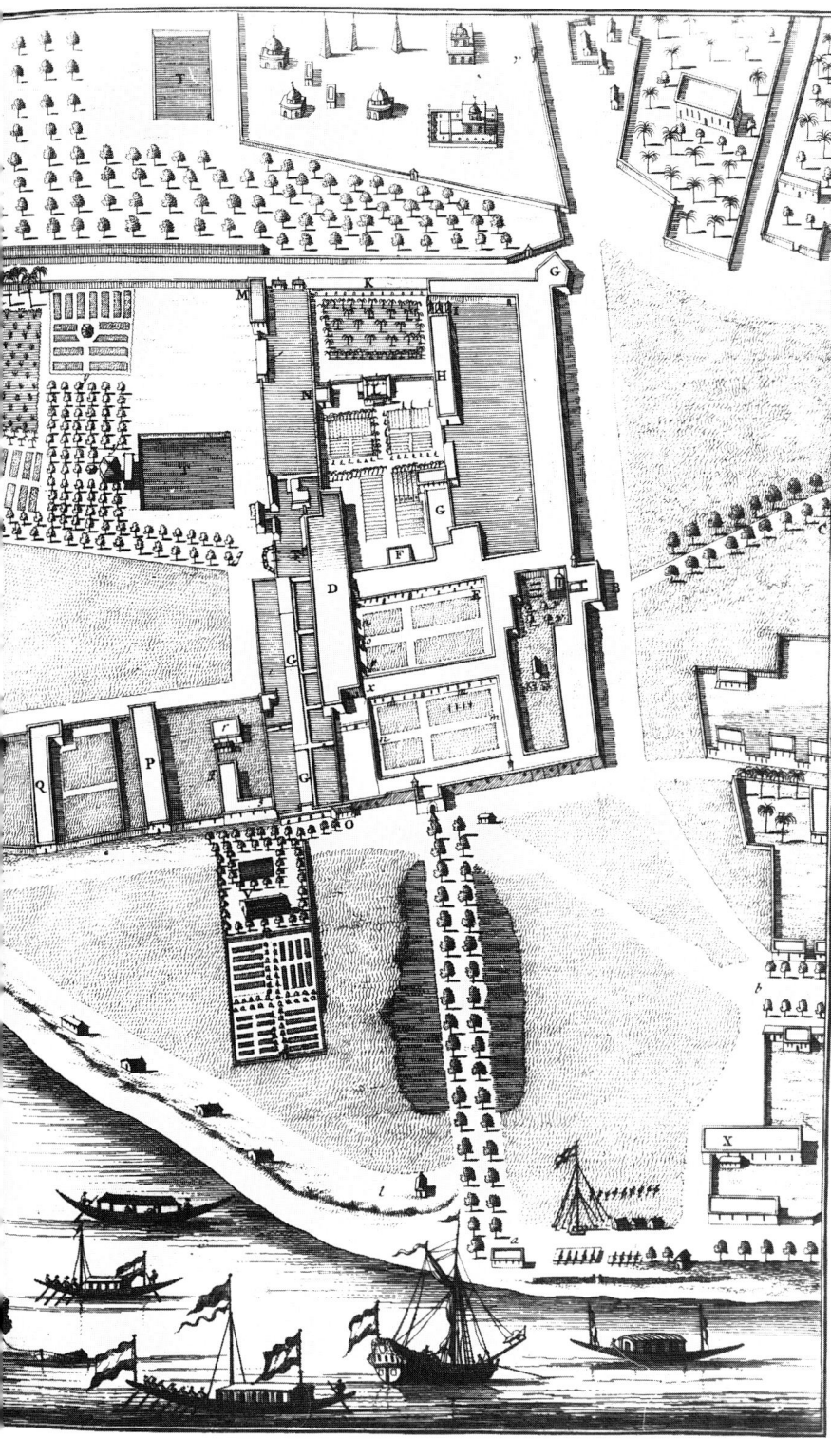

It can also be seen in the context of a positive policy of the Nawab in developing a port of outlet near his capital of Arcot. He did this by a series of administrative and fiscal measures which proved successful. On the other hand, the Madras authorities took punitive measures to restrict merchants domiciled in Madras from trading in San Thome. San Thome's trade grew in those very sectors in which the Madras trade was declining. It conducted a busy trade with Bengal, its trade with the ports of Burma, Tenasserim and western Malaya continued at an even pace. Its trade to Surat, though declining with all Coromandel trade to western India, did not totally disappear. Its coastal trade was always a feature of its strength. It is interesting to note that the Armenians, who received favoured treatment in Madras, continued to trade at San Thome, despite incurring the displeasure of the Madras authorities.[16]

It remains true that, before the period of political expansion, European ports of Coromandel were not dominant or even important in the commercial economy of Coromandel. To some extent, it could be argued that their importance diminished at the end of the seventeenth century. Through most of the seventeenth century, the major Companies had easy access to inland markets and, through their Indian merchant brokers, they interacted with these markets to a far larger extent than they were able to do in the eighteenth century. Now, while their coastal bases had undoubtedly expanded, they lost that access to the interior and looked oceanwards even more than they did previously. At best, they were suffering from the same malaise that affected Coromandel trade and Asian trade generally and sharing the difficulties that other ports of the Coast underwent. At worst, European ports stagnated and declined at a faster rate than Indian ports. The stagnation is true of English Madras and French Pondichery, the decline of Dutch Paleacat and Nagapatnam and English Fort St David.

This stagnation of the European ports runs directly in the face of the traditional view of the growth of European ports as city-states being the result of the establishment of European legal and administrative institutions and the security these afforded to persons and property. This caused, as the argument runs, a steady drift in the early eighteenth century of Indian merchant capital and enterprise to these ports. Whatever the case may have been in the other ports of the Indian Ocean, the evidence for Coromandel does not support these assertions. It was seen above that a crisis in the hinterland would lead to an immediate influx of population to or near the European port. Such a movement was sporadic and was caused by the push factor operating in the interior rather than the pull factor in the European port. That people in the neighbourhood of European ports found the law and order and security of property attractive enough to migrate cannot be sustained from the evidence.

This can be established from a close study of Madras where the English had extraterritorial rights from its cession in 1639. A mayoral court was established where Europeans and Indians could sue and be sued and to which Indians could resort voluntarily where both parties to a suit were Indians. The court was first set up in 1688, but for its first few years Indian litigants were very reluctant to resort to it, preferring by far their own system of arbitration by caste elders. Whenever a case came up before the mayor's court, Indians found its procedures strange and acutely destabilising of the social fabric of Indian merchant groups. Far worse, however, was the record of litigation between Indians and Europeans which were compulsorily heard before the mayor's court. This created situations in which Indians found themselves at a disadvantage in the conduct of suits against Europeans, arising from their ignorance of the laws of evidence, in inadmissibility of types of documentary and other evidence that came through their traditional systems and the reliance on European pleaders—a class which quickly grew up and throve around the European courts of Madras.

The worst feature of the system was that the highest court of appeal in the port was the governor-in-council and that, not infrequently, this body sat in judgment on appeals from cases in which the governor or one of the councillors was a party. Given that the governor and councillors were prominent merchants, dealing closely with a number of prominent Indian merchants of the port, it can be seen how heavily the dice were loaded in their favour. A number of governors appeared thus in litigation against Indians over commercial dealings and in a number of cases the court of appeal overturned judgments in favour of Indians given in the lower courts. The directors were acutely aware of this heavy-handed behaviour of their servants but were helpless to prevent it. When a governor was particularly oppressive in dealings with Indians, it inevitably affected the port's commerce adversely. Such is known to have happened in the times of Governors Winter (1661-65), Langhorn (1672-78), Master (1678-81), Hastings (1720-21), Macrae (1725-30), and Pitt (1730-35). Thus, far from being havens of the rule of law, these ports were no different in the nature of arbitrary government from other ports of the area. This certainly could not have been an attraction to such Indian groups as came to settle there.[17]

Finally, an index to the place of these ports in the region's commercial system is the circulation of currency and the operation of their mints. Every European power that settled along the coast asked and was given rights of minting coins current in the region. The Dutch coined pagodas and rupees in Paleacat, the English coined them in Madras and later the French were also given similar rights in Pondichery. All these Companies in the aggregate brought enormous quantities of silver and gold into the region but could not give wide currency to the coins minted in their own mints. This was, of course, governed both by economic and political factors. As long as hinterland governments were strong and economically viable, they could dictate exchange rates and discount coins minted in European mints, as they consistently did. But what is surprising is that they continued to do so even after they had lost their political and economic power. Even in a situation of economic weakness, these European-minted coins did not have currency beyond the confines of the European port.

Among European coins, the Dutch Paleacat pagoda had the most currency, particularly in north Coromandel because of the large investment they made in that currency from the early decades of the seventeenth century. Neither the English pagodas nor rupees were current outside their settlements, the rupees being transported to Bengal where they were exchanged at a lower than intrinsic value. The English Madras pagoda was not even current within the Madras city and had to be exchanged for Arcot and other pagodas, a situation that continued till the Carnatic wars.[18] Their influence in the Carnatic monetary system was very minimal indeed. The adverse consequences of this were visible when the Arcot coinage became debased in the 1730s and these debased coins gained currency in Madras and other European ports, driving the better Madras-minted coins into the hands of hoarders and bullion merchants. There was little the English could do to keep the coinage of their settlements pure.[19]

It cannot be assumed that before the Carnatic wars the European port-settlements on the Coromandel Coast were on a steady upward trend of growth and expansion or that they were able to operate as 'city-states', autonomous and challenging to the neighbourhood and hinterland. In many respects, they continued as alien intrusions, functioning in the interests of the European trade of the Companies and as a part of the Company trading system. In others, they shared the problems and the weaknesses of the states and economies in the neighbourhood. They were not in a position to dictate the course of events by any means but were reacting helplessly to more powerful forces beyond their control. There was still a good deal of dynamism left in the ports under Indian rule. Much less valid is the view that the European ports were havens of security and rule of law. The worst features of arbitrary rule and corrupt influence prevalent in Europe were reproduced here. In this respect, they had much in common with the volatile and unpredictable systems of neighbouring states. The security provided from external attack was negated by the venality of corrupt oligarchies. They lacked the political and economic base for a self-sustaining growth at the expense of their neighbours.

European port settlements in the Coromandel commercial system

The interaction of foreign traders and pearl fishermen in a seasonal industry: at Tuticorin, a pearl-trading post in South India.
From Hendrik Nieuhof *Joan Nieuhofs Gedenkwaerdighe Zee-en Lant-reize door de voornaemste Landschappen van West en Oostindien* Amsterdam, 1682.
Courtesy of Mitchell Library, State Library of New South Wales.

Notes

1. This is evident in almost all histories of the expansion of British dominion in India. A typical example is H.H. Dodwell *Cambridge Shorter History of India* Cambridge, reprinted S. Chand and Co. 1958, pp. 410-15. For a recent study with this underlying theme, see J. Richards 'European city-states on the Coromandel Coast' in *Studies in the Foreign Relations of India. Prof. H.K. Sherwani Felicitation Volume* Hyderabad, pp. 508-21, especially pp. 514-18.
2. See statistics in T. Raychaudhuri *Jan Company in Coromandel 1605-1690* The Hague, 1962, pp. 141-43, 219-20.
3. K. N. Chaudhuri *The Trading world of Asia and the English East India Company 1660-1760* Cambridge, 1978, Appendix 5, Table C2, pp. 508-10
4. I. B. Watson *Foundation for Empire. English Private trade in India 1659-1760* New Delhi, 1980, pp. 61-68, 90-97
5. Caul of Nawab Mir Muhamad Sahy to the VOC, 1 January 1647. Treaties and Grants to VOC, Mackenzie Collection. Private (India Office Library) 20.1
6. Memoir of Guillot, 19 September 1738. Mackenzie Collection Private 50
7. *Despatches to England*, 10 February 1970, p. 67, 22 January 1708, p. 93
8. *Despatches to England*, 29 August 1716, p. 94, 19 September 1718, p. 137, 17 September 1736
9. Farmer, Chief of St David to directors, 12 January 1711, Miscellaneous letters received, India Office Library E/1/3
10. Governor General and Council to directors, 1 December 1700, Algemeen Rijksarchief (The Hague) 1520, f.305
11. *Despatches to England*, 28 January 1737, p. 37, 25 August 1738, p. 88; *Despatches from England*, 21 March 1739
12. Data from *Diary and Consultation Books Fort St George, 1720-1730*
13. *Despatches to England*, 31 August 1734, p. 56, Public Consultations, Fort St George, 9 September 1734
14. *Despatches to England*, 22 September 1727, p. 68, *Despatches from England*, 14 February 1728, p. 6
15. *Despatches to England*, 31 August 1734, p.57, 28 January 1737, p.31
16. *Despatches to England*, 28 January 1737, pp. 30-31, Public Consultations Fort St George, 3 July 1739
17. This discussion of the legal system is based on the Mayor's Court Proceedings, Madras, 1720-1724
18. *Despatches to England*, 21 January 1724, p.93, 27 January 1737, p.65, *Despatches from England*, 17 February 1726, p.77, Public Consultations Fort St George, 2 April 1739
19. Public Consultations Fort St George, 2 April 1739, 7 April 1741

Further reading

Arasaratnam, S. *Merchants, Companies and Commerce on the Coromandel Coast 1650-1740* New Delhi, Oxford University Press 1986. A detailed study of Coromandel ports.

Arasaratnam, S. 'Society, Power, Factionalism and Corruption in early Madras 1640-1746' *Indica* 23 1&2 1986, pp. 113-34. Discusses the evolution of Madras society in the first century of its foundation.

Bowrey, T. *A Geographical Account of the Countries round the Bay of Bengal, 1669-1679*, ed. Sir Richard Temple, London, Hakluyt Society 1905, reprinted 1967. Most valuable of the contemporary travellers' accounts on the Coromandel ports.

Furber, H. *John Company at Work* Cambridge, Harvard University Press 1948. A pioneer study of the growth of private trade in Madras.

Havart, D. *Op en Ondergang van Coromandel* Amsterdam 1693. Contains much material on Dutch ports of Coromandel in the seventeenth century.

Love, H.D. *Vestiges of Old Madras* 3 vols, London, John Murray Ltd 1913, reprinted 1968. A chronicle of the growth of Madras, reproducing contemporary sources.

CHAPTER

Heather Sutherland

Eastern emporium and company town: trade and society in eighteenth-century Makassar*

Eighteenth-century Makassar (nowadays Ujung Pandang) was a hybrid town, created by the forcible grafting of a Dutch outpost upon an Indonesian port. But despite its position on the edge of Asia and its relatively small population it was no backwater. Makassar's economy was geared to the rhythms of world trade, its government was constantly striving to reconcile distant priorities with local realities, while social life reflected the tension and energy of a multi-ethnic settlement. Makassar was a place with far horizons; its influence and fortunes fluctuated with commercial tides, and most of its inhabitants were fed, directly or indirectly, by the flow of goods through its harbour or by the labour of its merchants and sailors. Neither the historical development of the town, nor the social structure and life of its population, can be understood unless its commercial basis is appreciated.

* This chapter makes grateful use of material from the Algemeen Rijksarchief (General State Archives, ARA), The Hague, and the Arsip National Republika Indonesia (Indonesian National State Archives, ANRI), Jakarta; I would like to record my thanks to the staff of both institutions, and also to Drs Ankie de Jonge for her painstaking assistance, and Barbara and Leonard Andaya for extensive comments on an earlier draft. Needless to say, they bear no responsibility for the following pages.

This chapter is, therefore, built up of three parts. First, a broad overview is given of the position of Makassar within the trading network of its region and beyond, in which its location on the southwesterly point of Sulawesi (Celebes) constituted the crucial factor. In order to understand the interest of the VOC in Makassar it is necessary to trace the town's rise to pre-eminence in the era before Dutch domination. The second part deals with the administrative policy of the VOC, its attempt to reshape Makassar and make it an effective instrument for the pursuit of its regional objectives — a policy dictated by the overall interests of the Company, but inevitably influenced by its inability to achieve full control over the surroundings of Makassar. Indeed, there was a large gap between the 'Company Town' as envisaged by Speelman and the social reality of Makassar described in the third part of the chapter. It is here that the continuities of the era before and after the arrival of the Dutch show most clearly, as the complexity of Makassar's population structure and the relations between its various ethnic and social groups reflected the inability of the VOC to totally transform regional trading networks. In consequence, Makassar remained an integral part of, rather than an alien intrusion in, the many-layered world of its region which, after all, was its *raison d'être*.

The trading world of Makassar

From its very beginning the development of Makassar has been inseparably linked with the seaborne trade of island Southeast Asia. It lies on the southwest peninsula of Sulawesi, within easy reach of the busy sealanes of eastern Indonesia. Makassar's appeal for traders lay in a combination of natural and political endowments. The anchorage was protected by the many small islands off the coast, while the beach ridges provided an admirably dry site for settlement. Fresh water was readily available, and fertile plains to the north and south were suitable for intensive rice cultivation. Javanese traders had probably been visiting the area for several hundred years before 1500, while Malays from the west began frequenting the waters in the later fifteenth century, perhaps following in the wake of Bajau or sea-nomads. The possibilities of the site were more fully exploited when, in the sixteenth century, the Makassarese-speaking rulers of the young state of Gowa added protection, freedom for foreign merchants and an orderly harbour administration to the port's attractions. These local circumstances, combined with the flourishing trade of the sixteenth century, proved most effective. Indeed, the rise of Makassar has been called 'one of the most rapid and spectacular success stories that Indonesian history affords'.[1]

The development of Makassar followed the established pattern of rising Southeast Asian entrepot states, in the tradition of Srivijaya and the great fifteenth-century Straits emporium of Malay Melaka. Although the classic distinction between Indonesian 'inland agrarian' and 'coastal maritime' centres

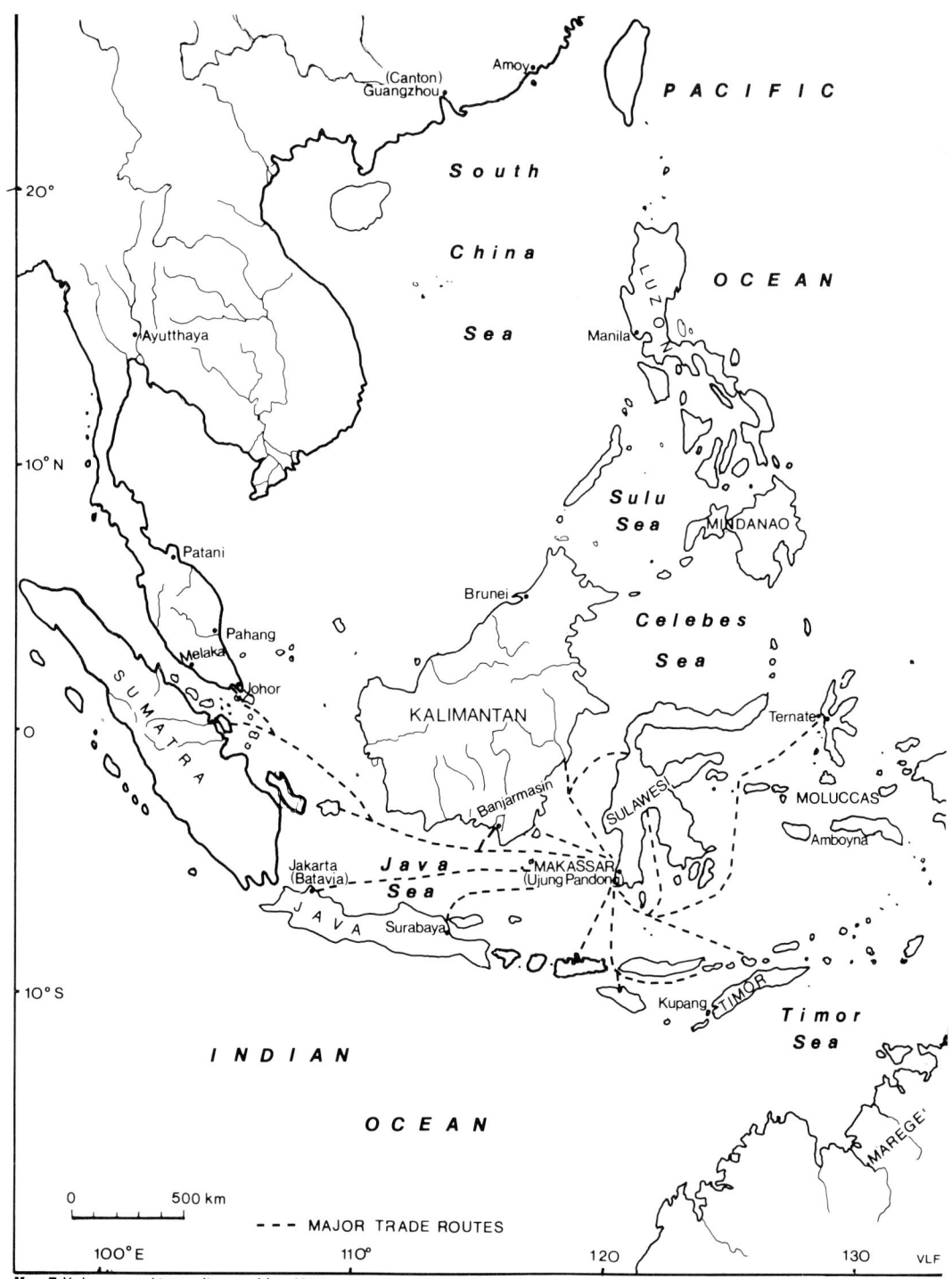

Map 7 *Makassar and its trading world, c.1750*

has been modified by recent recognition of the complex interplay between ports and hinterlands, the image of a harbour principality whose primary source of wealth was trade is still valid for towns like Makassar, and the role of long-distance commerce in early state formation is an important theme in recent research.[2] In this essay, however, we are less concerned with typologies or theories than with the social organisation of one specific town, Makassar, during one particular period of its history, when it was under the control of the Dutch United East India Company (VOC). However, continuities with the preceding state of Gowa run through the history of 'Dutch' Makassar, and can be traced in the economy, morphology and society of the settlement. The Gowan 'port' was the centre of the 'kingdom of the Makassara', and was usually given the name of its inhabitants. But Makassar was actually a cluster of villages sprawling along the beach, densely settled close to the sea and thinning out on the landward side, blending into the agrarian hinterland. The town focused upon the sheltered anchorage, which was protected by a complex of defence works. The most notable were the three forts of Ujung Pandang in the north, the central Somba Opu, between the mouths of the Jeneberang river, and Pankkukang to the south.[3] The heart of the kingdom, and hence of the settlement, was Somba Opu, whose brick walls are said to have been credited with attracting many foreign merchants to the town.

Somba Opu at its zenith is beautifully presented in a 1638 pictorial groundplan from the secret atlas of the VOC. The fort was the focus, facing west out to sea, with boat-filled streams on either side. Its walls enclosed two large palaces on piles, where the king lived, as well as the royal warehouses, a mosque and various fenced compounds each containing a number of houses. Close against the northern wall were the quarters of the foreign merchants: two blocks of Portuguese, one of Gujeratis. Adjoining them, but on the other side of the stream, was the 'large Bazaar or market', and to the north again was a large area of village housing and compounds, where not only Makassarese but also 'other nations' lived. (The 'kampung China' is not shown; there was one in Makassar at that time, but perhaps Chinese merchants were not very much in evidence, as turmoil in China was affecting overseas trade.) To the south, between the fort and another mouth of the Jeneberang, was the 'new bazaar' and houses, and all around were gardens and rice land.

Although Makassar was established as a major port under indigenous rule, its rise was nonetheless closely related to political and economic changes linked to European intervention. The Portuguese defeat of Melaka in 1511 had opened the way for a realignment of trading patterns. The dynamic ruler of Gowa seized this opportunity to build his capital into a strong regional trading centre, making full use of the knowledge and skills of both refugee Malays and Portuguese merchants.

Makassar maintained close ties with neighbours such as Maluku (the Moluccan 'spice islands'), Nusa Tenggara (the Lesser Sundas), Java and Kalimantan (Borneo). A vigorous trade developed between Makassar and Maluku, as rice (from South Sulawesi) and cloth (local and imported) were exchanged for

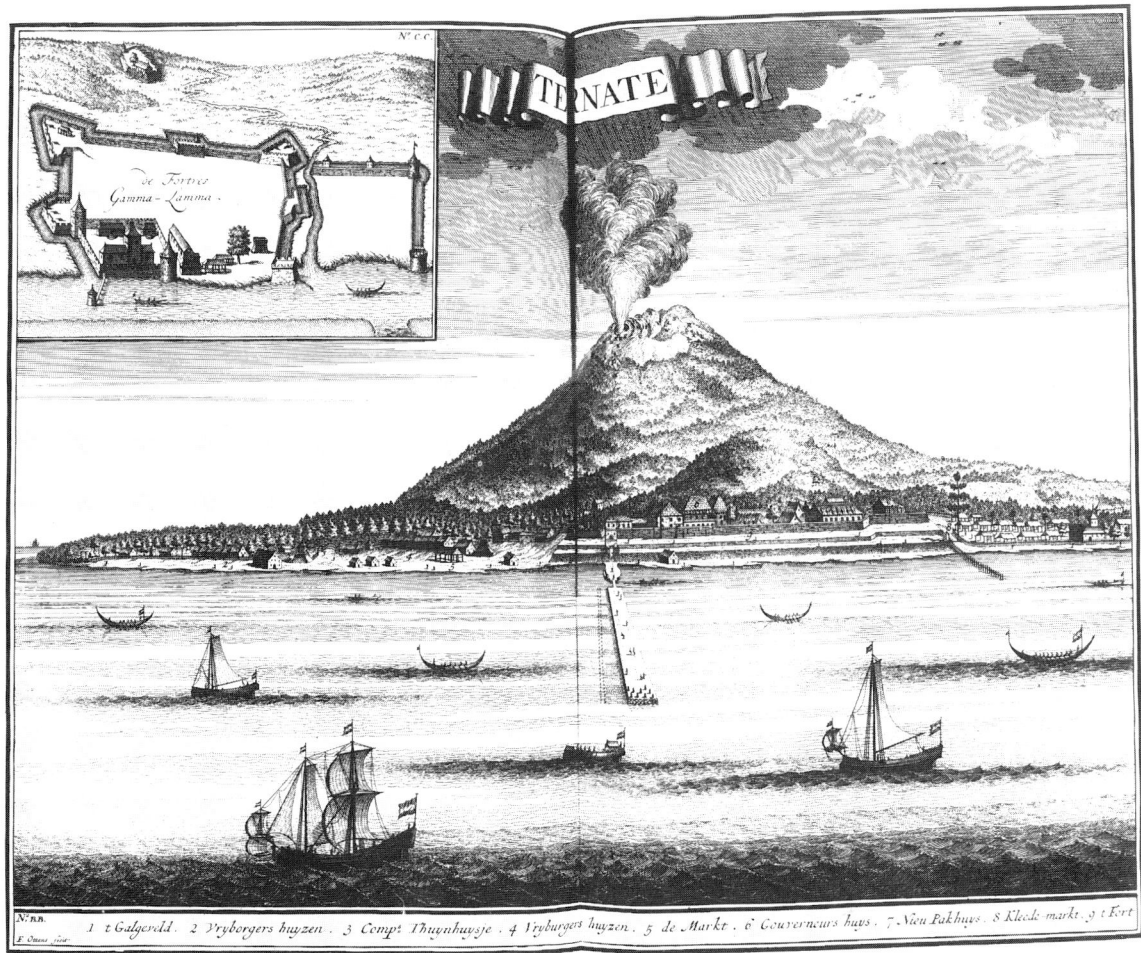

Ternate, one of the former major Sultanates of eastern Indonesia.
From **Francois Valentin** Oud en Nieuw Oost Indien Dordrecht, 1724-26.
Courtesy of Mitchell Library, State Library of New South Wales.

spices, above all cloves, nutmeg and mace (pepper was not grown on the islands). The spices attracted Malays from Johor, Pahang and Patani, Portuguese and Spanish, Gujerati and Chinese to Makassar. The northern Europeans came too; the Netherlands intermittently maintained a factory (trading post) there from the early seventeenth century, followed closely by the English and the Danes. Makassar received another boost when the Dutch conquest of Melaka in 1641 produced further refugees, and it continued to profit from the weakening of earlier indigenous trading powers based in Ternate/Tidore, Java and Brunei.

The foundation of Makassar's economy was regional trade, the accumulation of commodities through many-layered networks of political and economic transactions. At the most simple level local populations provided goods as tribute to their chiefs and rulers, or exchanged them to meet their own limited needs (particularly for such commodities as salt, metals and textiles, but later also for manufactures, coins, opium and guns). Spices were the most attractive for traders from afar, but slaves, sea and forest products were collected by apparently isolated peoples, who nonetheless thus supplied and obtained goods from the international market.

These deceptively simple deals fed into wider systems, with a whole scale of possible methods of linkage. Sometimes coastal populations formed a barrier between inland peoples and visiting merchants, and exploited their contact position to profit from the two-way trade. In more specialised situations the goods would be brought to a visiting trader, who might have local contacts (a wife and kinsmen, or an agent) to gather the commodities in anticipation of his arrival. Or merchants might settle for months on favourable coasts, sometimes as individuals within existing villages, but sometimes in groups, forming seasonal settlements which filled and emptied according to the monsoon regulation of trade. On a still more sophisticated level, the products were carried to town-based merchants who bulked them together for transport or sale. These commodities attracted buyers from India and China, who brought their own merchandise to exchange, while Indonesian spices and Chinese goods proved irresistible to European traders.

In the 1590s the first Dutch fleets had made profits of up to 400 percent on their cargoes of spices, but competition threatened prices and profits, so in 1602 the United East India Company or VOC was founded to protect the principle of buying cheap and selling dear. With the Company's sphere of interest, which extended from the Cape of Good Hope to Japan, it pursued its advantage as best it could, by free trade in competition with others if forced, but preferably via exclusive contracts with native rulers, or in a few instances, by establishing first political control, and then commercial monopoly.[4] In Indonesia, the most important areas under direct VOC rule were the Asian headquarters of Batavia (est. 1619) in West Java, and (since c.1660) all the spice islands of the Moluccas.

During the seventeenth century Gowa's bustling port and political influence were the major obstacles to effective Dutch enforcement of their spice monopoly in the Moluccas. Gowa's refusal to act against what it considered to be legitimate

'An Ambonese soldier': the exotic ferocity of the peoples of eastern Indonesia. From Hendrik Nieuhof Joan Nieuhofs Gedenkwaerdighe Zee-en Lant-reize door de voornaemste Landschappen van West en Oostindien Amsterdam, 1682. Courtesy of Mitchell Library, State Library of New South Wales.

commerce made Dutch intervention inevitable: the leak from the spice islands had to be sealed, political defiance in such a strategic region could not be tolerated. The Dutch found an ally in an exiled prince from South Sulawesi, whose kingdom of Bugis speakers had been defeated by their Makassarese neighbour, Gowa. In 1667 an alliance of VOC and Buginese forces under Cornelis Speelman succeeded, after a bitter war, in imposing the Treaty of Bungaya which established the Netherlands commercial and military hegemony.[5]

According to the terms of the Treaty, Gowa's main fortifications were to be destroyed, except for 'the northern fort Jumpandang'. Taking the name of his birthplace, Speelman called the restored Ujung Pandang 'Kasteel Rotterdam', and just as the more southerly Somba Opu had formed the nucleus for Gowa's Makassar, so eighteenth-century Makassar was focused upon the Dutch East India Company's castle.

Commercial interests had brought the Dutch to Makassar, and in this they were not alone. Like Somba Opu before it, eighteenth-century Makassar soon emerged as a motley town, populated by merchants and seafarers from all over Asia. For trade is not simply a movement of goods, it is also a social activity, linking individuals and communities in interlocking commercial networks. In the time before legal and political institutions could provide channels for the transfer of credit and protection for merchants, the most common underlying fabric for long-distance trade was provided by ethnic and generously defined kinship ties. Traders were members of scattered communities, where social ties reinforced economic links, and vice versa.[6]

The population of a trade-based town can never be understood in isolation. By definition, such a settlement is only part of a system or, more precisely, of various systems. In many cases Makassar's inhabitants could look across the seas to distant homelands and to related groups in other ports, for the trading beaches of Southeast Asia were home to a floating population of traders and sailors. More established merchants—Chinese, Malays, Indians, Bugis and Makassarese—were all members of wider diasporae, their peoples scattered over the seas, drawn by the chance of profit or driven by political crisis to settle in alien harbours.

Private European captains also followed this itinerant pattern, as they sought to exploit an economic niche between the great Companies (VOC and English East Indian) and the well-informed, low cost Asian networks. The British 'country traders' operating out of Indian ports were too successful for the Dutch; during the eighteenth century they pushed their way into all corners of the archipelago, exchanging textiles, opium and guns for the eastern exotica so desired by tea-rich China. While such vessels sought direct contact with producing areas, they also could rendezvous with local traders seeking attractive alternatives to the Dutch harbours, so bypassing both VOC monopolies and local taxes. The Company, having thus lost income to its arch rivals, redoubled its efforts to forcibly channel trade through approved ports under its own control.

From the 1670s the English East India Company had permitted private trade

Trade and society in eighteenth-century Makassar 105

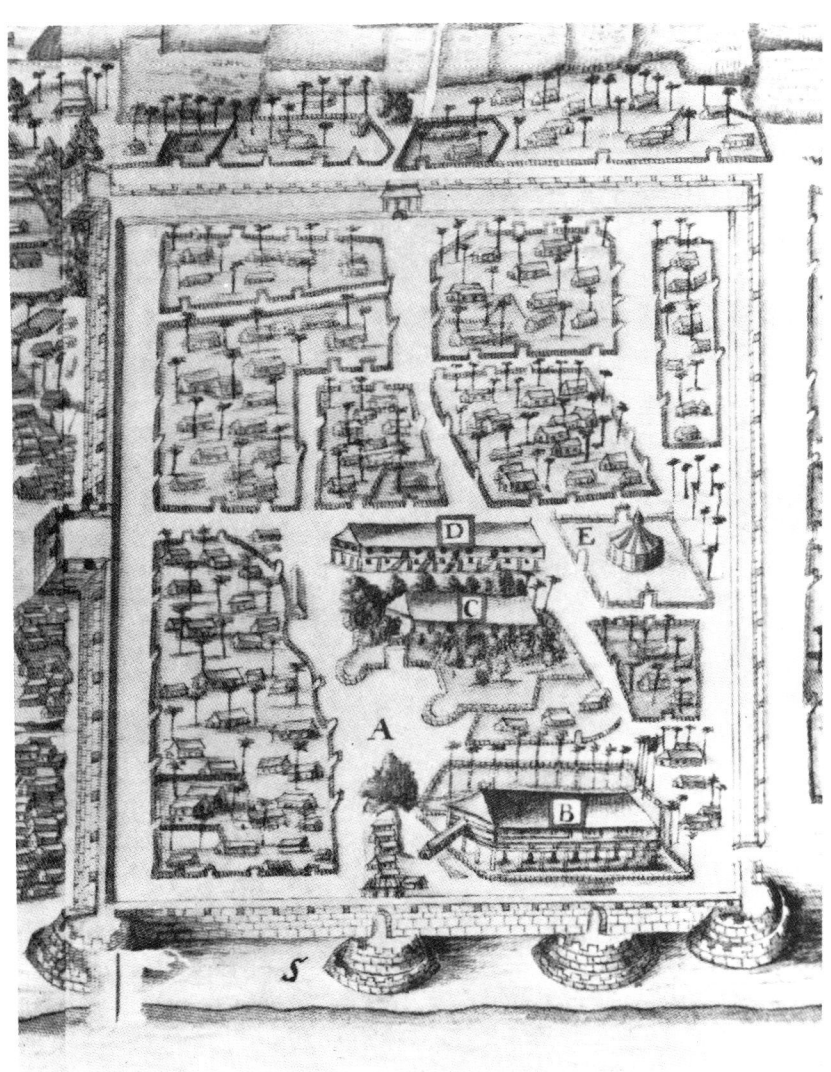

Somba Opu Fort, Makassar, eastern Indonesia (c. 1638). The focus of pre-Dutch Makassar, and one of the forts destroyed by Speelman.
VOC, Geheime Atlas, Algemeen Rijksarchief, The Hague.

in most of Asia, and profited from the new markets and routes the enterprising captains opened. But the VOC clung to its belief that if they could only contain trade within a straitjacket of their own design, then riches would flow once more into their coffers. Their hostility to the British, however, was political as much as it was economic; of far more immediate commercial importance was the recalcitrance of the Chinese. Trade with China boomed during the eighteenth century, and despite Dutch efforts (which included a failed attempt at direct trade with Canton, 1717-45), it proved impossible to bypass the junk captains. The best the Company could do was to try and force them to come to selected VOC ports. Free junk trade was banned in 1753, and apart from Batavia, the only approved harbours were Banjarmasin, which was allowed to receive two, and Makassar with a quota of only one vessel per year.[7]

In the later eighteenth century the arrival of the junk was the high point of Makassar's trading year. Before it came collectors sailed out to gather their sea and forest produce; local and Batavia Chinese formed *kongsi* (associations) to represent the Amoy merchants, while the chains of transactions necessary to gather together the outward cargo, and to distribute the inborne goods, guaranteed a welcome commercial stimulus. Moreover, the annual junk usually stayed several months in port (February to June for example), and it was huge compared to local craft. Chinese overseas junks could easily measure 400 *lasten* or 800 tons, carrying a crew of more than a hundred sailors as well as passengers. So not only traders benefited, but all the suppliers of services, from food-producers to gambling-den managers. The town was alive with activity when the junk came, but when the Chinese went to other ports, Makassar was quiet, and her traders sailed out to exchange their trepang and tortoiseshell for Chinese goods at some more favoured harbour.

The polyglot inhabitants of Makassar were mostly immigrants. Some came direct from their homelands, but others arrived after staying in trading settlements elsewhere in the archipelago, and no doubt were merely temporary residents. Many were far from their place of origin, so their cultural and social frame of reference could come to be defined more by the towns and the scattered seafaring communities of Southeast Asia than by their ancestral villages. But other newcomers were closer to home, drawn from the fishing and trading settlements of the Sulawesi coast, or the populous inland kingdoms.

The main inhabitants of the peninsula were the Makassarese and Buginese, who were organised in a number of states; further north were the coastal Mandar and the Toraja of the interior. By the seventeenth century the basic pattern of Sulawesi politics was already clear: a constant jockeying for position between fluctuating alliances of warring states. The competition between Makassarese Gowa in the west and the Buginese kingdom of Bone in the east was central, as each struggled to establish its hegemony over smaller states, such as Soppeng or Wajo'. If for the Dutch the primary motivation for their seventeenth-century wars with the Makassarese was to protect their interests in the spice islands, for their eventual allies, the chief Buginese state of Bone, cooperation with the VOC was simply a logical step in their long-drawn-out struggle against

Gowa. This constant strife between states did not stop with the establishment of Dutch Makassar. Although Gowa was no longer a force to be reckoned with, the great trading state of Wajo' was a serious threat to Makassar and Bone in the middle of the eighteenth century. Even in the areas ceded to the Company by the Treaty of Bungaya, such as the fertile Northern Districts, VOC control was often nominal, limited to a shaky garrison presence and the collection of a tithe on the rice crop.

The Dutch establishment in Makassar looked seawards, towards the shipping lanes; its only real interests in the peninsula were coastal trade and, of more importance, the rice of Maros in the north and Takalar to the south. These areas, probably opened for large-scale production during the sixteenth-century rise of Gowa, had long attracted ships seeking rice as a cargo for the Moluccas, or as provisions. After the defeat of Gowa the Dutch repeated the pattern of allocating the fertile plains to allies, who used slaves and followers to cultivate the land. These local Karaengs or lords paid the Dutch a part of the rice crop, but were free of any effective political control.[8]

In fact, the VOC could never completely dominate Makassar's surroundings or the trade of the region. For much of the eighteenth century it was an embattled outpost, helplessly watching the decline of Company trade, while anxiously placating mighty Bone and fighting to defend itself and its allies from ambitious local powers such as Wajo'. Even in their central task, the campaigns against violation of the trade monopolies, Dutch success was limited. Eliminating the Asian spice traders was relatively easy, given the restricted production areas, but for more generally available goods it was a different story, as the many creeks and beaches offered ample opportunity for private commerce, which only the VOC saw as illicit.

The Company's attempts to eliminate competition were resisted not only by Asian traders, but also by the *vrijburgers*, the retired or locally born Europeans who were allowed to settle in Company towns. A more powerful, if largely hidden, undermining of the monopolies came from the officials themselves. They had joined the VOC to become wealthy, and did not expect to do so by saving their salaries. Private trade and the abuse of office were the roads to riches, and much Company time and influence was used to arrange deals which were inimical to the VOC interest.

Of all Makassar's entrepreneurs it was probably the burgher merchants who suffered most from the VOC's heavy-handed attempts at mercantile management. Although free trade within Asia by burghers had been encouraged by J. P. Coen in the early 1620s, and was again promoted by Governor-General G. W. baron van Imhoff (1743-1750), it was usually seen as against the Company's interest and heavily restricted. Private traders were limited to secondary commerce which fed the VOC network, or to areas where the Company could not compete, or to low-profit activity. The governor and council in Makassar intermittently remonstrated with Batavia on behalf of local traders. They argued that a potentially flourishing economy was being squeezed to death by Company regulations and the regular closing of profitable routes to private merchants. Even when a given commodity could be legally traded, greater profits could often be earned in the more flexible irregular circuits. The private slave trade, for example, provided burghers with a good income. But even so, many slave traders preferred to deal illicitly, as their slaves were 'stolen' people who lacked the papers necessary for sale through approved channels.[9]

Although Makassar was an outpost, near the geographical limits of Dutch power, it had great strategic value for the VOC. It was the base for the cruising sloops and fast native-rigged *pancallang* which lay in wait for 'smugglers'; it was the diplomatic and military centre for the delicate negotiations necessary to protect Company interests in the polycentric world of East Indonesia. The town was very much part of all that world, and remained sensitive to all economic and political shifts, even if each community may have registered them slightly differently. For although Castle Rotterdam dominated the Makassar landscape, and other settlements clustered around the bastions, it would be a serious misperception simply to see eighteenth-century Makassar as a Dutch colonial town.

The VOC establishment provided security and a major source of income for the town dwellers: traders, merchants, artisans, sailors, fishermen, gardeners, market pedlars, brothel and toddy-shop keepers. This other Makassar was a multi-ethnic settlement with prosperous mestizo, Chinese and Malay elites doing business and politics with each other, with Buginese and Makassarese merchants, and with VOC employees (in their private capacities). To varying degrees the different groups were self-regulating, to some extent in symbiosis with the VOC, but in many respects going their own way. This patchwork of communities—separate yet in constant interaction—constituted the fabric of Makassar. Before we can understand this social reality, however, it is necessary to discuss VOC administrative policy; as will be seen, there was a considerable gap between theory and practice.

The company town

By the end of the seventeenth century it was clear that the Dutch, unlike the Portuguese, had decided that their settlements in the east should be based on ethnic separation rather than assimilation. But attempts at colonisation by European couples failed—settlers were squeezed between the monopolistic Company and Asian traders and farmers, so no feasible basis for an autonomous white community existed. Such small groups could not survive in isolation, and despite official barriers mixing occurred. In the absence of European women, men sought their wives and concubines among the mestizas, local women and slaves. As Boxer comments: 'Batavia, and in varying degrees the other Dutch settlements in Asia, thus presented the curious spectacle of a Dutch calvinist male society wedded uneasily with a large Indo-Portuguese female society.'[10]

While the general pattern of life in Makassar was similar to that of the VOC capital (and most of her institutions and laws were Batavia-derived), nonetheless there were also important differences. Makassar was simply an outpost in the Company's empire, albeit an important one. It had less than a quarter as many VOC employees as Batavia,[11] so it was harder to maintain clear boundaries and Dutch values. Accommodation to local ways led to ambiguities and deviations. Indeed, trying to write an account of the town is accompanied by a sense that reality is elusive: each attempt to focus upon the structure blurs the picture; each effort to pin down categories makes them shift.[12] Speelman's ideas concerning the proper form and development of Dutch Makassar are outlined in his invaluable Memorandum, written in 1669-1670. He decreed that the new town should consist of a well-fortified castle; *kampung* or 'native villages' with 'each nation under its own headman'; and 'a merchant town with the houses of foreigners and strangers'.[13] These three elements—castle, town and kampung—had been typical also of Somba Opu and many archipelago ports, and were to dominate the morphology of Makassar for almost 200 years. In the early eighteenth century Francois Valentijn described the merchant settlement as follows: 'The city is just a small market town (*vlek*) that is also called the Negory Vlaardingen, with only one large unpaved street, I think the Chinese street, and two or three smaller ones where the Dutch burghers, some Chinese under their captain, and some Makassarese and other natives live, and which can be closed and guarded by the Chinese and Burgher watch.'[14]

This walled settlement of Vlaardingen lay just north of the castle and south of the Kampung Melayu or Malay quarter; the beach lay to the west, while east were open fields and, along the High Path, the Company Garden. Close to the southern wall of the castle a further settlement grew in the early years of the eighteenth century, the new village or Kampung Baru, where the number of company subjects—natives, Christian Mardijkers (free Asians, often of slave origin) and burghers—almost equalled that of Vlaardingen. While the Company officials and garrison lived within the castle, some had houses in the burgher settlements, where they stayed with their family, slaves and retainers. Thus the basic pattern of fortified politico-military indigenous housing which typified so many early Asian cities repeated itself in Dutch Makassar. Each of these areas was clearly defined: the castle had its great stone walls, redoubts and gates, while Vlaardingen was surrounded by a more modest stockade. In both Vlaardingen and the *kampung* most people lived in fenced compounds containing several houses. In 1679 the VOC complained that a fire in Vlaardingen had burnt out some eighty houses, including the compound of Ince Buang and his family. This was a cluster of four large houses and assorted shacks where his followers, slaves and debtbondsmen lived—'all sorts of riffraff' (*een hoopen gespuys van volck*). A later source suggests about eight houses per compound and an average of eight people per house for the Malay quarter. In general, the Dutch preferred to segregate the various ethnic groups: hence, after the fire the 'Moor' (Indian Muslim) Ince Buang was moved from Vlaardingen 'to the Moorish quarter on the beach by the Bugis section', where his commercial coconut oil preparation promptly generated a new fire burning down much

Kampung Melayu, Makassar, eastern Indonesia, c. 1840. It is typical of the separate settlements which formed Indonesian port cities in the eighteenth and nineteenth centuries.
P. van de Velde, *Gezigte uit Neêrlands Indie*, Amsterdam, Buffa 1845, Koninklijk Instituut voor Taal-, Land- en Volkenkunde, Leiden.

of the Moorish, Bugis and adjoining Warorese quarters.[15]

The VOC had a most elaborate system of administrative specialisation and control, with rooms full of clerks laboriously copying tables of financial statistics, reports, resolutions and legal judgments. But the logistics of travel, between Batavia and Makassar, between Java and the Netherlands (where an exchange of letters took a minimum of eighteen months), combined with Makassar's small European population and proximity to powerful Indonesian neighbours, conspired to weaken metropolitan control and encourage accommodation to local mores. Moreover, the Company had no desire to meddle in the internal affairs of its Asian subjects.

The emphasis on ethnic segregation was based on both an eighteenth-century sense of natural order, and also on calculations of security. Fire, robbery and the possibility of armed attack preoccupied the Company; the high proportion of bamboo and thatched houses made arson both simple and dangerous, and the ensuing confusion provided ample opportunity for theft or violence. The best defence was held to be uncluttered and ethnically homogeneous settlements, with the most 'loyal' communities closest to the castle. Squatters' houses, unlicensed sheds or undergrowth could feed flames and shelter dangerous men, so regular decrees were issued to enforce open spaces. Indonesians were forbidden to stay in European settlements, where nightly patrols kept the curfew and checked credentials. Bugis and Makassarese were regarded as particularly violent and also as more susceptible to political subversion. The Malay *kampung*, just north of Vlaardingen, functioned as a buffer between the merchant town and the volatile Bugis quarter where smuggling, slave-dealing and intrigue were held to be common. Categorisation according to 'race' was fundamental to the Company administration of non-Europeans. Each ethnic group had its own headman, usually a wealthy merchant. The Chinese and Malay chiefs were called after military ranks (captain, lieutenant), while others bore local titles, such as *Galearang*. These leaders were responsible for good order within their own community, and had also to ensure that their followers met any obligations towards the VOC. The Dutch were outraged, for example, when Ince Mulut, or Maulud, captain of the Malays (1724-1728), refused to intervene to protect some Netherlanders under attack in a Bugis-Makassarese riot in 1726: this was seen as a serious dereliction of duty.[16]

If the Buginese and Makassarese were held to be the most dangerous inhabitants of the town, it went without saying that pure Europeans (especially Company men) were the most trustworthy, followed by mestizos, then Asian Christians (who might be Indian, Chinese or Indonesian—particularly Ambonese—in origin), Malays and Chinese. The explicit policy of the VOC was to ensure the domination of Company interests at all times; this meant that responsible posts should be held by those least likely to put personal or communal advantage before that of the VOC. So even the role of established burgher families was restricted to institutions such as the orphanage or the church council. For the VOC, outposts like Makassar existed to defend Company

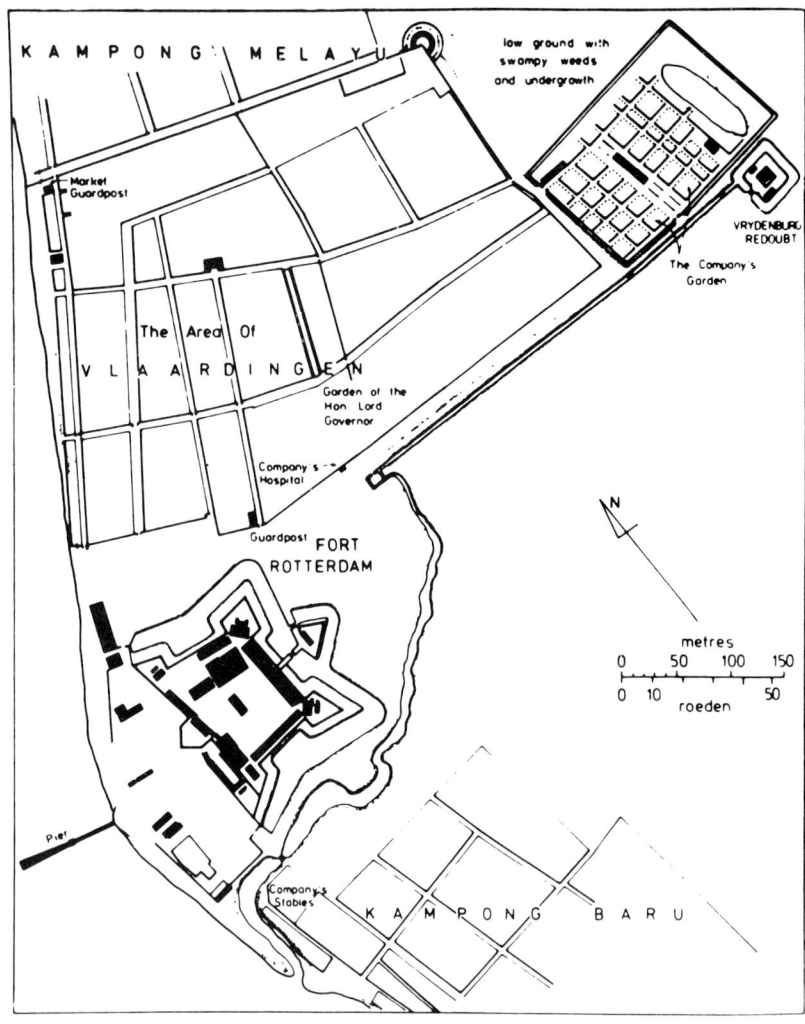

Map 8 Makassar: Fort Rotterdam and environs, seventeenth century

commerce, preferably without costing too much. Indeed, both the Gentlemen Seventeen in the Netherlands and the High Government in Batavia cherished the constantly expressed (and regularly disappointed) hope that the government in Makassar would be able to cover expenses with profits generated by the sale of VOC-imported goods, particularly textiles. Piecegoods from India and elsewhere were sold through the Company store and in auctions, to traders seeking stock for their journeys. But despite all exhortations from the High Government, which suspected Makassar's officials of mismanagement and corruption, Company imports continued to be undersold by Asian merchants and undermined by the private trade of its own officials. So although Makassar helped Batavia's economy by providing cheap consignments of slaves for the VOC labour force, on the whole it was a financial liability.

Besides Company commerce, Makassar also had its own local sources of revenue. Like most Asian and VOC settlements, a system of farms and monopolies (*pachten*) existed, in which the government surrendered its rights over selected economic activities in exchange for payment. In the late 1600s the only documented farm was the alcohol monopoly, for which burghers paid the considerable sum of over 1000 rds (*rijksdaalders*, 'rixdollars') per year. In some subsequent years the *pacht* climbed as high as 4000 rds, with prices depending less on the thirst of the garrison than on such imponderables as the interruption of the supply of palmwine by wars in the interior, on the competition from tea and coffee shops or, more predictably, on officials' private financial arrangements with the proprietors of illegal toddy shops or bidders for the monopoly. Most alcohol farmers were retired soldiers who, when they were in military service, had drawn an annual pay of around 24 rds, so the purchase of a monopoly was a major, though popular, investment.

The mid-eighteenth century saw a considerable shift from direct Company exploitation of taxes to farms. From 1745 the right to collect customs duties (on imports and exports) was sold to the highest bidder, producing a steadily increasing yearly revenue which exceeded 20 000 rds by the end of the century. Gambling joined drink as the next most important source of funds, at between two and three thousand rds per annum in the 1750s, while the market tax, Chinese head money and the slaughter tax (essentially on pork) were less significant.

Bad trading years were immediately felt by the monopoly farmers, and not only in customs revenue. Trade generated prosperity, and drew people to harbour and markets. More specifically, any major decline in the Chinese population lowered the value of the gambling and headmoney monopolies. This underlines the importance of Makassar's harbour and garrison functions, while the frequent suspicious queries from Batavia and Holland about the conduct of auctions, and the recurring complaints about unlicensed drinking and gambling dens, suggest that the administration of local finance was as susceptible to fraud and evasion as were the VOC trade regulations.

Apart from the *pachten* the government in Makassar also levied taxes on property, such as houses and ships, and on the sale of various goods. Payments on property generated more than 400 rds a year for Vlaardingen, where the total of real estate exceeded 80 000 rds in 1759; individual houses ranged from bamboo shacks to stone houses worth several thousand rds. The financial importance of these taxes, however, was slight compared to the harbour or alcohol monopolies.[17] As far as the Company was concerned, any involvement in town affairs was only justified in so far as it maintained a suitable environment for trade and garrison. In general the Gentlemen Seventeen and Batavia had no interest whatsoever in promoting local prosperity. On the contrary, they were always worried that a flourishing settled community would develop its own activities at the expense of the VOC. The high officials of the Company concentrated their attention on security and commerce, keeping the flow of goods moving and the ledgers up to date.

Specialists such as the *syahbandar* (harbourmaster), *fiskaal* (prosecutor) and *predikant* (Calvinist preacher) were important men for both the VOC and the town. They were officially responsible for the constant and usually fruitless attempts to combat the endemic illegal trade, evasion of monopolies, and debauchery so characteristic of the town. The harbourmaster, for example, maintained patrols and watchhouses on the beach to discourage smuggling, supervised the weigh-house, and inspected ships for contraband goods; he also maintained a register of incoming and outgoing vessels.[18] The *fiskaal* acted as head of the police and public prosecutor, catching suspected criminals, organising interrogation and presenting cases before the Council of Justice. Routine Company administrative efforts within the town focused on the Christian community, where the church with its charitable institutions and intermittent attempts at education was the bearer of European civilisation. Other services were provided by the militia (*schutterij*) and the town administration, which consisted of honorary block supervisors and chief firemen (*wijkmeester, brandspuitmeester*) and a lamplighter.

The burgher elite was active in the *schutterij* and also in charitable bodies, such as the *diakonij*, which supervised poor relief and the *weeshuis*, or orphanage. The directors of the orphanage not only supervised the housing and education of Makassar's relatively numerous Christian orphans, but also invested their inheritances, so they could look forward to a dowry or business capital on reaching their majority. The orphanage funds were used as a de facto bank, providing financial resources for burgher, Chinese and Makassarese traders alike as well as, on occasion, unsecured and lost loans for directors and their friends. The Makassar government intervened several times when scandal reached intolerable levels. But on the whole—even where the Christian community was concerned—the actual mechanics of intracommunal control were of little interest to the VOC, except when civil or criminal cases required legal action: the jurisdiction of the Council of Justice extended over Asians and Europeans alike.

Makassar society

When considering Makassar's inhabitants, it is necessary to follow Company usage, and make a rough distinction between the groups most closely identified with the VOC, and the more alien others. For most of the eighteenth century people were divided into several general categories. The first two divisions were that of 'Company servants, burghers and families' (which would include slaves) on the one hand, and the heterogeneous category of 'Makassarese, Buginese, Chinese, Ambonese, Bandanese, Moors, Peranakans and their slaves' on the other. This division paralleled that between Christians and heathens, since slaves—whatever their origins or beliefs—were simply subsumed in the census category of their owner. These two groups lived in the complex of settlements grouped around the castle, including Vlaardingen, Kampung Baru and the *kampung*. Beyond this cluster were areas under formal Dutch suzerainty, but in practice their fishermen and farmers were ruled by local chiefs or Karaeng; these were the territories of Galesong, Bulukumba, Bantaeng (Bonthain), Polombangkeng, Maros and the island Saleyar.

Around 1740 the combined population of castle, Vlaardingen and town *kampung* averaged around 5000. This figure increased to some 6000 in the 1760s and 1770s. Excluding the *kampung*, the population of the nucleus of Dutch Makassar (castle and Vlaardingen), remained relatively steady and increased slowly, from just over 2000 in the 1730s to almost 3000 by the 1780s. These figures indicate a stable and defined core population, but the reality was quite complex, as two very different sorts of community were involved.[19]

On the one hand there was the burgher population, derived originally from retired VOC employees (mostly soldiers or sailors), and their Asian wives and concubines. They formed a settled social group, earning a living in trade and commerce, with ties to both Dutch and Asian communities. In the first Makassar 'soulcount' for 1679 there were only two 'minties' (mestizo) men as opposed to forty male 'Nederlanders', but some ten years later the burgher community was already about 80 percent mestizo, a proportion which recurred and was probably fairly constant throughout the 1700s. During the late seventeenth and eighteenth centuries the mixed bag of labels from the early period were reorganised into a more defined hierarchy. The distinction between Dutch and mestizo was soon dropped, in favour of a more formal division between 'burghers' and employees of the VOC. At the same time, however, there was an inevitable tendency in the society to acculturation, to a less sharply graduated ethnic and cultural spectrum, where relative closeness to *kampung* or castle was influenced by social status.[20]

The strength of the Company establishment at Makassar waxed and waned depending on her economic and military fortunes. The small elite of fifteen to twenty 'qualified' officials—the governor, chief merchants, undermerchants and assistants—decided policy in Council and performed their specific administrative tasks individually. Below them was a middle-ranking group of similar size, skilled men such as the translators and harbourmaster, the teachers

The cosmopolitan character of Indonesian port cities: A Javanese trader of Batavia (Jakarta), Indonesia, c. 1680. In most port cities of Malaysia and Indonesia the different settlements included Javanese trade communities. This Javanese trader demonstrates a cultural style quite separate from the courtly world of the land-based kingdoms of Central Java.
From Hendrik Nieuhof Joan Nieuhofs Gedenkwaerdighe Zee-en Lant-reize door de voornaemste Landschappen van West en Oostindien *Amsterdam, 1682.*
Courtesy of Mitchell Library, State Library of New South Wales.

and *predikant*, hospital staff and artisans. The rest of the Company personnel, from five to eight hundred men, were soldiers and sailors, generally believed to represent the dregs of Europe.

The garrison and officials usually numbered eight to nine hundred men, but increased to more than 1500 when the political situation on the peninsula was threatening. Such temporary expeditionary forces were not included in the census, but more lasting reinforcements were. Crises in the security situation were reflected also in fluctuations in the non-European and burgher population groups, both within the central *kampung* complex around the castle and in more outlying areas under Company control.

During the wars with Wajo' (1739-1740) and the troubles in Gowa (1776-c.1790) the non-Christian population of Makassar, including the urban *kampung*, reached peaks of well over 4000 while for most of the eighteenth century there was a very variable 'heathen' (in reality, of course, predominantly Muslim) population count of between two and three thousand. During these same insecure periods the number of inhabitants in the outlying districts shrank dramatically (the total was less than 30 000 in 1780, as compared to well over 50 000 in 1760 and 1790). These figures emphasise that while the castle itself could provide relative safety for the settlements huddled around it, the Pax Neerlandica was far from guaranteed for more distant villages.

Such numbers can give us a general picture of the scale of settlement and population movements, but they tell us nothing of the town's social texture. Scattered references indicate that Makassar had a high mortality, skewed sex-ratios, widespread slave-holding and a kaleidoscope of ethnic categories. These factors combined to create a society which kept bursting out of its VOC framework, revealing the tensions, frustrations and dynamism born not of a static juxtaposition of Company garrison and Indonesian port, but from the interaction of the two.

In this context the walls, stockades and bamboo fences marking the boundaries between castle, *kampung* and compounds faded; only in the official middle-range vision did such limits seemed fixed and clear. A close look at the social reality of Makassar and, in particular, its patterns of residence indeed shows that the theory of ethnic segregation, as expressed in Speelman's precepts, was far from being realised. The castle, as a military base, was tightly controlled. The day-to-day problem there was to keep its inhabitants inside, rather than trying to keep others out—the soldiers tended to abandon their posts for nights of drinking, whoring and gambling, while higher officials sought the comfort of their houses and society in the settlements. Outside the castle walls, however, boundaries become more permeable, and inhabitants more variegated.

While Vlaardingen was essentially a Chinese and European settlement, the presence of Indonesians (particularly at night) gnawed at the government's sense of security. Despite regulations and placards, it was easy to arrange nocturnal visits, as the stockade was pierced by the back doors of houses close to the walls, and many residents had personal or business ties with Indonesians.

Moreover, by no means all burghers lived in Vlaardingen. Many mestizos—particularly the poorer members of the community—lived in the *kampung* among Asian neighbours. If we take 1733 as an example, and look at the annual taxation list on urban property, we can see who owned houses where, and what they were worth. The elite lived in the Tuinstraat, where just over half the houses were stone (twenty-one, as opposed to twenty of bamboo). Here was concentrated the property of two wealthy burghers, each of whom owned seven houses on the street, and paid 35 rds each in tax. But not everyone there was rich; two single women, probably representatives of the widows who were such a striking element in Makassar's society, lived in humble bamboo houses, and paid only a fraction of a rd each. The only obvious non-European on the Tuinstraat would seem to be Maria van Bima, whose name suggests she was an ex-slave from the island of Bima, who converted to Christianity as the common-law wife of some burgher. A second European street was the Middelstraat, but here we enter a lower economic bracket. Most houses are bamboo, and six are owned by women, four of whom are described as widows.

The busiest road in Dutch Makassar was the Chinese Street. Running close to the beach, it accommodated fifty households. Twenty-six houseowners bore Chinese names (twenty-three being Ko), of which almost a quarter indicated that their owners were heavily acculturated local Chinese, in many cases Muslim (*peranakan*). The rest of the inhabitants were European (including six female heads of households), except for one possible Makassarese.

Some concentrations of Europeans were also to be found outside Vlaardingen's stockade, such as the clusters of predominantly stone houses by the Dutch market (between Vlaardingen and the castle) and along the Hoge Pad leading to the Company Garden. But around the fringes of Vlaardingen and the castle, particularly on the southern side, were much poorer areas. Along the Koestraat, Breestraat and Langestraat at Kampung Baru were collections of bamboo housing inhabited by Asian Christians and ex-slaves, whose names suggest their origins; Maria van Bengal, Rachel van de Westkust, Badjo van Dompo and Maart (March) all probably began their Makassar lives involuntarily, while the recurrence of the Ambonese name Lehitu underlines the Christian element.

Nonetheless, these citizens of Makassar were still within the reach of the Company administration. More marginal were the *kampung* agglomerations under their own headmen, while the houses round the Bugis Market (about a half hour's walk north of the castle) and the warrens of squatters' sheds along the beach were virtually impervious to official European penetration.[21]

While the lists of houseowners indicate a clear clustering of residence by ethnicity and status, household composition was much more pluriform than might be expected. Since VOC employees often preferred to live outside the castle, many burghers rented houses or took in boarders, so while we know from the tax list that Abraham Fransz and Michiel de Vreede each owned seven houses in the Tuinstraat, we can only guess who lived in them. Details of domestic organisation are, however, both more important and more elusive.

In practice, the norm in Makassar was not that of the Calvinist nuclear family. Even in many parts of contemporary Europe extended households were common, and in Makassar this was further elaborated, both by the custom of living in compounds, with kin and followers, and by the pervasive influence of slavery. Poorer burghers often lived in bamboo dwellings on stilts, while the layout of many European-style houses showed specific Asian characteristics. The yard or compound was dominated by the main house, with a 'front gallery', followed by the main room and a 'back gallery', with kitchen, storerooms and slave quarters in the yard. Here also small industries were to be found, the workshops of artisans, or activities such as the preparation of foodstuffs and other goods, destined to be sold along the streets or through rented stalls in the Dutch Market.

Domestic inventories made in cases of intestate deaths or inheritance disputes can give us some insight into the household possessions of Makassar citizens. In 1767, for example, the Captain of Chinese and two colleagues inventoried the assets of one Niopanlong. This wealthy Chinese merchant's most valuable possessions were two houses on the Chinese Street, one stone (value 1500 rds) and one bamboo (240 rds) and three ships: two *perahu paduwakang* (one large, 150 rds, one small, 100 rds), and a *perahu pamayang* (40 rds). Luxuries (gold, silver and silks) were worth almost 1000 rds, while furnishings, which were Chinese in style, weapons and household goods came to about 1800 rds. Niopanlong's credit balance was increased by the value of trade goods in stock (2000 rds) and moneys owed him (c.1500), so his total assets came to an impressive 8800 rds. This was reduced, however, by his own debts to the burgher Voll and three Chinese, so that on balance he was worth 4122 rds. Niopanlong had been farmer of the market in 1764 and 1765, and had even been able to hold the import and export dues monopoly for 1765, in which he invested 12 000 rds, so it is fair to assume he was a relatively rich man. And indeed, the archives of court and orphanage show few estates as large as his.[22]

One notable absence in the list of Niopanlong's possessions is slaves; whether this is an oversight or not is hard to tell, but slaves, both as domestic assets and as trade goods, are a striking feature of virtually all mestizo and European inventories. We can gain an impression of a European household by looking through the detailed inventory from 1768 of Jan Adolph Kook, a blacksmith's mate in Company service. It is clear, despite the lack of valuations in the inventory, that he was a surprisingly wealthy man. Kook owned two stone houses (one in the Chinese Street), and a bamboo house in the Nieuwe Negory where his mother-in-law lived. He also owned five female slaves, one of whom had her oldest child living with her, and another had a son; one was from Makassar, two from Manggarai, and two were Bugis, as were his three male slaves, one of whom had a wife (also a slave) and three children. These nine adults were 'house slaves'; in addition Kook had a stock of 'trade slaves' at the time of his death: thirteen males and ten females, mostly from South Sulawesi and Nusa Tenggara. It seems probable that his wealth came more from his slave dealing than his salary, some twenty rds per month.

An impression of Kook's lifestyle can be gained from the very detailed description of each room of his house. The 'front gallery' had not only a pipe rack, but also a rack for *payung* (umbrellas), and an impressive seventeen chairs. But the real signs of ostentation emerge in the main house, where the reception room was furnished with hanging lights, racks of weapons, glass-fronted cupboards, tables and a couple of dozen chairs, and decorated with seven mirrors and thirty assorted paintings.

Our last eighteenth-century visit is to a Makassarese, Karaeng Tutolo, who lived in a bamboo house on stilts in the compound belonging to Karaeng Tujang in *kampung* Bulekang. (Although the title Karaeng is a high one, its frequent use in eighteenth-century documents suggests that it referred to a well-born Makassarese and not necessarily ruling nobility.) Karaeng Tulolo kept three women slaves in his house, two Balinese and one Makassarese, and two men. Another male slave, from Ende, was away in his *perahu* on a trading voyage to Bali. The furnishings of the house were relatively simple; there were four chairs—a sign of European influence—and a number of chests containing Makassarese clothes and weapons, mats and cushions, plates and Chinese porcelain and some simple silver jewellery.[23]

These three households give us an impression of relative prosperity and comfort; they are no doubt atypical, in that their importance required a proper inventory and VOC intervention. Each fits the stereotype of communal economic activity: the wealthy Chinese, the European slave dealer, and the relatively small-scale Indonesian trader. Although such detail is only illustrative, it does suggest the importance of trade, the significance of slavery, and differences in taste. As such, it gives us some sense of the daily lives of our subjects. Other documents can provide even less tangible, but fascinating, insights into contemporary behaviour and morality.

Both Portuguese predecessors and Asian neighbours in Celebes set examples of complex and far from puritan family life. The influence of slavery was pervasive, concubinage common, and the prolonged absences of men on trading voyages added to the flexibility of domestic arrangements. The effects can be glimpsed in official documents: a Company man's wife is caught violating curfew for a rendezvous with a Balinese soldier, while drunken soldiers returning after hours from a hunting expedition so gratuitously insult the *fiskaal* that he opens his blind eye and they all end up receiving heavy sentences for what was probably an everyday affair. Accounts of brawls in toddy shops, rumours of adultery, complaints about loose women and murders recur regularly in the files.

Drinking and to a lesser extent opium seem to have been the main recreations of Makassar's citizens and soldiers. More apparently modern indulgences were also noted: in October 1715 it was reported that 'various of our inhabitants, soldiers as well as artisans, have turned to the brewing of brown beer mixed with datura or marsh-marigolds, wild hemp and other sorts of maddening or crazy-making herbs'.[24] Attempts to enforce Calvinist morality upon such a seafaring and garrison community were doomed to failure. As early as June

1687 the governor and Council of Makassar sent a request to Batavia to be instructed on how to arrange civil and criminal affairs; adultery was common, they sighed, because 'many Netherlanders are married to sluttish native women, who walk out and leave them at the drop of a hat, and go into the bush and are never seen again'. A similar outrage was expressed ninety years later, when the government complained about the 'scandalous roaming around among the natives, by both married and unmarried Christian women'. Concubinage with slaves was regarded as normal, and the registration of children born of such unions was necessary to ensure their Christian status. Unacknowledged children followed their mother's status. Since, however, it was customary to free the mother of your children, most such children born of slave mothers would at least have been free. Both government and burgher elite were concerned about the souls of half-European children, of unknown fathers, who were doomed to sink into the *kampung* and follow the 'perfidious' teaching of Mohammed.[25]

An example of how a well-known mestizo family could develop is provided by the de Siso clan, descended from Daniel Dusisiaux from Vlissingen who arrived in 1728. He married a native woman, called Debora of Makassar, and his mestizo son Jan was a prosperous slave trader and captain of the burghers. Jan married three times, and had seven legal offspring; he also acknowledged two illegitimate children, one of them borne by the slave Clara of Sumbawa. One son, Alexander (b. 1766), who was also a leading citizen and slave trader, probably had five children, at least two of whom were by Asian mothers (Baba and Tjina).

Such a pattern is fairly typical; we see it again in histories like that of the Krookwits family. Jan Hendrik Krookwits arrived from Weteringen as a soldier in Batavia in 1722, and reached Makassar in 1740. His youngest and seventh son, Jan Hendrik, shipowner and trader, had several children by various mothers, such as the free native woman Mina of Makassar, the native Randa from Mandar and the slave Satima. One son, inevitably Jan Hendrik, who was born of the native woman Bintang of Mandar, chose for matrimony in 1808 (perhaps a sign of changing times?) and married Henriette Geertruida Claassen, daughter of one Hermanus and the free native woman Rananga of Makassar.[26] Such family histories make a mockery of the official emphasis on ethnic segregation and Calvinist morality.

The two officials most closely involved with regulating the mores of Makassar were the *predikant* and the *fiskaal*. Their job was not easy, and in many cases they probably adjusted to their environment. In fact, there were various periods when Makassar managed without any *predikant* at all, and some incumbents were eccentric to the point of insanity, or preoccupied with trade, particularly in slaves. The *fiskaal* could call upon the power of the eighteenth-century law, and criminals were regularly hung up with weights on their feet, broken on the wheel, flogged, branded and exposed to the birds of prey—behaviour which the Buginese and Makassarese found most barbarous. In a couple of instances the archives suggest that at times neither the public nor the governor and

Council appreciated attempts to impose a more rigorous morality.[27] The Company establishment in Makassar were less preoccupied with virtue than with trade. Their limited concern reflects not only an acceptance of a tolerant modus vivendi, but also the constraints upon Company administration which were imposed by both resources and expectations. Even in the two areas most closely associated with central VOC interests—security and trade—compromise was necessary. So Chinese might be allowed to join the watch, local princes consulted on security, headmen left to their own devices, and the ruler of Bone allowed to appoint a representative who assisted the *pachter* in port administration.[28]

But accommodation could only go so far. Company interests and Christian status had to be maintained, and although in practice it was quite possible to advance private trade at the expense of the VOC, and to recognise the useful qualities of non-Europeans, there were limits. The formal organisation of the town was predicated upon the economic dominance of the Company, while ethnic niches provided the social framework. But these principles could not be maintained. The problem was that neither the VOC nor the Christian community could compete effectively with Asian traders. There was an inherent and growing contradiction between the Company policy of controlling commerce and protecting Christian status, and the dynamics of Makassar itself, generated by local traders (including those from Wajo'), Chinese and Malays. These tensions sometimes surfaced in strained relations between burghers and the Company, and between Chinese and Malays.

The burgher population of Makassar was too few and too poor to support the proper urban institutions. In 1694 their *swacke getal* (small number) caused the government to introduce a paid rather than a citizen's night watch. In 1743 the government ascribed the low profits of the farm auctions to the absence of bidders because they were held in August when 'all burghers and freemen ... are sailing to Batavia or elsewhere'. On 12 May 1767 a resolution was passed to limit the mobility of burghers who were thought to be using trading trips as a way of avoiding communal responsibilities. And in 1780 it was acknowledged that the burdens of the watch and tax were too heavy for the citizens, and were contributing to their economic woes during what was in general a difficult time.[29]

A brawl in a toddy shop in May 1772 led to a confrontation between burghers and the government. A 'free native', Kamanjang, was returning from the Bugis Market with some trade cloth he had bought, and stopped to enjoy a jug of palmwine with his friends Balatong and Titus. Two burghers, much the worse for wear, were arguing in the drinking shop, and one enlisted Kamanjang's support. He was promptly accused of interference by the second man, Samuel Jansz, but refused to back down. Kamanjang then left the shop, his anxious friends remonstrating with him for talking back to 'such a respectable man'. Jansz thereupon emerged from the shop and without a word proceeded to beat Kamanjang severely.

Such incidents were common enough in Makassar, but this developed into something of a *cause célèbre*, either because tensions in the community were high, or because the *fiskaal* was unusually officious. He called Samuel Jansz up for punishment in the presence of the watch. The sergeant, Leendert Geesdorp, refused to assist in the punishment; he appealed to the crowd, saying that the burghers had had enough blood drained from them, and had no need to lose more to the cane just because of a native.

Such 'mutiny and rebellion' attracted the attention not only of the government in Makassar, but also Batavia, which suspected more was afoot and ordered an enquiry into burgher grievances. Makassar was unable to oblige as Geesdorp died a few days after Batavia's letter arrived. Whether or not the affair was simply a flash in the pan, or had deeper causes, is impossible to say, but burgher discontent was made explicit in April 1782. A group of prominent citizens (including Anthony Geesdorp) wrote a formal petition to the governor concerning unfair competition from VOC officials in the slave trade, which was they said 'the only way in which we can legitimately make a living'. They requested that the clandestine participation by Company men in this commerce be stopped. The governor, forwarding the petition to Batavia, stated in his defence, 'it is untrue and totally unknown to us that Company officials are attempting to monopolise the slave trade'.[30]

Throughout the eighteenth century, but particularly in the latter half, the burghers appeared as a struggling community. On the other hand, Malays, Chinese and local traders seemed to flourish, despite VOC attempts to dominate commerce. Company records regularly lamented the decline of Makassar's economy, but the number of local vessels using the port remains fairly constant (around 500 arrivals or departures per year), and Asian merchants willingly paid more each year for the monopoly on customs duties. The Company jealously strove to discourage local trade and shipping. Each year a list of vessels had to be sent to Batavia, and any increase in seagoing boats had to be explained away. By the end of the 1700s only three or four boats were listed. But the harbour master's register shows that whether or not ships were officially registered in Makassar, many were using the port. Unfortunately for both Company and burghers, it was Indonesians, Malays and Chinese (and perhaps VOC officials, in a private capacity) who seemed most active.[31]

From its beginnings in 1745 the monopoly on the collection of customs duties had been the most important farm, both in terms of its impact on local trade, and as a source of revenue. Conflicts between traders and the farmer could become intense, as happened in 1755 when a group of Batavia and Makassar Chinese felt that their associate, the captain of the junk, had been unfairly taxed. Competition between Chinese and Malays for the position of *pachter* could increase tension, and so in October 1766 it was decided that the customs monopoly was only to be given to Chinese, with the argument that others, particularly Malays, caused too much trouble and too many rows.

The Chinese victory proved shortlived. They may have been able to keep the Malays at bay until 1770, but from then until 1790 a Malay, Ince Sadulla, held the monopoly, except for a three-year stretch early on (1773-1775) when it reverted to a Chinese. Since virtually all other farms were Chinese-held, it was only to be expected that the loss of the most lucrative one should be the cause of some dissatisfaction. In 1781 a group of twenty Chinese merchants, of Makassar and Batavia, wrote to the governor accusing Ince Sadulla of violating the *pacht* conditions. Batavia, which was in any case unhappy that Makassar kept renewing Ince Sadulla's monopoly without public auction, asked for an explanation. The Makassar government defended Ince Sadulla on the grounds that 'he has held the *pacht* for years, and is used to getting along with the native kings and other powerful men, in particular with those of Bone, and should a Chinese or some other take over then we could expect daily squabbling'. Batavia must have been convinced, as Ince Sadulla kept the monopoly till the end of 1789, when it passed to a Chinese.[32]

Despite the vigorous and sometimes bitter competition between Malays and Chinese for positions of commercial power, the boundary between the two communities was blurred at the edges by the presence of the Muslim Chinese *peranakan* community. This very closeness was a cause of dissension. Thus, in November 1750, the captains of the Chinese Lijauko and Quepodang sent a formal letter of complaint to the governor concerning Malay conduct. They described how at the time of the conquest by Speelman the first captain of the Chinese, Ongwatko, was given authority over all Chinese, *parnakangs* and Malays. Because of old age his son (uncle of Lijauko) eventually took over as deputy, and in that period the Malays received the right to their own head, although without the status of captain. However, the governor then granted the request of the wife of Aru Palakka that Ince Tjoeka be made Kapitan Melayu; Ongwatko responded by requesting only that the new chief of the Malays have nothing to do with the *peranakan* Chinese, be they Muslim or not. But, wrote the suppliants, the present captain of the Malays was trying to assert his authority over the *peranakan*, thus violating both established custom and Company policy.

This complaint was promptly countered by an equally outraged missive from the Kapitan Melayu, complaining that Malay women marrying *peranakan* Chinese, or *peranakan* (sic) Malays marrying *peranakan* Chinese were treated by the Kapitan China as if they were 'his own people'. The Malay captain also called upon history to justify his claim, and added that he was convinced men were attaching themselves to the Chinese to avoid those Company services which fell heavily upon the Malays. More was involved here than mere status. Each captain had to call upon his people for both Company and personal services; fewer people meant less manpower to provide labour and funds for communal activities, such as maintenance of temples or mosques, and also fewer subjects to pay the petty fees and taxes which helped support the Kapitans. The Makassar government took the matter seriously, and finally decided the specific problem of the mixed marriages by applying the principle that wives should follow the nationality of their husband; this involved thirteen *peranakan* Malay women married to *peranakan* Chinese

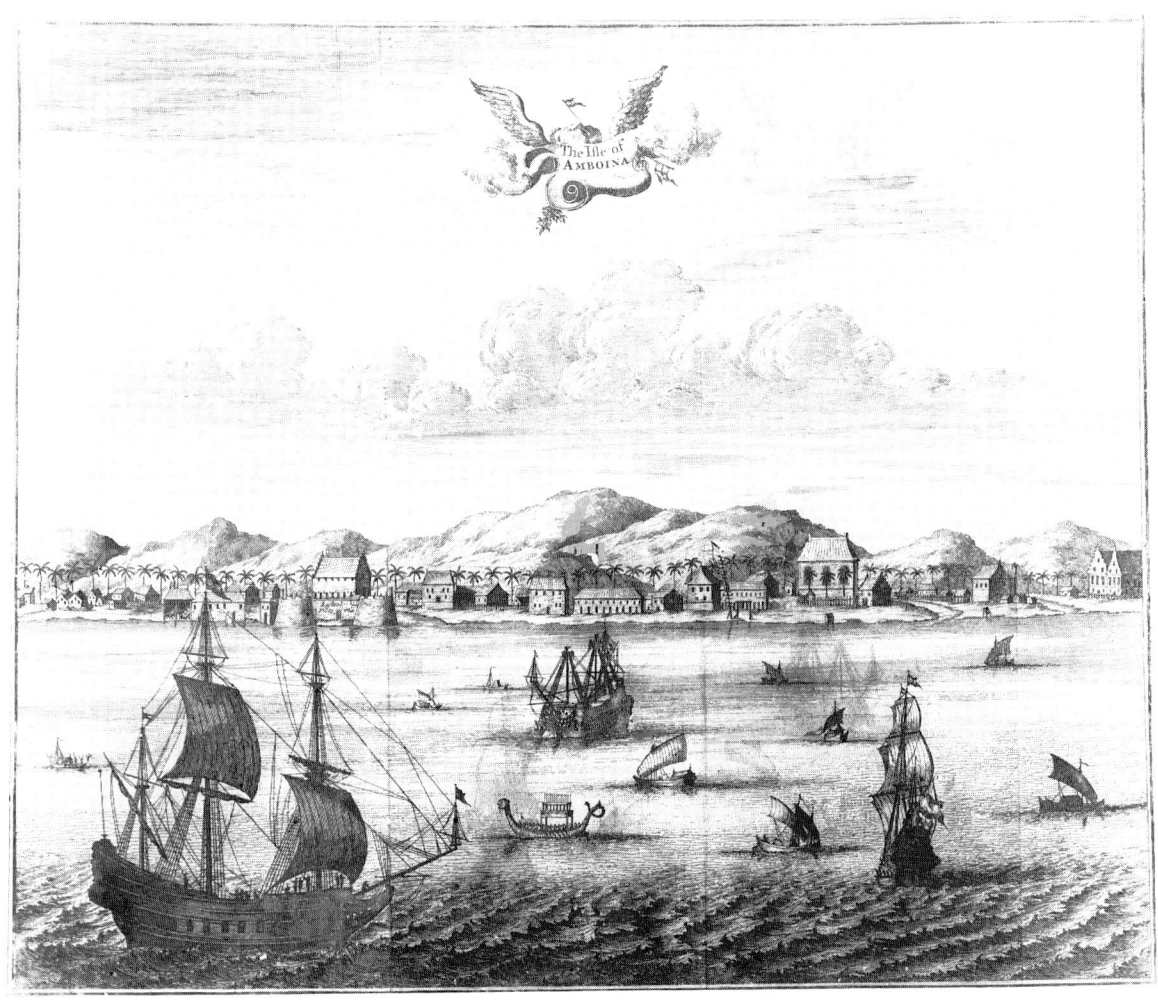

Amboina (Ambon), the mestizo port town of eastern Indonesia. This view of Ambon emphasises the Dutch and mestizo character of the architecture of this trade outpost.
From Hendrik Nieuhof *Joan Nieuhofs Gedenkwaerdighe Zee-en Lant-reize door de voornaemste Landschappen van West en Oostindien* Amsterdam, 1682.
Courtesy of Mitchell Library, State Library of New South Wales.

men, and six Malay men. Placed in a broader perspective, the dispute suggests not only intercommunal competition, but also a sharpening of ethnic boundaries.[33]

Conclusion

Centres and boundaries are essential to any definition of place, but each depends on the perspective adopted. What is of crucial importance to one individual or group can be peripheral to another. There was a VOC Makassar with its own institutions, regulations, ethics, politics, interests and domestic arrangements, just as there was also an identifiable Chinese or Malay or Bugis Makassar. The fences around the compound of an exiled prince or Malay merchant defined the nucleus of family and followers, just as Vlaardingen's stockade or the massive walls of the castle seemed to segregate the clusters of Europeans from their Asian environment.

But these boundaries were permeable. Vlaardingen's backdoors allowed quiet and frequent passage between settlements, and within the houses a polyglot population of slaves, concubines and children with kin in several communities blurred the lines between Christian and Muslim. Indeed, the very categories used to place Makassar's inhabitants within the social and legal systems, which seemed so 'natural', were maintained by deliberate choices. Flexibility of identity declined during the eighteenth century; this was perhaps clearest for the *peranakan* Chinese, who were often Makassarese-speaking Muslims, but was no doubt also true for other communities. The indications are that the formal structuring of ethnicity progressed under the VOC, and whereas changes in community and religion were probably relatively easy in indigenous society, with the rise of a more institutionalised administration labels became more firmly fixed.

Power in Makassar was concentrated in the hands of the Company officials; they could use their naval and military power to advance not only VOC policy, but also their own commercial interests and moral values. But their reach was limited. The internal life of the settled communities unfolded beyond their regulation, and many officials were dependent on local informants for their interpretation of the world around them. Nonetheless, they were involved and affected by this environment, as were their neighbours. For despite its formally segmented organisation Makassar was much more than the sum of its parts. Through the interaction of its inhabitants—which it both structured and symbolised—the port city realised both its own identity and its contribution to the dynamics of the region.

Notes

1. Anthony Reid 'The Rise of Makassar' *Review of Indonesian and Malayan Affairs* 17, 1983, pp.117-60; Kenneth R. Hall *Maritime Trade and State Development in Early Southeast Asia* Honolulu, 1985
2. On the history of the Malay region, including early trade, see Barbara Watson Andaya & Leonard Y. Andaya *A History of Malaysia* London, 1982; for background and comparative material, Karl L. Hutterer (ed.) *Economic Exchange and Social Interaction in Southeast Asia* Ann Arbor, 1977; and James F. Warren *The Sulu Zone. The Dynamics of Trade, Slavery and Ethnicity in the Transformation of a Southeast Asian Maritime State* Singapore, 1981. The traditional dichotomy of agrarian and maritime cities has recently been re-endorsed by T. Kathirithamby-Wells in 'The Islamic City: Melaka to Jogjakarta, c. 1500-1800' *Modern Asian Studies* 20, 1986, pp. 334-35, but see Chapter 2 in the present volume
3. Reid 'Rise'
4. The classic, and still unrivalled, account is C. R. Boxer *The Dutch Seaborne Empire, 1600-1800* London, 1965. See also F. S. Gaastra *De Geschiedenis van de VOC* Haarlem, 1982; Holden Furber *Rival Empires of Trade in the Orient, 1600-1800* Oxford, 1976; and M. A. P. Meilink-Roelofsz *Asian Trade and European Influence in the Indonesian Archipelago between 1500 and about 1630* The Hague, 1962
5. Leonard Y. Andaya *The Heritage of Arung Palakka. A History of South Sulawesi (Celebes) in the Seventeenth Century* The Hague, 1981
6. For a general account see Phillip D. Curtin *Cross-Cultural Trade in World History* Cambridge, 1984
7. Leonard Blussé 'Chinese Trade in Batavia during the Days of the VOC' *Archipel* 18, 1979, pp. 195-214
8. Reid 'Rise'; Heather Sutherland 'Power and Politics in South Sulawesi, 1860-1880' *Review of Indonesian and Malaysian Affairs* v 17, 1983, pp. 161-207, also discusses the region's history
9. Boxer *Dutch Seaborne Empire* ch.8, and Gaastra *VOC* ch.3 on slavery; Heather Sutherland 'Slavery and the Slave Trade in South Sulawesi, 1660s-1800' in A. J. S. Reid (ed.) *Slavery, Bondage and Dependence in Southeast Asia* St Lucia, 1983
10. Boxer *Dutch Seaborne Empire* p.262; also Jean S. Taylor *The Social World of Batavia; European and Eurasian in Dutch Asia* Madison, Wis., 1983; and F. Lequin *Het Personeel van de Vereenigde Oost-Indische Compagnie in Azië in de Achttiende Eeuw, meer in het bijzonder in de Vestiging Bengalen* 2 vols, Leiden, 1982
11. Gaastra *VOC* p.82; Heather Sutherland 'Mestizos as Middlemen? Ethnicity and Access in Colonial Makassar' in G. Schutte & H. Sutherland (eds.) *Papers of the Dutch-Indonesian Historical Conference held at Laage Vuursche, The Netherlands, June 1980* Leiden, 1982, pp.250-77
12. A major cause of this fluidity is our dependence on the VOC archives, which are in many ways disingenuous, calculated to deceive. Faced with conflicts between local realities and state policy—in town administration, social life and the regulation of trade—officials found that a blind eye was essential if their stay in Makassar was to be both pleasant and profitable. Missives and appendices were laboriously copied and sent off to Batavia twice a year, but their compilers were more anxious to make a good impression than to explain local complexities. In many cases Company officials preferred not to let their superiors know what was happening, but where Asian communities were involved they themselves often had very little real insight. Hence we have volume upon volume on trade and politics, but scant information on other aspects of society
13. Speelman's 'Notitie', Algemeen Rijksarchief, The Hague (henceforth ARA), Aanwinsten 1 November 1926, fol.704 ff
14. F. Valentijn *Oud en Nieuw Oost-indien* 1865-58 ed, The Hague, vol.3, p.116
15. Sutherland 'Mestizos'; ARA, OB (Overgekomen Brieven) 1680, VOC no.1358, ff.294-95; OB 1682, VOC no.1368, f.449
16. National Archives of the Republic of Indonesia (ANRI), Makassar Collection no.313/1, 'Papieren in de zaak Intje Moeloet'
17. Details on the *pachten* were given every year at the beginning of the report from Makassar to Batavia; the property tax ('the twentieth penny') appeared irregularly, but see VOC no. 2933, ff.96-101, and 3150, ff.275-77
18. A micro-computer data-base analysis of this register is being used in a current research project on Makassar's trade; see Heather Sutherland and David S. Bree 'The Harbourmaster's Specification: a pilot study in computer-aided identification of regional trade patterns in VOC Asia', paper presented to the Second International Conference on Indian Ocean Studies (ICIOS II), Perth 1984.
19. Population totals were given every year in Makassar's missive to Batavia; there are scattered very detailed early censuses from before 1730 in the archives, for example, for 1679 VOC no.1347, f.499 ff.

20 See Heather Sutherland 'Mestizos' and 'Ethnicity, Wealth and Power in Colonial Makassar: a historiographical reconsideration' in P. J. M. Nas (ed.) *The Indonesian City: studies in urban development and planning* Dordrecht, 1986, pp.37-55
21 VOC no. 2314; earlier years such as the OB for 1719 (VOC no.1910, f.109 ff.) show less homogeneity, with some Indonesians (Isaac from Bali, or the 'Free woman Jaria') among the citizens in the Tuinstraat
22 Papers of the *weeskamer*, Makassar, in ANRI, Makassar Collection 374/2
23 ANRI, Makassar Collection 309/2
24 OB 1716, VOC no.1867, f.51; the seeds and leaves of *datura fastuoso* (Malay *kacubong*, Makassarese *kucubu*) are narcotic in effect
25 For example, OB 1767, VOC no.3181, ff.51, 99-100; OB 1773, VOC no.3358, f.108; OB 1787, VOC no.3732, ff.51-53. On 'abominable' Islam OB 1773, VOC no. 3358, f.108. See also Taylor, *Social World of Batavia*.
26 Mr C. Christiaans of the Dutch Central Genealogical Bureau, ARA, The Hague, has generously provided information on Makassar families
27 Examples of conflict are, for the *predikant* OB 1749, VOC no.2717, ff.336 and OB 1763, VOC no.3958, ff.8-11; for the *fiskaal* OB 1753, VOC no.2818, ff.56-81, and OB 1766, VOC no.3150, ff.223-29
28 OB 1791, VOC. no.3905, f. 154
29 OB 1694, VOC no.1556, ff.699-700; OB 1744, VOC no.2606, f.52; OB 1768, VOC no.3210, ff.41-42; OB 1775, VOC no.3412, ff.6-7; OB 1781, VOC no.3580, ff.6-8
30 OB 1773, VOC no.3358, ff.86-89, 108; OB 1783, VOC no.3623, ff.82-89
31 For a preliminary study based on the registers see Heather Sutherland and David S. Bree 'The Trading Communities of Eighteenth Century Makassar', paper presented at the 10th Conference of the International Association of Historians of Asia, Singapore, October 1986
32 OB 1756, VOC no.2859, ff.181-90; OB 1767, VOC no.3181, ff.6-7, 89-90; OB 1782, VOC no.3598, ff.141-43, 153-56, and appendix to the appendices of the Resolutions; OB 1784, VOC no.3648, ff.4-5; OB 1787, VOC no.3732, ff.42-43
33 OB 1752, VOC no.2780, ff.85-89, 90-96; OB 1753, VOC no.2799, ff.199. See also 'De Kapitein Melajoe to Makassar (1920)' *Adatrechtbundels. XXXI: Selebes* The Hague, 1929, pp.110-112

Further reading

Blussé, Leonard *Strange Company: Chinese settlers, mestizo women and the Dutch in VOC Batavia* Dordrecht 1986. Essays on the Dutch East Indies capital of Batavia, concentrating on social mores and the Chinese, but giving a stimulating picture of the wider networks in the region.

Boxer, C.R. *The Dutch Seaborne Empire* London 1965. This classic remains the most lively and readable account of the Netherlands overseas expansion and society.

Bruijn, J.R., F.S. Gaastra and I. Schoffer *Dutch Asiatic Shipping in the 17th and 18th Centuries* vol. 1, The Hague 1987. An introduction to the definitive statistical and general study of shipping plying between the Netherlands and Asia in that period.

Gaastra, F.S. *De Geschiedenis van de VOC* Haarlem 1982. A concise and valuable summary, including recent work, on the organisation, development and social aspects of the VOC.

Meilink-Roelofsz, M.A.P. *Asian Trade and European Influence in the Indonesian Archipelago between 1500 and about 1630* The Hague 1962. A pioneering study presenting detailed analysis drawn from the Dutch archives, which reopened the discussion on the interaction between Asian and Western trading systems.

Reid, Anthony (ed.) *Southeast Asia in the Age of Commerce* vol. 1 *The Lands below the Winds* New Haven 1988. A stimulating introduction to the world of Southeast Asia before the establishment of European domination.

Taylor, Jean Gelman *The Social World of Batavia: European and Eurasian in Dutch Asia* Madison, Wisc., 1983. Recaptures much of the atmosphere of the multi-ethnic Indies capital, focusing on the role of women and the fabric of social life.

CHAPTER

Robert Y. Eng

The transformation of a semi-colonial port city: Shanghai, 1843-1941

Shanghae is by far the most important station for foreign trade on the coast of China ... No other town with which I am acquainted possesses such advantages: it is the great gate—the principal entrance, in fact—to the Chinese empire ... Junks come here from all parts of the coast, not only from the southern provinces, but also from Shantung and Peechelee: there are also a considerable number annually from Singapore and the Malay Islands. The convenience of inland transit is also unrivalled in any part of the world. The country, being as it were the Valley of the Yang-tse-kiang, is one vast plain, intersected by many beautiful rivers, and these again joined and crossed by canals, many of them nearly natural, and others stupendous works of art. Owing to the level nature of the country, the tide ebbs and flows a great distance inland, thus assisting the natives in the transmission of their exports to Shanghae, or their imports to the most distant parts of the country. The port of Shanghae swarms with boats of all sizes, employed in this inland traffic; and the traveller continually meets them, and gets a glimpse of their sails over the land, and at every step of his progress in the interior.

These observations, made by the British botanist Robert Fortune after a visit in 1843,[1] underscore the fact that Shanghai was already a major maritime centre before her emergence as a modern port city linking the hinterlands of the Yangzi (Yangtze) to the global economy of the nineteenth century. Perhaps more than any other Asian port city, Shanghai epitomises the thriving tradition of maritime Asia that antedated the intrusion of Western imperialism. Despite periods of maritime prohibition, imperial China had a highly commercialised and integrated economy with a flourishing sea trade. By the late eighteenth century Shanghai enjoyed a booming junk trade along four principal routes: the northern route to Tianjin, Niuzhuang and Yantai; the southern route to Ningbo, Shaoxing, Fuzhou, Chaozhou and Shantou; the central route along the Yangzi all the way to Wanxian in Sichuan; the interior riverine route to the hinterlands of Jiangsu, Zhejiang, Anhui and Shandong provinces; and the overseas routes to Japan, Korea and Southeast Asia.[2] Despite its commercial eminence, however, Shanghai was overshadowed in the Chinese urban hierarchy by traditional administrative centres such as Suzhou. The onset of Western imperialism would set in motion forces of change that not only vastly increased the economic importance and demographic size of Shanghai, but also its political significance. This chapter will build on the still epochal study of modern Shanghai—and, at the same time, pioneer in the field of port city research—of Rhoads Murphey;[3] more specifically, however, than Murphey's work it will focus on the transformation of its pivotal maritime sector under semi-colonialism and the consequences of this for the city as a whole: the development of port facilities and shipping services; the regional zoning of the port city; the rise of trades and services related to maritime commerce and port development; and, finally, the concomitant changes in population and social structure.

Before the Opium War of 1839-42, Sino-Western trade was restricted to the single port of Guangzhou (Canton). Britain's victory in that war permitted her to impose harsh terms on the Qing empire, including the payment of huge indemnities, the cession of Hong Kong and the opening of Shanghai and four other ports. It also ushered in an era of semi-colonial penetration of China, now exposed to be a hollow power and increasingly subjected to Western pressures and demands during the nineteenth century. Despite her retention of nominal political independence, China was forced to yield a series of concessions to the Western powers that impaired her sovereignty: the opening of additional treaty ports; the leasing of concessions in some of these ports to foreigners who resided in them and administered them without consulting either the Chinese government or the Chinese residents who constituted the majority of the population; the granting of extraterritoriality to foreign nationals who would be under the jurisdiction of their own laws and consuls rather than the Chinese authorities; the restriction of tariffs to 5 percent ad valorem; and the granting of most-favoured status to the Western powers, thereby allowing concessions extracted by one power to be extended to all.

The British choice of Shanghai as one of the ports to be opened after 1842 was dictated by glowing accounts of her commercial potential from earlier reconnaissances. As early as 1756, Pigou, an employee of the British East India Company, reported that Shanghai was a most suitable site for Sino-Western trade. In 1832, two Englishmen, Hugh Hamilton Lindsay and Charles Gutzlaff, visited Shanghai and came away with effusive reports of its commercial bustle and possibilities. Gutzlaff spoke of Shanghai as possibly the leading trade centre of China, while Lindsay described enthusiastically the immense junk trade and the superb harbour and wharving facilities.[4]

Macau. Although the format of many of these views of port cities is the same—boats in the harbour with the mountains in the background—depictions of Chinese ports such as this one attempt to identify the specific qualities of Chinese towns, which include the orderly architecture and the unique landscape in the background. For good measure the engraver has included the kinds of boats typically encountered in a Chinese port.
From Joan Nieuhof Het Gezantschap der Neérlandtsche Oost-Indische Compagnie aan den grooten Tartarischen Cham den tegenwoordigen Keizer van China Amsterdam, 1670.
Courtesy of Mitchell Library, State Library of New South Wales.

After Shanghai was opened to the West in 1843, it quickly supplanted Guangzhou as the leading centre of Sino-Western trade. Shanghai's share of that trade rose from 16 percent in 1846 to 50 percent in 1861 and 63 percent in 1871. Thereafter its share declined some as other ports developed their commerce, but from the 1880s through to the 1920s was always at or close to half of the total foreign trade of China (see Table 5.1).[5] During the 1930s Shanghai accounted for over half of China's total foreign commerce, far outdistancing Tianjin, China's second port, which accounted for just over 10 percent.[6]

Total trade at Shanghai rose from under 250 million Haikwan taels in the 1870s to over 1¾ billion taels in the 1920s (see Fig. 5.1). Much of this trade consisted of domestic goods going through Shanghai to other Chinese and

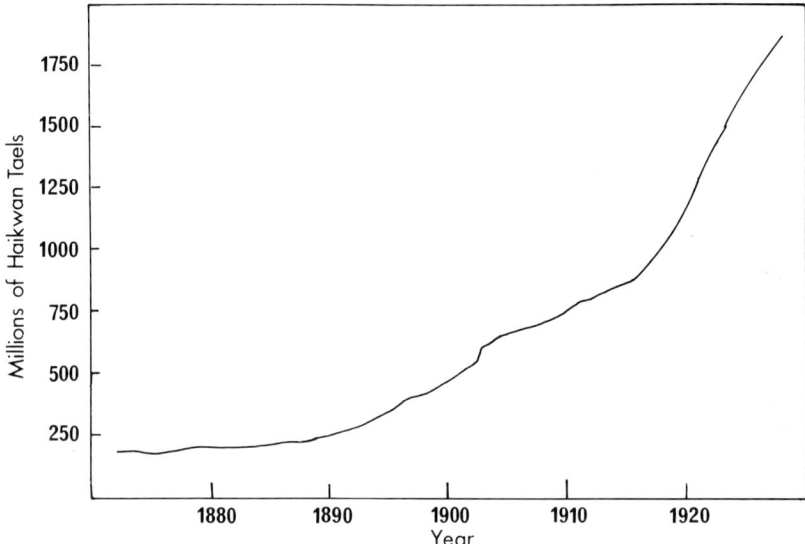

Figure 5.1
Value of total Shanghai trade, 1872-1928 (5-year moving averages)

TABLE 5.1
Shanghai's share of total foreign trade of China, 1870-1930
(% of total)

	Imports	Exports	Total Trade
1870-1880	85	59	62
1880-1890	58	48	53
1890-1900	56	52	54
1900-1910	54	48	51
1910-1920	51	45	48
1920-1930	50	40	45

Source: Cheng-siang Chen *Shanghai* Research report no. 38, Geographical Centre, Graduate School, the Chinese University of Hong Kong, Hong Kong, 1970, p. 11

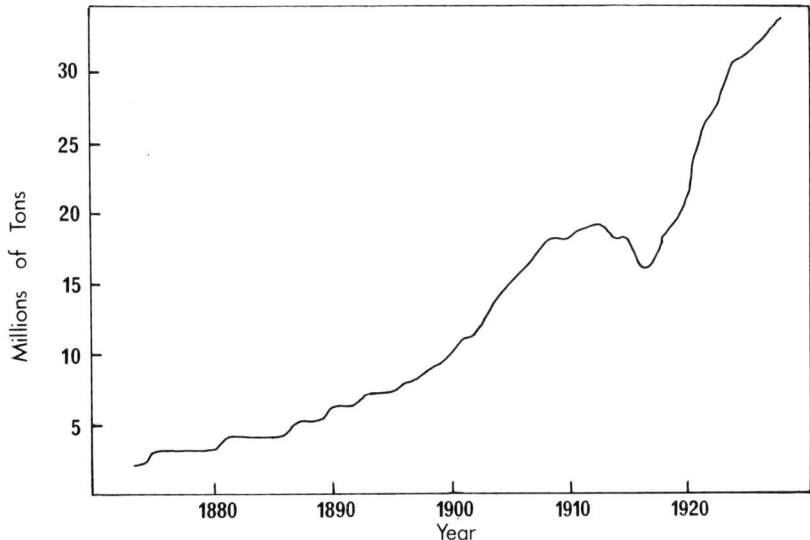

Figure 5.2
Total shipping tonnage entering and clearing Shanghai, 1873-1928 (5-year moving averages)

foreign ports and foreign imports en route to other destinations. In the decade of 1892-1901, for instance, re-exports accounted for 57 to 63 percent of total trade.[7] Concomitantly, total shipping entering and clearing Shanghai harbour rose from under 5 million tons in the 1870s and 1880s to over 30 million tons in the 1920s (see Fig. 5.2).

There were several reasons for Shanghai's rapid ascendancy. To begin with, the locational advantages of Shanghai at the mouth of the Huangpu (Whangpoo), a tributary of the Yangzi River, with easy access by water to the hinterlands of the immense Yangzi Delta, cannot be underestimated.[8] Moreover, Shanghai was ideally situated for sea transport as well. It lay close to the shipping route between the west coast of North America, Japan, China and Southeast Asia, and thus served as a focal point for East Asian shipping. It was roughly equidistant in shipping time and distance from western Europe and eastern United States, making it possible for merchants from those areas to compete on roughly equal terms with respect to transport cost and for Shanghai to serve as a major port of call for traffic going in both directions. Shanghai also lay approximately midway on the China coast between north and south; it could therefore act as the leading entrepot for carrying trade between these two regions.[9]

One often-cited advantage, however, the security of life and property that was offered in the Foreign Settlement and attracted Chinese mercantile presence and investment,[10] must be qualified. To be sure, the loss of legal and fiscal jurisdiction by the Chinese government in the foreign settlements, coupled with the presence of foreign gunboats along the Yangzi, served to

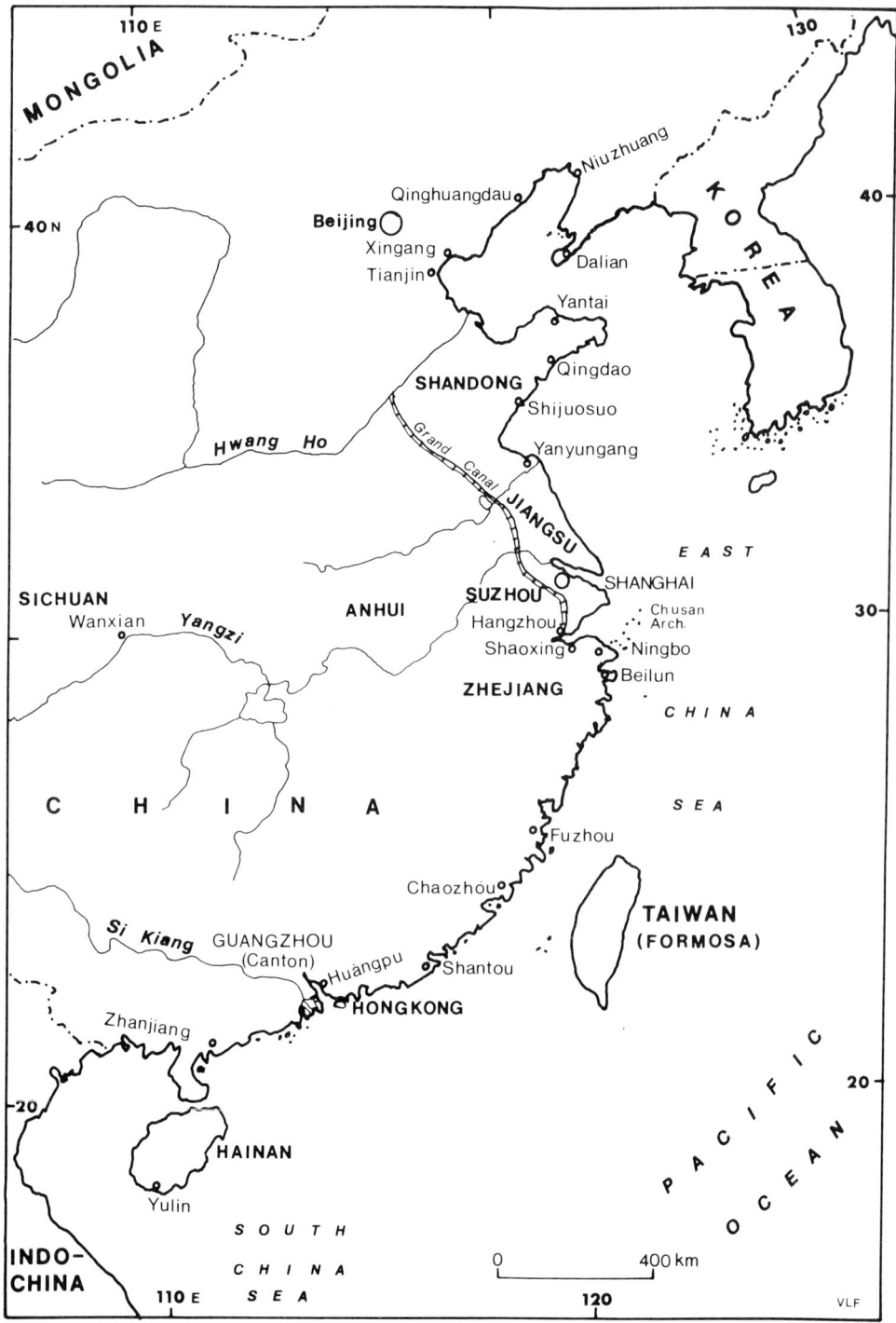

Map 9 Shanghai and maritime China

The transformation of a semi-colonial port city: Shanghai, 1843-1941

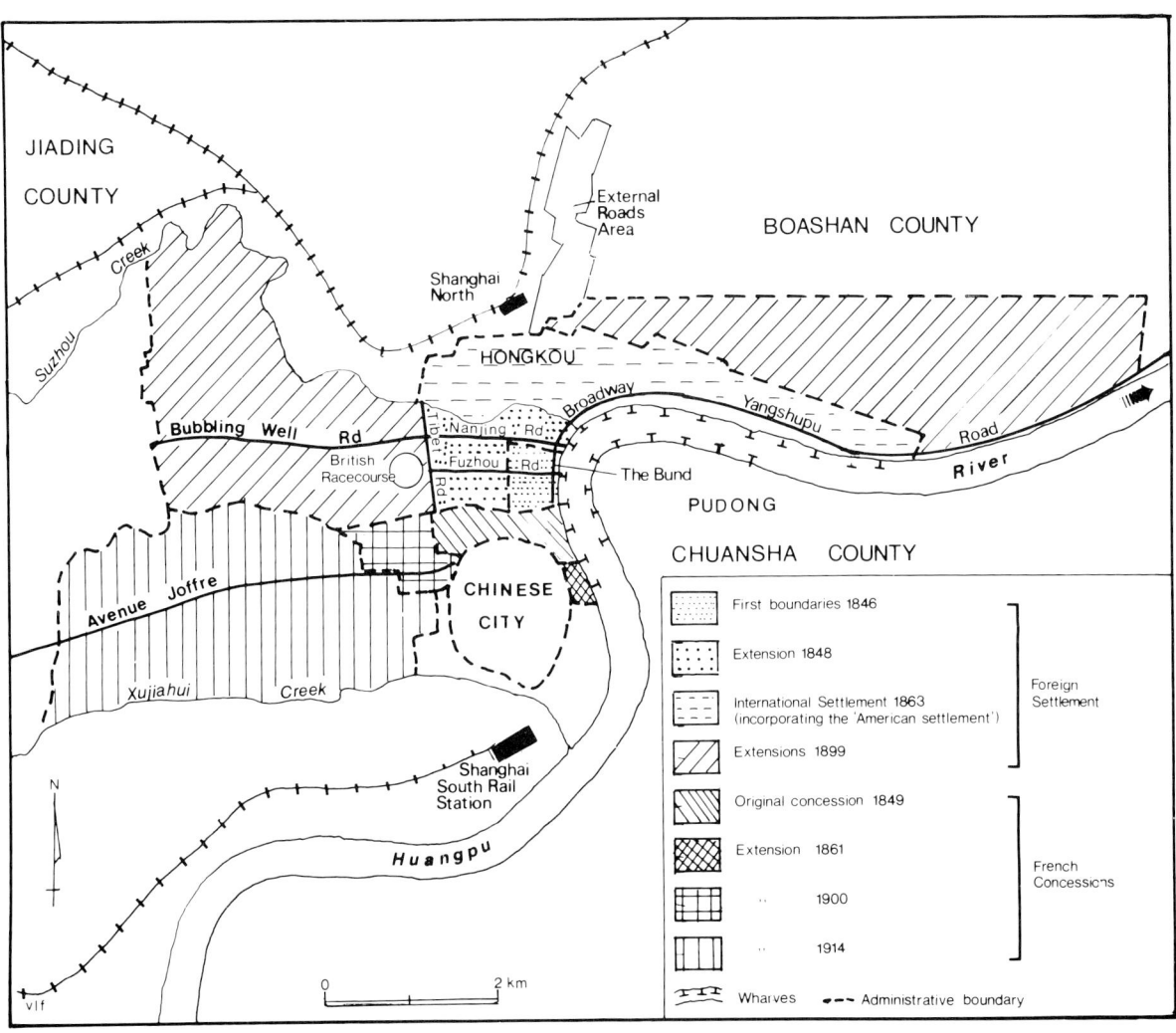

Map 10 Semi colonial Shanghai, 1843-1941

insulate the port city from the whims and arbitrary power of the Chinese authorities, particularly those warloads who vied for national and local power after 1916.[11] But the very privilege of extraterritoriality placed the Chinese at a severe handicap with respect to foreigners in the matters of civil and commercial litigation. The strong likelihood that a Western defendant was on social terms with his consul who would try the case made it improbable that a Chinese plaintiff would win a favourable judgment.[12] Secondly, social statistics and contemporary reporting attest to the fact that Shanghai had become one of the most crime-ridden cities of the world by the early twentieth century, where the rich especially were susceptible to blackmail, kidnapping and robbery.[13] Just as the locational advantages of Shanghai offset a poor harbour liable to silt and flood the banks, so too in the minds of the Chinese bourgeoisie the commercial opportunities offered in Shanghai's Sino-Western trade outweighed the risks of defraudment by Western factors and assault by Chinese criminals.

Before discussing the effects of Shanghai's opening on her port development, it should be pointed out that it actually consisted of three separate administrative areas, each with its distinctive government and legal basis: the International Settlement, the French Concession and the Chinese city. If the British selected the location of their original Settlement, an area 'bounded on three sides by defensible waterways and on the fourth by the navigable Whangpoo', largely on strategic grounds,[14] the subsequent expansion of the International Settlement was determined primarily by wharfing requirements. The area of the International Settlement expanded from 138 acres in 1843 to 5583 acres by agreements concluded in 1848, 1893 and 1899. Even so, further demands for space had to be satisfied through the construction of Extra-Settlement Roads in accordance with Shanghai's Land Regulations, which by 1930 amounted to 48.1 miles and encompassed an area of 7923 acres. The International Settlement was governed by the Shanghai Municipal Council, the charter of which provided for the annual election of its membership by ratepayers who paid rental on their property holdings. It was not until 1928 that the Chinese gained the right to vote and serve on the Municipal Council.[15]

The French Concession originated in 1844 as an area allotted by Chinese authorities where French nationals could lease land. It lay southwest of the Settlement and fronted the Huangpu. Later agreements in 1861, 1900 and 1914 extended the area of 164 acres in 1849 to 2525 acres. Unlike the Settlement, the government of which has been characterised as a 'representative oligarchy', the French Concession was governed through a 'bureaucratic autocracy' under the French consul-general, whose authority flowed directly from the French government in Paris.

The largest of the administrative areas of Shanghai was the Chinese city, which was delimited in 1906 to include not only the old Chinese walled city but also Nanshi (Nantao), Pudong (Pootung), Zhabei (Chapei), Jiangwan (Kiangwan) and Wusong (Woosung), with an area of 320 square miles. In 1930, the Nationalist government established the Chinese Municipal Administration of Shanghai.[16]

In the period following the opening of Shanghai in 1843, much of the overseas shipping had been monopolised by the British Peninsular & Oriental Steam Navigation Co. By the 1860s, as the Treaties of Tianjin and Beijing increased the number of treaty ports from five to sixteen and the Western powers gained the rights of inland and coastal navigation, Westerners were moving into the coastal carrying trade as well as the inland traffic. There was consequently a rapid rise in the total number of ships entering Shanghai and several new shipping companies were founded. The American firm of Russell & Co. established the Shanghai Steam Navigation Co. in 1861, and in 1863, two British companies, Wheelock & Co. and Shanghai Tug & Lighter Co., began shipping services. In 1866, the German firm Melchers & Co. entered the sea transport business. In 1867 Butterfield, Swire & Co., too, founded its own navigation company, the China Navigation Co., at Shanghai.[17] The China Merchants' Nagivation Company was founded in 1873 under the aegis of Li Hongzhang, the most powerful official of the empire, with the participation of the Chinese merchants Tang Tingshu, Xu Run, Sheng Xuanhuai and others. It increased its share of total tonnage sharply with the acquisition of the fleet of the Shanghai Union Steam Navigation Company in 1876.[18]

However, the China Merchants' fleet stagnated at about 23 000 tons from 1877 to 1893, while the China Navigation Co. increased its total tonnage from 8361 tons to 34 543 tons and the Indo-China Steam Navigation Co. (owned by Jardine Matheson & Co.) from 3109 tons to 23 953 tons.[19] China Merchants' and other smaller Chinese shipping companies were confined to internal shipping, but even there foreign companies had an advantage: goods carried on Western vessels were not exposed to multiple taxation and were subject only to the lower internal customs rates applicable to foreign goods.[20] The British remained the dominant force in shipping, although after 1900 their market share declined from over 50 percent to under 40 percent, and they came under the increasing challenge of the Japanese (see Figures 5.3 and 5.4).

The maritime orientation of Shanghai in large part determined the differential development of the three administrative areas of Shanghai and the mapping of the city into economic and residential zones. As shipping depended on docking and warehouse facilities, the British and American Settlements as well as the French Concession were initially established along a narrow strip of land along the Huangpu. Likewise the need to expand water frontage dictated the southward expansion of the French Concession in 1861, and the expansion of the International Settlement into Hongkou (Hongkew) in 1863.[21] It was necessary, however, to construct embankments to make the muddy tidal foreshores along the the Huangpu River and Suzhou (Soochow) Creek usable for buildings or wharves. This process of 'bunding' gave rise to the name for the famous Bund along the Huangpu frontage of the International Settlement from Suzhou Creek to the Yangjing Creek (Yang Ching Pang). The first jetties were constructed in the 1840s, in front of the foreign firms that lay along the waterfront. Since the clippers found it difficult to enter the waters and much of their inward cargo was contraband opium, goods were first transferred from the ships onto launches which docked at the jetties, where they could be directly unloaded into the warehouses of the import-export firms.[22]

The capacity of existing docking facilities was severely strained by the entry of Western ships in the coastal and interior carrying trades in the 1860s.

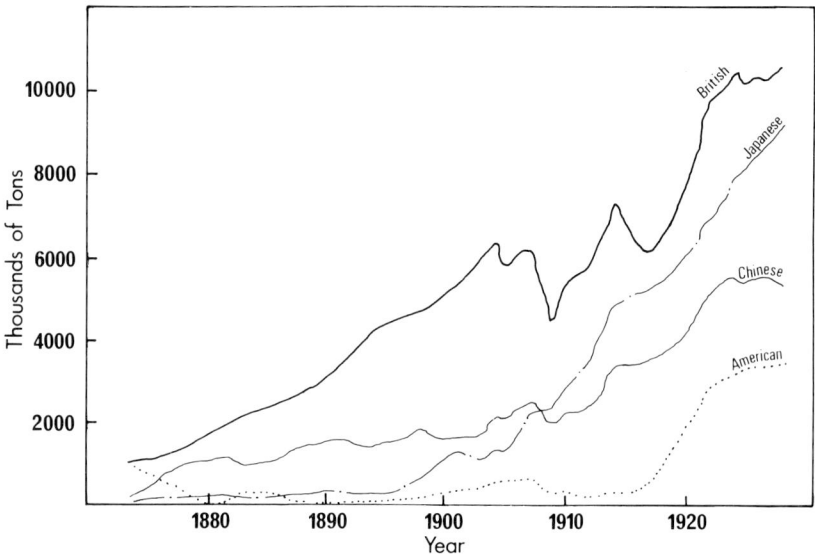

Figure 5.3
Total shipping tonnage entering and clearing Shanghai by nationality of registration, 1873-1928 (5-year moving averages)

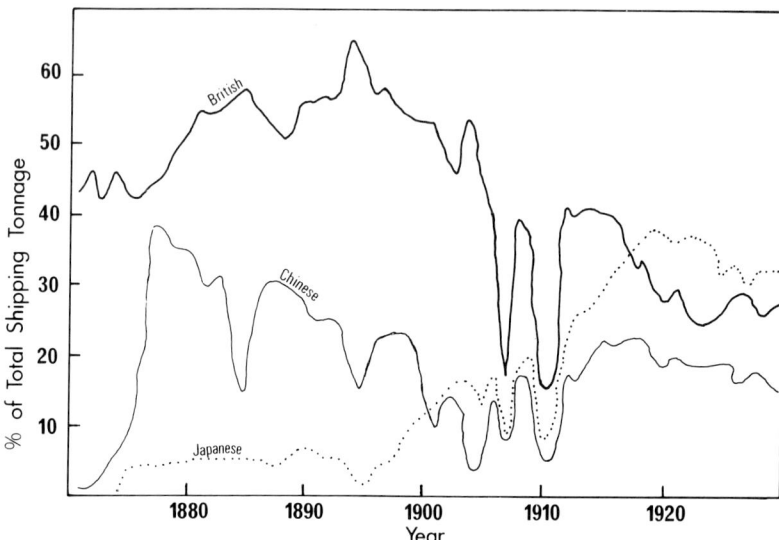

Figure 5.4
Share of shipping tonnage in and out of Shanghai, by nationality of registration, 1871-1930

Moreover, steamships with much larger dimensions were beginning to displace the clippers. Coupled with the rising overall volume of shipping, this necessitated a second wave of wharf construction. Rather than handling launches, these new wharves were designed to accommodate the steamers. Since the original waterfront was already occupied, new wharves were built in Hongkou and in the French Concession.[23]

The expansion of wharves accelerated in the 1870s, as the volume of shipping increased after the opening of the Suez Canal in 1869. The construction of these wharves was entirely dominated by Western firms.[24] By the end of the 1870s, many wharves had been built along the Huangpu in Hongkou, the waterfront of the French Concession and Pudong. The signing of the Treaty of Shimonoseki in 1895, after China's defeat by Japan, ushered in a third period of wharf construction, as China was forced to open up more treaty ports and permit the establishment of foreign factories. This phase continued into the 1920s. It involved not only the construction of many new wharves, but also the renovation and the extension of existing ones. Moreover, much of the construction took place outside the concessions in Pudong.[26]

The advantageous location of the International Settlement along the river helped to make it Shanghai's centre of commerce, finance, shipping and industry.[27] In contrast, the French Concession, with little room to expand along the river, had only 3800 feet of water frontage as compared to the 31 000 feet of the International Settlement; consequently it remained primarily a residential district with little commerce and industry. A second factor retarding the commercial progress of the Concession was the preferential treatment given by the French consul to French merchants in the registration of land deeds, with the result that other foreigners preferred the Settlement. It was not until 1914, after another extension of the Concession was negotiated with the Republican government, that the French relinquished control over the issuing of deeds and permitted other foreigners to register their deeds under their own consuls.[28] The Chinese municipality, on the other hand, grew in population as the native city and the foreign settlements overflowed with the booming of trade.[29]

At the same time, the silting of the Huangpu continued to be a worsening impediment to shipping. Because of the shift to large ocean steamers from the 1850s on, average tonnage and draught of ships entering and clearing Shanghai rose: in the 1850s, the average tonnage had been about 1000 tons and draught 12-13 feet; by 1880 tonnage had increased to 4000 tons and draught to over 20 feet. However, the port was becoming increasingly inaccessible to large ships. By 1905, the bar at the mouth of the river had only a depth of 15 feet at low tides.[30]

From 1850 on, the foreign firms of Shanghai repeatedly petitioned the Qing government to dredge the Huangpu to remove the sandbars and to deepen the channel. The government ignored these pleas for several reasons: it believed that the narrowing channels at Wusong presented a natural defence against foreign gunboats; it was reluctant to invest large sums of money in dredging

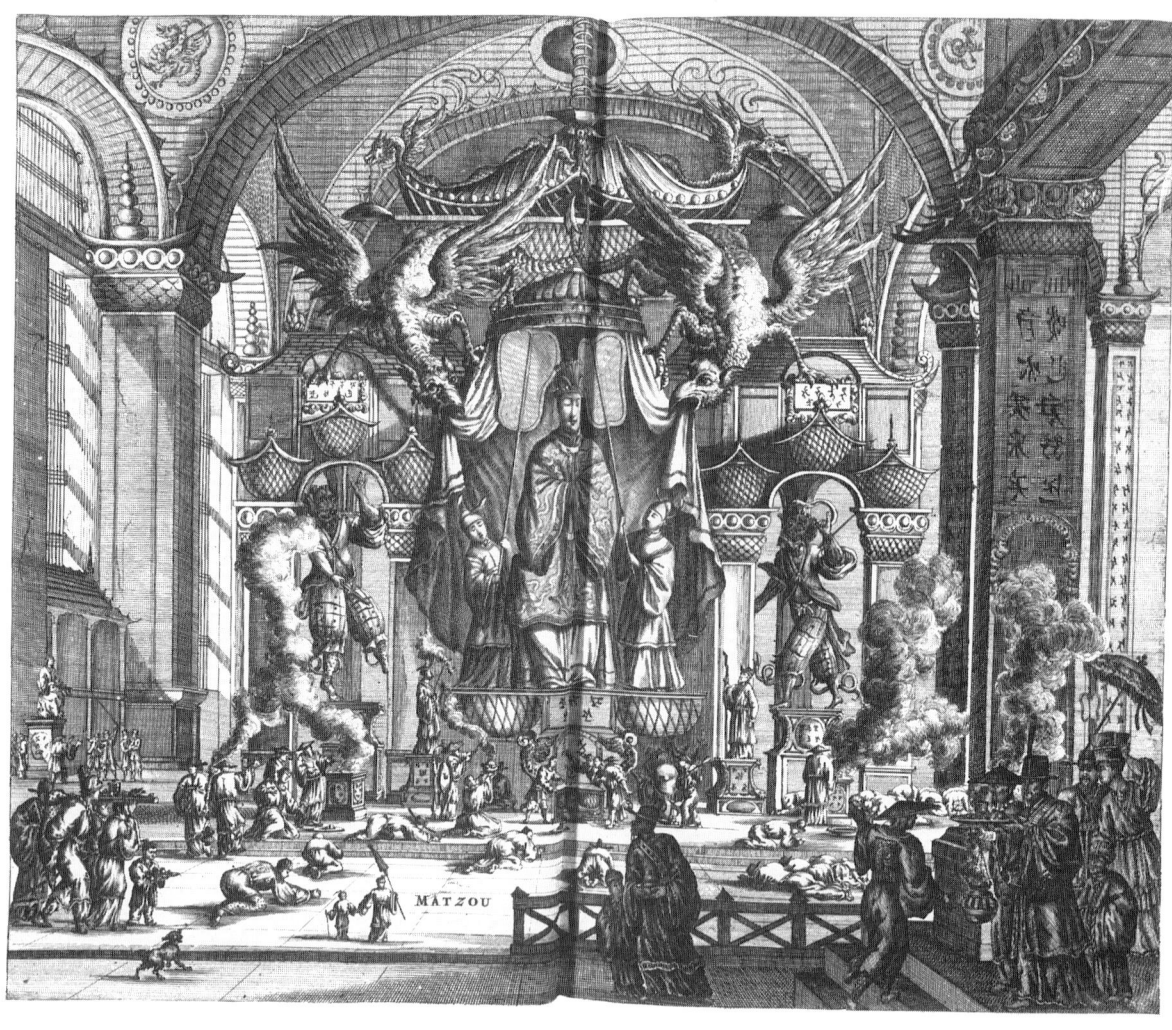

*The Matzou Chinese temple of Macau. This baroque version of a Chinese temple embodies many of the mysterious and impenetrable qualities of China which impressed foreign visitors, not only Europeans.
From Olfert Dapper Gedenkwaerdig bedryf der Nederlandsche Oost-Indische Maetschappye, op de kuste en in het keizerrijk van Taising of Sina Amsterdam, 1670.
Courtesy of Mitchell Library, State Library of New South Wales.*

projects that would bring little benefit to the smaller Chinese ships, including those belonging to the fleet of China Merchants' Navigation Co.[31] It was not until China's defeat in the Boxer Rebellion of 1900 that the Qing government was forced to accede to the establishment of the Whangpoo Conservancy Board. A 1905 agreement between China and the eleven Boxer Protocol powers set up the board, which was to be financed by China, directed by the Taotai of Shanghai and the commissioner of customs, and managed by foreign engineers. In 1912 insufficient resources led to a new agreement that the board should draw its funds from wharfage dues on the value of imports and exports, and from government sales of reclaimed estuarial land.[32] Between 1905 and 1930, approximately 33.7 million cubic yards of mud were dredged at the mouth of the Huangpu.[33]

Thus the continual rise of Sino-Western trade prompted and was in turn facilitated by the expansion of the water front and the dredging of the Huangpu. It also stimulated the growth of the population and changes in the social structure of the city. First we may note the influx of the Westerners (and later the Japanese), who though never constituting more than a tiny percentage of the total population, nevertheless profoundly influenced the character of the city by their presence, extraterritorial status and commercial and cultural activities.

In 1843 there were only twenty-three foreign residents, but already forty ships called at Shanghai.[34] As shipping and trade continued to expand during the subsequent decades, the number of foreign firms and residents connected with Sino-Western commerce grew. Within one year of Shanghai's opening in 1843, eleven firms were established. In 1854, ten years later, there were about 120 Western firms, almost all located along the Huangpu. By 1876, over 200 foreign firms engaged in trade at Shanghai,[35] and in 1903, over 600.[36] The oldest firms, including the British firms of Jardine Matheson & Co. and Dent and Co. and the American firm of Russell & Co., harked back to the pre-Opium War days when trade was confined to Guangzhou.[37] Almost to a firm they continued the profitable opium trade.[38] Most of the newer firms founded after 1843 got their starts in cotton textile trade.

Before the 1870s, the Western firms directly handled not only the import-export business, but also shipping, insurance and banking as well.[39] The rise of Sino-Western trade promoted greater specialisation and created the demand for various related services. One such service was pilotage. Pilots who guided the Western clippers safely into the Shanghai port were initially all Chinese. In 1855, the Western consuls and the Taotai of Shanghai agreed to the Pilot Regulations, which provided for the examination and licensing of pilots, now open to all nationalities. But revised regulations in 1859 limited the licensing of pilots to Europeans only; the exclusion of the Chinese was justified by Western claims that Chinese pilots could not be disciplined, and that some were in collusion with pirates.[40]

Not only were the Chinese barred from the pilotage business, but native junk traffic also declined in the face of Western competition, as Chinese merchants turned increasingly to Western vessels for the transportation of their goods for greater safety from the depredations of pirates. The Chinese shipping business was further damaged by government commandeering of ships during the great rebellions of the 1850s and 1860s.[41]

Another service that was stimulated by the growth of Sino-Western trade was ship repair and construction. During the 1840s and 1850s, the Westerners established nine ship repair yards in China; seven of these were located at Shanghai, an indication of the gravitation of trade there.[42] In 1900, Farmham & Co. and Boyed & Co., with a combined capital of 5.5 million taels and over 4000 workers, merged into the Shanghai Dock and Engineering Co. Ltd, the single largest foreign enterprise in Shanghai in the early twentieth century.[43] From the late 1860s too the Chinese initiated ship repair services. The first and the biggest of these, Fachang Hao, was founded in 1866 by Fang Juzan; it expanded into shipbuilding and other related services and employed over 300 workers by the 1870s. The majority of Chinese ship repair services, however, remained small enterprises dependent on subcontracting by the foreign companies. In 1895, even Fachang was forced to sell out.[44]

Banking services too were initiated in Shanghai from the 1840s to meet the needs of financing foreign trade. The first foreign bank in Shanghai was the branch of the Oriental Banking Corporation, established in 1847. In 1854, another British bank—the Chartered Mercantile Bank of India, London and China—also founded a branch office in Shanghai. The most prominent of the Western banks, the Hongkong & Shanghai Banking Corporation, began its operations in Shanghai in 1865; it had been founded by the joint capital of the British firms of Jardine Matheson & Co. and William Forbes & Co., the American firm of Russell & Co., and some German, French and Parsi merchants.[45] The withdrawal of German and French capital by the 1860s turned it into a British bank representing almost exclusively British interests; the ten biggest British firms in East Asia were represented on its board.[46] By 1936, there were over forty foreign banks and over 170 foreign insurance companies in Shanghai.[47]

With the signing of the Treaty of Shimonoseki in 1895, not only did Japan become an important foreign economic actor on the China scene, but foreign economic activities expanded beyond finance and import-export trade into direct investment in heavy industry, light industry and public utilities. The penetration of Western and Japanese capital into Shanghai was especially rapid after World War I: in 1928, according to the Social Bureau of the Chinese Municipality, foreign capital contributed over 64 percent of total industrial investment in Shanghai. By 1936, foreign firms were responsible for 85.3 percent of the consumption of electricity, and controlled 54.2 percent of docking facilities, 60.3 percent of cotton spindles and 70.9 percent of cotton looms. Moreover, Shanghai remained the principal arena of the Western economic presence in China; on the eve of the outbreak of the Second Sino-Japanese War in 1937, Shanghai accounted for 79.2 percent of all foreign banking capital, 81.2 percent of foreign investment in commerce and import-export trade, 67.1 percent of foreign industrial investment and 76.8 percent of foreign real estate investment.

The Western merchants and houses, however, could not have got very far without the collaboration of the compradors and the employment of large numbers of Chinese in communications, traffic industries and auxiliary services. The compradors were the indispensable intermediaries between the foreign and the domestic sectors. Their services were necessitated by the unfamiliarity of Western merchants with the Chinese language, commercial conditions and customs. Their duties and functions varied according to the nature of the Western firm. Compradors for foreign commercial concerns had the most diversified responsibilities: they were in charge of recruitment and supervision of the Chinese staff, the gathering of market information, and negotiations with other Chinese merchants. Those working for the Western banks were responsible for dealing with Chinese banks and currencies and bank drafts. Compradors employed by the shipping companies handled the collection of fees for transport of goods and persons. Compradors working for the warehouses were in charge of supervising the loading and unloading and the storage of goods.[49] It was not until the early twentieth century that foreign firms began to dispense with the compradors as they gained greater and direct knowledge of Chinese conditions.[50]

Not only did Chinese merchants provide valuable services to the foreign firms as compradors, but they also invested their capital extensively in foreign enterprises. According to Wang Jingyu's estimates, before 1895 Western enterprises absorbed about 40 million taels of Chinese mercantile capital.[51] As for the Shanghai Steam Navigation Company and the Yangzi Insurance Association founded by the American firm of Russell & Co., Chinese merchants contributed all but 60 000 of the total capitalisation of 1.4 million taels.[52] The eagerness of the Chinese to put capital at the disposal of the foreign firms, despite their lack of control over the actual management of these enterprises, was a consequence of extraterritoriality: they could thereby bypass Chinese bureaucratic interference and seek the protection of the foreign consuls.[53]

In turn, with excess capital derived from deposits, currency exchange speculations and foreign trade transactions, the Western banks regularly issued call money (called chop loans) to traditional Chinese banks (*qianzhuang*) so that the latter could supply working capital to Chinese commercial and industrial enterprises.[54] It was only from the 1910s that Western banks ceased to supply call loans to the traditional banks, which turned to modern Chinese banks for their working capital.[55]

While the penetration of Western shipping put many native launches out of business and the building of the wharves deprived many peasants of their lands and fishermen of their basis of livelihood, at the same time it created demands for stevedores and dockworkers that provided employment opportunities for these displaced workers, and proved over time to be increasingly a magnet for impoverished peasants from the interior. By the end of the nineteenth century there were close to 20 000 dockworkers; during the 1920s and 1930s, the number reached 50 000.

The growing foreign community of the International Settlement and the French Concession also required the services of an ever greater number of Chinese domestic and office workers. Little more than twenty years after the opening of Shanghai, a Chinese visitor to the International Settlement observed that 'several *li* along the [Huangpu] River were shipyards, godowns, jetties, and the residences of Western merchants. There were multitudes of natives of Guangzhou and Ningbo working there'.[57] By 1870, 4908 Chinese were working at the various Western factories, firms and residences in the International Settlement.[58] The population of all three administrative areas increased steadily; by 1930, there were about 1 million people residing in the International Settlement, over 400 000 in the French Concession and over 1.6 million in the Chinese city (see Fig. 5.5 and Table 5.2).

The Chinese bourgeoisie and working class expanded with the growth of export-oriented industries at Shanghai. The most important of these was silk-reeling, which manufactured raw silk for the silk-weaving industries of France and the United States from 1878 on.[59] In response to foreign demand and rising exports, the Chinese silk-reeling industry expanded steadily after the late nineteenth century, tripling its production capacity between 1900 and 1930 (see Fig. 5.6).

From the 1890s, industries producing for domestic consumption assumed a growing importance at Shanghai. The outbreak of World War I provided these industries with an impetus as foreign sources of supplies were cut off.[60] Foremost among them were cotton-spinning, flour-milling and tobacco. While the Chinese cotton-spinning industry had its start back in 1890 with the formation of the Shanghai Cotton Mill Company,[61] progress as measured by the total number of spindles was slow before the First World War. By 1921 production capacity, reaching a level of 509 000 spindles, had more than tripled the prewar level; it continued its precipitous rise until 1933, when 1.1 million spindles were in operation (see Fig. 5.7). By 1919 the number of flour mills in Shanghai rose to seventeen, with a production level of 8.4 million bags; flour exports rose from 990 651 piculs in 1912 to 4.4 million in 1918.[62]

Even in such industries, however, the link to foreign trade remained strong because of their dependence on imported raw materials and machinery. In the cotton-spinning industry, for example, by the 1920s about 60 percent of agricultural land in Shanghai county had switched from rice to cotton cultivation in response to the growth of Shanghai cotton mills and their demand for raw cotton; southeast Jiangsu produced about 200 000 tons of raw cotton. However, because of the short staple of Chinese cotton, it could be used alone only in the coarsest counts; consequently imported cotton from the United States and India must be used in combination with Chinese cotton, in order to spin most of the counts for which the local spinning mills were equipped.[63] Flour mills had originally depended on domestic wheat, but by the 1920s relied mostly on foreign wheat.[64]

Industrial consumption of energy too reflected a reliance on foreign supplies. By around 1930 Shanghai consumed about 2¾ million metric tons of coal

The transformation of a semi-colonial port city: Shanghai, 1843-1941

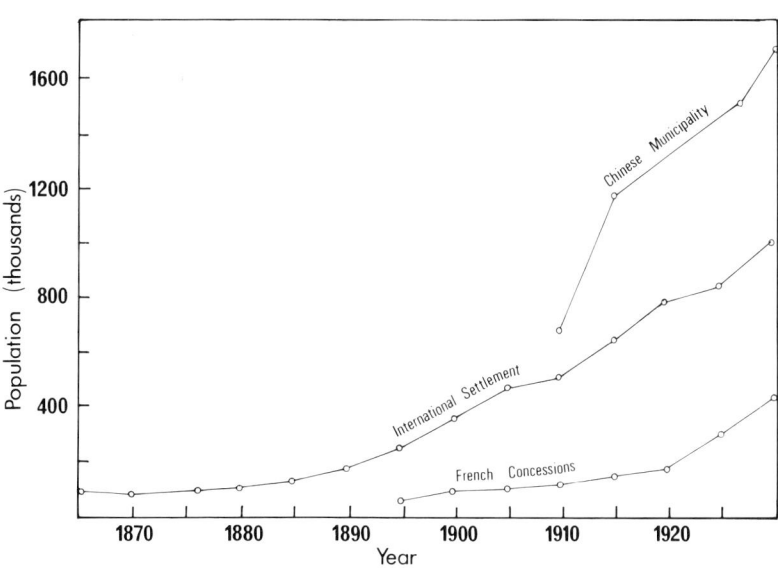

Figure 5.5
Population of Shanghai, 1865-1930

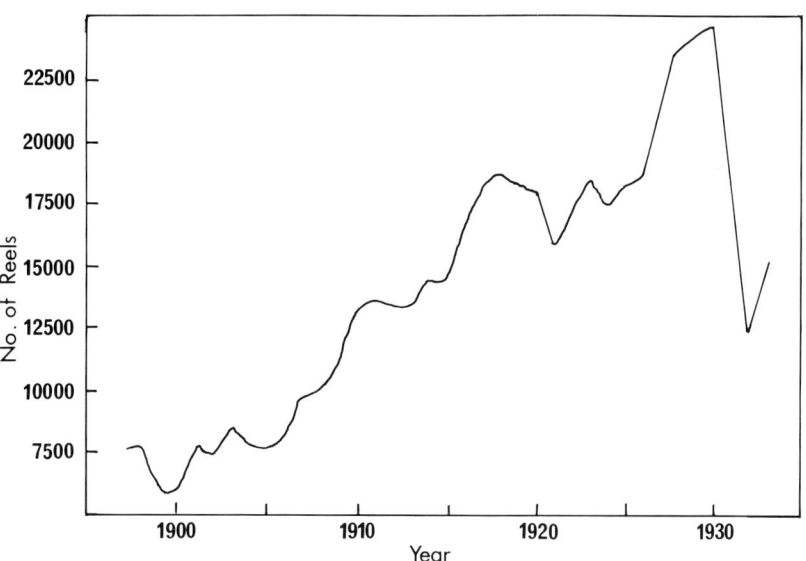

Figure 5.6
Production capacity of Shanghai silk filatures, 1897-1933

annually.[65] Coal deposits in the area near Shanghai—southwestern Jiangsu, Anhui and Jiangxi—were of poor quality and undeveloped; consequently the city must depend on imports from North China and from abroad, especially Japan. While Chinese coal accounted for 88.5 percent of total supplies in gross value in 1935,[66] in reality many of the Chinese mines were entirely or partly controlled by foreign capital, particularly Japanese. Totally Chinese-owned mines accounted for 44 percent of total coal production in China in 1928; the Japanese Southern Manchurian Railway Company owned and operated the Fushun mine near Mukden, the single largest coal field in China which alone contributed nearly one-third of total national output, as well as the Yantai mine in Shandong.[67] Kerosene and gasoline were mostly imported from the United States, the Soviet Union and the East Indies.[68]

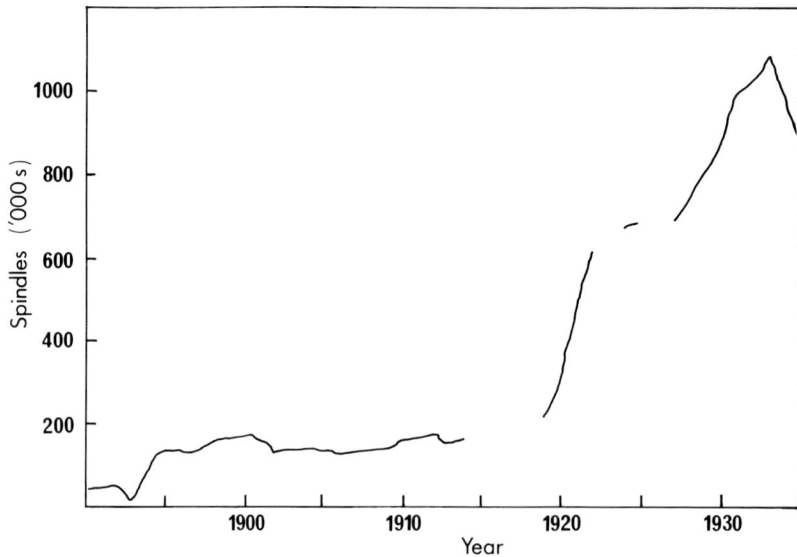

Figure 5.7
Production capacity of Shanghai cotton mills, 1890-1935

As the original areas of the International Settlement were already built up, new factories had to be located elsewhere, but with ready access to water transport. The Yangshupu district in the International Settlement, located along the Huangpu River below the mouth of Suzhou Creek, constituted the most important industrial area. Cotton-spinning and weaving mills and some engineering and chemical works dotted the riverbank below the stretch of wharves near the mouth of Suzhou Creek. A second important industrial region lay along the Settlement as well as the Zhabei sides of the Suzhou Creek, above the commercial area at its mouth and near the Nanjing-Shanghai Railway terminal. In the eastern part of this region were smaller Chinese establishments such as silk filatures, weaving sheds and knitting mills. A third concentration of large factories, including cotton, flour, oil and jute mills and chemical works, were situated along the upper reaches of Suzhou Creek beyond the boundaries of the Settlement and even beyond the area of external roads. An industrial zone of small Chinese-owned shops was found northeast of Zhabei, along the creeks and canals of the Hongkou district.[69]

The development of Shanghai as a port city was thus heavily conditioned by its semi-colonial character and maritime orientation, which dictated the expansion of port facilities, the rise of trades and industries related to shipping and the import-export business, the geographical spread and differential zoning of the foreign settlements. A high level of symbiosis between domestic and foreign factors ensued. The umbrella of extraterritoriality not only afforded commercial and political advantages to the foreigners (as manifested in the shipping business), it also prompted the foreign absorption of Chinese capital in search of security. The foreign firms relied on the services and financial resources of native compradors while foreign banks funnelled money back into Chinese enterprises through call loans to traditional Chinese banks. Domestic industries also depended to a great extent on foreign supplies of energy and raw materials. The possibility of a port-led industrialisation was thus stunted, as Shanghai failed to go beyond its primary role as an entrepot and integrate its economy more closely with the interior.

In 1937 the outbreak of the Second Sino-Japanese War led to the creation of 'Island Shanghai', which lasted until the attack on Pearl Harbor. Under the umbrella of neutrality, the International Settlement and the French Concession became a haven for Chinese refugees and capital fleeing the Japanese invasion. Ironically, wartime conditions promoted rapid economic expansion of Shanghai, as population more than doubled by the first half of 1940 as compared to before 1937, reaching a total of over 5 million people and creating an unprecedented level of demand. Refugee capitalists brought with them over 50 million yuan. Consequently, food and clothing industries and banking prospered. At the same time, Shanghai industry also benefited from demand from unoccupied and industrially backward China, and from the vacuum in the Southeast Asian market resulting from the preoccupation of the European powers with war and the boycotting of Japanese goods by the overseas Chinese.

As before the war, however, this industrial expansion was dominated by foreign capital, which in the first half of 1940 accounted for 67 percent of new cotton mills, 73 percent of spindles and 85 percent of looms. For reasons of security, Chinese banks deposited huge sums into the foreign banks, of which 27 were newly opened in response to the influx of capital. Dependence on foreign sources of raw materials was heightened, as the Japanese blockade made it difficult to secure supplies from the interior. Speculative fevers as manifested in the stockpiling of goods and the manipulations of the stock market added to the veneer of frenzied economic activity and apparent prosperity.

This era of 'Island Shanghai' was finally brought to an end with its invasion and occupation by the Japanese on 8 December 1941. Factories were put under the Japanese military or 'joint' Sino-Japanese management. Industrial activities came to a virtual standstill; by 1943 two-thirds of Chinese enterprises were closed, and by 1945 only a few maintained even partial production.[70] Ironically, the Japanese, who invaded China under the ideological guise of Pan-Asianism that would end Western imperialism and create a Greater East Asia Co-Prosperity Sphere, initially accentuated Shanghai's semi-colonial character and ultimately substituted direct Japanese imperialism for Western semi-colonialism.

In 1943, the puppet government under Wang Jingwei assumed control of the foreign concessions of Shanghai. The imperialist era in Shanghai came to an end in 1945 with Japan's defeat and full restoration of Chinese sovereignty. Since the communist revolution of 1949, Shanghai has continued to play a vital role in the national economy as China's leading industrial centre. Its maritime functions, however, were curtailed sharply: given the hostility of the United States, the Chinese policies of 'Lean to One Side' and self-reliance, and the turmoil of the Cultural Revolution from 1966, international trade, especially with the non-communist countries, remained at a low level.

But with the official proclamation of an end to the Cultural Revolution and a new policy of a 'Great Leap Outward' in 1977, relations with the United States and a number of non-communist countries were normalised, and international contacts and commerce have expanded enormously. Shanghai's maritime character has been revitalised. As China's total foreign trade rose from US$48 million in 1971 to $206 million in 1978 and $407 million in 1983,[71] Shanghai harbour's cargo-handling capacity was expanded steadily, from 57 million metric tons in 1976[72] to 113 million in 1985.[73] By 1985, with 30 percent of China's cargo-handling capacity, Shanghai has regained her place among the world's top ten ports.[74]

However, while Shanghai is still China's leading centre of foreign trade, her dominance is no longer as marked as before 1949. Shanghai's share of China's foreign exports has declined from 18 percent in 1981 to 13 percent in 1985; her overseas exports have fallen in dollar value at an annual rate of 4.7 percent over the same period.[75] Shanghai's maritime leadership may be challenged by a number of rapidly expanding ports. The northern port of Qinhuangdao, located along the Beijing-Shenyang Railway and with an ice-free harbour, has become China's leading energy-exporting port, where coal from Shanxi Province and petroleum from Daqing found their outlet to markets in South China and overseas.[76] In 1985 her cargo-handling capacity has jumped to 44 million metric tons, second only to Shanghai's.[77] In the south, the port of Guangzhou and the Special Economic Zone of Shenzhen, aided by proximity to Hong Kong and investment by overseas Chinese capitalists who are native sons of Guangdong Province, have been expanding their trade rapidly; in 1985, Shenzhen's foreign exports of US$5.6 million represented an increase of 47 percent over the previous year.[78] Nonetheless, despite the relative decline of her dominance, Shanghai is likely to remain China's leading port, and her re-emergence as a maritime centre is symbolic of Asia's recent assumption of the 'mantle of maritime leadership of the world'.[79]

TABLE 5.2
Population of Shanghai, 1855-1930 (thousands)

	International Settlement	French Concession	Chinese Municipality
1865	93		
1870	77		
1876	97		
1880	110		
1885	129		
1890	172		
1895	246	52	
1900	352	92	
1905	464	97	
1910	502	116	672
1915	639	149	1174
1920	783	170	
1925	840	297	
1927			1504
1930	1008	435	1702

Sources: All figures for the International Settlement and the French Concession except 1927 from Luo Zhiru *Tongzhibiao zhong zhi Shanghai* Nanking, 1932, Table 29, p. 21; the rest from Zhou Yuanhe and Wu Shenyuan, 'Shanghai lishi renkou yanjiu' *Fudan xuebao (shehui kexueban)* 4, 1985, p. 96.

Notes

1. Robert Fortune *Three Years' Wanderings in the Northern Provinces of China* London, 1847, pp. 121-22
2. *Shanghaigang shihua* Shanghai, 1979, pp. 17-20; Zhu Menghua 'Shanghai de shachuanye' *Shanghai difangshi ziliao* vol. 3, Shanghai, 1984, p. 64
3. Rhoads Murphey *Shanghai—Key to Modern China* Cambridge, Mass., 1953
4. Zhu Menghua 'Shanghai zhujie de xingcheng ji qi kuangchong' *Shanghai difangshi ziliao* vol. 2, Shanghai, 1983, p. 32; John E. Orchard 'Shanghai' *Geographical Review* 26, January 1936, pp. 5-6
5. Chen-siang Chen *Shanghai*, Research Report No. 38, Geographical Research Centre, Graduate School, The Chinese University of Hong Kong, Hong Kong, 1970, p. 11; Chen Liyi and Qian Xiaoming 'Jianguo qian Shanghai zai quanguo jingji zhong de dihui' *Shanghai difangshi ziliao* vol. 3, p. 14
6. *Shanghaigang shihua*, table on p. 219
7. Maritime Customs *Decennial Reports, 1892-1901* Shanghai, 1904, 'Shanghai', p. 472
8. Orchard 'Shanghai' pp. 7, 11-13; Murphey *Shanghai* pp. 45-49
9. Murphey *Shanghai* p. 51; Whangpoo Conservancy Board *Port of Shanghai* 9th rev. edn, Shanghai, 1936, p. 1
10. For example, the statements of the British and the Japanese Chambers of Commerce in Richard Feetham *Report of the Hon. Richard Feetham, C.M.G., to the Shanghai Municipal Council* Shanghai, 1931, part III, pp. 268, 282
11. Marie-Claire Bergere '"The Other China": Shanghai From 1919 To 1949' in Christopher Howe (ed.) *Shanghai: Revolution and Development in an Asian Metropolis* Cambridge, 1981, pp. 6-7
12. Ernest O. Hauser *Shanghai: City for Sale* New York, 1940, p. 70
13. See, for example, the crime statistics in The Shanghai Civic Association *Statistics of Shanghai* Shanghai, 1933.
14. Murphey *Shanghai* p. 33
15. Zhang Dachun 'Shanghai zhujie nianbiao' *Shanghai difangshi ziliao* vol. 2, p. 88
16. Robert W. Barnett *Economic Shanghai: Hostage to Politics 1937-1941* New York, n.d., pp. 4-7
17. Huang Wei *Shanghai kaibu chuqi duiwai maoyi yanjiu* Shanghai, 1979, pp. 117-18
18. Lin Jiehou 'Lunchuan zhaoshangju jianshi' *Shanghai difangshi ziliao* vol. 3, p. 72
19. Liu Huiwu *Shanghai jindaishi* vol. 1, Shanghai, 1985, p. 214
20. John Fairbank *Trade and Diplomacy on the China Coast* Stanford, 1969, pp. 317-21
21. *Shanghaigang shihua* pp.230-31
22. Ibid. pp. 230-32
23. Ibid. p. 234
24. Ibid. pp. 232-35
25. Ibid. p. 237
26. Ibid. pp. 237-39. The chronology of Shanghai's port expansion thus parallels closely that of the major 'fully imperial' ports in the Indian Ocean; see Frank Broeze, Peter Reeves & Kenneth McPherson 'Imperial Ports and the Modern World Economy: The Case of the Indian Ocean' *Journal of Transport History* 7, 1986, pp.1-20
27. William Crane Johnstone Jr *The Shanghai Problem* Stanford, 1937, p. 45
28. Ibid. pp. 98-99, 210
29. Ibid. p. 114
30. *Port of Shanghai* 9th edn, pp. 102-3
31. *Shanghaigang shihua* pp. 110-16
32. F.L. Hawks Pott *A Short History of Shanghai* Shanghai, 1928, pp. 156-58
33. Murphey *Shanghai* p. 39
34. Hauser *Shanghai* p. 21
35. Huang Wei *Shanghai* p. 25
36. Wu Zunyi *Qingmo Shanghai zhujie shehui* Taipei, 1978, p. 57
37. G. Lanning & S. Couling *The History of Shanghai* part I, Shanghai, 1921, pp. 464-68
38. C.A. Montalto de Jesus *Historic Shanghai* Shanghai, 1909, p. 49
39. Chen Wenyu 'Shanghai kaibu chuqi de yanghang' *Shanghai difangshi ziliao* vol . 3, pp. 198, 192
40. Lanning & Couling *History of Shanghai* pp. 379-81
41. Ibid. pp. 388-89
42. The other two yards were located at Guangzhou and Amoy respectively. Huang Wei *Shanghai* p. 113
43. Wu Xunyi *Qingmo Shanghai* p. 30
44. Liu Huiwu *Shanghai jindaishi* pp. 216-17
45. Huang Wei *Shanghai* pp. 115-16. A monumental *History of the Hong Kong and Shanghai Banking Corporation*,

46 by Frank H.H. King, is now being published, 4 vols., Cambridge, 1988
46 Xu Yanfei 'Huifeng yinhang ji qi maihan manji' *Shanghai difangshi ziliao* vol. 3, pp. 201-2
47 'Diguo zhuyi zai jiu Shanghai de jingji lueduo jianshu' *Shanghai difangshi ziliao* vol. 3, p. 10
48 Ibid. p. 1
49 Du Wenmin 'Jiu Shanghai de yanghang maihan' *Shanghai difangshi ziliao* vol. 3, pp. 219-20
50 Wu Xunyi *Quingmo Shanghai* pp. 104-5
51 Wang Jingyu 'Shijiu shiji waiguo chinhua qiye zhong de hua shang fugu huodong' *Lishi yanjiu* 4, 1965, p. 68
52 Nie Baozhang 'Cong meishang Qichang lunchuan gongsi de chuangban yu fazhan kan maihan de zhuoyong' *Lishi yanjiu* 2, 1964, pp. 94-98
53 Wu Xunyi *Qingmo Shanghai* p. 97
54 *Shanghai qianzhuang shiliao* Shanghai, 1960, 'Introduction', p. 9
55 Srinivas R. Wagel *Finance in China* Shanghai, 1914, p. 239; *Shanghai qianzhuang shiliao*, 'Introduction', p. 16
56 *Shanghaigang shihua* pp. 275-76
57 Huang Wei *Shanghai* pp. 120-21
58 Ibid. p. 121
59 See my article, 'Chinese Entrepreneurs, the Government, and the Foreign Sector: Silk-Reeling Enterprises in Shanghai and Guangzhou, 1861-1932' *Modern Asian Studies* 18, 1984, pp. 353-70
60 Maritime Customs *Decennial Reports, 1912-21* Shanghai, 1924, 'Shanghai', p. 26
61 *Decennial Reports, 1892-1901* 'Shanghai', p. 65
62 Tōa dōbunkai *Shina shōbetsu zenshi* vol. 15, Tokyo, 1920, pp. 793-94
63 *Decennial Reports, 1912-21* 'Shanghai', pp. 24-25, 30
64 *Decennial Reports, 1922-31* Shanghai, 1933 'Shanghai', p.26
65 Akira Nagano 'Development of Capitalism in China' in Institute of Pacific Relations *Economic Trends and Problems in the Early Republican Period* New York, 1980, pp. 79-80
66 *Port of Shanghai* 9th edn, p. 71
67 C. Y. Hsieh and M. C. Chu 'Foreign Interest in the Mining Industry in China' in *Economic Trends and Problems* pp. 48-49 and Table 1
68 *Port of Shanghai* 9th edn, p. 71
69 Orchard 'Shanghai' pp. 27-29
70 Wei Dazhi 'Shanghai "gudao jingji fanrong" shimo' *Fudan xuebao (shehui kexue ban)* 4, 1985, pp. 109-113
71 *Guide to China's Foreign Economic Relations and Trade: Import-Export Special* Hong Kong, 1984, p. 651
72 *Shanghaigang shihua* p. 350
73 *Zhongguo jingji nianjian (1986)* Hong Kong, 1986, p. vii-52
74 *China Handbook (1985-86)* Hong Kong, 1985, p. 250
75 Compiled and computed from figures in *Zhongguo jingji nianjian (1986)* pp. vi-238, vii-52, and *Guide to China's Foreign Economic Relations and Trade: Import-Export Special* p. 651
76 *China Handbook (1985-86)* p. 234
77 *Zhongguo jingji nianjian (1986)* p. vii-15
78 *China Handbook (1985-86)* p. vii-137
79 See Introduction to the present volume.

Further reading

Murphey, R. *Shanghai—Key to Modern China* Cambridge, Mass. 1953. The definitive modern study of Shanghai.

China. Maritime Customs *Decennial Reports, 1882-91* Shanghai 1893; *Decennial Reports, 1892-1901* 2 vols, Shanghai 1904, 1906; *Decennial Reports, 1902-1911* 2 vols, Shanghai 1913; *Decennial Reports, 1912-1921* 2 vols, Shanghai 1924; *Decennial Reports, 1922-1931* 2 vols, Shanghai 1933. A wealth of economic and political information on Shanghai and other treaty ports.

Howe, Christopher (ed.) *Shanghai: Revolution and Development in an Asian Metropolis* Cambridge 1981. A collection of authoritative articles on the recent history of Shanghai.

Lanning, G. and S. Couling *The History of Shanghai* 2 vols, Shanghai 1921, 1923. A classic history.

The Shanghai Civic Association *Statistics of Shanghai* Shanghai 1933. A compendium of useful social and economic statistics.

Shanghai difangshi ziliao 3 vols so far, Shanghai 1983- . A continuing collection of articles and reminiscences on the local history of Shanghai from the Chinese perspective.

distance shipping routes and the technology of the oceangoing steamer and, later, motorship. Through a combination of favourable geographical location and massive port construction Colombo was thus able for about half a century (from the early 1880s to the late 1920s) to be one of the busiest ports in Asia, indeed in the world. The explanation for this phenomenon lies primarily in the fact that it served both as the almost exclusive gateway to the export-oriented economy of Sri Lanka and as the central hub in the shipping network of the Indian Ocean, servicing a large part of the merchant fleets which traversed it. To explain how this came about and why Colombo could not maintain its pre-eminence is the purpose of this chapter. In order to accentuate both the general and the specific conditions affecting Colombo, it may be useful first to briefly survey the rise of two adjacent, but in their functions quite different, ports: Bombay and Singapore.

Bombay owes its prominence very much to its functions as a gateway to western India and an entrepot and transshipment point for the whole western Indian Ocean region. Its development as a port can be traced back to the year 1668 when it was transferred from the British Crown to the East India Company. To meet the immediate demands of trade the company constructed a customs house, a warehouse and a mole station capable of berthing small ships. A few years later Sir Gerald Aungier, the governor of Bombay, described the port as 'certainly the fairest, largest and securest in all these ports of India in a hundred, for tall ships may ride all the year safe with good anchorage'. The advantages brought about by the provision of such facilities not only made Bombay the headquarters of the East India Company but also helped to develop regular trade with the principal seaports of India, the Persian Gulf and East Africa. As Anglo-Indian trade expanded, Bombay, besides being the chief emporium of western India, also attracted to itself a larger share of the trade of British India than Calcutta and Madras, the country's other great ports.

In 1813 the monopoly of the East India Company was abolished, and the commerce of India was thrown open, the result of which also was to Bombay's gain as it attracted the traders of many other western Indian ports. A few years later steam navigation was started from Bombay. In 1829 the *Hugh Lindsay* became the first steamship to establish a regular service from that port to Suez. The success of this service led to the commencement in the 1840s of an ever larger and more intensive network of mail services in the Indian Ocean and East Asian waters which for a long time was to be dominated by the Peninsular & Oriental and British Indian Steam Navigation Companies.

The success of Bombay was achieved despite great disabilities in land-based transport facilities which precluded the hinterland being exploited to its maximum advantage. Here the breakthrough came in 1853, when the railway was introduced. In the expansion of the railway network that followed, Bombay was the focus of the main lines in western India and thus reinforced its hegemony as a port. The opening of the Suez Canal was the next major event as it shortened voyage time between England and Bombay from a hundred to twenty-five days.[1]

The revolutionary changes in transport infrastructure also resulted in an increasing number of India's industries being located in and around Bombay. In consequence of such developments nearly 40 percent of India's seaborne trade passed through that port by the end of the nineteenth century and it ranked as the second largest port of the subcontinent, closely behind Calcutta.[2] With regard to services to shipping, however, Bombay was of no more than minor importance. It had the Royal Navy Headquarters for the Indian Ocean, but despite its long tradition for shipbuilding and repair, carried and personified by the Wadia dynasty,[3] it was not able to maintain this role in the era of iron and steam. Located off the routes to the East and Australia, moreover, Bombay never became a fuelling port for transient traffic.

In contrast to Bombay, Singapore, on the eastern edge of the Indian Ocean, rose to pre-eminence more because of her advantageous geographical position in Southeast Asia and the Malay world (and to a lesser extent Australia) and less because of other factors. Its location was such that it was within easy reach from China, Indo-China and Thailand as well as from the Indonesian archipelago. It also lay athwart the natural shipping route between India and China and when the steamer arrived, it was the logical choice as a bunkering station in Southeast Asia.[4]

For the same reasons, the site proved to be ideal for Singapore to be a great ship repair yard in that part of the Indian Ocean. Quite apart from the heavy traffic traversing its region, the seasonal cyclones of the Bay of Bengal and the waters of Southeast Asia cause significant additional dangers. For many, even in faraway but expensive Australia, Singapore was the nearest dockyard. As the steamer tonnage passing through the Suez Canal to and from the Far East and Australia grew in leaps and bounds towards the end of the nineteenth century, so did Singapore's ship repair works expand. In fact so extensive did ship repair activities become that by 1899 no less than five dock companies were established in Singapore; the largest of them, the Tanjong Pagar Dock Company, alone owned five dry docks.[5]

Singapore's location in the Straits Settlements was exploited to the fullest advantage to make it the greatest entrepot in Southeast Asia. Established first as a centre where products of eastern and western Asia were exchanged, it subsequently became a convenient centre of trade for the Malay peninsula, Sumatra and numerous smaller islands. Then, as indicated earlier, Singapore, being located an easy sailing distance from Burma, Thailand, China and Indo-China, also served as a rendezvous for the merchants of those countries. In addition there were a host of other factors which further strengthened Singapore's role as an entrepot. The first was its status as a free port, there being no harbour, port, dock, town or light dues, while customs dues were levied only on opium, alcohol, tobacco and petroleum. The second was the commercial policy of the government which permitted the mercantile interests a complete freedom of trade that led to the setting up of powerful European agency houses, which firmly controlled Singapore's long-distance trade.[6] At the same time the city became the centre for Chinese mercantile and shipping enterprise in the region; as the foundation of Straits Steamship Company Ltd

(1890) was to show, short- and long-term interests of both communities were closely intertwined.[7] At the same time the Western agency houses invested heavily in the development of the Malayan rubber industry which further augmented Singapore's already growing commodity trade. The Chinese, on the other hand, developed the tin-mining industry of Malaya which also made Singapore its base.[8]

While the opening of Hong Kong and the development of Saigon by the French to a certain extent undermined Singapore's role as an entrepot, these adverse effects by the last quarter of the nineteenth century were more than counterbalanced by the development of Malaya's rubber and tin industries, for which Singapore became the main outlet. In 1918, for example, out of a total trade of $512.2 million the rubber exports alone amounted to $153.5 million and thereby indicated a significant trend in Singapore becoming a gateway to a hinterland as well.[9]

Thus, in contrasting mixtures as gateways and entrepots, Bombay and Singapore rose to pre-eminence; curiously, however, at the end of the nineteenth century Colombo with its relatively narrow hinterland attracted a substantially larger volume of shipping and ranked, after Hong Kong, as the greatest Asian port. The purpose of this chapter is to offer an analytical study of the rise of Colombo to that position of pre-eminence.

The island of Sri Lanka in the mid-nineteenth century had some sixteen outports and three main ports. Of the latter Colombo on the western coast, which was an open roadstead, handled almost the whole of the import/export trade of the country. Trincomalee on the eastern coast, although one of the finest natural harbours in the world and capable of providing shelter to a large number of ships throughout the year, was away from the main trade routes of the Indian Ocean and was therefore used more as a naval base than for commercial purposes. Galle on the southern tip of Sri Lanka, on the other hand, was centrally situated both in relation to the monsoonal wind regime and the steamer routes across the ocean. Consequently, with the advent of steamers, Galle became the premier port in Sri Lanka. Of a total of 790 249

TABLE 6.1
The tonnage of shipping using the ports of Galle and Colombo, 1855-79 (quinquennial averages)

	Tonnage of shipping Sri Lanka	Tonnage of shipping Galle	(b) as a % of (a)	Tonnage of shipping Colombo	(d) as a % of (a)
	(a)	(b)	(c)	(d)	(e)
1855-59	754 719	312 654	40.4	293 763	39.1
1860-64	931 034	406 885	43.5	356 490	38.5
1865-69	1 158 074	575 964	48.2	427 893	34.6
1870-74	1 785 203	903 703	50.3	668 871	37.2
1875-79	2 042 660	1 061 227	43.4	1 102 329	45.0

Source: Ceylon *Blue Books*

tons of shipping calling at Sri Lanka in 1860, Galle handled 45.5 percent, while the share of Colombo, through which almost the whole of the island's commodity trade flowed, was only 38.5 percent.[10] Table 6.1 shows that Galle maintained its lead until far into the 1870s.

Without a significant hinterland to generate cargoes, the supremacy of Galle over the other Sri Lankan ports hinged on the services it rendered to international shipping passing via Sri Lanka, most important of which were the British and French mail services to eastern India, Southeast Asia, China and Australia.

Galle's major function was as a port of call where shipping went for fuel, water, and provisions; and the beginning of the Australian branch line of the P & O (1859-1888) there, moreover, gave rise to a not unimportant transit and tourist trade; it should, nevertheless, be emphasised that the company handled very little else than cabin-class passengers and mail. The chances of Galle developing into a major ship repair yard was stymied by the competition from Calcutta, as homeport of the British India Steam Navigation Company, Bombay and, especially, Singapore. Thus, the ascendancy of Galle to greatness within the hierarchy of ports in the Indian Ocean lay purely in its ability to serve transient shipping. But by virtue of Sri Lanka's advantageous geographical position in the Indian Ocean, any of the main ports on the island had the potential to attract shipping passing her shores for those services.

Reference was made to the fact that despite the supremacy of Galle in terms of shipping tonnage, Colombo by 1860 was the gateway through which almost the whole of Sri Lanka's overseas trade passed. The reasons for Colombo's pre-eminence in this respect are to be found in the internal geography and transport infrastructure of Sri Lanka. The major Sri Lankan exports of coffee, tea and later rubber, grown in the wet-zone area, were served more economically by Colombo than by either Galle or Trincomalee. During Portuguese and Dutch times cinnamon, the staple export of the time, was grown in the vicinity of Colombo and hence Colombo became its main outlet. As the area under cinnamon expanded under Dutch times, to facilitate its export Colombo was linked with the cinnamon-growing areas with a network of artificial canals. But during the three centuries of Portuguese and Dutch rule, Colombo served only a narrow stretch of the southwest coast of Sri Lanka; it was under the British that Colombo's hinterland was subjected to a vast transformation.

In the 1840s coffee replaced cinnamon as the island's staple export. Coffee production collapsed in the 1880s, but by the 1890s tea had more than taken its place. By the first decade of this century coconut and rubber were added to the booming plantation sector. For all these commodities, Colombo was the natural outlet as it had been for cinnamon. Coffee was grown in the central hills; tea was grown later in substantially the same area; rubber was produced on the periphery of the tea belt; and coconut production for export was largely concentrated on the same coastal belt that has produced cinnamon for centuries. Colombo's share of the island's exports by value was about 80 percent in the 1860s, 85 percent in the 1870s and 95 percent in the 1890s.[11] A vital factor in its establishing this almost exclusive primacy was the city's domination of Sri Lanka's transport infrastructure.

The early development of coffee production had been greatly facilitated by a network of strategic military roads that stretched from Colombo to the central highlands. As coffee spread, that strategic network was extended and supplemented by new roads designed for specifically economic reasons. In the 1860s when the plantation coffee reached boom conditions the coffee area had some 615 miles of made roads and Sri Lanka as a whole had about 2500 miles of such roads.[12] Since the network of roads was designed primarily to assist the island's exports, it was largely centred on Colombo. Not surprisingly also, the first railway line in Sri Lanka (1867) linked Colombo and Kandy, and was built to serve the coffee plantations. Later as coffee and then tea moved more into the interior of highlands, further railway extensions were constructed. The first coastwise line likewise started from Colombo, reaching Kalutara in 1879 and extending later to Galle and Matara. Thus by the second half of the nineteenth century Colombo's position as Sri Lanka's gateway was reinforced by the expansion of the island's internal transport system rather than being undermined by Galle's rise as a coaling port.

Had hinterland been the only relevant factor, the growth of Colombo as a port would simply have reflected the development of Sri Lanka's plantation agriculture. But as Table 6.2 shows, it was much more than that.

TABLE 6.2
The tonnage of shipping using the Port of Colombo and the value of Sri Lanka's trade, 1858-82

	Tonnage of shipping using Colombo (in 1000 tons)	Total value of trade, Sri Lanka (in Rs. 1000)
1858-62	330	61 963
1863-67	409	85 605
1868-72	532	83 270
1873-77	937	106 339
1878-82	1 448	71 636

Source: Ceylon *Blue Books*

But the relationship between changes in the tonnage of shipping using Colombo and the value of Sri Lankan trade (most of which passed through Colombo) was far from exact. In particular, the volume of shipping more than quadrupled during the commercial stagnation of the eighties. Yet, while Colombo handled the bulk of the island's trade throughout the nineteenth century, it did not dominate shipping until the late 1870s. Only then it overtook, and then quickly outdistanced, Galle.

The explanation for this divergence is found in two factors. As referred to earlier, the early superiority of Galle over Colombo was not based on any great participation in Sri Lanka's export trades but arose solely from, on the one hand, the geography of the Indian Ocean and its favourable location for long-distance steamship liner services through it and, on the other, its qualities as a 'natural' harbour (as Hoyle would express it: its situation and its site).

The steamer was introduced to the eastern seas in the 1840s, but it was not until the 1860s that any qualitative change took place in the shipping that called at Sri Lanka. With the expansion of plantation coffee, the tonnage of shipping calling at Sri Lanka increased at rates as high as 43 percent, 137 percent and 61 percent during the three decades 1830 to 1840, 1840 to 1850 and 1850 to 1860 respectively, but the sailing vessel still dominated the scene.[13] In 1857, for example, out of a total of 876 563 tons of shipping calling at Sri Lanka steamers amounted only to 263 045 tons.[14] Even in that tonnage of steamers no great proportion was represented by cargo ships. The bulk of the steamer tonnage was contributed by the mail ships of the P & O in the Suez-Calcutta, Bombay-China and soon also Galle-Australia lines.[15] For these steamers not Colombo but Galle was the packet station, the port of call. Moreover, since those steamers were of small size they could still use the simple facilities provided for the sailing vessels of that era.

So long as the sailing vessel remained dominant, the ability of Sri Lanka to attract shipping for purposes other than handling her own overseas trade was obviously determined by her position in the network of sailing routes, and this network in turn was primarily shaped by the wind system of the Indian Ocean. The major features of that system were the southwest monsoon between May and October that dominated an area extending from the east coast of Africa to beyond the Philippines; the northeast monsoon that dominated the same area from October to April; a northerly monsoon that brought cyclones to Mauritius between December and March; the southeast trades that blew throughout the year between Madagascar and Australia; and the equally permanent westerlies that blew further south.[16]

At first sight, the effect of that wind system was of great navigational advantage for Sri Lanka, as the prominence of Taprobane in classical times already attested. Not only did Sri Lanka occupy a central position in the Indian Ocean but it was virtually the southern end of India. Although it was separated from the mainland by twenty miles of sea, Palk Strait was too shallow to be used by any vessels of considerable size. Therefore, the vessels that wished to round India had to round Sri Lanka. Because of the deepness of the seas around most of its coast, Sri Lanka is hardly affected by tides. It was easier, therefore, for small vessels to find convenient landing places. Above all, although Sri Lanka lay in the monsoonal area, it did not suffer the atmospheric disturbances that often marked inter-monsoonal periods in both the Arabian Sea and the Bay of Bengal. The cyclones that harassed the Coromandel Coast seldom or never reach the northeastern shores of Sri Lanka.[17]

But although Sri Lanka lay in the centre of the Indian Ocean and enjoyed conditions ideal for shipping, most of the major trade routes used by sailing vessels avoided it. They were those coming from Europe via the Cape to the Malabar coast; those coming round the Cape bound either for Australia or the Straits of Malacca; and those leaving the Coromandel coast and Calcutta for Europe. Consequently, Sri Lanka stood on three major trade routes. One was the route from Europe via the Cape to Madras, the other to Coromandel coast and Calcutta. Another was the route from Bombay to the Far East. But measured in terms of the shipping using it, by far the most important was the route between the Bay of Bengal and the Arabian Sea. Since Palk Strait was so shallow, all vessels of any significant size sailing from one side of India to the other had to sail round the southern extremity of Sri Lanka. As can be seen from Table 6.3 ships moving from different parts of India thus accounted for more than half the shipping using Sri Lanka during the 1860s.

TABLE 6.3
The distribution of tonnage of shipping using the ports of Sri Lanka among the major trade routes, 1860-69 (quinquennial averages)

	Tonnage of shipping calling on Sri Lanka	From and to UK	From and to British and Dutch possessions in Asia	From and to Far East and Australia	From and to the Middle East
1860-64	929 851	101 660	659 831	91 439	75 750
1865-69	1 198 054	130 804	798 517	123 258	112 909

Source: Ceylon, *Blue Books*

The bulk of Sri Lanka's imports of consumer goods (rice, curry stuffs, cotton cloths, etc.) was from India and it formed between 40 percent to 50 percent of the value of her foreign trade. And to carry that amount of trade with India it would not have demanded a tonnage of shipping as large as that given in Table 6.3. It is true that there were over 200 sailing vessels of less than a hundred tons owned by Indians and Sri Lankans in the transport of rice and immigrant labour. But a great number of them did not make more than six voyages a year. Dominant in the Indo-Sri Lankan trade, therefore, were the foreign-owned western-style sailing vessels. They were the largest class, averaging more than 500 tons, and hence it would not have required a large number to carry the commodity trade between Sri Lanka and India. Evidently, the tonnage of shipping was considerably made up of vessels not connected with Sri Lanka's own trade. One such category was that of P & O's mail steamers on the Suez-Calcutta line and the Bombay-China line which made Sri Lanka a coaling station.[18] Others were those of sailing vessels from Europe to eastern parts of British India, to and from the Bay of Bengal and Arabian Sea, and in trade between Bombay and China, many of which used Sri Lanka as a port of call.

For all those routes on which Sri Lanka was a port of call rather than a place of loading or discharge, Galle was more conveniently situated than Colombo. Not only was it nearer the southern extremity of the island that ships had to round, but it was particularly well served by currents, and for small vessels it had a good natural harbour provided by a bay well sheltered from the monsoons. It was natural, therefore, that throughout the period of sailing vessels Galle played an important role as a port of call in the Indian Ocean.

By the second quarter of the nineteenth century some steamers appeared in the Indian Ocean whose main function was to link India, the Far East and Australia; for such steamers Sri Lanka offered a valuable site for a coaling station. And partly because of its strategic position, coaling and other shipping services could be, and were, provided by Galle rather than Colombo. The early steamers were weak and their engines consumed great quantities of coal.[19] It was estimated that in the 1850s the average rate of coal consumption of steamers plying in the Indian Ocean was fifty-five tons per day in those sailing between Suez and Australia; forty-eight tons in those sailing between Aden and Calcutta, and thirty tons in those sailing between Bombay and China. Given the average speed of a steamer at nine knots and given also the rates of fuel consumption mentioned above, the amount of coal they would have needed for an unbroken voyage between the more important ports in the Indian Ocean would be as much as 720 tons between Aden and Calcutta; 505 tons between Bombay and Singapore; and 880 tons on the journey between Aden and Singapore.[20]

The carriage of such amounts of coal meant an uneconomic use of potential cargo space.[21] Consequently, unbroken voyages between those termini without a call for recoaling became rare and for recoaling on each of those routes Sri Lanka was the best located place. As long as steamers remained small enough, the natural harbour of Galle which was on the direct route was better situated than Colombo. The latter not only was an open roadstead but also some thirty miles off the shortest steamer routes; Trincomalee was no less than one and a quarter days' steaming distance from the main routes. Consequently, in the 1850s, Galle acquired a flourishing coal trade, and annually an average of about 50 000 tons, mainly from Cardiff, was imported. Once Galle was chosen as a coaling station, the shipping lines also used it for other purposes such as the transfer of mail and passengers from one route to the other.

In the 1860s the main lines of the P & O using the facilities offered by Galle were: from Bombay via Singapore to Hong Kong; from Suez and Aden to Madras and Calcutta, Singapore, Shanghai and Yokohama; and, finally, the branch line to Melbourne and Sydney. The French Messageries Imperiales (later Maritimes) used Galle for both its services to Pondichery and to Saigon. Because of the rapid rise of the steamer traffic across the ocean as well as around the coast of India, Galle's steamer tonnage increased rapidly.[22] Steamers contributed 201 120 of the 433 548 tons using the Galle harbour in 1858, 471 032 out of 560 606 in 1866 and 572 051 out of 621 729 in 1869.

Thus by the time the Suez Canal was opened Sri Lanka had two major ports each performing specialised functions.[23] The port of Colombo which was patronised largely by sailing vessels handled the island's commodity trade. Steamer-dominated Galle harbour, by contrast, had developed into an important coaling station and in terms of shipping tonnage acquired more importance than Colombo. The opening of the Suez Canal meant not only that the East-West trade in the future would be in steamers but also that the size of steamers would increase with the growth of international trade. In fact, in anticipation of the opening of the Suez Canal massive investments were being made in Europe in bigger steamers, which largely made use of the newly developed and more economical compound engine. To take full advantage of that increasing shipping tonnage and productivity in the Indian Ocean, Sri Lanka had to develop its ports. Suddenly, both Galle and Colombo were painfully inadequate.

As the number and tonnage of shipping calling increased, Galle harbour not only ceased to appear commodious but also seemed dangerous for steamers of large dimensions because of the presence of large sunken rocks, the removal of which proved to be difficult and costly. It was estimated in the 1860s that the harbour was incapable of accommodating half the tonnage of shipping visiting the port. As damages and delays to shipping increased it became apparent that Galle harbour should be improved. But it was not the only one that required improvements. In the sixties, although there were few steamers using Colombo, it could confidently be expected that with the opening of the Suez Canal the trade of Sri Lanka with Europe, Asia, the Far East and Australia would be carried in steamers. Since the meagre colonial revenues would have to bear the full cost of port improvements, it appeared that heavy investments on two ports within some seventy miles of the same coast was a waste of funds. Hence in the choice between Colombo and Galle for improvement, the plantation and commercial interests, who had formed a powerful pressure group in the legislature, were able to prevail upon the authorities to decide in favour of the former. Their argument rested principally on the point that since the cost of port improvement had to be borne by the general revenue, the port that served the merchandise trade of the island best should be the ultimate choice; but it is clear that it would have been well-nigh impossible and excessively expensive to relocate both Colombo's mercantile quarters and the island's transport infrastructure.

It was fully expected that Colombo, once it was made suitable for steamers, would become convenient as a port of call for the steamers which were visiting Galle. The results surpassed those expectations. By 1883 when the first stage of the port development programme (started in 1875) was nearing completion, out of a total shipping tonnage of 3 426 599 tons of shipping calling on Sri Lanka, Colombo's share was 81 percent, and that of Galle was 12.9 percent, whereas in 1869 Galle handled 51.7 percent of shipping calling on Sri Lanka, while the share of Colombo was only 33.6 percent.[24] Inevitably, the transfers of steam shipping from Galle to Colombo was accompanied by a shift of the coaling trade as well. In the sixties Colombo's share of the coal trade was not more than 11 000 tons per year, that of Galle never less than 50 000 tons. But by the 1880s Colombo's share had increased to 53 percent and by the opening years of this century it handled 98 percent of all coal imports to Sri Lanka.[25]

The diversion of Galle's shipping to Colombo was not the only result of the concentration of port investments on the latter after the opening of the Suez

Colombo: gateway and oceanic hub of shipping

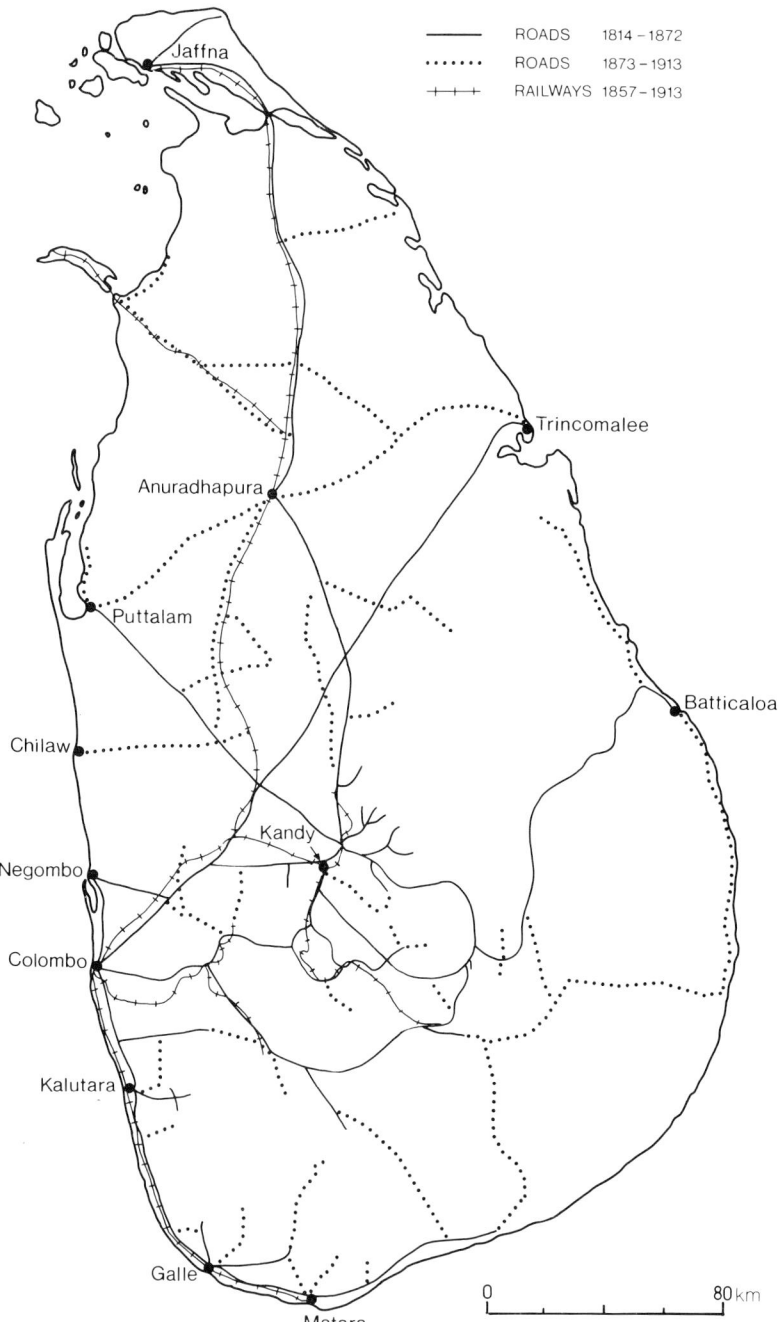

Map 12 The transport network of Sri Lanka, 1814-1913. Source: G. C. Mendis Ceylon under the British Occupation 3rd edn, Colombo 1952

Canal. Partly because of the strategic position of Sri Lanka vis-à-vis the steamer routes of the Indian Ocean (see map 11) and partly because of the excellent facilities claimed to have been provided, Colombo became the 'Clapham Junction' of the East. Between the periods 1883-1887 and 1893-1897 the volume of shipping calling at Sri Lanka rose spectacularly by 73.6 percent; the proportion of it calling at Colombo rose from 80.2 percent to 85.4 percent.[26] Total port revenue, total harbour dues and the yield on dues levied specifically on shipping, all doubled; and by the mid-1880s the general revenue of the colony was freed from the burden of servicing the loans raised for the harbour.

Significantly, with the combining of both gateway and port-of-call functions at Colombo, the availability of partly empty shipping tonnage had a stimulating effect on Sri Lanka's export industries. Indeed, shipping and trade moved and interacted in tandem: more trade demanded more shipping; more shipping promoted new branches of trade by keeping freight rates low. This interaction was vividly described by a contemporary as follows:

It is not the port and town of Colombo and the immediate neighbourhood, which exclusively benefit by the greater increased resort of mail, mercantile and calling steamers to the grand harbour. The benefits extend to all interests in the colony. Mail steamers and calling steamers which call mainly to coal and which in the latter case, are glad of a little cargo to drop here or carry away, are all competing for the freight we have to offer. As a result not only the tea, cinchona, cocoa, and the products of the European capitalists, but such absolutely native and largely native products as are yielded by the coconut and the areca palms, the cinnamon shrub, the lemer grass and the plumbego are carried to ports of sale at rates the lowest of which can be remunerative to the owners of the large fleets, which, by their resort to our harbour, have rendered Colombo one of the leading emporia of trade and navigation in the world.[27]

Given the enviable geographical position of Sri Lanka in the Indian Ocean, Colombo's rapid growth in shipping tonnage was facilitated further by factors such as the quality and efficiency of its port services. It had been a well-thought-out policy of both the colonial and imperial governments to maintain the sanitary conditions of Colombo, the motivation of which was the desire to have a clean port in a clean city. Frequent communications with India made the dockland area prone to the importation of epidemic diseases. The bulk of the grain imports of the country, on the other hand, came from plague-infested ports like Bombay and Rangoon. The bulk of the shipping used in the Eastern, Far Eastern and Australia trade and calling at Colombo was British and there was the danger of these infections being carried to the West. More importantly, the colonial government had the justifiable fear that if these diseases became endemic it would affect exports, because, by contrast to India, in Sri Lanka only Colombo could accommodate steamers of any size. For colonial as well as for imperial interests, the health of Colombo thus was of primary importance. To quote Governor Ridgeway:

The prosperity of Ceylon (Sri Lanka) is materially dependent on the prosperity of Colombo, practically its only sea port. Disastrous consequences would befall the whole country if Colombo were to become the home of epidemic disease, and therefore a foul port, and indeed the mischief would affect Imperial as well as insular interests.[28]

It was in view of these considerations that besides the measures introduced to improve the sanitation of Colombo, steps were also taken to provide the city with a pure and wholesome supply of water. The quality of water supplied to shipping at Colombo was so good that more ships took water from there than from all other regional ports. The revenue derived by the Colombo municipality on the sale of water, which formed 4 percent of its total revenue in 1887, the year in which the pipe-borne water supply was first introduced in the city, consequently rose to 8.8 percent in 1890 and to 14.2 percent at the eve of World War I.[29]

As no sufficient number of indigenous workers could be employed, the port was almost totally dependent on Indian immigrant labour. Although their supply was occasionally disrupted, a very high level of efficiency was generally maintained. The unexpected growth in the merchandise trade at the end of the nineties occasionally resulted in some congestion at warehouses and wharves, but in most years it functioned smoothly and with the maximum of efficiency; Colombo ranked as the greatest port in Asia for the expeditious dispatch of vessels. It is on record that at the eve of World War I a vessel arriving in port was moored and the operations of cargo discharge and coal bunkering and fresh water supply were all in progress after an hour from the vessel passing the harbour entrance. Coaling was carried out at the rate of 150 tons per hour compared with 110 tons at the beginning of the century and cargo-handling was carried out at the rate of a hundred tons an hour.[30]

This reputation for port efficiency helped Colombo to develop into an important transshipment point for goods and passengers. In contrast to most regional ports, Colombo was a central port of call in the Indian Ocean for all major steamship companies in the region. Although not a major terminus, it did become a real hub in the oceanwide network of liner services. Consequently, with the rise of plantation industries in the neighbouring countries, particularly the expansion of tea and rubber cultivation in the Presidencies of Madras and Travancore, Colombo's transshipment trade saw a rapid growth. In the early 1890s the amount of transshipment goods handled at the port did not average more than 300 000 packages a year, but the amount of such cargo handled at Colombo had doubled at the turn of the century and trebled by 1908.[31]

Far more important than transshipment, however, was the growth of Colombo's passenger traffic. This traffic fell into two distinct categories. The first was that of the Indian immigrant coolies for the plantations who had started coming since the beginning of the plantation coffee in the mid-1830s. The route used was that between Tuticorin (in South India) and Colombo and the tonnage of shipping involved to transport them was not very significant. The affluent European passengers that formed the second category consisted of two groups. There were the tourists whose numbers increased towards the end

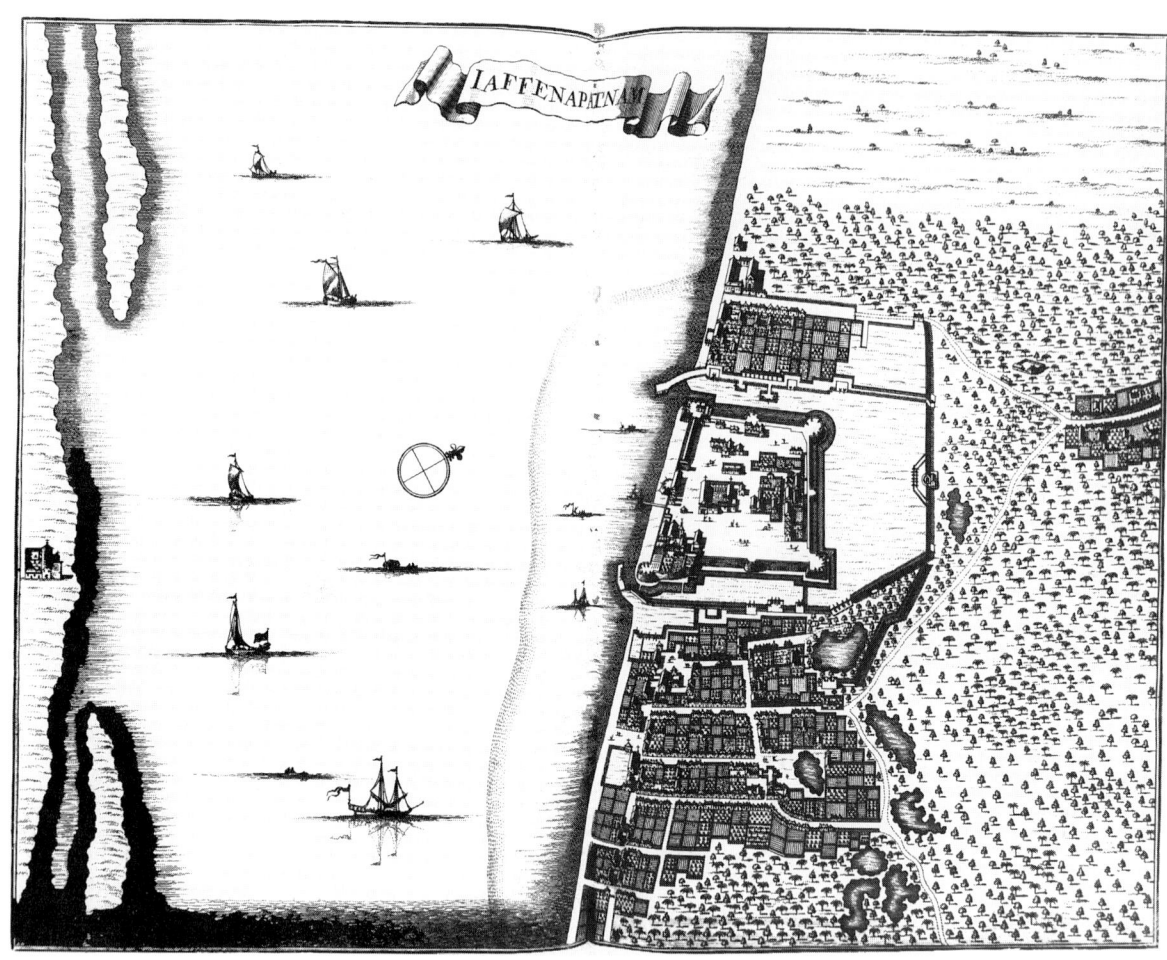

Jaffna, the lesser port of the island and centre of the Tamil community of Sri Lanka. In this distinctive view of Jaffna the key element of the town is the fort, and the rest of the town is quite small. From Francois Valentijn Oud en Nieuw Oost Indien *Dordrecht, 1724-26. Courtesy of Mitchell Library, State Library of New South Wales.*

of the century because of the large number of shipping lines calling on Colombo and the facilities the city provided for them. The attractions in Colombo and Sri Lanka were such that it was said to be challenging Egypt as a winter resort for the moderately rich European middle class. According to the records of the port surgeon, the number of such holiday-makers arriving in Colombo rose from less than 2000 in 1883 to 3086 in 1892 and to 6430 in 1905.[32]

More numerous than these were the passengers in transit staying for a few hours as sightseers or for up to a few days between leaving one vessel and boarding another. For short-term sightseers there are no statistics. But according to the commercial literature of the period, passengers staying in Colombo while in transit averaged about 25 000 a year by the end of the century.[33] For it was in Colombo that a traveller to any port in the Indian Ocean could find a vessel and it was through Colombo that many passengers from Europe or Australia passed to India.

Sri Lanka's central position together with Colombo's transformation into a large secure and modern habour made it within an astonishingly short span of three decades (1880-1910) into one of the leading ports of the world. As shown in Table 6.4 Colombo in the first decade of this century was the greatest Indian Ocean port in terms of the tonnage of shipping it handled, and in Asia it was second only to Hong Kong by a slight margin. Among the British imperial ports, Colombo ranked third, while worldwide it took the seventh position.

TABLE 6.4
World ranking of ports, 1910

Name of port	Tonnage of vessels entered
1 New York	12 154 780
2 London	11 605 698
3 Antwerp	11 005 761
4 Hamburg	10 944 909
5 Hong Kong	10 085 595
6 Rotterdam	8 600 496
7 Colombo	8 091 123
8 Liverpool	7 749 994
9 Marseilles	7 187 638
10 Singapore	7 045 193
11 Montevideo	6 936 983
12 Cardiff	5 771 475

Source: Administration Report of the Principal Collector of Customs, Colombo, for 1910

Although slightly checked by World War I, the trend in the growth of shipping, as well as of merchandise trade and coal imports of Colombo continued well into the later 1920s. The average tonnage of shipping entering the port, which was 14 202 000 in the period 1909-1913, declined to 8 652 000 in 1914-18, but then rose to 12 661 000 in 1919-23, and leapt forward to 19 620 000 in 1924-28. The average volume of imports and exports of merchandise trade for the same periods was 1 310 000, 1 368 000, 1 411 000 and 1 881 000 tons.

The volume of coal imports for the same years averaged 742 000 tons, 436 000 tons, 655 000 tons and 673 000 tons.[34] In the realm of shipping the importance of the route to and from India declined slightly in the immediate postwar years because of the restrictions in rice exports of that country following poor harvests, but that of the routes to Australia and the Far East continued to rise. The increasing volume of shipping in turn meant an increasing demand for coal, for shipping stores and for water.

An important development in the post-World War years, however, was the coming of the oil-burners which could not have been foreseen by the port planners of the late nineteenth century. Quite apart from introducing a new branch of trade, the switch from coal to oil also signalled the possibility that the dominance of Colombo as a leading port for international shipping in Asia could be undermined in the thirties unless its services were offered efficiently and at competitive rates.

It is unfortunate that the records are silent about the number of oil-burning vessels visiting the port before 1923. But the fact that in 1924 a total of 382 oil-burning vessels called at the port and the fact that the demand for oil increased by 20 percent over the previous year are ample proofs of the growing importance of the oil-bunkering trade at Colombo. But a comparison with Aden, however, shows a striking result, which is set out in Table 6.5.

TABLE 6.5
The oil trade of Colombo and Aden, 1924-32

Year	Colombo		Aden	
	Average oil imports (1000 tons)	Average no. of ships bunkering	Average oil imports (1000 tons)	Average no. of ships bunkering
1924-6	201	256	207	335
1927-9	214	318	351	540
1930-2	228	377	433	582

Source: Sessional Paper XIII of 1935: Report, Chairman Colombo Port Commission on oil dock.

In a decade during which oil imports at Aden had more than doubled, those at Colombo had remained almost stationary despite an increase of 50 percent in the number of vessels taking on oil, figures that suggested that many of the larger vessels were taking on enough oil at Aden to reach Singapore or vice versa. Nor was the sluggishness of the oil trade the only sign that Colombo's position as a great port of call in the Indian Ocean seemed to be in jeopardy. The decline in coal sales no doubt reflected mainly the switch to oil. But there was an ominous failure of the sale of shipping stores to recover after the depression. The value of sales had sunk from Rs.27 876 604 in 1929 to Rs.17 365 395 in 1932 and fell still further—Rs.15 619 219 in 1937,[35] although there had been some recovery in prices.

Figures of the sale of water were even more alarming. As referred to earlier, one of the attractions of Colombo as a port had been the quality and abundance of its water supplies, and sales of water to shipping had risen from some 24 million gallons a year at the end of the nineteenth century to nearly 120 million tons in 1929. By 1936 those sales had fallen to 87 million tons and threatened to fall further. The port commission put the blame firmly on the high prices charged by the municipality for water:

> Comparisons made from time to time with corresponding charges at neighbouring ports have revealed that the municipal charge in Colombo is the highest and that Colombo must suffer a substantial loss in its trade in water supplied to shipping until, and unless the charge levied by Municipality is reduced to a competitive level ... [T]he decreased consumption is overwhelmingly due to decreased intake by regular callers. This confirms the information supplied to this department by various shipping agents that their liners have distinct instructions to take as little water as possible, and where feasible, none at all in Colombo on account of the high cost of water.[36]

Perhaps the most distressing symptom of Colombo's decline was the position of its graving dock. Despite the cheapness of local labour and of materials imported from India, the dock did not succeed in attracting much commercial business. This was largely due to the prior claims on the dock made by naval vessels, which often used it for long periods (since speed of turnaround was not of any moment to naval vessels in times of peace), with the result that merchant vessels in difficulties were able to get nothing but temporary repairs sufficient to allow them to proceed to a neighbouring port where more permanent work could be done. Ships not actually in distress, such as those seeking cleaning and painting, were even less likely to visit Colombo for such purposes.[37]

These various problems led the port commissioners to utter a serious warning:

> It must be borne in mind that Colombo can no longer rest on its advantageous position in the trade routes of the East to attract shipping to its shores. Be it fuel or water, repairs or harbourage, there are well equipped ports in close proximity to Colombo offering efficient facilities at economic rates, and unless Colombo can offer similar attractions at competitive rates, it must ere long cede its position of ascendancy as a port of call. The increasing use of fuel oil for marine engine propulsion has enabled vessels to cover longer distances without stopping to re-fuel.[38]

Such a trend had, in fact, become visible since the early 1920s. Whereas in 1914-18 36 percent of the tonnage of shipping using Colombo was accounted for by ships which neither took nor unloaded cargo, in 1934-38 that percentage had been more than halved.

The situation at Colombo in the 1930s was further complicated by the fact that by that time the dimensions of the oil-burning vessels had greatly increased. For example, in 1938 out of 2166 steamers that called at Colombo, about 300 vessels were between 500 and 600 and about one hundred vessels were over 600 feet in length. Consequently, the existing berths were quite insufficient to accommodate the longer vessels and there had been a chronic congestion. To overcome this problem improvements in existing facilities were not any more sufficient; new alongside wharves would have to be constructed. The dearth of alongside accommodation, for instance, was so acute that to avoid frustration it became the common practice for ships to apply to local agents

TABLE 6.6
The percentage of shipping that entered and cleared at Colombo with working cargo, 1914-39 (quinquennial averages in 1000 tons)

	Total tonnage (a)	Tonnage with working cargo (b)	(b) as a % of (a)
1914-18	8 652	5 747	66
1919-23	12 661	10 798	85
1924-28	19 620	16 334	84
1929-33	22 791	19 524	86
1934-38	22 874	19 148	88
1939	20 741	18 510	90

Source: Ceylon *Blue Books*

for alongside berths well before their arrival at the port. Evidently the extent of such facilities at Colombo being limited, it was rare for such applications to be granted. In consequence, delays numbered fifteen in 1933, twenty-three in 1934, twenty-eight in 1935 and also in 1937.[39] Inevitably, these refusals and delays further undermined Colombo's popularity as a port of call for bunkers and other services which in addition to the longer-range capability of the diesel engine eroded its position as the hub for shipping in the Indian Ocean. The obvious solution seemed to lie in the modernisation of port facilities in tune with the advances in maritime technology and by 1939 the Colombo Port Commission planned to provide such facilities at an estimated cost of 12 million rupees.[40] The actual implementation of the plan, however, had to await the conclusion of World War II.

The example of Colombo during the sixty years or so until World War I shows clearly the advantages of a functional approach in the study of the development of ports. The solution of Sri Lanka's port dichotomy through the construction of a large and secure harbour at Colombo made it the maritime centre of both the island's economy and the Indian Ocean. While the rejection of Galle was conditioned as much by its specific disadvantages as by the terrestrial transport advantages and the vested interests of Colombo, port construction and then the handling of much larger tonnages of shipping had a profound influence on the economic and social life of the island's capital. The technologically and financially impressive response of the Ceylonese colonial government in financing and building the new harbour could, however, not permanently tie down shipping or isolate Colombo from external change.[41] The transition from coal to oil firing, the increasing efficiency of the marine steam engine and the introduction of the motorship with diesel power plants, however, seriously undermined both the quality of Colombo's facilities and port's strategic preeminence as the hub of the Indian Ocean. Not until the container age, and then under quite different circumstances, would Colombo be able to again expand its supra-regional functions.[42]

Notes

1. *Report of the Commission on Major Ports of India* New Delhi, Government of India, 1970, pp.7-8
2. About the ranking of major Indian ports in the 19th century, see Chapter 9 in the present volume.
3. R.A. Wadia *The Bombay Dockyard and the Wadia Master Builders* Bombay, 1955
4. *Singapore Port History*, compiled by the Port of Singapore Authority Singapore, n.d., p. 4
5. Ibid. p.7
6. C.M. Turnbull 'The European Mercantile Community in Singapore, 1819-1867' *Journal of South East Asian History* 10, 1969, pp.12-35
7. K. Tregonning *Home Port Singapore. A History of Straits Steamship Company Limited 1890-1965* Singapore, 1967, chs 1-2
8. B.C. Jayaswiya, Origins of the Ports of Singapore and Colombo and a Comparative Study of Certain Aspects of Operational Efficiency, unpublished Diploma in Ports and Shipping Administration, Department of Maritime Studies, University of Wales Institute of Science and Technology, 1980, pp.10-11
9. Ibid. p.13
10. Figures obtained from the annual Ceylon Government *Blue Book*
11. Compiled from the Customs Returns of the Principal Collector of Customs
12. Compiled from the Administration Reports of the Director of Public Works
13. Figures obtained from Ceylon *Blue Books*
14. Public Record Office (Kew), Colonial Office [henceforth CO], 54/337: Report on the extension and improvement of Galle Harbour, 14 November 1858
15. CO 54/354: Ward to Newcastle, 17 April 1860
16. C.N. Parkinson *Trade in the Eastern Seas* Cambridge, 1937, p.98
17. John Ferguson *Ceylon in 1903* Colombo 1904, p.94
18. Sessional paper XIV of 1871, *Memorandum on the Geographical Position of Ceylon*
19. Ibid
20. CO 54/337: Report on the extension and improvements of Galle Harbour
21. On the technological problems of the early steamers, and hence the need for subsidisation of lines over long distances see Frank Broeze 'The International Diffusion of Steam Navigation' *Economisch- en Sociaal-Historisch Jaarboek* 45, 1982, pp.77-95, and the sources mentioned there
22. H.L. Hoskins *Trade Routes to India* London, 1928, pp.255-61
23. CO 54/337: Report on the extension and improvement of Galle Harbour, Sessional paper IX of 1869; Ceylon *Blue Books*
24. Compiled from Ceylon *Blue Books*
25. Ibid.
26. Ibid.
27. A.M. & J. Ferguson *Ceylon Handbook & Directory, 1887-8* Colombo, 1888, p.145
28. Sessional Paper XXI of 1897: Quarantine Regulations in Ceylon
29. Compiled from the Annual Administration Reports of the Chairman, Colombo Municipal Council
30. Sessional Paper XIII of 1921, Harbour of Colombo, by A.D. Prouse
31. Compiled from Ceylon *Blue Books*
32. Annual Administration Reports of the Principal Medical Officer of Health for the relevant years
33. Ferguson *Ceylon in 1903* p.75
34. Compiled from Ceylon *Blue Books*
35. Ceylon *Blue Books*
36. Administration Report of the Chairman, Colombo Port Commission, for 1936
37. Sessional Paper XIII of 1921, Harbour of Colombo, by A.D. Prouse
38. Administration Report of the Chairman, Colombo Port Commission, for 1936
39. Sessional Paper XIII of 1935: Administration Report of the Chairman, Colombo Port Commission, 1937
40. Administration Report of the chairman, Colombo Port Commission for 1939
41. See Chapter 8 in this book, in which the primacy of external, 'maritime' influences on port development is argued
42. See K.S. Dharmasena 'Bombay and Colombo 1948-1984: A Study in Port Development with Special Reference to Containerisation' *The Great Circle* 9, 1987, pp.119-33

Further reading

Dharmasena, K. *The Port of Colombo 1860-1939* Colombo 1980 An analysis of the dramatic development of the Port of Colombo to the seventh greatest port in the world in 1910; discussion of the circular causation of increasing trade leading to more shipping and vice versa.

Vandendriesen, I.H. 'Some Trends in the Economic History of Ceylon in the Modern Period' *Ceylon Journal of Historical and Social Studies* 3 4 1960. Development of the first plantation crop, coffee, with the way the internal transport systems developed with Colombo as their maritime terminal.

Ferguson, A.M. and J. *Ceylon Handbook & Directory, 1887-8* Colombo 1888. An authentic account of the economy of contemporary Sri Lanka; shows how the vast fleets calling in to Colombo made it one of the leading emporia of trade and navigation in the world.

Gunasekara, H.A. de S. *From Dependent Currency to Central Banking in Ceylon* London 1962. An examination of the evolution and behaviour of the currency and banking system of Sri Lanka from 1825 to 1957.

Gunawardana, Elaine *The External Trade and Economic Structure of Ceylon, 1900-1955* Colombo 1965. An analysis of the development of Sri Lanka's tea, rubber and coconut export crops.

Panditharatne, B.L. 'Colombo: A Study of Urban Geography' PhD thesis, University of London 1960. First chapter discusses the geographical and strategic importance of Sri Lanka in the Indian Ocean and shows how it helped Colombo to emerge as a leading port in South Asia.

CHAPTER

Michael Roberts

The two faces of the port city: Colombo in modern times[1]

Almost all surveys of the development of Colombo city since the colonial era have dwelled on the commercial objectives of the imperial powers and, consequently, paid particular attention to the growth of a plantation economy in British times (especially from the 1830s) and the construction of the artificial harbour in the 1870s and 1880s which converted the port into a major Asian entrepot. Thus, a recent survey by ESCAP observes: 'Historically, urbanization in Sri Lanka has largely been a function of trade and commerce. The port capital city, Colombo, eclipsed all the other port towns that thrived in commerce and trade.'[2] Such perspectives, however, are misleading in the sense that they neglect to stress the links which any port city, necessarily, must have with the hinterland in which it is embedded. In consequence, the influences of the land in shaping the development and life of Colombo have often been played down or even overlooked. While there can be little argument that the city, as Dharmasena argues in the preceding chapter in this volume, was strongly affected by the development of steamshipping in the Indian Ocean and the opening of the Suez Canal, it is also true that the economic and social development of Sri Lanka made a profound impact on it. The purpose of this chapter will, therefore, be to trace other than those maritime themes in the shaping of its settlement pattern and socio-cultural life. The history of Colombo will be projected against the broad themes in the history of the island, such as the social use of its space and, in particular, the socio-cultural and ideological relationship between its major cities and the countryside.

The story of Colombo cannot be related without reference to the centrality of the southwestern lowlands for the history of Sri Lanka as a whole after the thirteenth century. It was in this region, where most of the population resided from that date, which could well be described in Pearson's terms as the 'littoral society', in which Colombo in its evolution from seaside village to capital port city was embedded.[3] C. R. de Silva categorically affirms that in the mid-sixteenth century 'Kotte was undoubtedly the most populous as well as the largest and richest kingdom in Ceylon'.[4] The first (and unreliable) census in the early nineteenth century records 47 percent of the total population (or 399 408 people) within this region.[5] Not only did the southwestern lowlands produce several important commodities, including cinnamon, areca nut and the various products of the coconut tree, but from about 1400 the Sinhalese king also chose to make his residence at Kotte, about nine kilometres from the waterfront and open roadstead of Colombo. Once the Western powers established themselves, the centre of Sinhalese resistance shifted first to Sitawaka and then to Kandy, while in British times the principal export crops (coffee, tea, and, to a lesser extent, rubber) were also largely grown in the highland interior. Nevertheless, the most significant socio-political movements among the Sinhalese majority on the island during the last 150 years have had their mainsprings firmly located within the southwestern lowlands: the Buddhist revitalisation movement dating from the mid-nineteenth century, the reformist nationalist agitation for constitutional devolution dating from about the 1900s (or earlier), the temperance movement of the early twentieth century, the upsurge of Sinhala Buddhist nationalism and the rise of the underprivileged in the 1950s, and the subsequent radical nativist insurrection of the Janata Vimukti Peramuna in 1971,[6] all drew their leadership from Colombo's surroundings, its 'littoral society'.

Today, as in the nineteenth century, the largest concentrations of people are in this region. The census of 1971 showed the continued migration into the Colombo District and documented the powerful pull which that region has exerted also after independence. In demographic terms Colombo is a primate city whose supremacy has increased over the years: in 1871 the municipal city of Colombo had only about twice as many people as the municipal towns of Galle and Kandy. By 1921, it had 244 163 people or six times that of Galle and Kandy, while as much as 42 percent of Sri Lanka's population classified as urban.[7] As a result of government policies promoting import substitution and selective industrialisation in the last three decades, and the expansion of factories in places such as Ratmalana, Sapugaskanda, Oruwala, Ekele and Katunayake, the urban sprawl of Colombo is even more significant. One can therefore properly talk of an, albeit ambiguously defined, metropolitan area called 'Greater Colombo'.

The primacy of Colombo (or 'Greater Colombo') is equally visible in the range and quantity of its economic functions[8] as in its political domination over the rest of the island. Clearly derived from its status as the seat of government which in turn was the result of its port function, Colombo's political dominance is also cultural and symbolic.

In order to understand what Colombo symbolised for Sri Lanka, one needs to be aware of other symbolic centres on the island: notably Kandy, Anuradhapura and the shrine at Kataragama.[9] The significant aspect of these other symbolic centres is their association with the Buddhist religion and, in the case of Kataragama, with Hindu and Muslim devotees as well. In contrast, Colombo's symbolic appeals are more heterogeneous and 'cosmopolitan'. This is to be expected, given its twin functions as hub for the political economy of the island and as gateway for its overseas trade and other linkages.

From about the eighth century A.D. Colombo, or Kolontota as it was then known, had a Moor trading settlement; and it would appear that in the early sixteenth century its population was 'predominantly Muslim'.[10] The census of 1824 records that the population of 'the town of Colombo' and its 'Four Gravets' was 31 188. Unfortunately, it does not describe the town's ethnic composition. But it is significant that the *district* of Colombo contained 13 421 Moors, 4550 Burghers (persons of mixed blood, descending from Dutch settlers) and 2453 Chetties, as well as smaller numbers of 'Malabars', 'Natookoteyas', 'Parewas', Bengalese, Malays, Europeans, etcetera.[11] It could, therefore, be speculated that at least two-fifths of the population of Colombo town was non-Sinhalese; probably, this figure was much higher, as most non-Sinhalese would have resided in the urban centre itself, thus making it a symbol of the changing relations of Sri Lanka with the outside world.

In the course of the nineteenth century, under British influence, the ethnic diversity of the city was augmented by the arrival of southern Indian labourers (many of them to work in and around the port) and traders and Parsee, Borah and Sindhi merchants; at the same time the Burghers in the small urban centres tended to gravitate to Colombo. With the improvement of interior communications and in particular, the opening of the Colombo-Jaffna railway (1905), the influx of Ceylon Tamils increased and several Tamil 'colonies' appeared within the urban scene.[12]

Employment opportunities in the fast-growing port city thus led to a demographic invasion from the landside, which could not but alter the ethnic and cultural structure of Colombo's population. In the census year 1921, the municipality of Colombo still contained more non-Sinhalese than Sinhalese, the ethnic distribution being as follows:[13]

Sinhalese	47 percent
Ceylon Tamils	5 percent
Indian Tamils	16 percent
Moors[14]	16 percent
Burghers	6 percent
Others[15]	8 percent

As befitted an emerging new city which attracted and exploited the labour of migrant workers, of whatever ethnic stock (including Sinhalese from the hinterland), a disproportionate number of the residents in 1921 were males: 61 percent or 149 595 out of 244 163 people. The labour force (including women classified as earners) was largely concentrated in the tertiary sector. Thus, those engaged in industrial occupations amounted to only 16 percent of the workforce, whereas 37 percent were in trade and transport, nearly 12 percent in domestic services and 11 percent in government service and the liberal professions.[16] This was in keeping with the character of Colombo at that stage as a port city and an administrative-cum-commercial centre.

The ethnic heterogeneity of Colombo during British rule has been highlighted here because this heterogeneity is now on the wane. Since the socio-political transformations initiated after independence in the 1950s,[17] the power and dominance of the Sinhalese has been making itself felt. Perhaps the most outstanding symbolic statement in this regard has been the reordering of space at Kataragama in the 1960s and 1970s which has established the political dominance of the Basnaike Nilame and *Kapuralas* and marginalised the Hindu organisations which had influenced the organisation of that area for centuries.[18] At a more materialist level this process is encouraging a Sinhalisation of the government services, the major area of employment in Sri Lanka;[19] as Dharmasena has shown, this process was no less marked in the port of Colombo itself.[20] In the result, the proportion of Sinhalese in the city of Colombo in the 1970s has grown to well over 50 percent.[21] After the anti-Tamil pogrom of 1983, it will be still greater. If we grant that, for some time past, the municipal city of Colombo has been effectively encased within Greater Colombo, then, the transformation within Colombo would appear yet more complete. For so long a foreign enclave in a Sinhalese countryside, Colombo is now being reclaimed by the Sinhalese; and yet more specifically, as we shall see, by the Low-Country Sinhalese.

Colombo's twentieth-century primacy as a port was not inevitable or foreseeable, either in an ecologically determinist sense or any other sense. In pre-colonial times and in the sixteenth century it was a partially sheltered bay, an open roadstead rather like Beruwala in recent times. As such, Colombo was merely one of the numerous little ports on the southwestern coast of the island.[22]

It had the advantage over the others, however, in being close to the seat of the Sinhala kingdom at Kotte. In a situation in which trade was subject to state regulation and in which cinnamon was a royal monopoly,[23] this became a factor of crucial importance. It attracted the Moorish merchants just as much as it was to direct initial Portuguese activities.

As the Portuguese meddled successfully in the affairs of the Sinhala state and gained control of territory within the island, they made Colombo, the place of their commercial activity as well as the natural point where their maritime strength could be brought to bear, their seat of government. Their political power in the south, however, was under constant threat: initially from the kingdom of Sitawaka located in the foothills and subsequently from the kingdom of Kandy centred upon the highlands; and throughout from rebellions in the lowlands. Driven back to the sea on several occasions, their seapower proved to be their saving grace in providing an unfailing channel of reinforcement. The necessary corollary of that seapower was a series of fortifications at strategic locations along the coast to hold the islanders at bay until such succour could arrive.

In accordance with this strategy Colombo had a Portuguese fort from early on in the sixteenth century. When the Dutch ousted the Portuguese in the mid-seventeenth century, they reorganised and strengthened the fort—even reducing its area in the process.[24] Thus, for a long time colonial Colombo, between the friendly sea and the hostile land, was both port and fort. Its citadel function did not end with the British conquest of the kingdom of Kandy, but continued till about the 1860s. Colombo, however, was not the only colonial citadel. The Dutch, whose strategic position on Sri Lanka differed little from that of the Portuguese, had numerous other forts along the littoral. One of these, at Galle, bestrode a little natural harbour that was far superior to Colombo's. Galle, too, was pre-eminently port and fort.

That Colombo should eventually outpace Galle in its development was conditioned by two interlinked factors, the one ecological and the other political. In the first place the priorities of the colonial powers were conditioned by the fact that, from about 1594, the centre of Sinhalese resistance was located in Kandy. Access to Kandy was most practicable from the west.[25] The route from Galle to Kandy was not only longer, but was barred by the narrow ridges and valleys of Morowak Korale and Sabaragamuwa, besides the steep range of mountains around Adam's Peak known as the Southern Wall. Influenced by ecological factors as well as political developments over time, therefore, the axis of political power ran from Colombo to Kandy. It was for this reason that one of the first steps taken by the British after they gained control of the Kingdom of Kandy was to build a bridged, all-weather road from Colombo to Kandy (completed between 1820 and 1832). Once the Central Highlands became a centre of coffee production (1830s to 1880s), the primacy of this axis was confirmed, albeit now transformed into one of economic significance—a conduit from the plantations to the port of exportation and, beyond that, the world market. This was consolidated when the first railway line, commenced in 1857, headed from Colombo to Kandy and was completed in 1867. By the mid-nineteenth century, indeed, Colombo was beginning to be the hub of a network of modern road and rail communications in support of its gateway function.[26] In time, however, this transport infrastructure also helped to stitch the island together.

Despite the advantages of Colombo, the 1860s and 1870s saw a prolonged debate among the British ruling elements as to whether Colombo or Galle would be a preferable location for a modern harbour—the need for which had emerged as a result of the long-term implications of steam navigation and the opening of the Suez Canal. As is shown in K. Dharmasena's chapter (p. 152), the vested interests of the mercantile and shipping community of Colombo gained the day. In any case, there were solid arguments against the choice of Galle: sunken rocks and treacherous currents made the path into the harbour a dangerous one, while a breakwater could secure only limited berthing space.[27] Construction of the new harbour at Colombo began in 1875 and its first stage was completed around 1883. Thereafter, Colombo's central-place functions burgeoned, while Galle withered and lay dormant.

The development of the port transformed the city in many ways—physical as well as social. One direct ecological consequence was the metamorphosis in the character of 'Colombo North', the part of Colombo north of the railway line. This part of the city had contained several elegant residential streets, both near the sea front in Mutwal and in and around the Pettah. It was also the location for the two most prestigious schools of that era—the Colombo Academy and St Thomas' College. The port development scheme and its associated industries, however, converted large segments (e.g. Kockchikade and Gintupitiya) into a dockland area and a warren of related working-class tenements and small businesses, while accelerating the transformation of the Pettah from a residential domain for the Burghers into a hive of shops and slums.[28] Nor did the sea air—that much-prized asset in the British colonial way of life—continue to be salubrious and invigorating. It brought coal dust and, over time, besmirched the elegant facades of the mansions in the locality.

The residential elite of Colombo, both European and coloured, therefore moved house, most of them to the south.[29] The favoured localities were Cinnamon Gardens and the Kollupitiya-Bambalapitiya seafronts. Cinnamon Gardens had been government plantations on the outskirts of the town in the late eighteenth century. When the British decided in the 1830s to terminate all government monopolies, this land came on the market. The Ceylonese elites who were emerging as a result of the expansion of opportunities associated with the plantation economy were in a position to invest in such land. In the 1870s the colonial government constructed a museum and a park in this area. And as the institutionalisation of leisure by the Victorians took root, several British clubs—the turf club, the lawn club, the golf clubs, and a cricket, a hockey and a football club—located themselves in and around this new suburb. These clubs debarred Ceylonese and blacks from membership. The emerging Ceylonese middle class, therefore, set up their own clubs—many of them located in the southern part of Colombo, and mostly in or near Cinnamon Gardens: one has only to pursue the history of such clubs as the Colts, the SSC, and the NCC to realise this.[30] It was not long before the Colombo Academy (now known as the Royal College) and St Thomas' College were moved to the southern part of Colombo: St Thomas' shifted to Mount Lavinia beyond the city limits in 1918 and Royal College relocated itself in the heart of Cinnamon Gardens by 1923.[31]

In early British times Colombo was a port, citadel and colonial power centre. Its role as the ultimate bastion of British power did not decline after the conquest of Kandy in 1815 or the completion of the Colombo-Kandy road in 1832. The massive rebellion in the Kandyan provinces in 1817-18 remained firmly etched in the British memory. They remained suspicious of the Kandyan headmen and Buddhist monks. There were intermittent scares of pretenders to the throne; and a rebellious insurrection with its embellishment of a monarchical pretender broke out in certain Kandyan districts in 1848.[32]

In these circumstances the fort of Colombo was an essential part of the British order. The fort was not merely a seat of administration, a maritime commercial hub and a residential nucleus. It was the foundation of British security. Its ramparts were not mere decor and the Racquet Court to the west of the ramparts (between the Fort and the Pettah) and the Galle Face Green and open ground to the south were military reserves which preserved an open field of fire.[33] And housed nearby in Slave Island and along the shores of the Beira Lake adjacent to the Fort were the British and Malay contingents which were to man this defence.

By the 1860s, however, the British felt much more secure. The 1848 insurrection had, in retrospect, proved to be a minor squib. The economy was booming. The communication network (including telegraph links) was vastly improved and growing apace. It was possible to view the Kandyan headmen in a different light and treat them as important links in the administration.[34] In the years 1869-71, therefore, the fortifications of Colombo Fort were demolished and the Ceylon Rifle Regiment, comprised mostly of Malay soldiers, was disbanded[35] — though a reduced British contingent remained and was eventually housed in the newly constructed Echelon Barracks in the Fort area itself.[36]

This, then, was an important landmark in Colombo's history. Its citadel function for the colonial power was no longer prominent. Colombo continued, however, to be the centre of symbolic display for the British, both in intended and unintended ways. Also in this sense, and not merely as a locus of decision-making, it remained a colonial power-centre. Together with the hill-station at Nuwara Eliya, Colombo provided the British with what Bourdieu would call 'symbolic capital',[37] the space in which they displayed their identity as the colonial power from overseas.

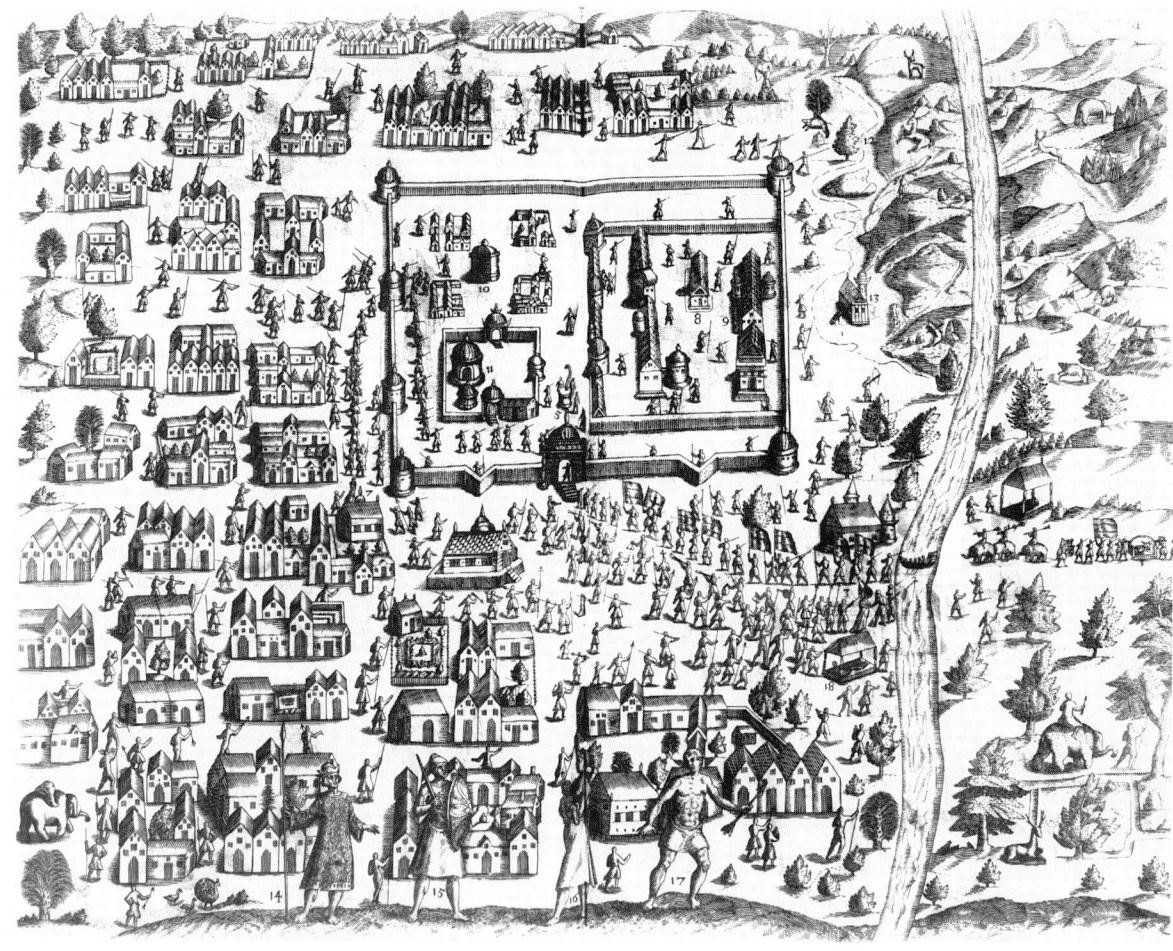

The inland capital of Sri Lanka, Kandy. While Colombo developed as a Portuguese, Dutch and English port, Kandy remained the political and religious centre of Sri Lankan society. This very early Dutch view of Kandy lays emphasis on the ceremonial and martial importance of a city situated in the mountains and hence impenetrable to European military actions. In the foreground we see the dress of 'typical' Kandyan aristocrats and warriors.
From Isaak Commelin Begin ende Voortgangh van de Vereenighde Nederlandtsche Geoctroyeerde Oost-Indische Compagnie *Amsterdam, 1646. Courtesy of Mitchell Library, State Library of New South Wales.*

While the ramparts had disappeared in the 1870s, the Galle Face Green remained. From the very outset this promenade area beside the sea had been used as a locale for the British gentlemen and ladies to take their airs, whether on foot or on horseback. It was

> Colombo's 'Park' or Prater—
> And here the world,
> Starched, brushed and curled,
> Appears at four or later.[38]

It also served as a parade ground and the site of colonial state rituals, whether in honour of the Queen's birthday or some special occasion. As such, it was a symbolic space: an embodiment of British dignity and culture, confidence and power. In the late nineteenth century military bands regularly provided musical entertainment at Galle Face during one evening each week.[39] Not surprisingly, the most toffee-nosed of the British clubs, the Colombo Club, which was founded in 1870-71, located itself in the building known as 'the Assembly Rooms' which stood at the southern end of the green. Soon afterwards, the Galle Face Hotel (built in 1897) arose as its neighbour;[40] many of its customers would be the Western passengers changing ships or interrupting their travels at Colombo port. In the interwar years of the twentieth century these two buildings found themselves looking across the green at what were perhaps more ambiguous symbols of British rule: a new parliament (completed in 1929) and the war memorial.

The symbolic ambience of Galle Face Green was augmented by the manifold leisure activities which occurred upon its 'hallowed' ground. In the course of the nineteenth century the full panoply of Victorian team games and spectator sports were played there. It would appear that cricket and horseracing were among the earliest of these pastimes, commencing about the 1820s (racing) and 1840s.[41] The horseraces became regular calendar events which attracted a substantial crowd of 'natives' who benefited from the fact that spectator space at this location was unstructured[42]—a condition which did not extend to the hierarchically patterned space at the Havelock Racecourse which came into operation in 1893. In enjoying themselves with such gusto, the male British residents of Sri Lanka effectively set themselves up as a class of leisured gentlemen. They believed, too, that such games as cricket, polo, soccer and rugger were exercises in character-building; and, as such, they treated these games as symbols of 'manliness', 'pluck' and 'bottom'.[43] Indulging in such leisure activities also demanded considerable organisation. The activities were institutionalised as clubs and associations. They called for appropriate and striking attire. There were appropriate times and places for each type of leisure activity, whether cricket, bridge or ballroom dancing. Both the day and the calendar year were marked out by several of these pastimes. And, as we have seen, the urban space of Colombo was marked out to accommodate such activities. By the late nineteenth century, therefore, the southern half of Colombo was very much of a garden city, rather in contrast with the cramped pattern of town houses which seems to have been characteristic of the Dutch urban centres in the eighteenth century[44] — the legacy of which remained in the Pettah quarter in Colombo and the Fort in Galle.

Several of these British games were introduced into the curricula of the leading schools in Sri Lanka. In this and other ways the games introduced through the gateway of Colombo helped induct the indigenous elites into westernised lifestyles. The success of the process of westernisation was linked with the dialectics of colonial opposition. However educated and however wealthy, members of the Ceylonese 'middle class' were excluded from most British clubs and subject to the racial arrogance of the white sahibs. They were mere 'half-castes' or 'natives'. In the late nineteenth or early twentieth century it was not feasible for them to challenge British rule in political terms without being labelled 'seditious'. In such a context, games became a convenient arena to allegorise political ambition.[45] As 'unserious activity', they could take on the British at their own games without risking political repression. The competition inherent in games was proper, a jolly good show, legitimate. The sports arena, therefore, was liberating: a realm in which one's autonomy could be expressed, one's self-respect built up. Thus, it was not long — from 1887 in fact — before the leading Ceylonese cricket club, the Colts, took on a combined team of European residents in what was billed as a 'test match'; this became an annual encounter which was eventually converted in 1905 into an 'European-Ceylonese' match.[46] It is partly in these terms, too, that one needs to review the reckless enthusiasm with which a few wealthy Sinhalese invested in racehorses and sought to make their mark in high society.[47] More subtly and compellingly than ever before Janus-like Colombo was becoming the meeting ground of the people of its fore- and hinterlands.

But it was not only in their pastimes that the Ceylonese middle class followed the British. Their eating habits, attire and consumerism, and even their naming practices, emulated British practice.[48] This tendency was quickly dubbed mimetic and represented as a process of denationalisation by such critics as the Anagarika Dharmapala, Ananda Coomaraswamy, Peter de Abrew and the Ceylon Social Reform Society.[49] It is a charge that is repeated by latter-day historians. The critique is not without validity: the Ceylonese middle class was strongly anglophile and, to this extent, represented the return on the British exporting their Western lifestyle to Sri Lanka. However, the emulatory practices of the middle class must also be understood as attempts to shore up their self-respect in the face of British racial superiority and, among the Sinhalese, as one facet of status rivalry among families and caste notables. Many members of this middle class had emerged recently from the ranks of the Karava, Salagama, Durāva and Wahumpura castes or from the menial segments (*vadakarana minissu*) of the superior Goyigama caste. Aware of the social discrimination to which their forefathers had been subject, and continuing to confront the snobbery, if not the machinations, of the Goyigama aristocracy,[50] these *arrivistes* used Colombo's space and social practice to express their new-found status and influence. The city of Colombo, and the Cinnamon Gardens in particular, became one of the prime sites for symbolic display. The construction of palatial mansions with neat driveways and gardens was just as much a part of this status competition as elegant dress, hansom cab or profligate wedding reception. These practices represented the extension of a principle—that of conspicuous consumption for symbolic purposes—that was firmly rooted in traditional Sinhala village practice.[51] But in Colombo it was played out with material forms and artifacts that were often of Western origin; spatially, perhaps the most striking marker of this influence was the craze for tennis which had established itself by the early twentieth century and led to a liberal sprinkling of private tennis courts in Cinnamon Gardens.

One of the legacies which Colombo's citadel function bequeathed to latter-day governments has been a stock of valuable real estate in the heart of Colombo, viz. the Galle Face Green precincts and Echelon Square. Since 1977 this has been put to new use under the aegis of the Urban Development Authority. The police and the army have been pushed out. The reorganised landscape has lost all trace of its maritime roots and may well be regarded as a symbol of the new capitalist order and Colombo's links with international capital. As a result of the reconstructions of the last thirty years, the most imposing buildings in the space between the old Queen's House in the Fort (now the President's House) and the Galle Face Hotel are the Central Bank, Ceylinco House (with banks and government houses) and a quartet of five-star hostelries, the Intercontinental, Galadari, Sheraton and Taj Samudra.

Overshadowed by all this and nestling in between is the old House of Parliament. 'Old' because the parliament has moved itself to Kotte: where it has been decked with an architectural form reminiscent of the palaces of Sinhala kings and been renamed Sri Jayawardenapura.[52] This is an explicit symbolic statement. It is not merely a case of localisation and Sinhalisation. The choice of Kotte was a representation of littoral, Low-Country Sinhalese power as much as it was an 'objective' solution to the overcrowding of functions in Colombo—a spatial shift of the capital and reaction against the over-dominance of primate port cities which Sri Lanka shares with several other non-Western nations. The political and cultural implications of the move to Kotte, however, are as much directed against the symbolic weight which is attached to Kandy, its Dalada Maligawa (the repository of the tooth relic) and Asala Festival (during which the tooth relic is taken in procession), as against the secular power of Colombo. These implications must be weighed in the light of the increasing prominence of the major temples in the area of Greater Colombo: those of Kelaniya, Kotte, Bellanwila and that new star in the firmament, the Gangarama, which is located beside the Heira Lake. Among other things, each of these temples has upgraded its annual processions (*perahara*). In the case of the Gangarama, in recent years the *Navam Perahara* held in February has been converted into a grandiose spectacle, almost outdoing the one in Kandy. And so, littoral society is gradually reclaiming its heart, when, for the first time in centuries, elephant dung has appeared in the heart of Colombo.

Although its port and portside industrialisation are more important than ever for its economic development, Colombo has thus, like so many of its Asian sisters, become an arena of confrontation between the forces of rapid economic growth and continued westernisation on the one hand, and the vigorous resurgence of traditional values on the other. Overshadowed as Sri Lanka at present is by other tensions, it may be long until a resolution of this collision between maritime and terrestrial vectors can be attempted. What is clear, however, is that by now Colombo's port has lost its previous supremacy in the city's socio-cultural life and that the city itself has gradually come to reflect the nation of which it is the gateway rather than the maritime world of shipping and trade which for a long time was its main *raison d'être*.

Notes

1. I wish to thank Messrs Ismeth Raheem and I.V. Edirisinghe for their cooperation in providing me with information and supporting documentation
2. ESCAP *Population of Sri Lanka* Country Monograph Series No. 4, New York, 1976, p. 76
3. M.N. Pearson 'Littoral Society: The Case for the Coast' *The Great Circle* 7, 1985, p. 1
4. C.R. de Silva 'The First Portuguese Revenue Register of the Kingdom of Kotte—1599' *The Ceylon Journal of Historical and Social Studies* 5, 1975, p. 84
5. *Return of the Population of the Island of Ceylon* Colombo, Govt. Press, 1827
6. Numerous publications document these activities. See K.M. de Silva *A History of Sri Lanka* Delhi, 1971, chs. 25-27; James Jupp *Sri Lanka—Third World Democracy* London, 1978, chs. 10-11; Michael Roberts 'Elites, Nationalisms and the Nationalist Movement in Ceylon' in M. Roberts (ed.) *Documents of the Ceylon National Congress and Nationalist Politics in Ceylon, 1929-1950* Colombo, 1977, chs. 3 and 5; and M. Roberts 'Meanderings in the Pathways of Collective Identity and Nationalism' in *Collective Identities, Nationalisms, and Protest in Modern Sri Lanka* Colombo, 1979, pp. 63-64
7. Computations from *Census of Ceylon, 1921* Colombo, Govt. Printer. In 1971 the city contained 19.8 percent of the population classified as 'urban'—an apparent decline which is in part due to changes in the classificatory system. However, 'Greater Colombo' contained nearly 44 percent of the urban population in 1971: ESCAP, *Migration, Urbanization and Development in Sri Lanka* New York, 1981, p. 20
8. For example, see ESCAP *Migration* p. 20; Godfrey Gunatilleke 'The Rural-Urban Balance and Development—the Experience in Sri Lanka' *Marga* 2, 1973, pp. 35-68; Percy Silva and Kusuma Gunawardena 'The Urban Fringe of Colombo: Some Trends and Problems concerning its Land Use' *Modern Ceylon Studies* 2, 1971, pp. 39-68; and Gavin W. Jones and S. Selvaratnam 'Urbanization in Ceylon, 1946-63' *Modern Ceylon Studies* 1, 1970, pp. 199-212
9. On this theme see H.L. Seneviratne *Rituals of the Kandyan State* Cambridge 1978; Deborah Winslow 'A Political Geography of Deities: Space and the Pantheon in Sinhalese Buddhism' *Journal of Asian Studies* 18, 1984, pp. 273-91; Bruce Kapferer *A Celebration of Demons* Bloomington, 1983; and the many publications by Gananath Obeyesekere, most of which are conveniently listed in the bibliography in his *The Cult of the Goddess Pattini* Chicago, 1984. Sri Lankans of most religious persuasions who desire therapeutic aid and godly favours are liable to visit the central shrine of the diety, Kataragama (also known as Skandha and Murugan), to make vows. In popular belief Kataragama is not fussy about the motives behind a request as long as the supplicant reveals total devotion to him
10. Revd. S.G. Perera 'Colombo' *The Easter Annual* 1926, p. 32; B.L. Panditharatna 'The Harbour and Port of Colombo: A Geographical Appraisal of its Historical and Functional Aspects' *Ceylon Journal of Historical and Social Studies* 3, 1960, p. 128
11. *Return of the Population of the Island of Ceylon, 1827* pp. 57-58 and 54. My figure for Burghers is an amalgamation of those for 'Burghers', 'European descendants' and 'Toeppas'.
12. There were no middle-class Tamils in Wellawatte, then on the outskirts of the city, till about the mid-1880s; the first of these appears to have been an advocate named W. Muttyah (see Colombo, Dept. of National Archives, lot 33/2733). Strikingly, during the mid twentieth-century Wellawatte has tended to be regarded as a 'Tamil' suburb.
13. *Census of Ceylon 1921* vol. 1, part 1, pp. 40, 112, 191 and vol. 4, pp. 166-68. 'Sinhalese' includes a small (1.6) percentage of Kandyan Sinhalese
14. Including Indian Moors. My decision has been influenced by the fact that in subsequent years—or so I speculate—most of the Indian Moors that did not return to India have been able to merge with the indigenous Moor population
15. Includes 'Europeans' (1.1%) and Malays (2.3%)
16. *Census of Ceylon 1921* vol. 1, part 2, p. 77. Cf. Chapter 9 for similar figures on India's major port cities at the time. Direct comparisons are, unfortunately, not feasible because of the different categorisation of workers used in both countries
17. See K.M. de Silva *History* chs 36 and 37; Jupp *Sri Lanka*; and Mervyn de Silva '1956: The Cultural Revolution that Shook the Left' *Ceylon Observer* Magazine Edition, 26 May 1967
18. Information communicated personally by David Brooks on the basis of his fieldwork at Kataragama in 1981-82
19. C.R. de Silva and Vijaya Samaraweera 'Leadership Perspectives 1948-1975. An Interpretative Essay' *Ceylon Journal of Historical and Social Studies* 4, 1974, pp. 29 and 39; Michael Roberts 'Meanderings', pp. 70-72, and 'Report

of the Committee for Rational Development' in *Lanka Guardian* 1 November 1983
20 K. Dharmasena 'The Port and Dock Workers of Colombo 1860-1960', *The Great Circle* 7, 1985, p. 112
21 *Census of Population and Housing, Sri Lanka 1981* Colombo, Department of Census and Statistics, January 1984
22 C.R. de Silva 'First Portuguese Revenue Register' p. 103 and *passim*; and Michael Roberts *Caste Conflict and Elite Formation. The Rise of the Karava Elite in Sri Lanka, 1500-1931* Cambridge, 1982, pp. 18-32
23 De Silva 'First Portuguese Revenue Register' p. 97
24 E.B.F. Sueter 'Old Colombo' *The Times of Ceylon Christmas Number* 1913, pp. 66-68, and Revd. S.G. Perera 'Old Colombo' *Ceylon Observer Annual* 1937, n.p.
25 It was possible to approach Kandy from the east from Batticaloa, but this entailed marches through malaria-ridden and sparsely peopled jungles. Constantine de Sa led an invasion of Uva (the southeast of the highlands) via Sabaragumuwa in 1630. This ended in disaster. See C.R. de Silva *The Portuguese in Ceylon, 1617-1638* Colombo, 1972, pp. 105ff
26 There were about 1050 miles of metalled road by 1863. By 1935 there were nearly 5000 miles of road and over 900 miles of railtrack: Wickremeratne 'The Development of Transportation in Ceylon, c. 1800-1947' *History of Ceylon* 3, Colombo, 1973, p. 312
27 K. Dharmasena *The Port of Colombo, 1860-1939* Colombo, 1980, pp. 13-15 and Donovan Moldrich *Ceylon in Our Times, A Ceylon Cold Stores Diamond Jubilee Publication* Colombo, 1969, pp. 34-35
28 See Walter E. Pine 'The Slums of Colombo' *Times of Ceylon Sunday Illustrated* 15 and 22 February 1925; *Administration Report of the Colombo Municipal Council 1924*; and Dharmasena *Port of Colombo* ch. 6
29 Pockets of middle-class housing remained in the northern part of the city, especially in Kotahena
30 See S.P. Foenander *Sixty Years of Ceylon Cricket* Colombo, 1924. Also see any of the large-scale maps of Colombo in the early twentieth century or the descriptive information in George J.A. Skeen *A Guide to Colombo* Colombo, 1906, as compared with his earlier compilation in 1887
31 *The History of Royal College* Colombo, 1932, p. 124; and W.T. Keble *A History of St. Thomas' College* Colombo, 1937
32 For the background to these events, see K. Malalgoda 'Millennialism in Relation to Buddhism' *Comparative Studies in Society and History* 12, 1970, pp. 424-41; and K.M. de Silva 'The "Rebellion" of 1848 in Ceylon' *Ceylon Journal of Historical and Social Studies* 7, 1964, pp. 144-70
33 C. Brooke Elliott *The Real Ceylon* Colombo, 1938 edn, pp. 12-13. For description of the Fort area and the Beira scene in early British times, see the works of Percival (1803) and Cordiner (1807)
34 K.M. de Silva *History* pp. 316-17. Indeed, from the 1870s the British administration promoted several aristocratic Kandyan families as a conservative bulwark and a counterweight to those educated Ceylonese (mostly Ceylon Tamils and Low-Country Sinhalese) who pushed for administrative and constitutional reform
35 A.M. Ferguson *Sir W.H. Gregory and Sir James Longden and their Predecessors in the Government of Ceylon* Colombo, 1878, pp. 46-47, 50. At a public meeting in Kandy on 21 June 1873, a gathering of Europeans 'deprecated the entire removal of the troops stationed there' (ibid. p. 50)
36 Five blocks were constructed between 1870 and 1877, the sixth block of the Barracks being added in 1901. See J.T. Rea *Building in Ceylon* Colombo, 1918, p. 12
37 Pierre Bourdieu *Outline of a Theory of Practice* Cambridge, 1977, esp. pp. 171-83
38 V.M. Hamilton and S.M. Fasson *Scenes in Ceylon* London, 1881
39 Elliott *Real Ceylon* p. 13
40 W.E. Pine 'The Colombo Club Jubilee Celebration 1921' in *The Times of Ceylon Christmas Number, 1921* pp. 41-42 and Rea *Building* p. 13
41 Foenander *Sixty years* pp. 1-2, and 'The Turf Club of Ceylon' *Times of Ceylon Christmas Number, 1910* pp. 33 and 36. A racemeet was held in Kandy in 1821: J.P. Lewis, *Ceylon in Early British Times*, Colombo, 2nd edn, 1915, pp. 56-57
42 For early descriptions of the races, see J.L.K. Van Dort 'Colombo Races on Galle Face in the Forties' *The Times of Ceylon Christmas Number, 1919* pp. 60 and 61, and J.P. Lewis 'The Colombo Races of 1854' *Ceylon Literary Register* Oct. 1919 and Jan. 1920, vol. V, pp. 86-101, 157-63
43 See W.F. Mandle 'Games People Played: Cricket and Football in England and Victoria in the Late Nineteenth Century' *Historical Studies* 15, 1973, pp. 511-35; K.A.P. Sandiford 'Sport and Victorian England: A Review Article' *Canadian Journal of History* 18, 1983, pp. 111-17; and J.A. Mangan *Athleticism in the Victorian and Edwardian Public School* Cambridge, Mass., 1981

44 For descriptions of Dutch Colombo, see Sueter 'Old Colombo'; and A. Daalmans 'A Belgian Physician's Notes on Ceylon in 1687-89', trans. D. Ferguson, *Journal of the Royal Asiatic Society, Ceylon Branch* 1887, pp. 1-34

45 Don Handelman 'A Note on Play' *American Anthropologist* 76, 1974, pp. 66-68. The quotation that follows is from this article

46 Foenander *Sixty Years* pp. 158, 162

47 E.g., A.E. de Silva Jnr, E.L.F. de Soysa and E.C. de Fonseka

48 For some illustrations, see Yasmine Gooneratne *English Literature in Ceylon 1815-1878* Dehiwala, 1968, pp. 36-39 and 48-63, and Arnold Wright (comp.) *Twentieth Century Impressions of Ceylon* London, 1907, pp. 510-913

49 See the *Ceylon National Review* 1906 et seq.; Dharmapala *Return to Righteousness*, ed. by A. Guruge, Colombo, 1965, and de Abrow *Eastern Learning* Colombo, 1919

50 For the background and for illustrations, see Roberts *Caste Conflict* pp. 46-74, 89-77, ch. 6; and esp. pp. 150-59 and 330-35

51 See G. Obeyesekere *Land Tenure in Village Ceylon* Cambridge, 1967, ch. 9, and Michael Roberts 'A New Marriage, An Old Dichotomy: the "Middle Class" in British Ceylon?', in K. Indrapala (ed.) *The James Thevathasan Rutnam Felicitation Volume* Jaffna, Jaffna Archaeological Society, 1975, pp. 45-51

52 See *Sri Lanka's New Capital—Sri Jayawardenapura* Colombo, Urban Development Authority, 1982. The alternative name is of ancient usage in the Sinhala language (e.g., see B. Gunasekera (ed.) *The Rajavaliya* Colombo, 1953, p. 53) and its coincidence with the name of President J.R. Jayewardene is accidental. This coincidence may, however, have contributed to its attraction. Young J.R. Jayewardene was among those who encouraged the Ceylon National Congress to hold its annual conferences in outlying centres in the Low-Country such as Mirigama (1940), Dummaladeniya (1941) and Kalaniya (1942), where the conference grounds were given such names as 'Swaraj Pura' and 'Gamani Matha Pura'. See Roberts (ed.) *Documents* vol. 2, pp. 1371-1470

Further Reading

Dharmasena, K. *The Port of Colombo 1860-1939* Colombo 1980. A competent description of the growth of the port which uses the available printed documents. Not designed as a theoretical piece.

ESCAP *Population of Sri Lanka*, Country Monograph Series No. 4, New York 1976. A revealing set of maps and statistical tables, in great part the fruit of an excellent team of researchers at the University of Colombo (e.g. Kusuma Gunawardena, Hiran Dias, Percy Silva).

Foenander, S.P. *Fifty Years of Ceylon Cricket* Colombo 1924. This descriptive work is rare and provides useful data relating to a field which is of social and cultural significance in all British colonies. No history of Westernisation and the ambiguities of colonial domination should neglect the field of leisure.

Roberts, Michael *Caste Conflict and Elite Formation: The Rise of a Karava Elite in Sri Lanka, 1500-1931*, Cambridge 1982. A piece of historical sociology with a broad sweep. Among other facets, it describes the processes of elite formation and uses a comparative methodology to reveal how it came about that the Karava caste provided so many of the new *arrivistes* in British Ceylon. In doing so it underlines the dominance of the southwestern littoral in the emerging political order.

Seneviratne, H.L. *Rituals of the Kandyan State* Cambridge 1978. Describes and analyses the grand Asala perahara (procession) at Kandy. Of central importance for understanding the nature of the Sinhalese kingdoms of pre-colonial times and the centripetal religio-political ideology which they perpetuated.

de Silva, S.B.D. *The Political Economy of Underdevelopment* London 1982. A global survey of the sociology of underdevelopment which focuses especially on the plantation colonies and deploys much Sri Lankan data. Particularly useful for understanding the role of merchant capitalism in the dependencies.

B.S. Hoyle

Maritime perspectives on ports and port systems: the case of East Africa

CHAPTER 8

The historical and economic interdependence of the numerous regions of the Asian littoral and the Indian Ocean region—stretching from China and Japan to Southwest Asia (the Middle East) and East Africa—is essentially based upon the sea, and especially upon the ships, the port cities and the technologies which successive generations have developed in order to use and exploit the resources of land and sea areas. Navigators approaching their shores are today, as in the past, very much aware of the diversity of port facilities available, of the character and relative commercial vitality of each port city, and of the advantages and dangers of each in terms of trade or navigation. Each seaport there, as elsewhere in the world, occupies a unique location in relation to its hinterlands and to the network of sealanes with which it is connected, but at the same time seaports share many common characteristics in physical, economic and technological terms. Every seaport is perceived by the governments and peoples of the countries which it serves as an element in national and international transport systems, and as one of a number of gateways through which external trade may be routed. From a maritime standpoint the perspective of the ship operator is focused on the commercial and navigational characteristics of a port in comparison with other ports, in the context of the competitive position that each port strives to maintain and enhance. From both the landward and the seaward sides, therefore, perspectives on ports involve contextual analyses and comparative assessments; and the port selection process is a complex matter with far-reaching implications for regional development and for transport systems.

Functioning essentially as a critical node within a multimodal transport system, a seaport is first and foremost a central place of economic and cultural interchange. As a gateway standing at the interface between land and water transport networks, a seaport originates and grows in response to demands from many sources and as a reflection of inter-relationships that extend over wide areas and substantial time-periods on many different scales.[1] The basic function of a seaport is transport integration; but in the performance of this function a seaport may also grow into a major urban centre, an important source of employment, and an influential factor in national and regional development. In Asia, as in Africa or Latin America, port cities can fulfil and have fulfilled critical roles in the processes of economic, social and political change; in order to do so efficiently, they must be able to respond rapidly to changing demands from both the landward and maritime sides.

The study of seaports and port cities may be approached in a variety of ways. From a geographical viewpoint, several major recent publications have emphasised the value and complexity of maritime as well as terrestrial perspectives.[2] It is also increasingly recognised that the problems of ports and port cities, particularly in terms of their inter-relationships with processes of socio-economic and political change, are today nowhere more critical than in the less-developed countries of the so-called Third World. Asia and the Indian Ocean provide in this context a wide range of fascinating and complex problems associated with ports and port cities. This chapter is concerned with selected aspects of one relatively discrete element of the world system, the East African realm; as such it may be taken as an example for similar studies elsewhere in, for example, South and Southeast Asia or, *mutatis mutandis*, China, Japan, and especially Southwest Asia with which it was, historically, so closely connected. For a long time an integral part of a western Indian Ocean trading system dominated from the Arabian peninsula and, to a lesser extent, India, East Africa only in this century came to occupy a position more distinctly its own in the world economic system. Three specific approaches are adopted. First, some theoretical underpinnings derived from transport geography are outlined as a means of emphasising the fundamental importance of maritime perspectives in seaport study. Second, the concept of changing port hierarchies is used to illustrate the significance of historical interpretations of port development. Third, the impact of recent innovations in maritime technology is discussed, with specific reference to containerisation. Illustrations are drawn mainly from Kenya and Tanzania, but frequent references to Asian port cities where appropriate may illuminate conditions there.[3]

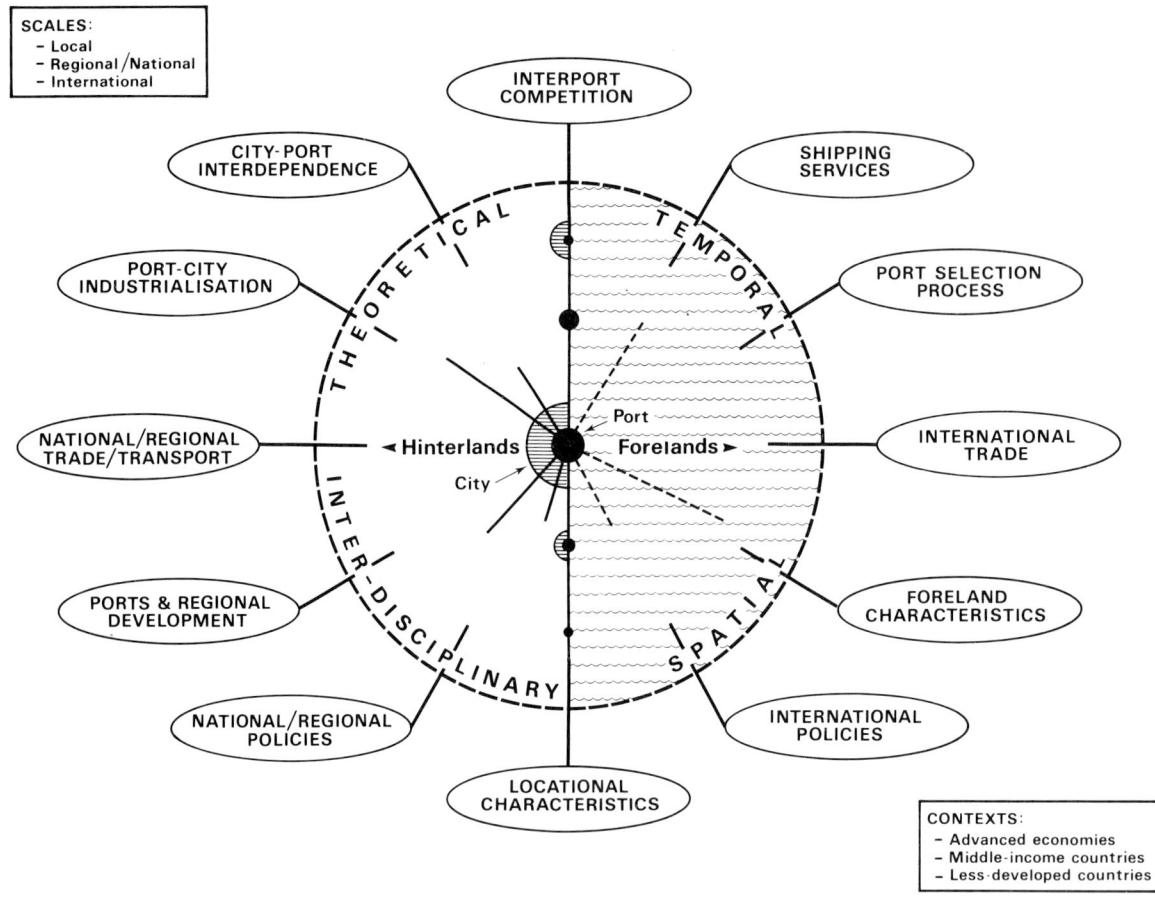

Figure 8.1
Some elements in port geography. Reproduced from B. S. Hoyle and D. Hilling (eds.) Seaport systems and spatial change *Chichester, 1984, p.2; by permission.*

Theoretical perspectives

The study of seaports is basically concerned with what happens at the waterfront, across the frontier between land and sea, wherever trade is regularly carried out, whether in a technologically primitive context or in a context of advanced transport systems. Figure 8.1 is an attempt to show, in a very simplified way, some of the main elements involved in the geographical study of seaports and seaport systems.[4] In this model, the port is represented as a node located at the land/maritime interface along with other ports which have experienced differential development. Ports are shown to vary in size and in the extent to which they are associated with urban development, and interport competition is affected by locational characteristics of various kinds, notably the conditions of land and water sites and the characteristics of hinterland transport systems.

A basic division in port geography is between those elements derived from the hinterlands and those derived from the maritime side. On the landward side, important research areas are suggested by the box-labels: city-port interdependence, port city industrialisation, transport networks and trade patterns, relationships between ports and regional development, and the impact of policy formulation and decision-making at various levels on the port development process. On the maritime side, port development is first and foremost dependent upon ships—in the dual context of ship design and shipping services—and upon the process of port selection as perceived in the past by the founders of port settlements and today by the ship-operating companies who use port facilities. The global and regional patterns of international trade are obviously an important influence, as are the specific characteristics of foreland areas beyond the seas with which ports are linked. The international political dimension includes bilateral relations, group arrangements such as those of ASEAN (notably unsuccessful in the formulation of a coherent shipping policy), OPEC or those between the EEC and Afro-Asian countries, and global policies derived from the United Nations and its agencies. These elements, relating to both economic and more specifically shipping relations, are all open to investigation at various scales ranging from the local to the global; all relate to countries and areas throughout the development spectrum from the most advanced to the least developed; and all are subject to interpretation in several dimensions, four of which are indicated in Figure 8.1: theoretical, temporal, spatial and interdisciplinary.

Spatial dimensions of port development have traditionally emphasised four sets of factors associated with the water situation and the land situation, and with the land site and the water site. Of these, the water site often provides the initial stimulus to development, but unless conditions in the other three categories are favourable the settlement is unlikely to prosper. The level of port development, measured in terms of cargo-handling capacity or the volume and value of commodity flow, is chiefly a reflection of the land situation—the extent and pattern of economic development in the hinterland, including transport development—rather than of the land or water site. Nevertheless, the land site constitutes a direct control over the pattern of urban growth, and where factors in all four categories are broadly favourable—as at Tokyo, Bombay, Colombo or Mombasa (Kenya)—there is direct correlation between the level of port development and the extent of associated urban growth. In all cases, however, the port function lies at the root of the physical expansion of the port city in terms of location, layout and size.

From an oceanic perspective the general water situation is often a substantial positive or negative influence. Technological changes, too, can transform the water situation of a group of seaports. The opening of the Suez Canal in 1869 dramatically altered the maritime/geographical context in which the seaports of Asia and the Indian Ocean found themselves; and in the 1970s the inclusion of many Asian and African seaports in new regional and global containerised sea-transport networks became a significant dynamic and differentiating factor.

The coasts of many countries such as India, Indonesia, Malaysia, Saudi Arabia, or Kenya are generally lacking in good natural harbours, but today this physical characteristic cannot be said significantly to impede their economic progress. As development has proceeded, the pattern of port location has been adjusted, partly by the continued growth and sometimes the increasing dominance of established ports (such as Bombay or Calcutta), partly by the decline into relative insignificance of formerly well-located ports (Surat, Zanzibar and Melaka are good examples), and also by the construction of new ports as at Jeddah, Colombo, and Madras, or more recently Port Kelang (Malaysia), Paradeep and Haldia (India), Nacala (Mozambique) or Sattahip (Thailand).[5] In many cases such innovations are based upon artificially constructed harbours, located where port facilities are needed but where natural harbours are not available; in other cases, such as Colombo, Shanghai or Jeddah, it has meant the complete transformation of existing but inadequate facilities.

The wholesale modernisation of inadequate natural harbours often involved port development on a substantial scale. But the specific topographical and environmental conditions of the new water site also exerted a great measure of control over the physical form and pattern of urban development associated with the port. Two striking examples of such morphological dynamism are the drowned river valleys of Mombasa (Kenya) and Dar es Salaam (Tanzania), the two (amongst many other traditional dhow harbours) sites chosen in the last quarter of the nineteenth century by Western interests as the main gateways for their steamships of the East African coast. This port selection process, ultimately, was one of the most important physical aspects of the wider process of commercial and political penetration of Africa by external forces whose succession to Swahili and Arab power, and subsequent temporary dominance of East African affairs, was based substantially if not primarily upon sea power.

Historico-genetic studies have long been important in explaining how present-day port functions and layouts have developed from past decisions; and economic analyses have emphasised the distinction between sea-*ports* as transport nodes and seaport *terminals* as locations for industries based on bulk imports.[6] Whereas some types of seaport study are concerned with the port area itself or with aspects of its hinterland structures, the emphasis of this chapter is on the maritime side of the waterfront, that of shipping technology and organisation. It is always important to emphasise the question of ship design in terms of its impact on ports, and to exploit the insights to be gained from comparative studies of groups of ports. On the local scale it can be seen that, as seaports develop, they normally move downstream towards deeper water, and that port-industrial development often involves an extension of the port areas beyond the original coastline; shortage of space, as at Jeddah, Singapore, Hong Kong or Kobe, can also necessitate land reclamation for port expansion itself. On the continental or global scale, in contrast, every port is an element in an international system of maritime transport which uses the interconnected oceans or world lake; every port serves the same world fleet of shipping (or similar sections of it) and therefore has the same incentives to maintain and enhance its competitive position. In practice, the application of this theoretical argument is complicated by tariff barriers and other political intervention, and by the difficulties of matching resources and markets to the optimum benefit of the system as a whole.

These theoretical perspectives share a common concern for the maritime elements in port study while insisting that a port is essentially defined by its function as a transport node at the land/sea interface. Studies of real-world seaports and their multifarious problems in consequence must preserve a balance between terrestrial and maritime factors that are in many respects interdependent. Yet in more general terms it is widely recognised that the design of shipping, rather than the condition of harbours, has always been the principal pacemaker in sea-transport developments. The gateway must be selected, designed and adapted to accommodate the ocean carrier, not vice versa, and in that sense it is certainly the maritime perspective that is predominant.

Seaport hierarchies in historical perspective

The principles of port development stress that a port is essentially a dynamic phenomenon, changing in its morphology, functions and status over time. In Asia, as in Africa and elsewhere, no port is an isolated phenomenon, for each belongs to a port complex within which individual ports are functionally interrelated. Viewed from the maritime side, ports linked in trading terms to the same forelands are related (for example, the oil-exporting ports and facilities of the Gulf), as are ports which share a common political or economic hinterland (such as the port complexes of Japan, Malaysia/Singapore/Indonesia, India or in Europe the so-called Havre-Hamburg range on the eastern littoral of the Channel and North Sea). Within each regional or subregional complex ports will never be totally equal, whatever criteria of measurement are adopted, and can therefore be ordered into a hierarchy. Within such a hierarchy the specific character and functions of each port can, of course, change over time because of the differential impact of factors influencing port growth.

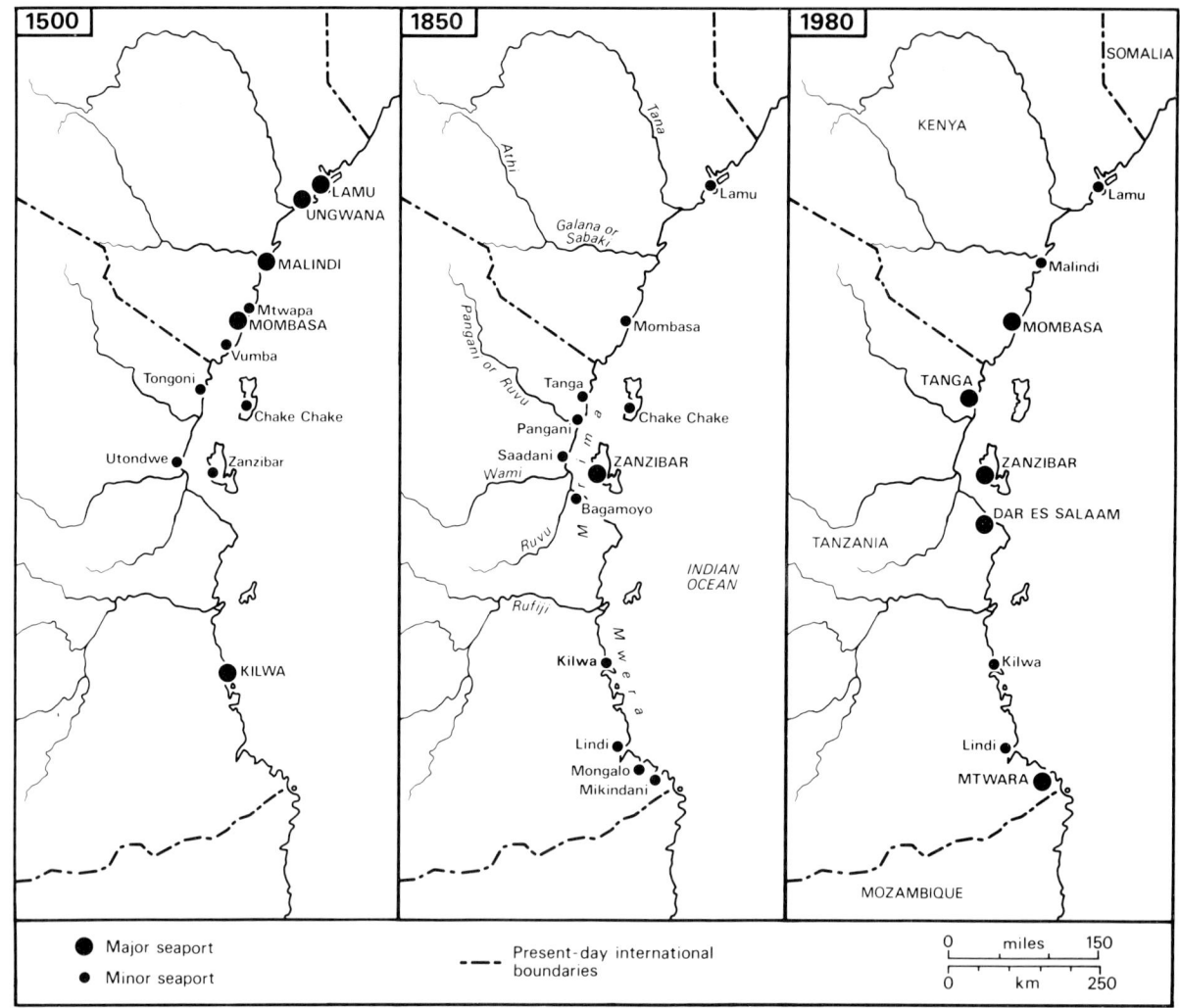

Map 13 The seaports of East Africa, 1500, 1850 and 1980, Reproduced from B. S. Hoyle Seaports and Development: The Experience of Kenya and Tanganyika New York/London, 1983; by permission.

Within a specific port hierarchy there may be a tendency towards *port diffusion* or toward *port concentration* along a coast, or there may be an *unstabilised port structure*. A port which successfully maintains its competitive position over a lengthy period of time (as Bombay, Jeddah, Singapore and Mombasa have done, in different contexts) may be described as a centre of *sustained port dominance*.[7] In the twentieth century the factors affecting port development have generally encouraged specialisation and concentration, to the continuing disadvantage of smaller ports. This has clearly been the experience of most Asian countries as larger modern seaports have developed rapidly and smaller, more numerous, seaports have tended to stagnate or at least to decline in relative significance. Over much longer periods of time, however, it is possible to recognise alternating periods of concentration and diffusion in the evolution of a port complex. In some areas, the interpretation may be that a long-term trend towards concentration has been periodically interrupted to yield a cyclical evolutionary sequence in which concentration alternates with some form of diffusion. Elsewhere a flexible system of diffusion of port activity may be the norm over many centuries, yielding to a form of concentration only when investment in modern port facilities requires the stabilisation of a formerly fluid pattern.

A study of the growth of port activity on the East African coast before the present century reveals a series of interacting processes on the mainland, on the offshore islands, and in the wider spaces of the northwestern Indian Ocean.[8] Using the seasonal reversal of monsoonal winds to which sailing vessels were skilfully adapted, a long succession of maritime traders came to the shores of East Africa from the Middle East and India, beginning as early as the first century A.D.[9] From the south came the Portuguese in the fifteenth century, followed by other Europeans and by Americans in the nineteenth. In the interior of East Africa, indigenous trading networks developed, at first in relative isolation but later more expansively. At the coast, seaports were initially almost exclusively oriented towards the trade circulations of the Indian Ocean, but they gradually came to fulfil more effectively the classic seaport role as intermediary nodes linking land and sea transport networks. As the trading systems of the East African interior were extended to include the coastlands, and as the variety and intensity of Indian Ocean trade increased, the coastal ports modified their commercial orientation and became, effectively for the first time, growth points in the maritime facade of a major part of Africa now integrated into trading systems of the world as a whole.

Interactions between the maritime world of Southwest and South Asia, on the one hand, and those of the coastlands and interior of East Africa, on the other, thus produced over time a series of contrasting hierarchies of ports (Map 13). In the absence of alternative evidence we can only assume an initial period of relative concentration upon the mysterious pre-Islamic port of Rhapta, and a diffusion of small-scale port activity along the coast in the early Islamic period. The fuller development of Swahili civilisation in the fourteenth and fifteenth centuries included a concentration of port activity at Lamu, Malindi,

Mombasa and Kilwa, but the impact of the Portuguese engendered an era of relative decline and port diffusion in succeeding centuries. The rise of Zanzibar as a major nineteenth-century entrepot under the Omani Arabs clearly represented renewed concentration, but this was supported by the diffusion of a series of outports located at important mainland caravan terminals such as Bagamoyo. Throughout these periods the construction of substantial port facilities was scarcely necessary, and flexibility of port sites customary. Towards the end of the nineteenth century, however, technological factors brought about a crystallisation of the traditional patterns of port development and led to the establishment of a more centralised system which forms the basis of the present-day hierarchy.

The twentieth century has seen a new beginning on several mainland sites, representing a diffusion of port activity in a new technological era, and an increasing concentration of activity on the principal modern East African seaport of Mombasa (Kenya) (Map 14). Around the turn of the century there occurred a geographical shift from a series of small harbours or open roadsteads used by Arab dhows (such as Mombasa Old Harbour, Pangani and Bagamoyo) to the harbours which now contain East Africa's major seaports (Mombasa-Kilindini, Tanga, Dar es Salaam). This move was made both possible and necessary by the change from sail to steam propulsion, by the increasing size and manoeuvrability of ships, and by the start of railway building from the coast to the interior. Amid the complex processes of political and economic change experienced in late-nineteenth-century East Africa, the new technology of maritime transport was a factor of critical importance; it created more certain and effective links with the world beyond the northwestern Indian Ocean and also gave the impetus to the growth of new gateways for the entry of overseas goods, people and ideas. In Mombasa, interestingly, the new port city was created side by side to the traditional Swahili centre[10] — a physical arrangement which resembled so many of the European plantings along the Asian littoral.

Numerous problems have arisen throughout the former colonial world (not least in Asia, Africa and Australia) as a direct result of the politically motivated historical process of port selection by external powers. One of the most common of such problems is the conflict between port-related functions and urban development. The early growth of the modern port cities of East Africa, like that of similar settlements in many parts of Asia, was an expression of the economic power and aims of the European nations which established themselves in these areas in the eighteenth and especially the nineteenth century. During the earlier phases of European involvement in East Africa the coastal settlements were the obvious points of political, economic and cultural contact between coloniser and colonised. The port towns provided the main gateways through which intensifying contact developed, the chief filters through which the new transforming influences passed, and they logically became at least initially the main foci of European administration. The selection and use of port cities as political capitals has been the common experience of many parts of the world that have received the tide of European expansionism. But the convenience of the colonial administrators and traders in maintaining contact with their homelands, while exploiting and developing new hinterlands, has in many cases become the inconvenience of modern urban planners; for the multifunctional character of favoured port sites has created excessive demands on the limited potential which these sites often provide. A colonial system of port city capitals is, of course, extremely difficult to change once well established, as the experience of Pakistan, Australia and Brazil have shown. In many of the coastal nations of the African continent as a whole, as in all Australian states, the capital city and the major port city still share the same location. That this is much less frequently the case in Asia is partly a reflection of the greater degree of political maturity now characteristic of Asian countries, but also a function of their much larger average area in comparison with the fragmented condition of the African continent and significant differences in the manner in which European and indigenous powers interacted during the age of imperialism.

The capacity of a given site to absorb not only expanding port development but also rapid urban growth is essentially limited in most cases, especially if the site has been inherited from an era when urban centres and transport systems operated on a much more restricted scale. The physical site conditions which, from a maritime viewpoint, encouraged the establishment of some Asian and African ports in the past, and which still today encourage port expansion, do not, unfortunately, necessarily also favour urban development. A site with defensive attributes important in medieval times, for example, does not always lend itself particularly well to modern urban or port growth, as a comparison of the contrasting fortunes of Lamu, Mombasa and Kilwa in East Africa demonstrates. Such a comparison brings into consideration not only the specific site of a port town but also its more general situation; collectively, its topographical and strategic locations must incorporate both maritime and landward perspectives. It might therefore be argued that the main reasons why Mombasa, rather than Lamu or Kilwa, has emerged as a successful modern port city have more to do with situation than with site and reflect hinterland conditions more clearly than maritime influences in modern times. Lamu and Kilwa, in contrast, although they have access to capacious deepwater harbours, have not developed either as ports or as cities, mainly because their hinterlands are not well endowed with resources nor well connected by modern transport networks.

Mombasa has experienced not only traffic congestion in the port areas but also severe urban development problems, to a large extent due to the characteristics of the original site of the port and the town on the northeastern shore of Mombasa Island (Map 14). The extension of the modern port facilities in Kilindini Harbour onto the mainland at Kipevu, and the spread of urban development to Nyali and Likoni (northeast and southwest of the Island, respectively), have introduced transport problems that are proving expensive and difficult to resolve. Dar es Salaam (Tanzania) (Map 15) suffers from similar congestion in the port, in spite of very substantial extensions to the deepwater facilities during the 1970s; moreover, in urban terms the city has traditionally and more typically combined in one location the political, economic and cultural functions that in Kenya are divided between Mombasa as the principal seaport and the inland political capital of Nairobi. The establishment of a new and more centrally located political capital for Tanzania at Dodoma may conceivably remove some of the pressures upon Dar es Salaam, but it is unlikely to have much direct impact in the critical area of port efficiency. Readers of this volume may care to consider whether there is any validity in comparisons between these East African examples and the somewhat larger-scale cases provided by Asian countries such as Pakistan or Malaysia.

Technological perspectives

Seaports, like cities and transport systems, invariably reflect the technologies of the past during which they were designed and developed as well as the technologies of today. As maritime transport systems have evolved, the degree of intermodal integration has gradually become more sophisticated and the efficiency of movement across the land/sea interface has been enhanced. The seaports of East Africa, like those elsewhere, have absorbed and utilised technological innovations over many years, and most of these innovations have come by sea. Today, the physical layout of a modern seaport reflects this process of sea-derived technological change linking the most traditional with the most sophisticated methods of cargo-handling, each technological stage being represented (in the past, or today) by an appropriate range of physical facilities at the water's edge. The analysis of seaports in terms of the technological basis of their activities is of course central to an understanding of modern port operations and management, and to an appreciation of the practical problems that confront port authorities today.[11]

Two major technological revolutions within the global maritime transport system have profoundly affected the development and character of seaports throughout the world. The first was the nineteenth-century change from sail to steam propulsion—a development which had a dramatic impact upon the character and even upon the location of seaports in many different countries. The second was the coming of the container. Major changes in cargo-handling methods have become increasingly widespread in recent years, and the rising importance of bulk handling installations has reflected technological pressures for the further refinement of transfers across the quayside. In this context, the use of standard-sized containers as a basis for transport systems linking inland terminals through ocean ports and sealanes became the dominant trend in the 1960s and effectively revolutionised cargo-handling techniques in the seaports of all advanced countries.[12] During the 1960s and early 1970s a high proportion of break-bulk ocean cargoes was unitised, port operation became increasingly automated and the overall productivity of world liner shipping was improved.

A controversial issue during this period was the extent to which less-developed countries in Asia and Africa would find it in their interests to adapt their port systems to the so-called 'container revolution'.[13] The main argument for increased containerisation of cargoes is that the pace is inexorably forced by the advanced countries, in the sense that ship operators involved in trades to and from less-developed countries require port facilities in those countries that match up at least to a rising world minimum level. Ports which do not conform to this standard, it is argued, are likely to find themselves seriously disadvantaged in terms of competition for trade. Against this view there is the argument that containerised transport systems are most economic when used to facilitate the multidirectional flow of high-value goods in quantity between advanced countries, and that their extensive use in less-developed countries is at present inappropriate. The relevance of the new maritime technologies to the economies and port systems of less-developed countries is still to some extent an open question, and the incorporation of Asian and African ports into this system has certainly presented many economic and technical problems; but there is no basic reason why these problems should not be overcome in circumstances where participation in the global maritime container network is seen as clearly advantageous.[14]

In the later 1960s and early 1970s the conversion of the Europe-Australia and Europe-Far East trades was a major factor in the rapid if somewhat unsteady growth of the world container transport network. As the major trades between advanced countries were containerised close to the limits of their potential, more rapid progress was made towards the containerisation of cargoes at ports in less-developed countries, particularly in the fast-rising economies of Southeast Asia and in India where Cochin played a significant dynamic role. By the mid-1970s the lessons of this process began to have a substantial effect upon the seaports of other less-developed areas including East Africa. The rates of increase in containerised throughputs were unexpectedly high at many ports and the view that container shipping services would develop rapidly only until trades between advanced countries were saturated with capacity was abandoned. World fleets of container ships continued to expand and today, in spite of the global economic recession, container traffic is increasingly penetrating the ports and hinterlands of virtually all parts of the Third and 'Fourth' Worlds.

The potential for the development of container services in the seaports of less-developed countries in Asia and Africa is of course related to a variety of factors, but reflects most directly the volume and character of general-cargo throughput. The extent to which this potential is realised depends upon the development of shipping services and port installations, but also requires coordinated planning between ship operators, land transport authorities, and government departments. Maritime factors, in the form of the pattern of shipping services and the character of general cargo trades, are the chief determinants of the development of container traffic at most ports, but in many countries the state of the inland transport network linking ports and hinterlands provides an important constraint upon the way in which the container transport system can operate. In order to work at maximum efficiency, container services are designed to link inland consignors with inland consignees. If inland transport systems are unable adequately to handle container traffic, this factor alone can seriously affect the efficient operation of the system. Ideally, container terminals require not only efficient rail and road links but also a series of efficiently operated inland container terminals at carefully selected points in traffic-generating zones within their hinterlands. The development of such an infrastructure is a point of high priority with many Asian governments, especially India.[15] It will be of great interest to observe how China will respond to this latest challenge across her maritime frontier.

During the 1970s container traffic became a very important component in the activity of all major Asian and African seaports, and substantial numbers of containers were also handled at many relatively minor ports. The establishment of USA-India and Europe-India/Pakistan full container services in the mid-1970s was an important development; major West African ports (Dakar, Abidjan, Lagos) were incorporated soon afterwards within the world container system. Developments in East African seaports came slightly later, and before the mid-1970s very few containers were seen in the area. From 1975 onwards, however, the growth of container traffic at Mombasa and Dar es Salaam has been remarkably rapid (Table 8.1); and it is quite clear that East Africa has crossed an important threshold in technological terms in this context. The experience of this particular part of Africa's maritime facade in responding to the challenge of containerisation is a useful indicator of an important trend now characteristic of many parts of Africa, Asia and other Third World areas.

East African seaports are now linked by container services with a variety of destinations in the Middle East, Southeast Asia and Japan, as well as with European and North American ports. Initially, as in most ports in less-developed countries, almost all containers handled were stuffed and unstuffed in the ports themselves, but as the system has expanded it has become possible to handle an increasing number of containers at inland depots. In Kenya the most obvious location for such depots is Nairobi; but other areas where traffic concentration is likely to warrant additional depots include western Kenya, southern Uganda and Rwanda. No inland container depots have yet been developed in Tanzania, but container traffic through Dar es Salaam to extranational hinterlands in Zambia and Burundi has grown considerably. Inland container depots in East Africa are rail-dependent, but the movement of containers by road transport is increasing.

The further development of container facilities and the growth of container throughputs is likely to increase the degree of concentration of traffic within the East African seaport complex at the two major terminals. In this context the recent experience of East African seaports is representative of a much broader canvas: only a selected number of economically important or strategically located Third World seaports have as yet been able to become

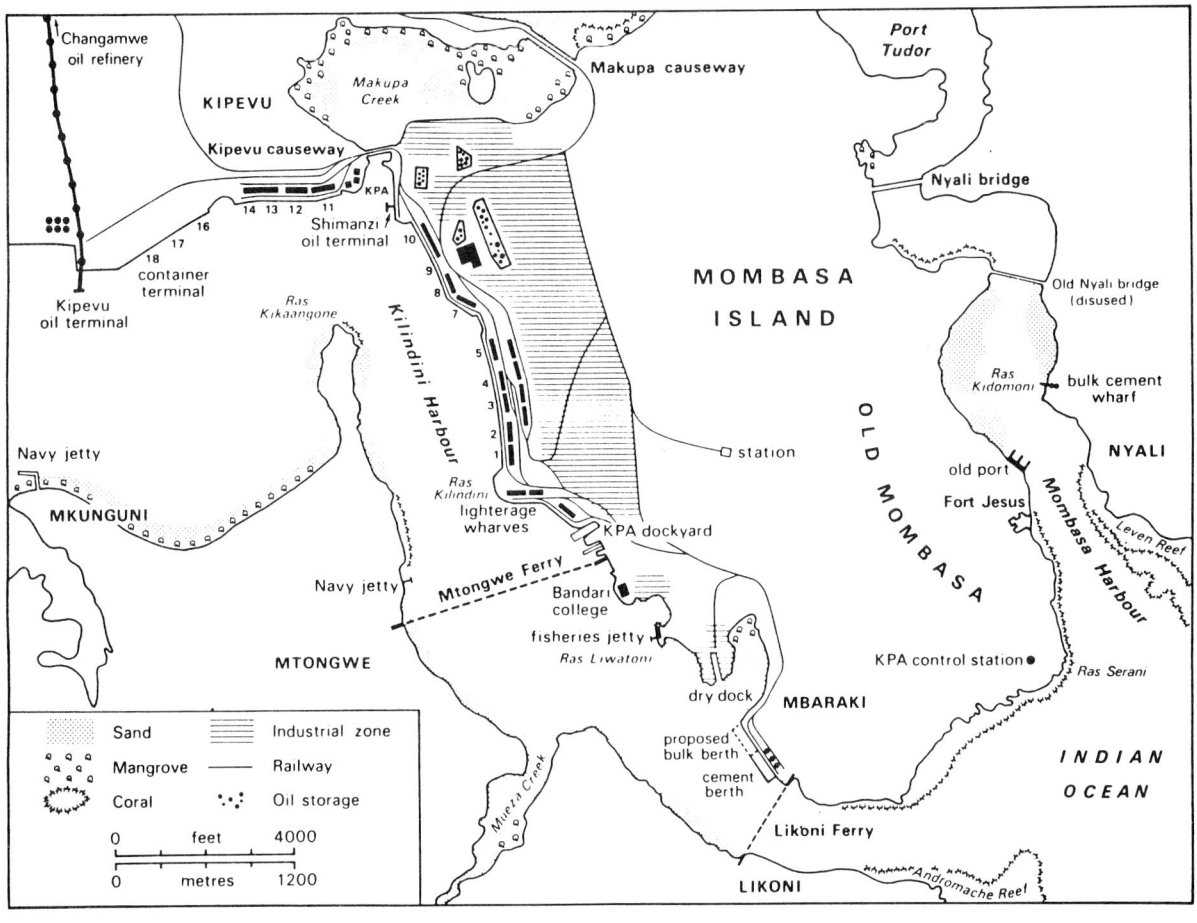

Map 14 The port of Mombasa, Kenya. A substantial area to the west of that shown is scheduled for future industrial development.

fully involved in the new world maritime transport system based upon the through-transport concept. Containerisation, like all earlier technological innovations in maritime transport, tends to operate selectively, to reduce the number and increase the relative importance of major ports, and to reduce the relative status of minor ports unable to attract sufficient traffic based on the new technology. Conversely, ports which—for whatever reason—wished to maintain or improve their hierarchical standing and thus were selected for the transition to containerisation, had to make significant commitments in terms of both finance and space. At the same time the economics of modern port development, the logistics of national-scale economic geography, and the legacies of port layouts and systems conceived in past times, often combine to produce serious congestion and considerable delays to ships awaiting berths.

In an era of rapid technological change, port systems in Asia and in Africa (as elsewhere) have responded in various ways to this fundamental problem of congestion and delay. From both the landward and maritime sides of the waterfront it is possible to detect a retreat from the traditional port areas. One symptom of this withdrawal within the port cities themselves is the increasingly widespread disquiet concerning pollution from port-related industries. Environmental pollution, including of course pollution of the sea, has not yet received as much attention as it deserves in the developing countries. On the landward side, within the framework of the nation-state, the removal of the national political capital function from its traditional cityport location (as in Pakistan or Tanzania) is at least in part a response to the problems of overconcentration of functions in a location originally selected and developed as a port. From a maritime perspective, the unsuitability of some Asian and African seaports for the handling of bulk cargoes and the accommodation of large bulk carriers has led to a variety of technological responses, including the use of undersea pipelines and offshore mooring buoys for oil traffic and the development of specialised terminals to serve specific systems of resource exploitation linking producer countries with overseas markets.

Demands for new ports have arisen in many countries in recent years as resources previously unexploited have been tapped, as regions hitherto underdeveloped have been incorporated more fully within modern economies, and as major new foci within the global maritime trading system have emerged. Pressure on existing facilities has led to major expansion schemes at ports such as Shanghai, Singapore and Hong Kong; large general-cargo ports such as Bombay and Madras have acquired more modern facilities; and some smaller-scale ports such as Port Kelang, Dubai and Dar es Salaam have seen rapid growth. In general, the consolidation and improvement of the existing port system has been the usual formula as is shown at Manila or Karachi. Nevertheless there have been various new port developments and proposals in several parts of Asia and the Indian Ocean, from the dramatic and costly artificial island ports developed in Japan and the Middle East to the new industrial port city growth poles projected for Manda Bay (Kenya)[16] and Pulau Batam (Indonesia)[17] as well as satellite ports such as Nhava Sheva opposite Bombay.

Maritime perspectives on ports and port systems: the case of East Africa 203

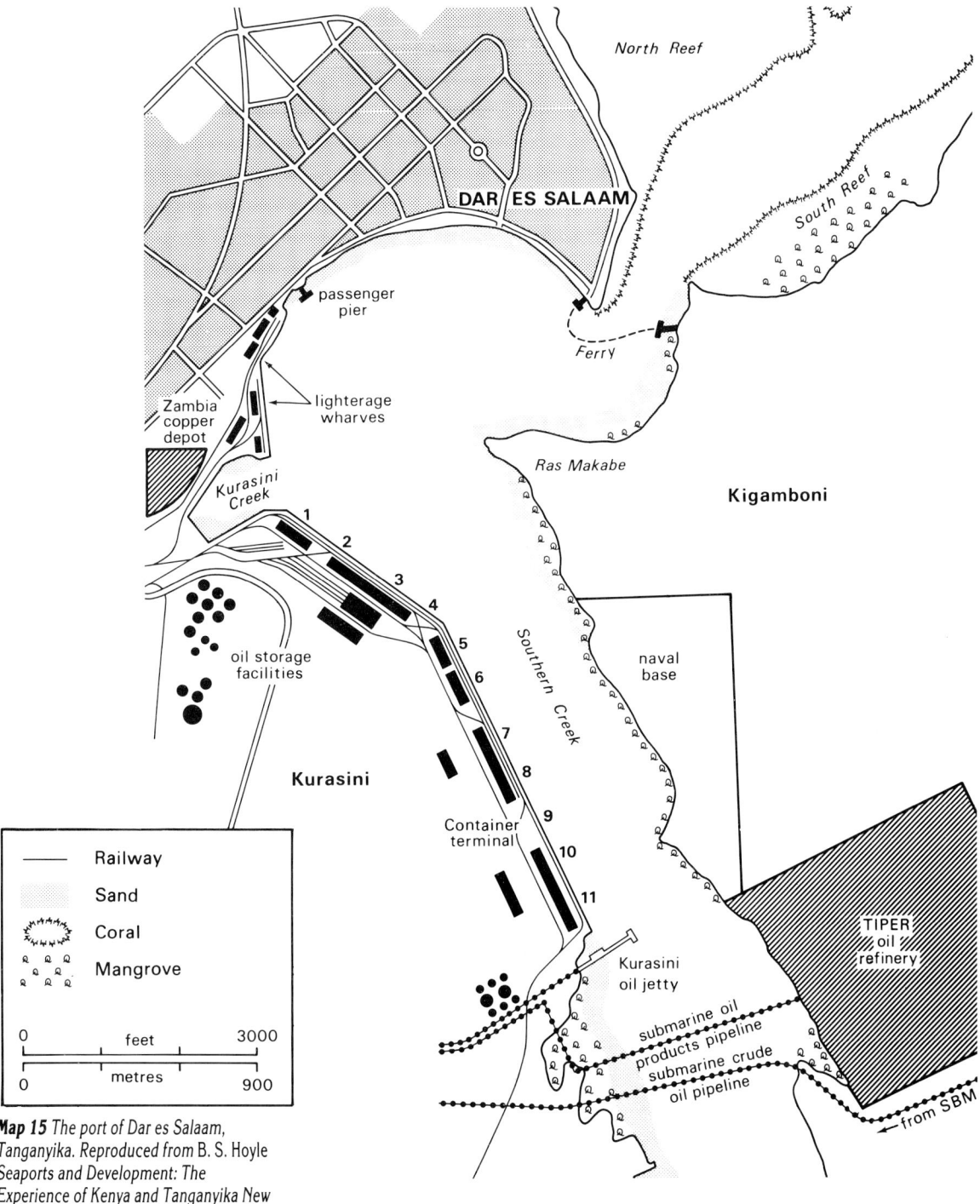

Map 15 The port of Dar es Salaam, Tanganyika. Reproduced from B. S. Hoyle *Seaports and Development: The Experience of Kenya and Tanganyika* New York/London, 1983; by permission.

Conclusion

An attempt has been made in this chapter to survey some aspects of East African seaports, in the past and today, with particular reference to maritime perspectives and to ways in which sea-derived factors and influences have affected processes of change and development. The theoretical, historical and technological themes discussed have underlined the importance of maritime factors in the port-selection process and in the ways in which ports respond differentially to factors affecting spatial, economic and political change. The political significance of seaport location and development, in terms of both the space economies of East African countries and their military strategies, is implicit in these themes and should not be overlooked. For although the countries of modern Africa, in general, possess very limited commercial or naval sea power, some eastern African seaports possess substantial strategic significance. Examples include Mombasa (Kenya), Maputo (Mozambique), Berbera (Somalia) and Assab (Ethiopia), which could conceivably become critical in the context of West-East relations, just as Aden and Kuwait, Singapore and Hong Kong have done, in very different contexts, in the past.

Today the seaports serving the modern economies and societies of East Africa are part of an interlocking global maritime transport system. Physically they lie on the shores of the Indian Ocean, but functionally they belong to the outer edges of the world network of sealanes, to the periphery of the global system whose three cores lie in Western Europe, North America and East Asia. What happens at the quayside in East African ports, in terms of commodity movements, is in the first instance a reflection of the condition of their hinterlands; but events, ultimately, are largely a result of initiatives taken elsewhere, beyond the seas, in areas of the world where economies are more powerful and technologies more advanced. In this perspective, the port cities of East Africa have much in common with others in the Third World, amongst which many in Asia still rank.

TABLE 8.1
Container traffic at major East African seaports, 1975-83

	1975	1976	1977	1978	1979	1980	1981	1982	1983
Mombasa									
No.* of containers handled:									
imports	0.6	1.6	2.3	4.7	8.0	15.5	22.0	27.4	41.7
exports	0.4	1.6	1.9	4.0	6.4	14.2	19.1	27.0	38.4
total†	1.3	3.4	4.6	9.1	15.2	30.4	42.7	55.1	80.1
Dar es Salaam									
No.* of containers handled:									
imports	0.2	0.3	0.8	1.1	2.4	4.7	9.8	15.1	14.1
exports	–	–	–	–	1.9	4.5	8.2	11.2	12.3
total†	0.2	0.3	0.8	1.1	4.3	9.3	18.0	26.3	26.4

Sources: Kenya Ports Authority, Tanzania Harbours Authority
Notes: * In thousands
† Including transshipment

Notes

1. The concept of the seaport as a gateway has been developed particularly by J. H. Bird. See 'Seaports as a subset of gateways for regions: a research survey' *Progress in Human Geography* 4, 1980, pp. 360-70; and 'Gateways: slow recognition by irresistible rise' *Tijdschrift voor Economische en Sociale Geografie* 74, 1983, pp. 196-202.
2. Two standard and essentially complementary texts on the geography of seaports and maritime transport are J. H. Bird *Seaports and seaport terminals* London, 1971 and A. D. Couper *The geography of sea transport* London, 1972. More recent contributions to this field from Italian and French authorities include A. Vallega's two volumes, *Per una geografia del mare* Milan, 1981 and *Ecumene oceano* Milan, 1984 and A. Vigarie's earlier study *Ports de commerce et vie littorale* Paris, 1979. See also A. D. Couper's edited work *The Times Atlas of the Oceans* London, 1983.
3. A similar approach is adopted by the present author in a paper entitled 'Gateways from the sea: some maritime perspectives on African seaports' presented to a conference on 'Africa and the Sea' held at Aberdeen in 1984. A volume of papers from this conference has been edited by Dr J.C. Stone and published by the University of Aberdeen African Studies Group under the title *Africa and the sea* Aberdeen, 1985. Certain paragraphs in the central section of the present chapter are based on the Aberdeen publication and I am grateful to the editor for permission to reuse in this way.
4. This diagram was first published in B.S. Hoyle and D. Hilling (eds.) *Seaport systems and spatial change: technology, industry and development strategies* Chichester, 1984, p.2, and is reproduced here by permission.
5. An overview of nineteenth/early-twentieth-century port building is offered by F. Broeze, P. Reeves & K. McPherson 'Imperial ports and the modern world economy: the case of the Indian Ocean' *Journal of Transport History* 7, 2 Sep. 1986, pp. 1-20. A fascinating—and negative—example in Japan during the same period is H. Masuda 'Japan's Industrial Development Policy and the Construction of the Nobiru Port: The Case Study of a Failure *The Developing Economies* 18, Tokyo, 1980, pp. 333-63. Details of the development of the port of Sattahip are to be found in R. Robinson 'Industrialization, new port and spatial development strategies in less-developed countries: the case of Thailand' in B.S. Hoyle and D.A. Pinder (eds.) *City port industralization and regional development: spatial analysis and planning strategies* Oxford, 1981, pp. 305-321. The opening of a new port complex at Iloilo (Philippines) was reported in *Lloyd's Maritime Asia*, August/September 1986, p. 40
6. See Bird *Seaports and Seaport Terminals*
7. These ideas on dynamic port systems were first elaborated by the late Dr Babafemi Ogundana in the context of Nigerian seaports. See his chapter on 'Patterns and problems of seaport evolution in Nigeria' in B.S. Hoyle and D. Hilling (eds.) *Seaports and development in tropical Africa* London, 1970, pp. 167-82; and his related paper 'The location factor in changing seaport significance in Nigeria' *Nigerian Geographical Journal* 14, 1970, pp. 71-88
8. The summary account of the East African case study given here is based upon a more extended treatment in B.S. Hoyle *Seaports and development: the experience of Kenya and Tanzania* New York and London, 1983, ch. 3: 'Seaport hierarchies'
9. The earliest documented account of the trading systems of the northwestern zone of the Indian Ocean, linking the Middle East with India and eastern Africa, is *The Periplus of the Erythraean Sea*. A new edition of the *Periplus*, edited by G.W.B. Huntingford, was published in 1976 (London, Hakluyt Society, 2nd series, vol. 151). Amongst the many works dealing with the maritime history of the western Indian Ocean one should maintain the classic G.F. Hourani *Arab Seafaring in the Indian Ocean in Ancient and Early Medieval Times* Princeton, 1951; A. Toussaint *History of the Indian Ocean* London, 1966, chs. 3-5; Ph.D. Curtin *Cross-Cultural Trade in World History* Cambridge, 1984, chs. 5-6, and K.N. Chaudhuri *Trade and Civilisation in the Indian Ocean* Cambridge 1985, ch. 2
10. On the social development of Mombasa since c.1800 one should see F.J. Berg, Mombasa under the Busaidi Sultanate, PhD thesis, University of Wisconsin, 1971; K.K. Janmohamed, A History of Mombasa, c.1895-1939, PhD thesis, North-western Univerity, 1978; and H.J. de Blij *Mombasa; An African City* Evanston, Ill., 1968. A significant study covering the one half of the port city's population that, besides prostitutes, is usually overlooked is M.A. Strobel *Muslim Women in Mombasa, 1890-1975* New Haven/London, 1979
11. For a general consideration of these problems see B. Slack 'Technology and seaports in the 1980s' *Tijdschrift voor Economische en Sociale Geografie* 71, 1980, pp. 108-113
12. Generally on containerisation see H.L. Beth et al. *25 Years of World Shipping* London, 1984, ch. II, pt. 3, and H.J. Witthöft *Container* Herford 1977

13 See, for example, Witthöft *Container* pp. 24-25, but also the increasingly more contemplative annual reports of the major liner shipping companies involved in the overseas trade of lesser developed countries
14 A very recent example is that of the Assam tea industry which was, for a long time, hampered by the restrictive conditions of its antiquated land transport system. See, for example, *Fairplay* 26 June 1985 and *Lloyd's Maritime Asia* May 1986, p. 50
15 *Lloyd's Maritime Asia* October 1986, p. 47, and April 1987, pp. 21, 23 and 31
16 The proposal to develop a new port city at Manda Bay on the north Kenya coast does not seem to be economically sound, but may become so in due course. The case is discussed in detail in B.S. Hoyle 'Cityport industrialisation and regional development in less-developed countries: the tropical African experience' in Hoyle and Pinder (eds.) *Cityport industrialization and regional development* pp. 281-303

Further reading

Bird, J.H. *Seaports and seaport terminals* London 1971. An essential overview of theoretical viewpoints by a noted authority on the geography of ports and port systems.

———— 'Gateways: Slow Recognition by Irresistible Rise' *Tijdschrift voor Economische en Sociale Geografie* 74, 1983, pp. 196-202. Pursues the idea of seaports as gateways.

Hoyle, B.S. *Seaports and development: the experience of Kenya and Tanzania* New York/London 1983. Provides the only detailed geographical analysis of East African ports in their Indian Ocean context.

Slack, B. 'Technology and Seaports in the 1980s' *Tijdschrift voor Economische en Sociale Geografie* 71, 1980, pp. 108-113. A key paper on the subject.

CHAPTER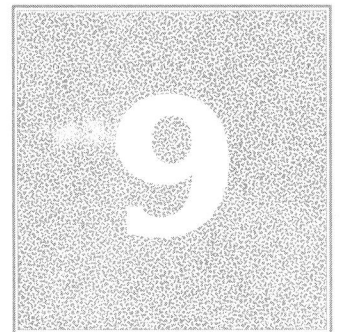

Atiya Habeeb Kidwai

Port cities in a national system of ports and cities: a geographical analysis of India in the twentieth century

The purpose of this chapter is to discuss some of the major conceptual problems involved in the use of the term 'port city' as first outlined in 1982 by Reeves, Broeze and McPherson,[1] through a statistical analysis of the major ports and port cities of India in the twentieth century; as within this period the politico-economic imperatives before and after independence were so totally different, it has, whenever necessary, been divided in its colonial and post-colonial segments. Before a description of the method used is given, it may be useful to briefly summarise the salient issues involved. The starting point of Reeves and associates was their observation that in the existing historiography port cities all too often had been treated either as 'ports' or as 'cities'; the physical conjunction of the two terms apparently had not resulted in a concomitant emergence of the specific concept of the 'port city'. They emphasised the need for this conceptualisation if the term were to be usefully employed in historical analysis. Such conceptualisation, according to them, could be achieved only if a proper appreciation were given to the role played by the port in determining the structure and functioning of the city identified as a port city.

The preliminary stage of any analysis of port cities must be to invest the term with meaning. The first questions to be asked, therefore, should be:

1 Which cities are (or, in what period, were) port cities and which cities are/were not port cities?

2 What is the nature and extent of economic, socio-cultural and political interaction between the port (as a social entity) and the city (as a social entity)?

3 In what ways and forms does the social structure of port cities change?

This chapter will, by taking India as a case study, attempt to probe into the first of these queries. Its conceptual starting point will be the definition proposed by Reeves and associates of the port city, viz. that it is an urban settlement with specific characteristics derived from its maritime functions of exchange, enterprise and transport. These functions differentiate the port city from other urban settlements in the region and determine its physical, economic and social configuration. It is also stressed that the port and the settlement associated with it evolve over time; that there is a balance between the functions and the settlement; and that a port city can (and does) move beyond that stage.

The development of seaports in any economy involves the interplay of a wide range of factors. Many of these factors are associated directly or indirectly with the physical environment, others with economic or political conditions or with technological changes—the latter both internal and external/maritime. Moreover, these factors gradually organise a country's ports into an integrated system, wherein ports are hierarchically arranged and have a prescribed role and a hinterland. Over time these roles change, the fortunes of individual ports fluctuate and their hinterlands expand or contract. Finally the point is reached in this evolutionary process, when the port system gets webbed in with the national or regional city system. The concept of the port city becomes especially useful for the analysis of this historical juncture, which, as the case of India clearly shows, broadly coincides with the growth of modern ports in colonial and less developed countries.[2]

A geographical/statistical investigation of port cities, based on the systemic approach outlined above and in consonance with the concept given by Reeves and associates, must rest on the use of both qualitative and quantitative indices, suitable both for the identification of these cities in India's national systems of ports and cities, and for their differentiation from ports (with an urban nucleus) on the one hand and cities (which were once primarily ports) on the other. These indices should also be useful in indicating the historical moment when port cities are transformed into such 'general' cities. They should, therefore, be based on data that lend themselves to a cross-national time-series analysis of ports and cities in terms of both their hierarchical position and their economic base. For the purposes of this chapter a port city may, therefore, be redefined as that settlement which, first, maintains its rank both amongst the system of ports and the system of cities,[3] and, secondly, which does not diversify its economic base to the extent that the port-generated economic activities in the city no more remain its dominant economic functions. In the following pages this definition will be put to the test on the major ports of India, which country with her long history of inland and maritime trade presents an illuminating case study for the analysis of the processes which pattern a port system and enmesh it with the overall urban system of the country.

Few countries of the world, indeed, have witnessed changes in their port system of such magnitude as India, where the configuration has changed from century to century; even the shifting port system of East Africa outlined in Hoyle's chapter shows less dramatic alterations. The country's existing port system began to evolve in the seventeenth century in response to European trade which was then making its presence felt in the subcontinent. European traders initially patronised the Mughal ports on the western coast where they were permitted to trade freely with Indians. Lahiri-Bunder, Cambay, Broach, Somnath, Dwarka, Diu, Rander and Surat were the important imperial ports of this time.[4] Port paramountcy remained with Cambay and Lahiri-Bunder throughout the sixteenth century.

At the beginning of the seventeenth century, Surat, situated on the navigable Tapti, began to grow in importance. It was chosen as the site for the earliest trading 'factories' not only by the Portuguese who came here first, but also by the English, the Dutch and the French East India Companies. It was the hub both of the sealanes of the Indian Ocean and the inland caravan routes, and dominated the foreign trade of India for over a century.[5] The second most important trading 'factory' during this period was Broach. These two Gujerat 'factories' gradually became the base of the British East India Company which soon started a keen trade in spices. The Malabar coast provided two rare spices, cardamom and cinnamon, and was also the second great supplier of black pepper at this time. A large number of small ports developed in quick succession in response to this trade and dotted the western coastline.[6] Surat, however, continued to be the premier port of India. It was only in 1667 that the Company was able to establish their independent port at Bombay. Strenuous efforts were made to attract trade to the island. But the Company's dream of making Bombay an effective rival to Surat remained unfulfilled for more than a century and the island's long struggle to supplant the northern rival may be said to have lasted even beyond 1759 when Surat was captured by the English forces.

Between 1660 and 1680 the centre of gravity of the Company's commercial policy moved to the south, from Surat to Madras, which had been established in 1638. As Arasaratnam shows in Chapter 3, the road to hegemony in Coromandel was not an easy one for Madras. Ironically, around the time when it was in the ascendancy, its primacy in India was challenged by Bengal when from the early eighteenth century the focus of Western traders shifted to the products of northeastern India. Bengal emerged as the premier trading region of the Company as it offered three staple products (cotton muslins, raw silk and saltpetre), which were of great commercial importance for European trading companies.

The growth and development of ports on the northeastern coast of India, like the opening up of the trade in that region, was a slow, steady and gradual process. Geographically the eastern coastline is less indented than that of the western coast and is also full of banks and shallows which render navigation by traditional methods in the area perilous. The rivers disgorging on the east coast tend to change their courses too frequently and since they were, at that time, the principal means of communication, port towns developing on their banks or mouths could easily become ephemeral. In the Mughal period Satgaon, Hugli, Chittagong, Anjaner, Jalesar and Balasore were the principal seaports. Satgaon remained the chief port of Bengal until the emergence of Hugli. Founded by the Portuguese in 1579, Hugli had experienced rapid growth and for a century remained the most flourishing and the most populous of the trading ports of Bengal. It, however, conceded its place in the early decades of the eighteenth century to Calcutta, which from the swamps and marshes of lower Bengal emerged as a regional port and a budding metropolis.

In 1757 the Company established its political supremacy in the sub-continent after the Battle of Plassey; in consequence, the period between 1757 and 1813 recorded major changes, both structural and quantitative, in the Indian trade.[7] The Company attempted to enforce a monopolistic trade in traditional Indian export goods of fine textiles, opium, foodstuffs, precious metals and some manufactured products. Catering to this trade, and in a well-balanced symbiosis between Company and private interests, Calcutta grew from an enclave port on the edge of a vast, though relatively inaccessible, hinterland to become the trading centre of an empire. The volume of Calcutta's trade with England soon equalled the total trade of the remainder of the Company's settlements in the entire East.[8] Port primacy shifted from Madras to Calcutta where it remained well into the nineteenth century. During the last hundred years it has moved between Bombay and Calcutta.

During the Raj period India was gradually drawn into the orbit of the world capitalist system. One of the major objectives of the British government in India during the nineteenth century was to promote the overseas (Western) trade of the country by creating a modern system of ports as well as other transport and communication infrastructure, so that the commercial penetration of the colony could be intensified. A network of railways and roads was constructed from the ports to the interior parts of the country. Gradually the focal points of these transport networks became major population centres which, in turn, grew into primate metropolitan cities.[9] The spatial organisation of India's national economy has also after independence been controlled by these primate cities.

In the post-Independence period the biased economic policy which had characterised the development of transport in colonial India gave way to a more comprehensive and positive approach to economic and social development. The need for economic independence was asserted by both planners and politicians. This not only meant the breaking up of the ties which had hitherto bound economic development to the interests of the parent country but also stressed the necessity to create preconditions for sustained growth. This fundamental change in economic thinking strengthened the desire to

A geographical analysis of India in the twentieth century

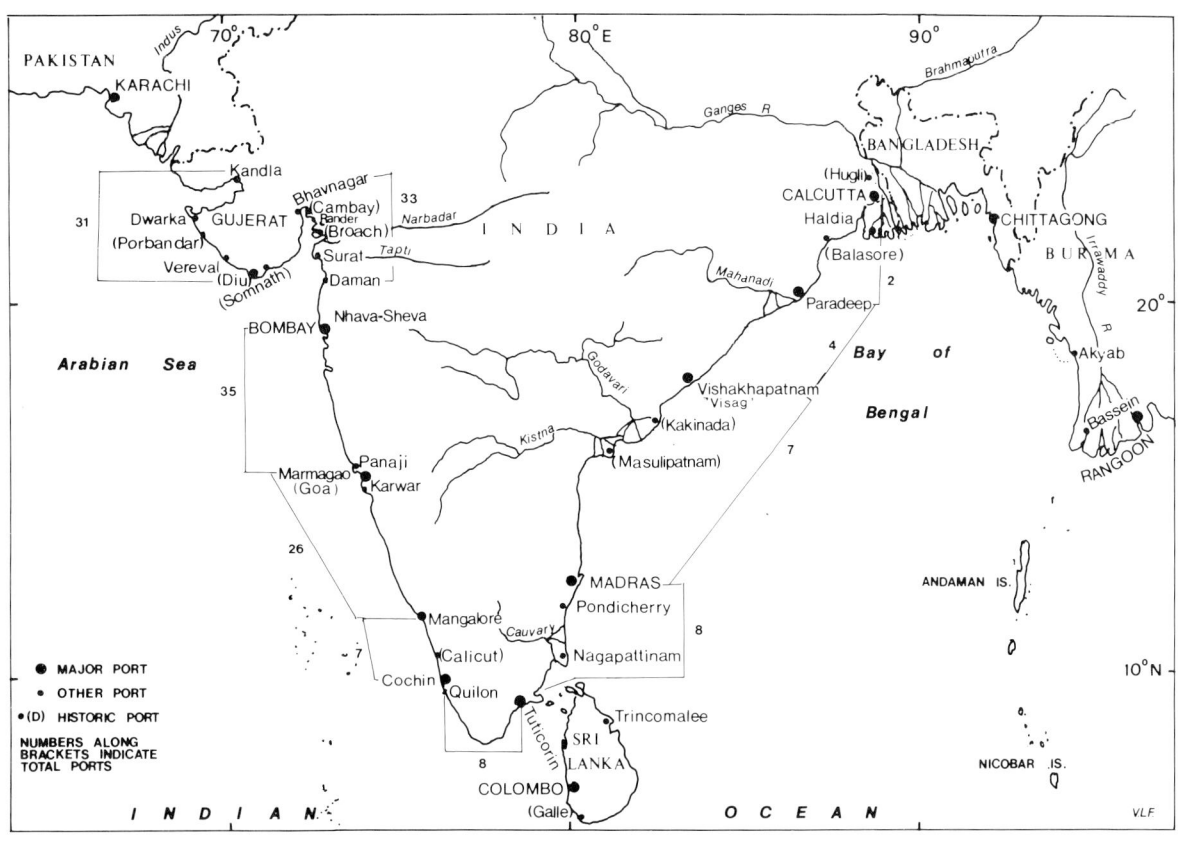

Map 16 The ports of India, twentieth century

improve India's infrastructure, diversify her economic base and embark upon a systematic policy of industrialisation. This ideological and political commitment also gave a strong impetus to the development of ports. Consequently, considerable change has occurred in the patterning of large ports on the 5560 kilometres which comprise the west and east coasts of the country. Besides twenty-two intermediate ports and 204 minor ports India now (1988) has eleven major ports; until Independence this status had been given to only five: Calcutta, Madras, Bombay (and Karachi), and newcomers Vishakhapatnam (1917) and Cochin (1920). The cargo-handling capacity of the ports has increased manyfold and integrated links have been established among all modes of transport for the quicker and better functioning of the ports, vitally desirable because at present the share of seaborne trade of the country is more than 95 percent of her total trade in any given year. The major ports are administered by the central government, the others by their respective state governments. Some of the major ports have recently been chosen as 'growth poles' and thus become sites for the development of industrial complexes. As a result they have acquired the potential of transforming themselves into major port cities of India.

The hierarchical ranking of ports, port cities and cities

Ports are usually arranged in a hierarchy with respect to the volume of their traffic measured in terms of tonnage, as this is a much better indicator of port activity than the value of goods imported and exported. Though imperfect, especially if it fails to distinguish between general and single-commodity specialised ports, this is still a convenient criterion of comparing the relative significance of ports. Table 9.1 provides a summary of the ranking as well as the historical variability and changes in ranking for the ten largest ports in India (as in 1980) for which complete time-series data are available from 1920.[10] These figures indicate that India's ports broadly fall into three categories: five ports (Bombay, Madras, Marmagao, Kandla and Paradeep) show relative stability, varying only by one position or maintaining their position; two ports (Vishakhapatnam and Tuticorin) show extreme variation, with the former gaining by ten positions and the latter losing by five. Three ports, finally (Calcutta, Cochin and Mangalore) show moderate variation, with Calcutta losing three ranks. Considering the average deviation in the rankings, Vishakhapatnam has shown the maximum deviation, while still gaining in rank. Cochin and Mangalore show moderate deviation and have also gained in rank. Calcutta and Tuticorin show significant deviation too, but they slipped in the rankings.

For an analysis of the ports in terms of their ranks amongst the system of cities in the country, we refer to the study of Swain on Indian ports.[11] In his study Swain found that rank correlation values between the volume of cargo handled by ports and their population size was as high as 1.00 up to 1911

TABLE 9.1
Variability of ranks of major ports in India, 1920-80

Ports	1920	1930	1940	1950	1960	1970	1980	Average rank	Range of rank	Net: gain/loss
1 Calcutta	1	2	1	2	2	2	4	2.42	4	-3
2 Bombay	2	1	2	1	1	1	1	1.28	1	+1
3 Madras	3	3	3	3	4	4	3	3.28	1	0
4 Karachi	4	4	4	—	—	—	—	—	—	—
5 Tuticorin	5	5	5	5	8	9	10	6.71	5	-5
6 Nagapatnam	6	6	10	—	—	—	—	—	—	—
7 Dhanus Kodi	7	7	9	—	—	—	—	—	—	—
8 Cuddalore	8	12	14	—	—	—	—	—	—	—
9 Cochin	9	8	6	4	6	6	6	6.42	3	+3
10 Calicut	10	9	12	—	—	—	—	—	—	—
11 Chittagong	11	14	8	—	—	—	—	—	—	—
12 Mangalore	12	13	12	7	9	10	9	10.28	6	+3
13 Porto Novo	13	10	13	—	—	—	—	—	—	—
14 Telicherry	14	11	15	—	—	—	—	—	—	—
15 Vishakhapatnam	15	13	11	6	5	3	5	8.28	10	+10
16 Marmagao	*	*	*	*	3	2	2	2.33	1	+1
17 Kandla	*	*	*	*	7	8	7	7.33	1	0
18 Paradeep	*	*	*	*	*	7	8	7.50	1	-1

Source: Derived from data on total cargo handled by the ports in respective years. Government of India, *Basic Port Statistics*
Notes: — data not available
* had not emerged as major ports

and 0.75, 0.89, 0.82, and 0.89 respectively in 1921, 1931, 1941, and 1951. This indicates that large ports until the 1950s were also large cities.

This situation, however, soon altered. Correlation values dropped dramatically to 0.54 in 1961, 0.45 in 1971, and 0.40 in 1981. The main cause of this divergence was the emergence of new ports like Marmagao, Kandla and Paradeep which are primarily bulk-exporting ports and have only very small populations. Individually, Kandla and Paradeep have very low values, viz. 0.17 and 0.00 respectively. For almost all other major ports, however, the correlation value has remained high between 1920 and 1981.[12] The figure for Calcutta is still relatively high (0.69) but less than those of the other ports. This indicates that, relatively speaking, in Calcutta city growth is becoming more pronounced than port growth and that it is losing its character as a port city and is emerging as a general city. In Kandla and Paradeep, by contrast, port growth dominates; they are largely ports without a sizeable population and may not yet be characterised as port cities.

The suggestion that Calcutta has evolved from a 'port city' into just a 'general city' can further be substantiated through an analysis of the major ports in the country in terms of their position within their port complexes, that is, the totality of the ports covering the particular hinterland which they serve. This analysis is also important because ports vie for hegemony within their regional complexes and rival ports influence each other's fortunes. The structure of port complexes develops, as is also shown by Arasaratnam and Hoyle in this volume, through a process of changing port hierarchies, in which the ranking of ports changes over time and the composite pattern of the complex shows an alternation of concentration and diffusion. As Rimmer has shown for New Zealand, some ports may nevertheless remain leaders over successive periods of concentration and diffusion.[13]

TABLE 9.2
Percentage shares of cargo handled by the major ports in their respective port-complexes, 1915-20 to 1981-85

	1915-1920	1921-1930	1931-1940	1941-1950	1951-1960	1961-1970	1971-1980	1981-1985
Calcutta	97.9	98.1	83.5	94.4	80.3	51.4	45.1	42.2
Bombay	88.4	85.9	81.7	66.6	85.9	72.9	72.6	73.0
Madras	52.7	60.6	54.4	74.1	72.0	83.6	75.5	75.0
Karachi	99.8	99.9	99.4	—	—	—	—	—

Source: Derived from data on total cargo handled by the ports

The percentage share of cargo handled by the major ports in their respective port complexes between 1915-20 and 1980-85 is given in Table 9.2. It is clear from that table that amongst the four primate ports Calcutta has experienced the greatest loss in its relative share in the total cargo handled by the complex of which it is the major participant (Bengal-Orissa). Between 1915 and 1950 Calcutta handled, on average, more than 90 percent of the total cargo of its complex. This share was reduced considerably after Independence, viz. to 80 percent during 1951-60. This trend continued unabated until in 1971-75 its share amounted to only 47 percent; by 1985 it had further dropped to c.40 percent. This reduction can be attributed mainly to the silting of the approaches to the port of Calcutta and the consequent diversion of the hinterland's cargo through other ports to relieve congestion. Moreover, the new port of Paradeep in Orissa started handling much of the bulk cargo which was earlier passing through Calcutta itself as well as that from newly opened extractive industries. The share of Calcutta is likely to decline further once the new port of Haldia comes into full operation by the late 1980s and as containerised traffic increases, which cannot be handled by the riverine port of Calcutta.

The trends followed by the Madras port complex (the classical Coromandel coast of Tamil-Nadu with Andhra Pradesh) were contrary to those of Calcutta, as the share of Madras had increased rather than diminished with time. Between 1915-20 and 1981-85 its share rose from 52.7 percent to 75.0 percent. The main reason for this trend is that the facilities at Madras port were adequately improved so that no need to divert traffic to other ports was felt.

Bombay (covering the whole western coast from Kerala to Hyderabad) has followed the path of Calcutta but has been able to maintain its regional supremacy, though in a slightly reduced form. (The building of the modern port of Cochin impinged statistically on it from the 1930s, but also diverted cargo from Madras' South Indian hinterland.) Karachi, finally, can be called the true primate amongst the ports of pre-Independence India as it has no rivals of any significance in Sind; it still maintains this absolute hegemony in Pakistan.

One more indicator of the changing balance of India's national port system is that through a calculation of the deviation from each port's status in the national port hierarchy and its ranking according to Haggett's formula.[14] This analysis indicates that almost all the ten major ports (Calcutta seems to be the only exception) show a positive deviation, which means that their influence in the national system of ports is becoming stronger. Minor ports on the other hand show negative deviation and there is, indeed, a sharp contrast in the figures for the major and the minor ports. This indicates a considerable degree of port concentration at the expense of the smaller ports. But, at the same time, a break in the pattern of cargo concentration amongst the major ports is taking place. Only two major ports showed a positive deviation in 1950-51, whereas that number increased to eight in 1985. The primacy of ports like Calcutta has thus been reduced to a great extent, while intermediate ports like Marmagao, Paradeep and Vishakhapatnam (which are basically single-commodity facilities for bulk exports like iron ore and coal) raised their capacity faster than the national rate. This supports the conclusion that the prime port cities are losing their primacy amongst the system of port cities and are tending to become 'general cities'. In the system of cities, however, they still reign supreme.

On the basis of this analysis we may conclude that Calcutta is now more of a city than a port city; Bombay in some respects is in the process of transformation from a port city and Madras is a true port city as it has been able to maintain its importance both in the system of ports and the system of cities. Amongst the newer ports Mangalore is following the path of Calcutta and Vishakhapatnam of Madras. Tuticorin, Marmagao, Kandla and Paradeep, finally, are ports rather than port cities.

The economic structure of port cities

Seaports, in their purest form mere 'gateways', often emerge as a vital factor in the economic growth of the vicinity or the cities which grow around them; they have the potential of becoming foci for the agglomeration of port-based manufacturing and for the growth of different types of auxiliary and downstream activities. These activities may have been initially related to the port industry such as packaging, storing, reprocessing etc., but later on tend to attract a variety of ancillary activities to the settlement. Especially in developing countries ports are often designed to become the growth poles at which economic development is concentrated.[15] Consequently, a high percentage of new industry in these countries is located in the ports.

With the passage of time the port grows both in terms of population and functions, both economic and non-economic. As the population grows and the ancillary functions become self-propelling, the port spins off webs of interlinkages around it and new ancillary functions develop. This diversification transforms the port from being merely a node in the transport system into a port city. A third stage is reached when the port-generated functions are no more the main propelling functions in the city's economy and lose in significance to other economic and non-economic activities which develop unhinged from the port. When these functions dominate the city's economic and social life, it loses its character as a port city and becomes a 'general' city.

To determine whether in a port city the port is still dominant or whether it functions as no more than a subordinate system, the relative importance and magnitude of the port's functions must be gauged. The indicators selected for this analysis are: first, the proportion of the port workers in the total number of workers of the city as well as in the total number of workers engaged in transport activities;[16] if these proportions decrease, this implies that the port function, relatively speaking, is losing its significance; second, the occupational structure of the port cities, in order to identify their broad economic characteristics as well as the changes over time in those characteristics. Both yardsticks should yield some specific indication of the development of ancillary port activities.

From Table 9.3 we find that in the primate ports of Bombay, Calcutta and Madras, though the total number of port workers, as well as their percentage

TABLE 9.3
Port workers, total workers and transport workers in the major ports of India, 1961-86

Ports	Total port workers[1] (in '000)		% of port workers to total workers[2]			% of port workers to transport workers		
	1961	1986	1961	1971	1981	1961	1971	1981
Bombay	42.5	41.7	3.6	1.9	1.4	30.7	15.6	14.4
Calcutta	29.1	27.8	1.7	1.3	0.9	15.4	12.3	9.7
Madras	14.3	12.3	2.5	1.4	1.1	21.3	8.2	9.2
Tuticorin	4.0	2.4	0.9	1.3	N.A	6.3	8.9	N.A
Cochin	5.9	6.8	6.4	5.3	3.8	40.3	33.1	26.2
Mangalore	0.3	1.4	0.4	1.2	1.2	5.2	10.5	11.7
Vishakhapatnam	9.5	11.9	17.5	9.9	N.A	80.8	39.3	N.A
Marmagao	1.8	3.7	6.6	14.2	N.A	42.3	30.8	N.A
Kandla	0.8	3.5	17.6	39.7	N.A	59.1	75.6	N.A
Paradeep	N.O	2.6	N.O	16.2	N.A	N.O	38.4	N.A
Haldia	N.O	3.4	N.O	N.A	N.A	N.O	N.A	N.A

Sources: 1 Annual Reports published by respective port authorities
2 Census of India, 1961, 1981
Notes: N.O. = Not operational
N.A. = Not available

share in the total transport workers in these cities, is quite substantial, they form quite an insignificant part of the total city workers. Moreover, their number as well as their percentage share, both in the transport and total workers, has declined between 1961 and 1981. In the newer ports, however, the number of port workers is not high but it forms a substantial part of the total city workers and a major part of the total transport workers. A comparison of the data on port workers in 1961 and 1986 indicates that in most of these newer ports the trend of growth is positive as opposed to the negative rate of growth observed in the primate ports.

TABLE 9.4
Sectoral distribution of workers in the primate ports, 1872-1981

	Bombay			Calcutta			Madras		
	L_s	L_t	I_t	L_s	L_t	I_t	L_s	L_t	I_t
1872	4.0	90.7	2226	12.3	78.9	639	26.3	70.9	269
1881	6.4	90.2	1416	9.9	83.2	835	29.5	65.7	223
1891	7.8	89.5	1145	14.9	77.6	517	—	—	—
1901	9.6	88.2	915	21.6	70.2	324	29.5	66.2	224
1911	23.3	74.9	321	18.6	73.3	393	31.5	42.1	203
1921	26.2	72.6	276	20.9	70.2	336	24.3	72.9	300
1971	45.3	53.1	115	43.3	56.3	222	34.2	65.3	195
1981	44.6	53.8	121	44.3	53.4	121	37.5	58.2	155

Source: Based on data on occupational characteristics of workers, Census of India, 1872-1981
Notes: L_s proportion of workers employed in secondary sector
L_t proportion of workers employed in tertiary sector

The data on occupational structure is available for three ports (Calcutta, Bombay and Madras) for the ten decades between 1872 and 1971 and for all ports for 1961, 1971 and 1982. In Table 9.4 the percentage distribution of the total workers into secondary (L_s) and tertiary (L_t) sectors and the index of tertiarisation (I_t), which indicates the number of tertiary sector workers per 100 secondary workers, is given for the three major ports for the period 1872-1971.[17] The data indicate that the share of the secondary sector has increased considerably: from 4.0 percent to 44.6 percent in Bombay, from 12.3 percent to 44.3 percent in Calcutta and from 26.3 percent to 37.5 percent in Madras. The substantial decline in the I_t values further brings out the structural changes that have taken place in these port cities.

How much of this industrialisation is related to the port? The extent of this linkage can be assessed through an analysis of the structure of the secondary sector. From the data in Table 9.5 we find that, though these 'port cities' have a substantial share in the total industrial establishments found in all the metropolitan cities in India (69.2 percent in 1901 and 44.9 percent in 1971), their industrial structure is not much different. The consumer goods sector proliferates and the capital goods sector is only slightly above the metropolitan average. In terms of types of industrial establishments, those belonging to food and textile industries are most numerous, followed by metal, machinery and chemical products.[18]

TABLE 9.5
Industrial structure of the primate ports of India, 1901, 1971

		Capital goods	Intermediate goods	Consumer goods	Transport Equipment	% share in total establishments
		% are in terms of total industrial establishments				
Bombay	1901	0.2	13.1	83.1	3.7	20.8
	1971	13.6	13.8	67.6	5.0	19.4
Calcutta	1901	1.7	20.1	77.4	0.7	39.9
	1971	14.7	13.9	67.5	3.9	18.6
Madras	1901	0.9	16.8	79.2	3.1	11.5
	1971	10.9	15.6	57.7	15.8	6.9
All metropolitan	1901	0.6	15.8	81.3	2.3	100.0
cities	1971	9.8	23.1	61.8	5.4	100.0

Source: Based on data for industrial establishments, Census of India, 1901, 1971

Historically, there is no doubt that in the earlier phases of the development of the primate ports the port function did provide an impetus to industrial growth linked to shipbuilding and repairs,[19] but the situation changed dramatically after the 1850s. For this 'underdevelopment' two factors were largely responsible: with the triumph of the metal and steam-engined ships, Indian shipbuilding faded into insignificance,[20] and, as the railway network started branching out from these ports after 1853 and connected them to the national space economy, it was no more the port facility but the transport connectivity and the infrastructural base available in them that attracted some industries. These industries were, by and large, small, consumer-oriented and those which seek an urban and not necessarily a port location.[21] Industrial growth in Calcutta, Bombay and Madras gradually became unhinged from the port function and port growth. As opposed to this, the newer ports of Paradeep, Vishakhapatnam, Haldia and Kandla have become the foci of port-linked industrialisation based on fertilisers, iron and steel, petrochemicals and free-trade zones respectively. Consequently the port function in these cities will continue to remain important.

The services in the tertiary sector linked to the port function are primarily related to trade, finance, insurance, brokerage and transport. In this general survey it has not been possible to trace the development of these functions in each of the ports under consideration. However, on the basis of the data given in Table 9.6 one may conclude that in the three major port cities, services relating to trade and finance occupy about a quarter of the workers in the tertiary sector. But the other services like non-professional, personal and social overhead, which have only tenuous links with port activities, also proliferate. On the other hand, we find that in 1971 in the smaller ports like Marmagao,

Kandla and Paradeep, transport engages about 40 to 50 percent of the tertiary workers and trade and commerce between 10 and 22 percent. Professional services in them are less developed as compared to the larger port cities.[22]

TABLE 9.6
Percentage distribution of workers engaged in the different activities of the tertiary sector in the primate port cities of India, 1961, 1971
(Percentages are in terms of total tertiary workers)

		Social overhead	Personal Professional	Personal Non-professional	Community	Financial	Trade Wholesale	Trade Retail	Unspecified
Bombay	1961	37.5	3.4	22.2	2.3	5.5	3.6	22.2	3.2
	1971	38.8	3.6	19.3	2.7	10.0	3.5	22.6	—
Calcutta	1961	35.5	3.1	22.3	2.5	4.6	4.6	21.7	5.6
	1971	35.4	4.1	21.3	2.0	7.5	7.3	24.2	—
Madras	1961	36.3	3.7	15.3	4.1	7.1	2.4	17.4	13.4
	1971	57.0	2.5	12.7	3.4	3.5	1.5	19.0	—

Source: Based on 3-digit classification of occupations. Census of India, 1961, 1971

Conclusion

The main conclusions which can now be drawn are fourfold. First, and most importantly, in terms of relative ranks and growth trends, no consistent pattern has been followed by the Indian ports. But in the colonial period the general tendency has been that the major ports have both absolutely and relatively shown a positive growth in the national port system, whereas the intermediate and minor ports remained stagnant or experienced insignificant growth. This pattern changed in the post-Independence period when the major ports showed a relative loss of cargo handled in comparison to the intermediate ports.

Second, the relationship between the ranks of the ports in terms of cargo handled and their ranks in terms of population size has been weak, particularly in the post-Independence period. This indicates that some cities like Calcutta, which started as primate port cities, are now general cities and have lost their primacy in the system of ports. Some ports, however, have maintained their position in both port and city ranking; these, Bombay, Madras, Vishakhapatnam and Cochin, can be called port cities.

Third, in terms of the industrial and service sectors, the old ports like Calcutta, Bombay and Madras have acquired a diversified structure resembling that of any metropolitan city. The economic structure of new ports, by contrast, is less diversified.

Fourth, in the ports where the port function dominates the economy of the city the rate of growth of employment generated by the port is higher irrespective of the total volume of port labour. Consequently, although the total number of workers in the old established ports like Calcutta and Bombay is high, the rate of growth of the labour force involved is low.

It should, finally, be pointed out that these conclusions only give a very generalised picture of reality and are based on a limited analysis of restricted data. This analysis is neither complete nor comprehensive as the broad span of the subject demands a more profound historical treatment than is provided here. Each of the ports considered in this study should be subjected to detailed micro-level studies so that issues raised will prove to be very useful for geographical research in the Third World where port-based regional development strategies are still popular, where functional and spatial ties between cities and ports have not yet loosened as they have in the more advanced countries, and where ports will continue to be transformed into port cities.

Notes

1. Peter Reeves, Frank Broeze & Kenneth McPherson 'Port-cities: The Conceptual Problems', paper presented at the Maritime History panel of the Australian Historical Association Conference, University of New South Wales, Sydney, August 1982
2. See Frank Broeze, Peter Reeves & Kenneth McPherson 'Imperial ports and the modern world economy: the case of the Indian Ocean' *Journal of Transport History*, 7, Sept. 1986, pp. 1-20
3. The changes that take place in the ranks of ports or settlements can be ascertained through the measures of the degree of variability of ranks. These are (i) average rank of the port/city, i.e. its average position in the port/city hierarchy; (ii) average deviation of the ranks which is the average of the relative change of position of a port/city. This measure indicates the degree of consistency of the position of a port/city in the system of ports and settlements; and (iii) range of a port city's rank which indicates the number of positions over which the rank has varied
4. M.N. Pearson 'India and the Indian Ocean in the Sixteenth Century' in Ashin Das Gupta & M.N. Pearson (eds.) *India and the Indian Ocean* Calcutta, 1987; see also H.V. Naqvi *Urbanization and Urban Centres under the Great Mughals (1556-1707)* Simla, 1972
5. Ashin Das Gupta *Indian Merchants and the Decline of Surat c. 1700-1750* Wiesbaden, 1979; O.P. Singh *Surat and its Trade in the Second Half of the 17th Century* Delhi, 1976; and B.G. Gokhale *Surat in the Seventeenth Century* London, 1979
6. K.N. Chaudhuri *The Trading World of Asia and the English East India Company (1660-1760)* Cambridge, 1978, p. 50
7. K.N. Chaudhuri 'Foreign Trade and Balance of Payments (1757-1947)' in Dharma Kumar (ed.) *The Cambridge Economic History of India* vol. 2, New Delhi, 1982, p. 806
8. R. Pearson *Eastern Interlude* Calcutta, 1933, p. 176
9. Atiya Habeeb, Characteristics and Processes of Urbanization in Colonial India. A Case Study of Calcutta and its Hinterland (1872-1921), PhD thesis, School of Social Sciences, Jawaharlal Nehru University, New Delhi, India, 1979
10. The source of data for the pre-independence period has been the *Accounts Relating to the Seaborne Trade and Navigation of British India* published by the Imperial Records Department by order of the Governor General in Council, Commercial Intelligence Department, India (1881-1951). For the post-independence period data has been collected from the *Indian Ports Statistics* and *Basic Port Statistics* published by the Transport Research Division, Ministry of Shipping and Transport, Government of India (1951-1986). As stated in the text, the volume of the throughput of ports was taken as the criterion for their ranking; for a three-pronged one, based on value as well as volume of trade, and the volume of shipping, see J. Bird *Seaport Gateways of Australia* London, 1968, pp. 1-6
11. Bijay K. Swain, A Geographical Analysis of seaports in India (1881-1981), PhD Thesis, Centre for the Study of Regional Development, Jawaharlal Nehru University, New Delhi, pp. 108-114
12. Ibid. pp. 108-114 and 161
13. P.J. Rimmer 'The Changing Status of New Zealand Seaports' *Annals of the Association of American Geographers* 57, 1967, pp. 83-100
14. The formula used for determining the ranks of the ports is as follows:

$$Cr = \frac{Ci}{R}$$

    where Cr = Cargo of the rth port
    Ci = Cargo of the largest port
    R = Rank of the rth port.
    See Peter Haggett *Geography: A Modern Synthesis* New York, 1975, p. 358
15. See, e.g., B.S. Hoyle & D. Hilling (eds.) *Seaport Systems and Spatial Change: Technology, Industry and Development Strategies* Chichester, 1984, and Hoyle's chapter in this volume
16. This is considered to be quite an appropriate method of gauging the importance of port activities because most of the Indian ports, at least the older ones, still use labour-intensive methods of operating. The perhaps more accurate method using investment and production data for port enterprises cannot be used as the necessary

data are not available for all ports on a comparable and consistent basis.
17 Following the method used in Yeves Sabolo *The Service Industries* Geneva, International Labour Organization, 1975
18 Food and textile industries, on an average, have employed 40-50 percent and metal machinery and chemical products 10-15 percent of the manufacturing workers in the three primate ports between 1872 and 1971
19 At Kidderpore, Calcutta, between 1780 and 1805 no less than 110 vessels were launched (H.E.A. Cotton *Calcutta Old and New* Calcutta, 1907, p. 167); see, for Bombay, R.A. Wadia *The Bombay Dockyard and the Wadia Master Builders* Bombay, 1955 and also, more generally, J. Phipps *A Collection of Papers Relative to Shipbuilding in India . . .* Calcutta, 1840)
20 Frank Broeze 'Underdevelopment and Dependency: Maritime India during the Raj' *Modern Asian Studies* 18, 1984, p.431
21 Atiya Habeeb Kidwai 'The Gateway Cities of Asia: Calcutta 1800-1981', mimeographed paper, Association for Asian Social Science Research Councils, New Delhi, 1987
22 Professional services occupied about 18 percent of tertiary workers in Cochin and about 10 percent in Mangalore in 1981. For others ports the data is not available.

Further reading

Chaudhuri, K.N. *The Trading World of Asia and the English East India Company (1660-1760)* Cambridge 1978. Very useful as an introduction to early European trade and commercial settlements in Asia.

Hilling, P. and B.S. Hoyle *Seaports and the Economic Development of Tropical Africa* London 1970. Provides a good list of concepts and statistical methods used in port geography.

Kidwai, Atiya Habeeb 'Gateway Cities of Asia: Calcutta 1800-1981' Association of Asian Social Science Research Councils, New Delhi 1987 (mimeographed). An historical analysis of the growth of Calcutta in the context of its port, capital and primate city functions.

Swain, Bijay K. 'A Geographical Analysis of Seaports in India (1881-1981)' PhD thesis, Centre for the Study of Regional Development, Jawaharlal Nehru University, New Delhi. A time series analysis of port hierarchies based on trade data with an emphasis on recent trends in port development.

CHAPTER 10

Rhoads Murphey

On the evolution of the port city

Our understanding of any subject grows through a combination of specific studies of particular examples and efforts to frame the larger context, from the concrete to the general, or as some would prefer, from 'facts' to 'theories'. 'Fact' is a notoriously hard notion to define, but there is certainly a continuum, and a necessary connection, between the particular and the general. And while recognising that every place, every individual combination of circumstances, interactions, and observable results is unique, few would argue that there is no basis, or no need, to attempt to go beyond that by generalising. Each study of individual settings can be seen as material for comparison, and for building a larger picture of similar or related settings which have enough in common to form a pattern, whatever the variations among them. The papers collected here range from what might almost be called theoretical efforts to generalise about broad patterns and to pursue or refine universal concepts, to relatively micro-level studies of individual places and their particular character and evolution. Both are valuable, and both are necessary to advance our understanding of a phenomenon which has always attracted the imagination:

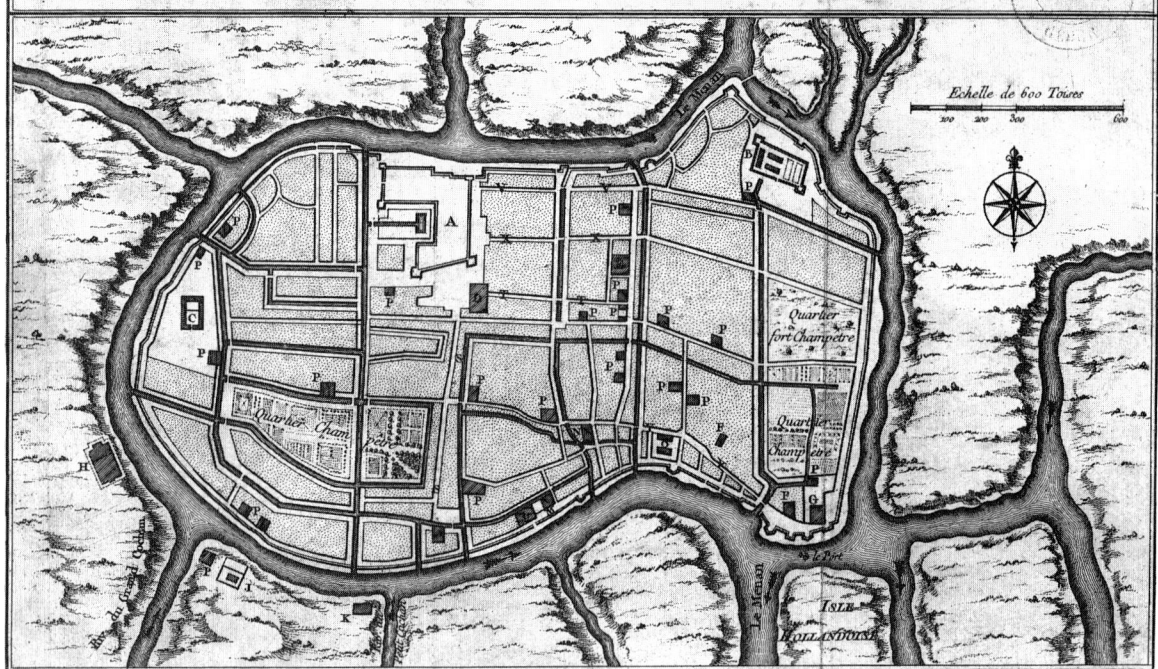

Ayutthaya, Thai capital. Unlike many views of Ayutthaya, this map does not depict any of the major buildings or the surrounding community; it shows the bare essentials of the walled city as the French saw it.
Courtesy of Cartes et Plans, Bibliothèque Nationale, Paris.

port cities, centres of exchange where different cultures and different environments meet, the boundary between land and sea. They, and their fascination, are older than Jeddah, and older than Venice, where in the centuries of its maritime-based greatness the Doge performed an annual ceremony of throwing a gold ring into the sea to celebrate the marriage of the city with the clearly perceived source of its wealth. Venetians, and many other seaport people, would have responded to the title of this book.

However much individual cases may resist being squeezed into one or even several large categories, the validity of the port concept as a centre of land-sea exchange is undeniable, as is the generalisation that this process has been and remains a major source of livelihood, and a major force for culture mixing or cosmopolitanisation, in a very long list of cities around the world, from the early beginnings of man's use of the sea to haul goods and people over long distances. The exchange of goods, cultures, and people which is the basis of all ports leads to a variety of results, differing as circumstances differ from place to place, and yet produces as it must a range of common urban characteristics which amply justify our lumping port cities together under a single generic label. They have enough in common to warrant distinguishing them from other kinds of cities. And yet the line is not always easy to draw. Many of the modern world's biggest cities, for example, London, New York, Shanghai, Istanbul, or Buenos Aires, began as ports or with land-sea exchange as their major function, but have since grown disproportionately in other respects so that their port functions are no longer dominant and they are more important as manufacturing, financial, service, or administrative centres. Their evolution is typical of many places, indeed of virtually all of the largest cities which still also serve as ports: Tokyo, Jakarta, Calcutta, Philadelphia, San Francisco, Kuwait, and so on. It would I think be arbitrary, and not really useful to efforts toward defining or understanding what a port city is, to eliminate all these and their parallel cases because their port functions are no longer, or in some cases have never been, dominant. They remain different kinds of places from non-port cities, and their port functions, however less important now, account for that difference even though stevedores, shippers, pilots, ship chandlers, and their co-workers may now be a tiny fraction of the total urban workforce.

Port functions, more than anything else, make a city cosmopolitan, a word which does not necessarily mean 'sophisticated' but rather hybrid. A port city is open to the world, or at least to a varied section of it. In it races, cultures, and ideas as well as goods from a variety of places jostle, mix, and enrich each other and the life of the city. The smell of the sea and the harbour, still to be found (sometimes with an effort!) in all of them, like the sound of boat whistles or the moving tides, is a symbol of their multiple links with a wider world, samples of which are present in microcosm within their own urban areas. Nor can it be argued that the more recent rise of manufacturing, administration, or other urban functions to greater prominence is not a direct result, wholly or in large part, of the earlier role of the city as a port, a role which in nearly

*Manila: A walled Christian outpost in the jungle. In this image of Manila the fort is quite separate from the rest of the community, and most of the shipping is shown as European.
From* François Valentijn Oud en Nieuw Oost Indien Dordrecht, 1724-26. *Courtesy of Mitchell Library, State Library of New South Wales.*

all of them continues to contribute to the flourishing of the greater city which has grown up around them. Port cities become industrial and financial nodes, service centres, and political capitals *because* of their water connections and the urban concentration which arises there and later draws to it railways, highways, and air routes. Water transport, especially by sea, means cheap access, the chief basis of all cities and of all urban functions.

Indeed, as a city loses most of its port functions, it loses these qualities, perhaps most of all its cosmopolitanism. Ports are centres of concentrated exchange, a process which has merely been accelerated by railways, highways, and air routes. Sea transport routes and exchange centres have also been transformed by the advent of powered vessels whose most economic size and draught have continued to increase. Many formerly important ports have become economically and physically less accessible or even inaccessible as a result. Bypassed by most of their former enriching flow of exchange and hybridisation, they have become cultural and economic backwaters, the opposite of cosmopolitan, or have acquired the character of museums of the past: Charleston and Savannah, Salem, Bristol, Plymouth, Lübeck, Narbonne, Surat, Galle, Melaka, Soochow, and a long list of earlier prominent port cities bypassed by 'progress' in Southeast Asia, Africa, and Latin America. One other victim of the progress of concentration has been piracy, although its demise (perhaps better 'near-demise', since it still exists in the Caribbean, the Melaka Straits, and elsewhere where ships are occasionally boarded and their crews robbed, and in altered form as hijackings) resulted also from inability to compete with fast and heavily armed naval and police vessels on the side of the law as well as the increased speed and size of the prey. Well into the nineteenth century, however, piracy was an endemic problem in many parts of the world, and ports were often moved farther up-river and/or heavily fortified to protect against them, as can still be seen for example in most older ports of the Mediterranean, the Caribbean, the China and Malay coasts, and much of Southeast Asia, traditional centres of piracy.

What constitutes a port city is hard to derive from statistical data on employment, economic categories, or even trade flows, especially for the world beyond Europe and North America where the data are often poor at best but in any case do not adequately distinguish port-related from other functions. Anyone who has tried to work with what Asian data there are, especially before the present century, knows what a truism that is. But for many ports, again especially those in the major population concentrations of Asia, the chief data are those for external trade, often recorded and published by foreign agencies or colonial governments. Much, probably most, of domestic trade went unrecorded or at best underrecorded, particularly in China and to an extent also in India and Southeast Asia. What evidence we have suggests, however, that domestic trade, including transit and entrepot trade, was greater at all periods than external trade, as was and remains true for most ports everywhere. Shanghai, for example, did most of its trade with other Chinese ports and inland cities, especially if one includes Hong Kong, Japanese-controlled Taiwan (from

1895) and Manchuria (after 1931). Calcutta traded mainly with other parts of India, and so on.

One of the things which help to blur the distinction between what is and is not a port city is the multiple nature of all cities. A city cannot exist without providing a *range* of goods and services to a wider area tributary to it, to which it is tied by virtue of its superior access. This is of course the area commonly referred to as the city's hinterland, to which one must add for ports the area tributary to it by sea, appropriately labelled its foreland (or recognised by Weigend and others as part of its overall *umland*). Different cities or ports commonly, however, share given hinterlands and forelands to varying degrees, competing with each other within them and overlapping or interfingering one another's coverage, some with competitive advantages for certain goods or services, others for others. Often this has to do with merchant or financial, guild or kin networks for particular goods, including overseas connections as well as domestic ones. But most of any city's population or work force is engaged in providing goods and services for the city itself. The city provides basic goods and services (including, for example, financial or insurance services) for the wider area tributary to it. These may be sold and exported, or people may come to the city for them. Trade with extra-urban areas is clearly part of the basic function in this sense, even if only in the form of goods-handling, as are the city's people engaged in it in any capacity, including transport and transshipment. Each basic worker, however, requires food, housing, clothing, and a variety of other goods and services, as do non-employed family members. Estimates of the ratio of basic to service workers range from 1:4 to 1:8, and do of course vary in reality from one kind of city to another.

No city can be simply a port but must be involved in a variety of other activities, including additional basic as well as service functions beyond the handling of water-borne trade and its integration with land transport. It also provides other goods and services, related to or growing out of its port functions, to a wider tributary area. A port has strong advantages of access for drawing to it raw materials, distributing goods in any form, and providing wider services. Many ports also take advantage of the need for breaking bulk where land and water transport meet and where loading and unloading costs are thus minimised to further refine raw materials in transit or to turn them into finished goods. The major example here is oil refining, commonly located in a port, although the same is true of most ore refining and of most processing of important foodstuffs. These things would not happen there without the port, and the connection is extremely close, almost a further stage of the unloading and sorting or repacking which is an essential part of any land-sea exchange. Are these refining or processing enterprises to be excluded from port functions? If so, how? Can or should one distinguish between unloading a tanker into one set of refinery tanks, and loading a land carrier out of another set? It is a logical progression from refining and processing to other kinds of manufacturing which similarly re-sort and re-combine materials entering the port in order to ship them out in altered form. It is not easy to draw a line

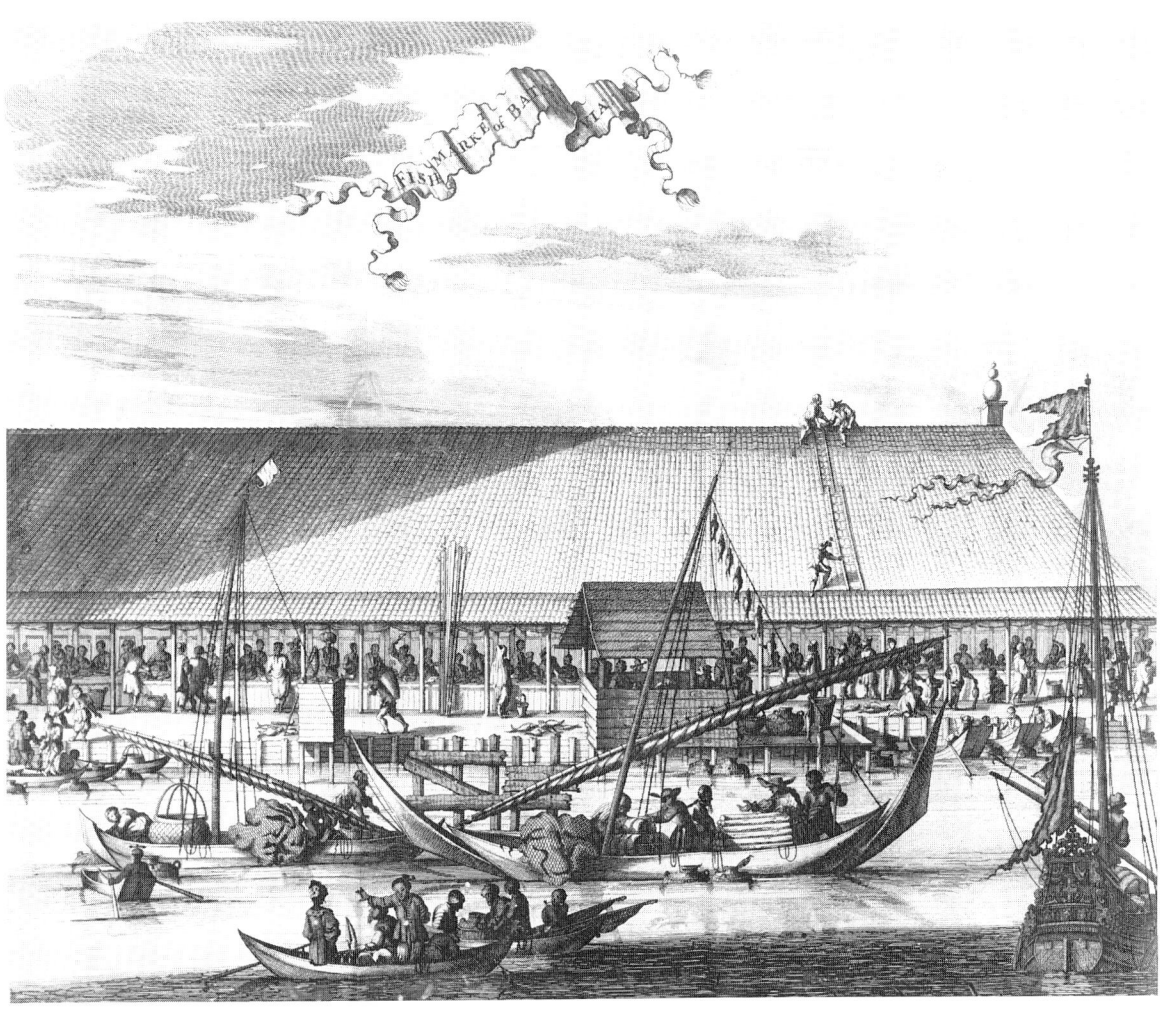

The fishmarket (pasar ikan) at Batavia (Jakarta), Indonesia. The size and complexity of a port city such as Batavia saw the development of specialised marketing and the use of canals as a means of transport between marketing centres.
From Hendrik Nieuhof *Joan Nieuhofs Gedenkwaerdighe Zee-en Lant-reize door de voornaemste Landschappen van West en Oostindien* Amsterdam, 1682.
Courtesy of Mitchell Library, State Library of New South Wales.

around what a port is or is not in these terms, since all ports handle, unload, sort, alter, process, repack, and reship most of what they receive. It is not necessary to labour this point, or to extend it further into other manufacturing or services (insurance, brokerage, travel agencies, and so on), to suggest that a city may, as most do, become involved in a great range of functions not immediately involved with ships or docks, and yet can still legitimately be regarded as a port city.

One way of guessing how important port functions are or have been in explaining the rise and development of a city is to look at its morphology, as some of the papers in this volume do explicitly. All port cities begin at the edge of the harbour, where land and water meet, and may consist for a time mainly of docks, storage facilities, ships, stores, services to sailors, and housing and basic services for the resident population, which however necessarily include general merchants or shippers and their offices. As port trade increases these may be joined by banks, insurance offices, assayers, customs officials, police, and so on but all grouped immediately around the waterfront, which is the city's access to the wider world it serves. The first big expansion away from the waterfront comes as white-collar groups move laterally away from the bustle of the port as their incomes rise, a process greatly accelerated by the coming of railways. This new form of transport also makes it possible for manufacturing to locate away from water even though it usually remains dependent on the port for much of its supply and distribution. Administrative services, for the city or for the wider area it may govern as an important centre with good access, usually remain close to the harbour but may move a few blocks away. From the late nineteenth century, as part of the overall process of urban growth in a railway and automobile age, the city may explode outward into residential suburbs and peripheral or nodal areas of manufacturing and retailing.

Nearly all cities which began as ports and where port functions remain important still show this evolutionary pattern clearly. In most of them the chief commercial and administrative centre of the city remains closely articulated with or even grouped along its waterfront: the centre of New York in these terms is lower Manhattan cradled between its two rivers where the island narrows, the City of London and the City of Westminster along the Thames, Shanghai along the Bund, the commercial, financial, and administrative centres of Boston, Philadelphia, Bombay, Calcutta, Madras, Singapore, Bangkok, Colombo, Manila, Hong Kong, Tianjin, Yokohama, and most other great port cities still grouped around or only a few blocks away from their harbours even as each city has enormously expanded outward away from the water as its port functions have nourished its transformation into a metropolis. Even a casual visitor to any of these cities can hardly mistake not only their port origins but the basic role which the port and harbour still play, symbolically and appropriately at the centre of the stage even of the contemporary city, or running through or beside its heart.

Port and harbour are however two very different things. Most ports have poor harbours, and many fine harbours see few ships. Harbour is a physical concept,

'Prau of the Sultan of Batchian' (eastern Indonesia). By the late nineteenth century European depictions of indigenous shipping in Asia were confined to images of exotic and technologically more backward (in European eyes) vessels. From F. H. H. Guillemard *The Cruise of the Marchesa to Kamschatka and New Guinea* London: John Murray, 1886. Courtesy of Mitchell Library, State Library of New South Wales.

a shelter for ships; port is an economic concept, a centre of land-sea exchange, which requires good access to a hinterland even more than to a sea-linked foreland. As the size and draught of ocean carriers has increased, most of the harbours which were adequate earlier—including small lagoons or simply a stretch of beach where boats could be drawn up—can no longer be used and port traffic concentrates in a few which can be kept usable. Even in the best such harbours constant dredging is necessary. But it is landward access which is critical, access to a hinterland which is productive of goods for export and which demands imports. Given good landward access and a productive hinterland, an artificial harbour can be built even on a low featureless coast with no deep water near the shore, as at Tianjin or along much of the coasts of West Africa or the Persian Gulf. At others, or before an artificial harbour is built, ships anchor well offshore and do their loading and unloading by lighter, as was even more common in earlier centuries, dangerous, expensive, and time-consuming but responding to the pull of landward access to a productive trade area. More commonly, a poor harbour will be expensively improved and dredged, enlarged, or provided with breakwaters, as for example at Madras or Colombo, or simply put up with through what dredging is possible, as for most river ports. Ports at river mouths, including many of the world's largest, must contend with the most intractable harbour problems of all: limited space, shallow water, often difficult access from the sea, and heavy chronic silting, especially at deltaic sites, as most of them are, although estuarine ports (Philadelphia, Buenos Aires, London, Hamburg) are better off. Most river ports have had to develop outports for deeper draught vessels in the modern period: Cuxhaven, Gravesend, Haldia, or Woosung, but these rarely become more than way stations or minor functional satellites to the original port city, where the bulk of commercial functions remains.

The distribution of ports everywhere shows an evolution from a great number of small and widely scattered places to a few large ones where maritime trade is now concentrated. Asia is in fact one of the best examples, and the historical process there, as elsewhere, has had less to do with the quality of harbours than with landward access. Bombay displaced Surat, but not primarily because of the enormous superiority of its harbour, which in fact at the time when this shift took place was too wide and too deep for the shipping of the period; it was attractive as a more nearly independent base for the Company's trade. Its later growth rested on its landward access, especially with the defeat of the Marathas and the subsequent building of railways, opening the whole of western India to Bombay. The city's growth was also accelerated by the finally successful suppression of the piracy which had long plagued the west coast and restricted foreland access. The smaller ports of Southeast Asia—Aceh, Makassar, Ternate, and so on—each serving relatively small hinterlands, no longer offered the trade volume to attract large carriers, and hence their harbours have not been improved to keep pace with modern shipping.

River and deltaic ports, including many of Asia's largest, grew despite the dismaying problems of their harbours because the river and the valley it created

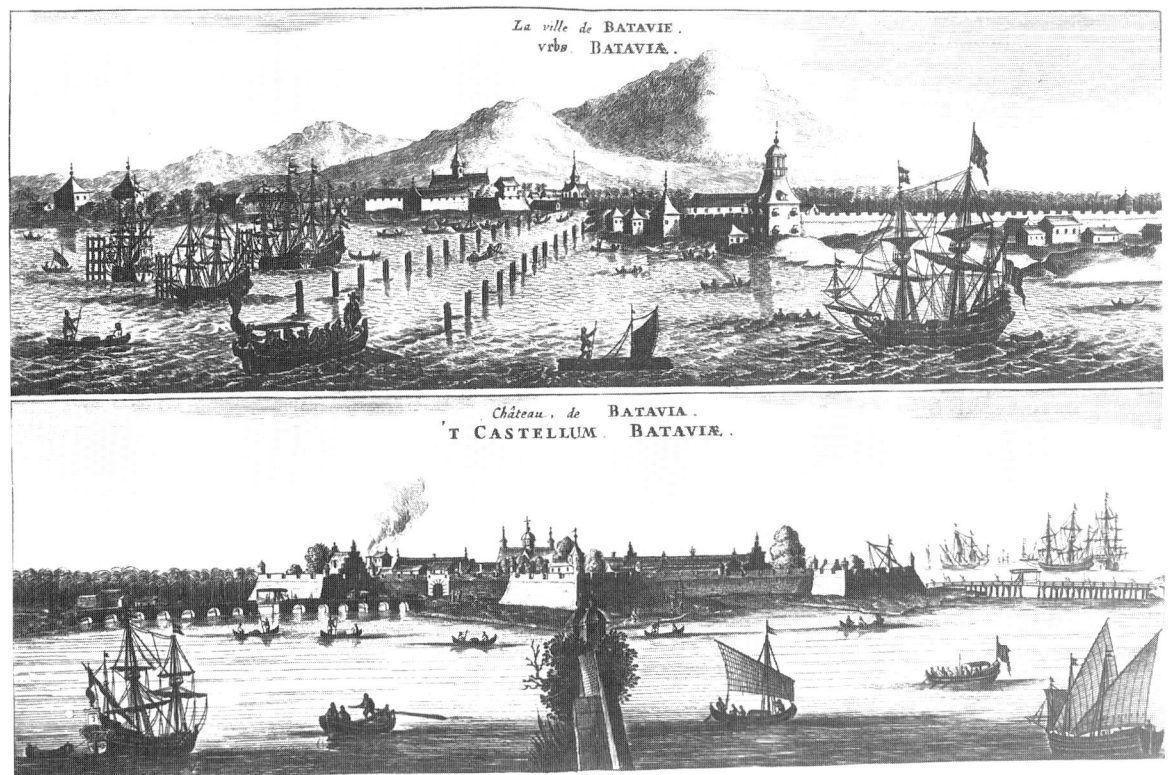

Batavia (Jakarta), Indonesia, city and castle. These two complementary views of Batavia contrast the lively nature of the trading aspect of the city with the authority of the old castle, the political underpinning of that trading life.
From Joan Nieuhof *Het Gezantschap der Neêrlandtsche Oost-Indische Compagnie aan den grooten Tartarischen Cham den tegenwoordigen Keizer van China* Amsterdam, 1670.
Courtesy of Mitchell Library, State Library of New South Wales.

and nourished offered both a productive hinterland and an easy avenue of access, by water or by rail and road along the valley route. How else can one explain the immense port traffic of pitifully poor harbours like Calcutta's or Shanghai's, or the fact that Calcutta has consistently rivalled Bombay with its superb natural harbour and Shanghai far outdistanced the fine harbours of Qing dao, Dalian or Fuzhou? Colombo won out over Galle and Trincomalee, the latter especially with one of Asia's finest harbours, because its superior access to the cinnamon, tea, rubber, and coconut-producing areas amply justified the artificial enlargement of its originally shallow, exposed, and tiny lagoon. Even so, traffic often backs up there, as at Madras, and at both one can see long lines of ships anchored off the coast waiting for their turn to enter the harbour and unload or load. It seems a ridiculous situation, and certainly a severe problem, but the landward access of both ports, and their concentration of port facilities, leave shippers with little alternative.

Where maritime trade seeks to connect with productive land areas it develops an entrance. The port thus created is a powerful magnet for improvements in land transport, focused on the port like the spokes of a wheel. Given this multiple access, as any port city must have to survive, it naturally develops additional functions in manufacturing, administration, and other services for which its situation gives it strong advantages. But of all such basic functions, it is hard to avoid concluding that the port component remains the most basic even if others become in time larger employers or earners of capital.

As the Introduction to this volume rightly points out, Westerners and even their ships and trade remained less important than Asians and the trade they carried and controlled for several centuries after da Gama's voyage to Calicut. Colonialism and semi-colonialism, far from 'creating' the port cities which served as funnels for exports to the metropolitan countries, merely overlaid a long pre-existing system of trade and ports engaged for many centuries in both domestic and external commerce. In India Westerners founded what became the dominant modern ports, but their later dominance resulted in large part from their attracting trade to them at the expense of earlier ports elsewhere, many of them with harbours inadequate for nineteenth- and twentieth-century shipping. In most of the rest of Asia (Java and Malaya were qualified exceptions) Westerners moved into or expanded existing ports, fixing their own settlements and trade functions there because they were already established commercial centres of land-sea exchange and hence the best places for the effort to tap the domestic market. I have argued elsewhere[1] that the foreign presence of this sort in China produced much less economic change or alteration of trade flows than the foreigners then or now thought they were doing, in large part because the external trade, which was largely under their control, was progressively fully recorded and growing (though part of the growth was a growth in statistics only), while the probably larger domestic trade and most of that very considerable part which remained in Chinese hands in Chinese vessels was not.

The revisionism gathering force in recent years which attempts to see modern

On the evolution of the port city

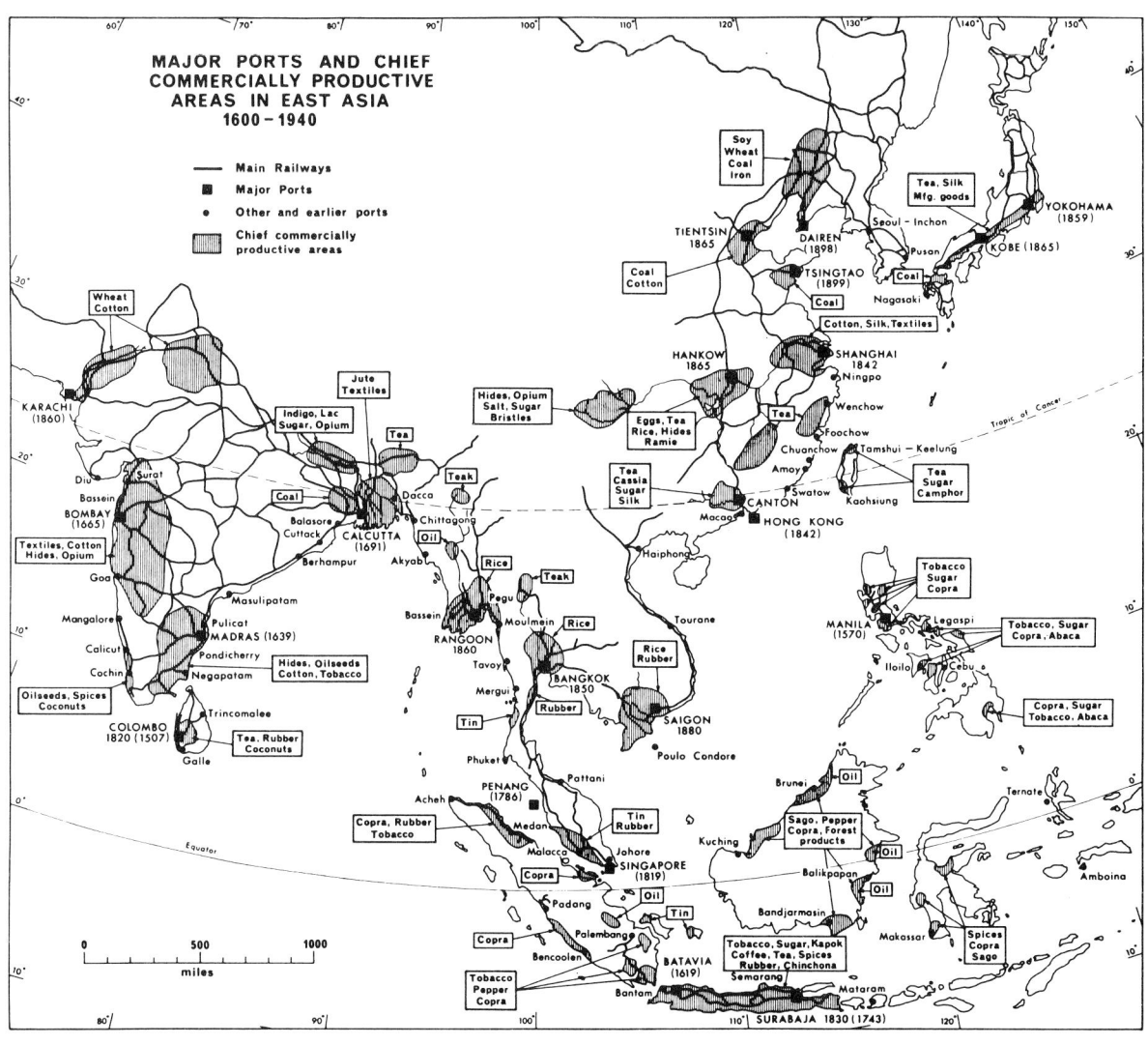

Map 17 Major ports and chief commercially productive areas in East Asia, 1600-1940

Asian history as such rather than as the story of the Western impact is appropriately reflected in this volume. A closer look at each port's hinterland and foreland connections, as urged in Chapter 1, will often reveal the extent to which in much of Asia each continued to serve trade flows which had existed for centuries before the arrival of the Westerners and which in the larger countries, notably China, were only in part taken over or deflected to Western markets. In any case, Asian entrepreneurs, as well as Asian workers, remained prominent and competitive with foreign entrepreneurs in the growing economic life of most of these ports. 'Traditional' business groups and their methods proved fully capable of successful operation even in that Western-dominated setting. Throughout the colonial period Asians remained the overwhelming majority in all of the port cities, and were far from being simply servants or workers. Some prospered as collaborators, some as imitators of the West, but many as indigenous traditional-style merchants, competing effectively with outsiders in dealing with a market which, after all, they knew best.

Ports flourished, as they had for centuries before, by attracting the widest volume of traffic from all comers, local and distant, indigenous and foreign. Early ports established by Westerners in Asia, or where they tried to win the upper hand, succeeded mainly to the extent they were able to draw to them a variety of Asian and even rival European traders. Dutch and French efforts to exclude rival European and Asian ships and traders proved self-defeating, as in the Arasaratnam account of Dutch Paleacat versus the more open policy at Madras in the seventeenth century; other Dutch and French ports, and later French ports in Vietnam, suffered from the same shortsighted policy. Arasaratnam rightly emphasises also the fluctuating fortunes of ports in this earlier period as Westerners managed to differing degrees to build relations with local states and commercial networks, and picked as patrons or partners successful or less successful contenders in the continually shifting balance of intergroup rivalry characteristic especially of South and Southeast Asia, and for a time, until about 1615, of Japan. But early and late, the chief basis of port success was the ability to attract trade and traders, from as many groups and both near and distant areas as possible. For the larger countries by far the greatest trade volume was with the indigenous market, and through indigenous merchants, including coastal and riverine trade, much of it in traditional Asian vessels, as well as overland. For most of the ports, including those which became the largest, the transit, re-export, the entrepot trade continued to be a larger part of the total volume than direct export and import.

Yet all of them also exhibit a highly varied mix of peoples and cultures, reflecting their widespread connections and enhancing their fascination for the student as cosmopolitan centres of ferment, social mobility, innovation, and stimulus, open doors on the world and major crossroads of its traffic in ideas and people as well as in goods. In each country ports have also always attracted people from different regions, offering them new economic opportunity and blending them into its cosmopolitan mix as each grew for much of its history through immigration as much as by natural increase, a process which still continues: up-country and low-country Sinhalese, Ceylon and Indian Tamils, Moors, Burghers, Indians, Chinese, and more distant foreigners in Colombo, as Roberts points out, people from every Chinese province in Shanghai and from every Indian state and language group in Calcutta or Bombay, from every Japanese prefecture in Tokyo, from all parts of Indonesia in Batavia/Jakarta, and so on. Many of the successful among these urban recruits lived, as Roberts again points out, in Western or semi-Western style, following the then dominant model of success as *arrivistes*, dancing to jazz bands in the foreign concession areas, building houses and gardens in the colonial port version of Western architecture, sending their children to English or American mission or mission-founded schools, learning to play cricket, sharing the English passion for horseracing, and often losing touch with their traditional cultures. Chinese nationalists came to call them 'running dogs', but their opposite numbers in fully colonial India, Ceylon, and parts of Southeast Asia probably went even further down the Western path and away from their own cultural patterns. Many, probably most, of the Asians who rose to wealth and prominence in the rapidly growing port cities were not only *arrivistes* but parvenus, people whose origins were humble or obscure but who made their way rapidly upward in the dynamic and fluid situation of the port cities where change was concentrated, progressively displacing formerly or traditionally dominant groups, first in these cities and increasingly in each country.

Eighteenth-century Makassar, as described in Chapter 5, is both a microcosm and a harbinger of what was to continue on a larger scale all over nineteenth- and twentieth-century Asia. This includes the system whereby each of the many ethnic groups, Celeban and foreign, in Makassar governed itself, an established pattern long before the Western imposition of extraterritoriality with precedents going back to at least classical times in the West as well as in the East. Makassar's bewildering mix of peoples and cultures is typical of port cities, including most of those in Asia, though given the fragmented as well as the open maritime nature of Southeast Asia foreigners were proportionately more important there. Makassar's morphology of fort, European settlement, and a variety of separate ethnic communities spontaneously self-segregated and each with its own headman, with open space preserved between European and Asian settlement areas, was equally typical. The same essential pattern was repeated in port cities throughout Asia. Forts were absent in most Chinese and Japanese ports in the absence of full colonialism, but were especially necessary in the troubled political landscape of post-Mughal India and Southeast Asia, the latter with the additional problem of widespread piracy from its almost infinite bases among the islands of the archipelago, through which passed rich streams of trade to prey on.

There has been a continuing argument, however, about how important in explaining the rise of colonial ports was the relative security which they offered, either in terms of forts and military protection or through the force of law and the treaty port order under extraterritoriality. Westerners understandably felt at risk in the early centuries of their Asian presence as alien minority competitors in areas which were also often politically disordered. Trade could not take place without some security for goods in storage or in transit to and from the hinterland, a major consideration especially in the spread of the Company's control inland in India and for its protection of each port as soon as this was possible. There seems little doubt that Asians, especially merchants, found foreign-dominated ports in all areas attractive as places where they could reduce the risks of banditry and civil war for themselves, their goods, and their fortunes under not merely the walls of a fort but under the sanctity of private property, which few indigenous powers respected so highly. In times of civil war or famine larger masses of refugees also flooded into the relative security of these ports, but this was usually a temporary flow, repeated periodically but receding when more normal conditions returned. European strength at sea was also important in attracting Asian cargoes to their ships, where they were more likely to arrive despite pirates or other oceanic hazards, especially after the advent of steam. Insurance agents recognised the difference by offering lower rates for shipments by Western vessels, and later by any powered ships. Within the port cities under European domination, order was often better kept than elsewhere, and the array of lower-cost financial services, reflecting lower risks, was similarly attractive. Nearly all of the colonial or semi-colonial ports were sited so as to provide or enhance protection by water, on which Western naval vessels could also offer the intervention, and the symbol, of their power, in defence of trade and property, as important to Asian as to Western entrepreneurs.

But the rule of Western law under extraterritoriality in its many forms was not necessarily always an attraction, as Arasaratnam points out for early Madras, which like most of the colonial ports had such a system from its inception in 1639. Indian (and later Chinese) merchants were understandably reluctant to live under it or to submit disputes to foreign-loaded justice. Only where the choice was between some kind of legal order and chaos did the foreign-dominated order appeal, especially where it differed from the indigenous alternative also in respecting private property, contracts, and the secure amassing of wealth. Even if Asians were often at a disadvantage in a foreign court, that might be preferable to lack of any protection against the rapacity of the traditional state, or against chronic banditry and political chaos. In balance, for most Asians at most periods until the Second World War, the colonial ports were more attractive on such grounds than repellent, as detailed examination of the evolution of many of them, and the pattern of 'voting with the feet', makes clear.

The argument about the importance of legal security to the flourishing of a port reached its climax in the discussions about the rendition of extraterritoriality and other special rights in the China treaty ports beginning in the late 1920s, when the British Concession at Hankow was returned to China in 1927, continuing into the 1930s as the writing on the wall grew clearer for Shanghai and all the other treaty ports. The abandonment of special privilege was of course resisted, but as others pointed out, German loss of these

Meimbun, Sulu Island, southern Philippines: A nineteenth-century trade backwater, but still in the heart of the pirate and trade zone of island Southeast Asia.
From F. H. H. Guillemard The Cruise of the Marchesa to Kamschatka and New Guinea *London: John Murray, 1886. Courtesy of Mitchell Library, State Library of New South Wales.*

privileges, including extraterritoriality, with the First World War did not seem to have hampered them as trade competitors after 1919, when in fact they won a larger share of trade at Shanghai than they had before the war. Nor was extraterritoriality necessary to maintain a foreign military presence or a foreign-dominated municipal government in the treaty ports, which together continued to ensure greater protection of property and contract there for all merchants and their trade than in the deteriorating political landscape of China outside the ports, even though treaty port justice in the courts struck many Chinese as far from even-handed. One example was the pattern for rich Chinese to live in the International or French Settlements where they and their families felt themselves safer from extortion, expropriation, ruinous taxation, or kidnapping for ransom, where they could indulge their taste for conspicuous consumption, make money in commerce, attend the races and other forms of gambling, and store their wealth in foreign banks.

The discussion about the rendition of foreign privileges (they called them 'rights') was swept away by the Pacific war, but the best concise conclusion was probably that of the foreign-published *China Weekly Review* for 4 December 1926 (p. 15): 'Shanghai would have been a great city had there never been a foreigner in the place. It would continue to be a great city even if the foreigners should vacate their modern buildings and go home.' The writer might have added that, like nearly all the treaty ports, Shanghai was a major port before 1843, and, we can now add, remained so after the 1949 revolution expelled the foreigners, as it still is under sole Chinese management. Special privilege probably attracted some of the foreign merchants, and gave them at least a perceived advantage, as did colonial control over ports elsewhere in Asia, but the foreign political order had little if anything to do with the growth of the ports which prospered. Indeed where it was exercised over-protectively, as noted above for French and Dutch ports, it was counterproductive. Trade flows were determined primarily by the freest and easiest access, the network of connections between hinterlands and forelands, a network in which Asians remained the major players.

It is fully appropriate to stress, as several of the papers in this volume do, especially those by Arasaratnam, Reid, and Sutherland, the indigenous context of the rise of port cities in Asia. Arabs, Greeks, and Romans arriving in India before and after the birth of Christ found ports there, as the Arabs found them eastward to the China coast, already highly developed. Earlier still, the port of Lothal served a flourishing trade by sea between the Indus civilisation and Sumer. Indeed the Indian Ocean and the Arabian Sea were probably the first areas of open ocean to see the beginnings of long-distance navigation. South India's extensive maritime connections with peninsular and insular Southeast Asia were based in major ports on the southeast coast such as ancient Puhar, a sea link in which other ports in Malabar and Gujerat also had a part as well perhaps as late Mauryan and post-Mauryan ports in Bengal. The maritime landscape of Southeast Asia is hazy in this period, but ports on the China coast were major centres of coastal trade at least by Han times, and by T'ang and Sung were involved also in extensive trade with Japan, the Philippines, Java, the Indo-China peninsula, and Malaya. Each of these many ports rested on internal trade networks feeding goods to it by land and distributing its imports. At Puhar (near modern Madras) and Zayton (Zhuanzhou) in Fukien we have textual evidence for specifically organised special quarters for each nationality or cultural group of foreign merchants where each foreign community lived under the jurisdiction of its own appointed headman over a thousand years before the modern Western use of foreign concessions and extraterritoriality. Many of these earlier ports had extensive dock and warehouse areas, separate quarters for offices, residences, and designated market areas for specific goods, and many were marked by lighthouses and other navigational aids.

When the Europeans arrived in Asia by sea, such ports and their trade connections had thus been established for many centuries, changing no doubt over time but part of a longstanding system. For the early part of the Western presence, as I have argued elsewhere,[2] and indeed for most of the period labelled by some 'the age of da Gama', these indigenously founded ports continued to dominate the sea trade of Asia. Even Goa, Melaka, and the Canton estuary (if not Macao) were already thriving ports before the Portuguese. Although Batavia, Madras, Manila (to a degree), Bombay, and Calcutta had been founded by Westerners by or before the end of the seventeenth century, they did not begin to dominate the trade of their respective areas or to reach large size at the expense of the indigenous ports until considerably later. Elsewhere in Asia Westerners continued to trade in competition with local and other foreign merchants only in long pre-existing Asian ports such as Aceh, Makassar, Canton, or Nagasaki, and only much later founded a few new ports themselves, such as Hong Kong, Tsingtao (Qingdao), or Yokohama. But in East Asia as a whole, Western merchants and their trade remained overwhelmingly concentrated in port cities which had existed as such for many centuries before the Westerners arrived and which continued to be dominated at least numerically by indigenous merchants, who provided the essential links with the markets of each country and region and the networks which served them, in which kin and guild connections were of primary importance.

However, the nineteenth century saw the advent of steam and steel, at sea and on land, setting in train a process of trade and urban concentration in a few major ports which I have described in more detail elsewhere.[3] This resulted also from the rapid increase in the size and draught of the most economical ocean carriers, which were too big to use most of the earlier ports, whose harbours were inadequate and whose landward connections did not tap a market producing a large enough flow of goods to sustain a major port by the new standards. This process saw the reduction to minor local importance of the great majority of these lesser ports: Calicut, Patani, Bantam, Wenzhou, and so on, and the concentration of most port business in a few giants in each country, served by rail and/or by inland and coastal steam navigation. Areas previously tributary to the smaller local ports instead now sent their exports and received their imports by such means to and from Karachi, Bombay, Colombo, Madras, Calcutta, Rangoon, Bangkok, Singapore, Saigon, Batavia, Manila, Hong Kong, Shanghai, Tientsin, Tsingtao, Dairen, Kobe, and Yokohama. It needs to be stressed, however, that in all of them, despite Western sovereignty or special privilege, indigenous merchants and their internal networks remained essential parts of each port's commercial life as well as numerically dominant. That in itself insured a considerable degree of continuity with not only the distant past but with the two centuries or more after da Gama. These Western-founded ports remained, in other words, largely Asian, serving Asian markets through Asian networks which had long been in place.

What was different about the nineteenth century was the enormous and rapidly increasing volume of trade passing through these newly concentrated centres, their newly augmented links with a wider world by sea (including the 'modernising' West), and hence their role as funnels through which external forces for change flowed into each port and were disseminated by each along its lines of internal trade and communication. One may agree that such a process is discernible even in the sixteenth and seventeenth centuries—notably the Portuguese role in Malabar, the *fan kuei* at Canton, the Dutch at Nagasaki, the Spanish at Manila, the Dutch at Batavia. But the wave of exogenous influences into each country through these port centres of the nineteenth century was on a far greater scale and became different not only in degree but in kind, tempting one to speak, as one cannot of earlier periods, of the 'transformation' of each Asian country through the agency of its newly dominant port cities.[4]

One aspect of that transformation was the progressive reversal of the traditional Asian pattern of inward-centredness in each country. Traditionally the largest Asian cities, including the national capitals, were inland, close to the ecumene and/or the centre of population and production in each country, or in China close to the most threatened landward frontier. Delhi, Anuradhapura, Kandy, Pagan, Mandalay, Ayutthaya, Angkor, Jogjakarta, Ch'ang An, Kaifeng, Beijing, Kyoto, all illustrate this pattern, as do nearly all large pre-nineteenth-century Asian cities. But by 1900, the largest cities in each country were instead all ports, in the smallest countries the only big cities. Their growth was clearly due to their port functions in an age of greatly expanded overseas trade, but they had also become in each country the chief centres of intellectual ferment and of institutional as well as economic change (including industrialisation), centres whose influence extended widely inland to different degrees in each country, along the trade routes which had fed their rise. They were windows on a wider world abroad, and replicated in themselves many aspects of that wider world, in ideas, in new commercial, social, and political institutions, and ultimately in the stirrings of nationalism.

In such senses, they were indeed 'transforming', playing a different and far larger role than their sixteenth-, seventeenth-, or eighteenth-century prototypes (if that is in fact the correct label for eighteenth-century Makassar, seventeenth-century Manila, or sixteenth-century south Indian ports).[5] I have argued in *The*

Outsiders that although the Western aims in Asia were essentially uniform, their success in 'transformation' differed sharply from area to area, as a reflection of the strikingly different Asian contexts, most notably as between India and China. And yet in many ways Shanghai played the same kind of role as Calcutta and its parallels. Even though it did not produce wholly comparable results in the age of foreign domination, its influence for change, as a model, as a goad to Chinese smarting under foreign humiliation, as a window on the world overseas, and as a nursery of revolution and revolutionaries, was in the end perhaps even more 'transforming' as seen from the perspective of China now. One may say that modern China was to a large extent made in Shanghai— as much at least as modern India was made in Calcutta or Bombay, modern Japan in Yokohama-Tokyo, modern Indonesia in Batavia, and so on. Certainly the current patterns, development trends, and priorities of Asian countries were not made in their traditional inland centres, nor in the sixteenth-, seventeenth-, or eighteenth-century port cities. But one can still see important continuities, and it is right to call attention to them.

If one is to understand the port phenomenon and to discern consistent or recurring patterns, or if one is to see individual cases in a larger context which can often pick out or draw attention to what is important, study must be comparative, and must range over many centuries of change, as the papers in this volume do. Makassar or Colombo, Bombay or Shanghai are appropriate objects of study not only for themselves, their immediate contexts, and their uniquenesses but for how they can help toward building a picture of port cities in Asia as a generic whole. There is already an extensive literature in this field, and in recent years it has begun to grow more vigorously. Most of it still consists of individual port and trade network studies, although it ranges widely over the centuries from the fourteenth or fifteenth to the present, albeit with more emphasis on South and Southeast Asia than on the single-state systems of China and Japan, while Korea is hardly represented at all. Part of this of course reflects the circumstance that the countries of East Asia were effectively closed to substantial foreign participation in normal overseas trade until the mid-nineteenth century, with relatively minor exceptions as at Canton and Deshima. But ports in these countries continued to flourish without major participation by foreign merchants, including in the Chinese case extensive trade with Southeast Asia as well as a massive coastal and riverine commerce. More work, in addition to the studies already published, needs to be done on these ports before the outsiders became prominent there, as well as in the treaty port and contemporary periods where most attention has been centred. As more individual studies accumulate, and over a wider geographic and historical spread, the comparative analysis which is essential to a generic understanding of port cities becomes easier, and more compelling. The present volume is a major and welcome step in that direction.

Dobbo (Aru), eastern Indonesia, 'in the Trading Season'. Once colonialism and the international economy had established the major patterns of trade in Asia, many areas such as eastern Indonesia were reduced to the status of sleepy backwaters.
Illustration by T. Baines, from Alfred Russel Wallace The Malay Archipelago: The Land of the Orang-Utan, and the Bird of Paradise *London, 1869.*
Courtesy of Mitchell Library, State Library of New South Wales.

Notes

1   *The Outsiders: The Western Experience in India and China* Ann Arbor, 1977
2   'Traditionalism and Colonialism: Changing Urban Roles in Asia' *Journal of Asian Studies* 29, 1969, pp. 67-84; and *The Outsiders*
3   'Traditionalism and Colonialism'; *The Outsiders; Shanghai: Key to Modern China* Harvard Press, 1953; 'Port Cities and the Transformation of Asia: Colombo as Prototype' in D. Basu (ed.) *Colonial Port Cities in Asia* forthcoming 1988
4   This point is further developed in *Shanghai: Key to Modern China* and in my 'Port Cities and the Transformation of Asia'.
5   These points are further developed in the works previously cited, and in my 'The City as a Centre of Change: Western Europe and China' *Annals of the Association of American Geographers* 44, 1954, pp. 349-62; see also my 'Urbanization in Asia' *Ekistics* 21, 1966, pp. 8-17.

INDEX

Numbers in bold indicate illustrations

a. concepts historical events, etc.

air transport   3 (terminal), 23
automobiles   230

Battle of Plassey   **1757** 210
boatbuilding   60, 61, 67
Buddhist, Buddhism   174, 179, 183 (festivals)

caravan routes   209
Christians   109, 111, 118, 122,126
cities
   administrative cities   55, 130, 176
   ceremonial cities   34
   colonial cities   34-9, 179
   general cities   23, 37, 44, 45, 61 see also port cities, metropolitanisation
   hierarchy of cities   22-3, 34,130, 174-5, 207-22
   historiography on   30-2
   multiple nature of   228
   primate cities   4, 18, 22, 34, 175, 210, 215, 219
   the traditional Asian city   55, 57, 242
   urban culture   31
   urban planning   1
coal mining   146 (China), 215 (India)
compradors/collaborators   19, 143, 236
containerisation   17, 19, 21, 22, 45, 170, 189, 192, 198-206, 214

Cultural Revolution   148
cyclones   155, 159

dock workers, see ports, labour force

eurocentricity of sources and literature   8

First Opium War   16, 130
fishing   3, 60, 67, 106, 108, **229**
foreign concessions in China   130, 136, 139, 238-40, 241
forts   **41, 62**, 79-80, **81, 84,** 85, **88-9**, 100, 104, **105**, 109, 112 (map 8), 115, 117, 126, 177, 179, 227, **233**

Great Proletarian Revolution   16
Greater East Asia Co-Prosperity Sphere   148

Haggett's formula of ranking   215, 221
hajis   4
Hindus, Hinduism   12, 90, 176

inland transport   13, 40, 44, 129, 154, 157-8, 177, 191, 195, 200, 210, 228, 232, 234
inter-Asian trade in western hands   77, 80
Islam, Islamic   1, 8, 12, 17, 77, 90, 109, 117, 126, 195
life-style of expatriate Europeans   19, 37, 64, 120, 178-9, 181-3, 237; imitated by local 'arrivistes'   178-9, 181-3, 237
'littoral society'   18, 48, 174, 184
localisation   183

maritime archaeology   8
Meiji Restoration   6, 45
migration, migrants   8, 12, 45, 160, 165
modernisation   1, 4, 6, 16 see also technological change and transformation
monsoons in Indian Ocean   159, 195
Muslims see Islam

overseas trade, general   3, 6,14, 34, 57, 71, 104, 129-30, 227
organisation of trade in Makassar   102
'trading beaches'   104
trading commodities, general   12, 42, 57
   alcoholic beverages   155
   beans   57
   cardamom   209
   ceramics   60
   cinchona   164
   cinnamon   157, 164, 174, 177, 209
   cloves   57, 102
   coal   23, 144-6, 148, 161, 168
   cocoa   157, 164
   coconut oil   57, 164, 174
   coconuts   57
   coffee   157, 177
   coins   102
   copper   61
   copperware   61
   cotton   144, 160, 209
   dried fish   57

foodstuffs 57, 210
gasoline 146
gold 87
grain 87
guns 102, 104
honey 57
indigo 90
iron ore 23, 24, 215
ironware 61
kerosene 146
krises, swords 61
lead 61
mace 102
manufactured goods, general 102, 210
metals 87, 102, 210
minerals 82
nutmeg 102
oil (edible) 90
oil (petroleum) 3, 24, 148, 155, 168
opium 102, 104, 137, 155, 210
pearls **95**
peas 57
pepper 57, 209
plumbego 164
rice 12, 57, 90, 98, 100, 107, 160
rock phosphate 24
rubber 156, 157, 165
salt 57, 102
saltpetre 209
silk 144, 209
silver 87
spices 12, 82, 102, 107, 160, 209
sugar 57, 90
tea 157, 164, 165
textiles 57, 80, 82, 83, 90, 100, 113, 210
tin 61
tobacco 155
tortoise shell 106
wheat 144
woollens 87

passenger traffic 3, 26, 42, 161, 165
Pax Neerlandica 117
piracy, pirates 142, 227
port functions defined 11, 152-4, 188-93, 225, 229-30
 administration 98, 212
 'Anyport' model 39
 coaling stations 161, 168
 construction of harbours 4, 40, 137-41, 154, 162, 167, 170, 178, 192, 230-4
 docks see wharves, etc
 and economic development 189, 215, 220
 facilities 23, 34, 40, 87, 130, 137, 139, 152, 164, 188, 192, 196, 198, 212
 forelands 11, 39, 104, 152, 182, 193, 228, 234, 240
 gateway ports 152, 164, 193
 general ports 23, 202
 hierarchy of ports 11, 17, 19, 21, 22-23, 39, 48, 132, 148, 152, 157-8, 189, 193-8, 200-2, 212-5

 hinterlands 11, 39, 152, 156-8, 182, 188, 191, 193-8, 208, 228, 232, 236, 240
 jetty ports 23
 labour force (incl. dock workers, etc) 40-42, 48, 143, 165, 216-7, 225
 location 14, 21, 34, 98, 133, 154, 155, 158-9, 164, 191-3
 modernisation 6, 21, 23, 192
 'natural harbours' 17, 156, 160, 177, 192, 230-2
 oil bunkering 168
 outports 232
 pilotage, pilots 141-2, 225
 port selection 189, 191, 192, 234
 port systems 11, 13, 21-2, 37, 193-8, 208, 209-12
 ports of call 152, 161, 162, 164, 168-9
 provisioning 40, 83, 230
 shrinking of port sectors 23
 site 24, 34, 130, 136, 191-3, 197, 230-4
 traditional ports 21-2, 130
'port city' concept discussed 1-4, 9, 9-11, 13-14, 24-6, 29-53, 207-9, 223-45
'port city', methodologies for study of 9-14, 17, 21, 22, 24, 42, 192-3, 207-9, 243
 colonial port cities 6, 18, 32, 34, 42, 54, 240
 concubinage 64, 120
 cultural life 42, 44-5, 65, 225, 227
 cultural revitalisation 26, 183
 duties levied on trade 57-60, 82, 87, 92, 111-3, 123-4, 130, 137, 155
 economic development 212, 215-20, 225-7, 228
 economic groups, occupations, activity
  agency houses 156
  commerce, merchants 34, 35, 42, 44, 77-94 passim, 98-108 passim, 141-3, 155, 178, 22
  commercial elite 4, 44, 67, 178, 240
  commodity markets 55, 83, 100, 102
  communication industries 42, 143
  craftsmen 65-7, 69
  financial services, banks, etc 34, 39, 42, 44, 57, 83, 93, 142-3
  insurance 142, 228
  manufacturing 61
  maritime industries, general 11, 42-4, 230
  ship repair 142, 155, 157, 169, 218
  shipbuilding 42, 142, 218
  shipowning 39, 42, 137-41, 155-6
 entrepots 3, 4, 54, 57, 98, 152, 155-6, 165
 ethnic segregation 34, 55, 108-14, 115, 117-8, 121, 124-6, 130, 196, 237
 ethnicity 126
 extraterritoriality 136, 141, 143, 147, 237, 238-40, 241
 folklife, popular culture 44
 functional diversification 12, 22, 23, 34, 39, 42, 45, 142-3, 197-8, 225-7
 gateway function 121, 21, 32, 39, 40, 54-5, 130, 156, 184, 241-3
 hierarchy, 207-22
 hinterland, relationship with 4, 12, 18, 22, 34, 37, 39, 45, 48, 100, 107, 144, 173-87, 188-206, 228
 housing 42, 109, **110**, 114, 118-20, 178-9
 industrialisation, general 6, 16, 21, 22-3, 39, 142-7, 184, 193,

202, 216-20, 225-7, 242; in free trade zones 19, 148, 218
 labour force 12, 14, 42, 60-74, 144, 176, 216-20; wages and costs 61-4
 maritime (external) influences 21, 139, 173-4, 184, 188-206 passim, 208, 242
 maturity 19, 45
 mestizos 115, 118, 119, 121
 metropolitanisation, development into general cities 22, 23, 37, 208, 213-5, 215-20, 225
 mixed marriages 108, 115, 121, 124
 morphology, spatial development 14, 19, 22, 34, 35, 37, 100, 108-12, 178-82, 191, 192, 230; maps 2 (10, Jeddah), 4 (47, Yokohama), 8 (112, Makassar), 10 (135, Shanghai), 14 (201, Mombasa), 15 (203, Dar es Salaam)
 museums 44
 non-colonial port cities 6, 24, 45
 origins 13, 14, 16, 98
 political role 19, 45, 242
 port sector, defined 42
 power structure in pre-colonial port cities 55, 59-60, 64-71
 prostitution 64
 public health 42, 164-165
 regional hegemony 12, 18, 39, 75-96 passim, 98-102 see also hinterland, relations with
 security offered under western law, discussed 85-6, 92-3, 94, 108, 133-4, 134, 237-40
 slaves 63-4, 65, 67, 69, 115, 117, 119, 120
 social life 14-16, 19, 44-5, 108-126 passim, 136,174-87, 225, 236-7
 stripping away of political functions 19, 23, 183, 197-8, 202
 tertiarisation 23, 143, 176, 217, 220
 women 64, 108, 115, 118, 119, 120, 121, 124, 128
 zoological gardens 44
private trade
 East India Companies and 79, 80, 104-6, 107-8, 113
 servants of the EIC and 79, 87, 90, 93
 servants of the VOC and 123, 126
 'vrijburgers' (ex VOC servants) 107, 111, 113, 114, 115, 122

qianzhuang (traditional Chinese banks) 143

railways 21, 146, 148, 154, 158, 179, 200, 210, 234
replica voyages 8
river transport 129, 130, 137, 210, 234
road traffic 23, 158, 177-8, 179, 191, 195, 200, 210, 234
rubber industry, Malaya 156

seafaring (*see also* shipping and ships)
 Aceh 60
 Asian, modern 6-8
 Asian, traditional 8-9, 160, 195, 210, 240-1
shipping (*see also* seafaring and ships)
 general 3, 12, 13, 23, 55, 154, 188, 198, 232, 234
 bulk shipping 45, 202
 container shipping see containerisation
 African 204
 Asian 6, 38, 54-5, 77-92 *passim*
 British 137, 164
 Chinese 16, 106, 129-30, 137, 141-2
 European/western 12, 16, 137, 241

Indian   75, 80, 82-3, 86, 87, 90, 160
Japanese   6, 17, 137
Portuguese   65, 69
Shanghai   129-49 *passim*
Sri Lanka   40, 152-72 *passim*
ships
  clippers   137, 139, 141
  dhows   21, 192, 196
  galleys   65
  junks
    Chinese   16, 22, **31**, 57, 65, 106, 129, 130
    Javanese   57
  mail steamers   17, 154, 157, 159, 161, 164
  motorships   154, 168, 169, 176
  pancallang   108
  prahus   22, 119, 120, **231**
  sailing vessels (Asian)   **38, 78**
  sailing ships (western)   17, 159, 160, 195, 238
  steamships   17, 21, 137, 139, 154, 155, 159, 161-4,168, 169, 170, 173, 196, 218, 238, 241
silk industry   144
slaves
  as passengers   12, 102, 108, 113, 119, 121
  in port cities   63-4, 65, 67, 69, 115, 117, 119, 120
symbiosis of western and Asian business enterprise   8-9, 13, 75-96 *passim*, 155-6, 234, 236, 240, 242

technological change (*see also* modernisation and transformation)   12, 45, 65, 189, 198, 202, 208
textile mills   44, 142, 144
tin mining industry, Malaya   156
tourists   165-7
trade *see* overseas trade
trade diaspora   8
trading commodities *see* overseas trade, trading commodities
transformation, of Asia (*see also* modernisation)   242-3
Treaty of Beijing *(1860)*   137
Treaty of Bungaya *(1667)*   104, 107
Treaty of Shomonoseki (1895)   139, 142
Treaty of Tianjin (Tientsin, *1860*   137
treaty ports, China   130, 139, 238
trepang fishery   14, 106

'Vasco da Gama period'   6, 8, 234, 241, 242

War of Austrian Succession   90
western impact on Asia, discussed   6-9, 234-6
World War I   165, 167, 170, 240
World War II   170, 238, 240

b. geographical names

Abidjan   200
Aceh   55-7, **56**, 60, 61, 63, 64, 65, 67, 69, 82, 232, 240
Adam's Peak (Sri Lanka)   177
Aden   22, 27, 152, 161, 168, 204
Africa   4, 37, 45, 189, 192, 193, 196, 199, 200, 202, 204, 227
Ambon (Amboina)   **62, 123**
Amerapura   61
Americas, the   3, 26, 45
Amoy   106, 150
Ampenan   64
Amsterdam   53
Andhra Pradesh   214
Angkor   242
Anhui   130, 146
Anjaner   210
Antwerp   167
Anuradhapura   175, 242
Aqaba   24, 27
Arabia   55, 189
Arabian Sea   159, 160, 240
Arakan   57
Arcot   92, 94
Asia
  allegoric illustration, frontispiece   5
  general character of   3
  'maritime Asia'   3-4, 6-9, 16, 24, 26, 48, 129, 149
  port cities indicated   map 1 (2), map 17 (235)
  urbanisation   32-3, 34-5, 37, 51, 53, 54-5, 212-5, 217-20, 225-7, 241-3
Asian Seas, the   2 (map 1), 3, 21, 188
Assab   204
Assam   206
Association of southeast Asian Nations (ASEAN)   191
Atlantic Ocean   6, 8
Australasia (Australia and New Zealand)   39, 40
Australia   14, 17, 26, 27, 45, 155, 157, 159, 160, 161, 162, 167, 168, 196, 197, 199
Ava   55
Awaji   27
Ayutthaya   55, 57, 60, 63, 64, **224**, 242

Bagamayo   196
Baghdad   19
Bahrain   11, 28
Balambangan   57
Balasore   210
Bali   27, 64, 120, 128
Baltimore   39
Banda *see* Nera
Banggai   60
Bangkok   6, 24, 45, 63, 65, 230, 242
Banjarmasin   57, 67, 106
Bantaeng (Bonthain)   115
Banten (Bantam)   **25, 46**, 55, 57, 63, 67, **70**, 74, 241
Basra   6, 23, 27
Batavia (Jakarta)   6, **36**, 37, **41, 43**, 65, 74, 102, 106, 107, 108-9, 111, 113, 114, **116**, 121, 122, 123-4, 127, 128, **229, 233**, 237, 240, 242, 243
Battacilao   186
Bay of Bengal   8, 75, 82, 155, 159, 160
Beijing   19, 148, 242
Benadir coast   21
Bengal   57, 61, 87, 90, 94, 118, 127, 209, 214
Berbera   204
Beruwala   176
Bijapur   85

Bima   18
Birnlipatnam   77
Bira peninsula   60
Bombay   6, 11, 13, 17, 19, 22-3, 37, 44, 45, 152, 154-5, 156, 157, 159, 160, 161, 164, 171, 192, 195, 202, 209, 210, 212-20, 222, 230, 232, 237, 240, 242, 243
Bone   106-7, 122, 124
Borneo (*see also* Kalimantan)   60, 61, **68**
Boston (USA)   39, 45, 230
Brazil   197
Bremen   53
Bristol,   227
Britian *see* Great Britain
British Empire   40
Broach   209
Brunei   55, 57, 64, 102
Buenos Aires   45, 225, 232
Bulukumba   15
Burma   55, 61, 92, 155
Burundi   200
Busan   24

Cairo   55
Calcutta   13, 19, 22-3, 24, 32, 34, 37, 44, 45, 90, 152, 154, 155, 157, 159, 160, 161, 210, 212-20, 222, 225, 228, 230, 237, 240, 242, 243
Calicut   213, 234, 240
Canbay   209
Cambodia   55, 57
Canberra   45
Canton (*see also* Guangzhou)   8, 27, 106, 241, 242, 243
Cape of Good Hope   102, 159, 160
Cardiff   161, 167
Caribbean (region)   37, 227
Carnatic   13, 86, 87, 90, 94
Celebes *see* Sulawesi
Central Highlands (Sri Lanka)   177
Ceylon *see* Sri Lanka
Ch'ang An   242
Channel   193
Chaozhou   130
Charleston   227
Chennapatnam   79
China,
  coastal trade   129, 240-1
  general   3, 6, 16, 17, 19, 22, 51, 21, 52, 55, 65, 67, 90, 100, 102, 104, 129-51 *passim*, 155, 157, 159, 160, 161, 188, 189, 200, 227, 234, 236, 238, 240, 243
  'maritime China'   map 9 (134)
  overseas trade   6, 11, 16, 106, 240-1
Chittagong   210, 213
Cholon   37
Cochin   23, 199, 212-20, 222
Cochinchina   65
Colombo
  general   11, 14, 17-19, 21, 40-42, 44, 45, 48, 50, 53, 152-72 *passim*, 173-87 *passim*, 192, 230, 232, 234, 242, 243
  'Greater Colombo'   19, 175, 176, 183, 185
  transport network: map 11 (Indian Ocean, 153), map 12 (Sri Lanka, 163)

Coromandel coast 12, 13, 16, 21, 75-96 *passim* (with map 6 on 76), **84**, 159, 160, 209, 214
Cuddalore 80, 83, 85, 213
Cuxhaven 232

Dakar 200
Dalian (Dairen) 234, 242
Daqing 148
Dar es Salaam 19, 192, 196-8, 200, 202, 203 (map 15), 204
Deccan 87
Delhi 242
Demak 55
Deshima 8, 243
Devanapatnam 80
Dhanus Kodi 213
Diu 209
Dobbo (Aru Islands) **244**
Dodoma 198
Dompo 118
Dubai 202
Dummaladeniya 187
Dwarka 209

East Africa (*see also* Swahili coast) 3, 11, 21, 39, 75, 159, 188-206 *passim* incl. map 13 on 194), 209
East Indies (*see also* Indonesia) **5**, 14, 146
East Asia (*see also* Northeast Asia, or China, maritime) 8
Egypt 4, 167
Ekele 175
Ende 120
England *see* Great Britain
Ethiopia 204
Europe
  general 26, 160, 162, 167, 199, 200, 204, 227
  northern 55, 193
  urbanisation and urban studies 30
  European Economic Community 191

Far East *see* Northeast Asia
Fort St David, 79-80, 85, 86, 92
Fort St George (Madras) 79, 85, **88-9**
France 6, 13, 144
Fremantle 26, 45
Fushun 146
Fuzhou 130, 234

Galesong 15
Galle 17, 156-62, 170, 174, 177, 227, 234
Glasgow 44, 50
Goa **33**, 241
Golconda 82, 85, 86
Gowa 98, 100, 102-4, 106-7, 117
Gravesend 232
Great Britain 6, 13, 154, 160
'Greater Colombo' *see* Colombo
Grisek 55, 60, 61, 67
Guangdong (province) 148
Guangzhou (*see also* Canton) 23, 130, 141, 148, 150, 151
Gujerat 209, 240

Gulf (Arabian/Persian) 8, 20 (map 3), 21, 22, 28, 77, 154, 193, 232

Haldia 192, 212-20, 232
Hamburg 44, 50, 52, 53, 167, 232
Hankow 238
Havre-Hamburg range of ports 193
Hejaz 4, 6
Hobart 40
Holland *see* Netherlands
Hong Kong 16, 37, 42, 130, 148, 152, 156, 161, 167, 193, 202, 204, 227, 230, 242
Huangpu (Whangpoo), river 133, 135 (map 10), 136, 137, 139, 141, 144, 146
Hugli **91**, 210
Hyderabad 214

Iloilo 50, 53, 205
India
  general 3, 17, 19, 27, 34, 40, 51, 55, 69, 102, 113, 144, 154, 157, 159, 160, 161, 167, 169, 192, 193, 195, 199, 200, 207-23, 227, 228, 234, 237, 238, 240, 243
  ports and port system of 21, 22-4, 75-96 (Coromandel, incl. map 6 on 76), 171, 207-23 (incl. map 16 on 211)
  seafarers 8
  urban system of 207-23
Indian Ocean 3, 8, 17, 19, 21, 24, 39, 40, 53, 80, 83, 150, 153 (map 11), 154, 155, 156-64, 168, 170, 172, 173, 188, 192, 195, 202, 204, 205, 240
Indochina 155, 241
Indonesia (*see also* East Indies) 34, 98, 155, 192, 193, 243
Indus, river 240
Iraq 6, 19, 24, 28
Irrawaddy, river 61
Islamabad 45
Istanbul 225

Jaffna **166**, 175
Jakarta (*see also* Batavia) 45, 225, 237
Jalesar 210
Jambi, river 61
Jambi, town 57, 63
Japan 4, 6, 17, 21, 27, 45, 51, 55, 102, 130, 133, 139, 142, 146, 147-8, 18, 189, 193, 200, 202, 205, 236, 237, 241, 243
Java 55, 57, 60, 61, 100, 102, 111, 234, 241
Jeddah 1-4, 6, 9, 10 (map 2), 16, 22, 24, 26, 28, 90, 192, 193, 195, 225
Jeneberang, river 100
Jiangsu 130, 144, 146
Jiangxi 146
Jinji 80, 85
Jogjakarta 127, 242
Johor 57, 102

Kaifeng 242
Kalaniya 187
Kalimantan (*see also* Borneo) 100
Kalutara 158
Kandla 212-20

Kandy 158, 174, 175, 177-8, 179, **180**, 183-4, 186, 187, 242
Karachi 19, 23, 202, 212, 214, 215, 242
Karikal 83
Karimata 60
Katagarama 175, 176, 185
Katunayake 175
Kenya 189, 192, 196-8, 200, 204, 206
Kerala 214
Kharg Island 23
Kilindini Harbour (Mombasa) 21, 196, 197, 201 (map 14)
Kilwa 196, 197
Kobe 24, 44, 193, 242
Kolontota 175
Korea 8, 130, 243
Kotte 19, 174, 177, 183
Kuala Lumpur 19
Kuwait 23, 27, 28, 44, 204, 225
Kyoto 242

Lagos 200
Lahiri-Bunder 209
Lamu 195, 197
Latin America 37, 189, 227
Launceston 40
Lesser Sunda islands (Nusa Tenggara) 100, 119
Ligor (Nakhon Sithammarat) 55
Liverpool 50, 167
Lombok 64
London 40, 167, 225, 230, 232
Lothal 240
Lübeck 227

Ma'alla (Aden) 22
Macau **131, 140,** 241
Madagascar 8, 27, 159
Madras 13, 22-3, 32, 34, 45, 79-96 *passim*, 88-9, 154, 160, 161, 165, 192, 202, 209, 210, 212-20, 230, 232, 234, 236, 238, 241, 242
Madura 82
Madurai 34
Makassar (*see also* Ujung Pandang) 11, 12, 14-16, 55, 57, 63, 65-7, 97-128 (incl. map 7 on 99, map 8 on 112), **105, 110**, 232, 237, 242, 243
Melabar coast, **78**, 87, 159, 209, 240, 242
Malay world (*see also* Southeast Asia, maritime world of) 3, 53, 129, 155
Malaya 92, 155, 156, 227, 234, 241
Malaysia 19, 192, 193, 198
Malindi 195
Maluku *see* Moluccas
Manchuria 228
Manda Bay 202, 206
Mandalay 242
Mandar 121
Mangalore 212-20, 222
Manggarai 119
Manila 45, 55, 63, 90, 202, **226**, 230, 241, 242
Maputo 204
Marmagao 23-4, 212-20
Maros 107, 115

Martaban 63
Masulipatnam 77, 83, 86
Matara 158
Mataram 57, 67
Mauritius 159
Mediterranean 45, 227
Meimbun (Sulu Islands) **239**
Mekka 4
Melaka, river 69
Melaka, town/city 55, 57, **58-9**, 63, 64, 69, 74, 82, 98, 100, 102, 127, 192, 227, 241
Melbourne, 161
Middle East *(see also* Southwest Asia) 55, 160, 188, 195, 200, 202
Mina al Ahmadi 24
Minangkabau 60
Mindanao town 69
Mirigama 187
Mocha **7**, 8, 90
Moluccas 8, 57, 100, 102, 107
Mombasa 21-22, 192, 195-8, 200, 201 (map 14), 204
Montevideo 167
Montreal 53
Morowak Korale 177
Mount Lavinia 179
Mozambique 192, 204
Mughal Empire 80, 82
Mukden 146
Muscat 27, 53
Mylapore *see* San Thome

Nacala 192
Nagapatnam 80, 82, 87, 92
Nagara 61, 67
Nagasaki 6, 241, 242
Nagore 87
Nairobi 198, 200
Nakhon Sithammarat (Ligon) 55
Nanjing 146
Narbonne 227
Nera, Banda **66**
Netherlands *also* Holland) 13, 27, 111, 112, 113, 128
New Delhi 45
New York 23, 39, 40, 53, 167, 225, 230
New Zealand *(see also* Australasia) 214
Nhava Sheva 202
Nigeria 205
Ningbo 130
Niuzhuang 130
Nobiru 28, 205
North America 133, 200, 204, 227
North Sea 193
Northeast Asia *(also* East Asia *or* Far East) 3, 14, 22, 40, 80, 142, 154, 155, 160, 161, 162, 168, 199, 241, 243
Nusa Tenggara *see* Lesser Sunda islands
Nuwara Eliya 179

Oman 27, 196
Organisation of Petroleum Exporting Countries (OPEC) 191

Orissa 214
Oruwela 175

Pacific Ocean 6
Pagan 61, 242
Pahang 55, 57, 102
Pakistan 197, 198, 200, 202, 215
Paleacat 13, 80, **81**, 82, 83, 85, 87, 92, 93, 236
Palembang 55, 57
Palk Strait 159, 160
Pangani 196
Paradeep 23-4, 192, 212-20
Paris 40, 136
Pasai 55, 57, 69
Patani 55, 57, 61, 64, 102, 241
Pearl Harbor 147
Pechili 129
Pegu 5, 57
Perak 61
Periaman 60
Perth 45
Philadelphia 39, 225, 230, 232
Philippines 8, 45, 159, 241
Plymouth 27
Pnompenh 55
Polombangkeng 115
Pondichery 13, 77, 82-3, 85, 86, 92, 93, 161
Port Kelang 192, 202
Porto Novo 83, 86, 90, 213
Puhar 240, 241
Pulau Batam 202

Qatar 28
Qingdao (Tsingtao) 234, 241, 242
Qinhuangdao 148
Quezon City 45

Rander 209
Rangoon 26, 45, 64, 164
Ratmalana 175
Red Sea 1, 4
Rhapta 195
Riyadh 19
Rotterdam 44, 53, 167
Rwanda 200

Sabaragamuwa 177, 186
Sadraspatnam 83, 87
Saigon 37, 156, 161, 242
Salem 227
Saleyar 115
San Francisco 53, 225
San Thome 13, 86, 90, 92
Sapugaskanda 175
Satgaon 210
Savannah 227
Sattahip 192, 205
Saudi-Arabia 3, 19, 28, 192
Scotland 44
Shandong (Shantung) 129, 130, 146

Shanghai 6, 14, 16, 23, 24, 32, 34, 53, 129-51 (incl. map 9 on 134, and map 10 on 135), 152, 161 192, 202, 225, 227, 230, 237, 238-9, 240, 242, 243
Shantou 130
Shantung *see* Shandong
Shaoxing 130
Shenyang 148
Shenzhen 148
Si Satchanalai (Suwankhulok) 60
Siam *(see also* Thailand) 55, 57, 64, 65
Sichuan 130
Sind 215
Singapore 17, 26, 28, 37, 44, 53, 129, 152, 154, 155-6, 157, 161, 167, 193, 195, 202, 204, 230, 242
Sitawaka 174, 177
Somalia 204
Somnath 209
Soppeng 106
South Asia 3, 14, 189, 195, 236, 243
Southampton 44
Southeast Asia *(see also* Malay world), maritime world of 3, 11-12, 14, 21, 22, 27, 37, 49 (map 5), 54-74, 75, 79, 82, 90, 98-108 (incl. map 7 on 99), 127, 128, 130, 133, 147, 155, 157, 189, 199, 200, 227, 232, 236, 237, 240, 243
Southwest Asia *(see also* Middle East) 3, 6, 75, 87, 90, 188, 189, 195
Soviet Union 6, 22, 146
Sri Jayawardenapura 19, 45, 183
Sri Lanka 17-19, 40, 45, 48, 53, 154, 156-64 (incl. map 12 on 163), 170, 172, 173, 174-87 *passim*, 237
Srivijaya 98
Steamer Point (Aden) 22
Strait of Malacca 159, 227
Straits Settlements 155
Suez 17, 159, 160
Suez Canal 17, 139, 154, 155, 161, 162-4, 174, 178, 192
Sukhothai 60
Sulawesi 60, 98, 100, 104, 106, 119
Sumatra 57, 61, 155
Sumbawa 121
Sumer 240
Sunga Puar 61
Surabaya 55, 60, 61, 67, 69
Surakarta 67
Surat 8, **15**, 87, 92, 209, 227, 232
Suwankhalok (Si Satchanalai) 60
Suzhou 130, 227
Swahili coast *(see also* East Africa) 3, 8, 28, 195
Sydney 22, 23, 26, 44, 45, 161

Taiwan 37, 227
Takalar 107
Tamil-Nadu 214
Tanga 196
Tanjore 82, 87
Tanzania 19, 189, 192, 197-8, 200, 202
Taprobane 159
Tapti, river 209
Tasmania 40
Tellicherry 213

Tenasserim 61, 92
Ternate 55, **101**, 102, 232
Thailand (*see also* Siam) 6, 12, 60, 155, 192
Thames, river 230
Tianjin (Tientsin) 26, 130, 132, 230, 232, 242
Tidore 102
Tientsin *see* Tianjin
Timor 57
Tokyo 11, 23, 192, 225, 237, 243
Tondi 77
Travancore 165
Trincomalee 18, 156, 157, 161, 234
Tsingtao *see* Qingdao
Tuban 67
Turawan 60
Tuticorin **95**, 165, 212-20

Uganda 200
Ujung Pandang (Makassar) 45, 97
United Nations 191
United States of America 6, 22, 30, 36, 133, 144
Upeh 69
Uva 186

Vancouver 27
Venice 225
Vietnam 236
Vishakhapatnam 212-20
Vlissingen (Flushing) 121

Wajo 106-7, 117, 122
Wenzhou 241
West Africa 3, 200, 232
West Asia *see* Southwest Asia
Weteringen 121
Woosung 139, 232

Yangzi Kiang, river 16, 129, 130, 131
Yantai 130, 146
Yokohama 6, 47 (map 4), 161, 230, 241, 242, 243

Zambia 200
Zanzibar 26, 28, 28, 192, 196
Zayton (Zhuanzhou) 241
Zeelandia 37
Zhejiang 130
Zhuanzhou *see* Zayton

c. names of persons, companies, ethnic groups, etc.

Agung, sultan of Mataram 67
Albuquerque 69
Arasaratnam, S. 9, 12, 13, 16, 21, 209, 214, 236, 240
Aru Palakka 124
Aungier, Sir Gerald 154
Ambonese **103**, 111, 115, 118

Americans 195
Arabs
  general 1, 196, 240
  in India and further East ('Moors') **43**, 53, 175, 176, 177
Armenians 87-90, 92

Bajau (sea nomads) 98
Balandier, G. 34
Balinese 120
Bandanese 115
Barbosa, Duarte 69
Basnaike Nilame 176
Basu, Dilip Kumar 4, 32, 35
Baughman, James 52
Bengalis 70, 175
Bird, James 39, 40, 205
Blussé, Leonard 37
Borahs 175
Bourdieu, Pierre 179
Boxer, C. R. 108
Boyed & Co., shipyard at Shanghai 142
Braudel, Fernand 55
British
  expatriates 19, 177-83
    at Shanghai 136, 137
    on Sri Lanka 177-83
British (English), East India Company [E/C],
  general 104-6, 130, 154, 209-10, 238
  in Coromandel 13, 34, 75-96 *passim*
British India Steam Navigation Company 154, 157
Broeze, Frank 4, 9-11, 19, 22, 207
Bugis, Buginese 104, 106, 109-10, 115, 118, 119, 121, 122, 126
burghers (descendants of the Dutch on Sri Lanka) 175, 176, 237
Butterfield, Swire & Co., Shanghai 137

Ceylon Rifle Regiment 179
Ceylon Social Reform Society 182
Ceylonese 18-19
Chartered Mercantile Bank of India, London and China 142
Chettis 53, 175
Chicago school of sociology 30
China Merchants' Steam Navigation Company, Shangai 137, 141
China Navigation Company, Shanghai 137
Chinese
  in Makassar 100, 102, 104, 106, 108-9, 111, 113, 114, 115-26 *passim*
  overseas 53, 61, 63, 64, 65, 103, 106
  peranakan (Chinese converted to Islam) 115, 118, 124, 126
  in Shanghai 129-30, 136-7
  in Singapore 44, 53, 155-6
  in Thailand 12
  working with westerners in China 16, 143, 240
Chiu, T. N. 42
Chulias 86
Coen, J. P. 107
Colombo Academy 178, 179

Colombo Club 181
Colts Cricket Club (Colombo) 182
Coomaraswamy, Ananda 182
Crawfurd, John 61, 65
Curtin, Philip D. 8

Dampier, William 69
Danish East India Company 79
Davis, John 60
De Abrew, Peter 182
De Silva, C. R. 174
Delaware conference 39
Delprat, D. A., Amsterdam shipowner 53
Dent & Co.,Shanghai 141
Dharmapala, Anagarika 182
Dharmasena, K. 9, 11, 17-18, 21, 40-2, 173, 176, 178
Durava, Sinhalese caste 182
Dutch
  general 16, 55, 61, 65, 67, 157, 242
  'Mardijkers' **36**, 109
  at Makassar 97-128 *passim*
  mestizos (see also burghers) 115, 118, 119, 121
  on Sri Lanka 175, 177
  vrijburgers (ex-VOC servants) 107, 111, 113, 114, 115, 118, 121, 122, 123
Dutch East India Company [Vereenidge Oost-Indische compagnie, VOC]
  general 14, 113
  in Batavia **41**, 102, 108-9, 113, 114, 121, 123, 242
  in Coromandel 13, 75-96 *passim*
  Gentlemen Seventeen 113, 114
  in Japan 242
  in Makassar 14-16, 97-128 *passim*
  in the Moluccas 102
  in Surat **15**
  on Taiwan 37
Dyster, Barrie 40

East India Companies (*see also* British India Co., Danish East India Co., Dutch East India Co., French East India Co.)
  general 6, 9, 209
  in Coromandel 13, 76-96 *passim*
Eng, Robert Y. 9, 14, 16
English (*see also* British) 61, 87-90
Erasmus University, Rotterdam 44
ESCAP (United Nations Economic and Social Council for Asia and the Pacific) 173

Fachang Hao, shipyard at Shanghai 142
Fang Juzan, Chinese entrepreneur at Shanghai 142
Farmham & Co., shipyard at Shanghai 142
Farsi, Mohamed Said, major of Jeddah 1-3, 9, 16, 26
Finlay, James & Co., agency house 52
Forbes, William, & Co., agency house 142
Fortune, Robert 129
Fox, Richard 30, 32
French
  at Saigon 37, 156
  at Shanghai 136, 139, 142
French East India Company, in Coromandel 13, 75-96 *passim*

Galle Face Hotel, Colombo   181
Germans
   in northern Europe   55
   at Shanghai   142
Goyigama, Sinhalese caste   182
Greeks   55, 240
Guillaume, X.   37
Gujeratis   70, 100, 102
Gutzlaff, Charles   130

Hadhramis   53
Han dynasty   240
Hastings, EIC Governor of Madras   93
Hong Kong and Shanghai Banking Corporation   142
Horvath, R. J.   34
Hoyle B. S.   9, 11, 13, 21-2, 39, 40, 75, 159, 209, 214
Hugh Lindsay, steamer   154

Ibn Khaldun   1
Ibn Muhammad Ibrahim   64
Imhoff, G. W. Baron van   107
Ince Buang, merchant at Makassar   109
Ince Mulut, captain of Malays at Makassar   111
Ince Sadulla, customs *pachter* at Makassar   123-4
Ince Tjoeka, captain of the Malays at Makassar   124
Inchcape Group   52
Indians
   Muslim ('Moors')   109-10, 115, 175, 176
   overseas   53, 90, 104, 111, 237
Indo-China Steam Navigation Company   137
Iskander Muda, sultan of Aceh   65

Jamsetjee Jeejeebhoy, Bombay entrepreneur   53
Janata Vimukti Perumana   174
Japanese   137, 141, 142, 148, 227-8
Jardine Matheson & Co,   6, 47, 52 *The Thistle and the Jade*), 137, 141, 142
Javanese   25, 69, 98, **116**
Jayewardene, J. R.   187

Karaeng Tutolo, Makassar   120
Karava, Sinhalese caste   182
Kidwai, Atiya Habeeb   9, 11, 19, 21, 22-4
King, Anthony D.   4, 35
Konvitz, Josef W.   51
Kooiman, Dick   37
Kook, Jan Adolph, burgher of Makassar   119

Langhorn, EIC Governor of Madras   93
Leur, J. van   60
Lewandowski, Susan   32, 34, 35
Li Hongzhang, Chinese statesman   137
Lijauko, captain of the Chinese at Makassar   124
Lindsay, Hugh Hamilton   130
Lobe, Karl   42

Macrae, EIC Governor of Madras   93
Makdum Nina, merchant of Porto Novo   86
'Malabars'   175

Malays   65, 98, 100, 102, 104, 108, **110**, 111, 122, 123, 124-6, 175, 179
Mandar   106
Marathas   80, 85, 86, 232
'Mardijkers'   **36**, 109
Marshall, Peter   37
Master, EIC Governor of Madras   93
McCoy, Alfred W.   53
McGee, T. G.   34
McPherson, Kenneth   4, 9-11, 19, 22, 207
Melchers & Co., Shanghai   137
Messageries Impériales/Maritimes   161
Mohammad, the prophet   121
Moorhouse, Geoffrey   13
'Moors' (*see also* Arabs, in India and further East, and Indians, Muslim)   **43**, 175, 176, 177, 237
Mughals   80, 82, 85
Mumford, Lewis   50
Murphey, Rhoads   4, 9, 24, 32, 34, 130

'Natookoteyas'   175
Niopanlong, Chinese merchant at Makassar   119
Nippon Yusen Kaisha   53

O'Connor, R.   55
Ongwatko, captain of the Chinese at Makassar   124
Oosterhof, J. L.   37
Oriental Banking Corporation   142
Othman, caliph   4

'Parewas'   175
Park, Robert E.   30
Parsis   175
Pathans (Perso-Afghans)   86
Pearson, M.N.   18, 48, 174
Peninsular & Oriental Steam Navigation Company (P & O)   137, 154, 157, 159, 160, 161
peranakan (Chinese converted to Islam)   115, 118, 124, 126
Phoenicians   55
Pigou, W. H., EIC official   130
Pirenne, Henri   30
Pires, Tomé   57, 61
Pitt, EIC Governor of Madras   93
Portuguese
   black, Asian, 'Indo-Portuguese',   **33**, 61, 65, 108
   general   6, 18, **33**, 63, 65, 77, **78**, 82, 86, 87, 100, 108, 120, 157, 177, 195-6, 209, 210, 242

Qing dynasty   130, 139, 141
Quepodang, captain of the Chinese at Makassar   124

Redfield, Robert   32
Reeves, Peter   4, 9-11, 19, 22, 207
Reid, Anthony   9, 11-12, 14, 240
Rigdeway, Governor of Ceylon   164
Rimmer, P. J.   39, 214
Roberts, Michael   9, 14, 18-19, 48, 237
Romans   240
Ross, Robert   35-6
Royal College, Colombo   179

Royal Navy (Great Britain)   155
Rudolph, Wolfgang   44
Russell & Co., Shanghai   137, 141, 142, 143

Saint Thomas' College, Colombo   178, 179
Salagama, Sinhalese caste   182
Santa Cruz, University of California at, conference   32-5, 53
Scandinavians   6
Schinckel, Max von, Hamburg business man   53
Schouten, Joost   60
Shanghai Cotton Mill Company   144
Shanghai Dock and Engineering Company   142
Shanghai Steam Navigation Company   137, 143
Shanghai Tug & Lighter Company   137
Shanghai Union Steam Navigation Company   137
Sheng Xuanhuai, Chinese entrepreneur at Shanghai   137
Sindhis   175
Sinhalese   18-19, 174-9
Smith, Michael Peter   30
Solomon, Robert   40
Southern Manchurian Railway Company   146
Spanish   102, 242
Speelman, Cornelis   98, 104, 109, 117, 124
Stoianovich, T.   40, 45
Straits Steamship Company   155
Sung dynasty   241
Sutherland, Heather   9, 11, 12, 14, 240
Swain, Bijay K.   212
Symes, M.   61

Tagore, Dwarkanath, merchant at Calcutta   53
Tamils
   traditionally living on Sri Lanka (Ceylon Tamils)   18, 175, 176, 237
   recent immigrants in Sri Lanka   18, 42, 165, 176, 237
T ang dynasty   240
Tang Tingshu, Chinese entrepreneur at Shanghai   137
Tanjong Pagar Dock Company, Singapore   155
Tata, Jamsetji Nusserwanji, Bombay entrepreneur   52
Telkamp, Gerard   35-6
Tindall, Gillian   13
Tönnies, F.   30
Toraja   106
Tunijallo, king of Makassar   66
Tunipalangga, king of Makassar   65-6
'Tupas' *see* 'Mardijkers'

United Arab Shipping Company   28
University of California *see* Santa Cruz
University of Commerce, Kobe   44
University of Glasgow   44
University of Hamburg   44
University of Southampton   44
University of Sydney   4

Venetians   55
Vliet, Jeremias van   60
VOC, Vereenigde Oost-Indische Compagnie *see* East India Companies, Dutch

Wadia family, Bombay 155
Wahampura, Sinhalese caste 182
Walchand Hirachand, Bombay entrepreneur 52
Wang Jingwei 148
Wang Jingyu 143
Warorese 111

Weber, Max 30, 50-1, 55
Weigend, Guido 39
Whangpoo Conservancy Board 141
Wheelock & Co., Shanghai 137
Wiegand, Heinrich, Bremen entrepreneur 53
Winter, EIC Governor of Madras 93

Wirth, Louis 30
Wolters, O. W. 55

Xu Run, Chinese entrepreneur at Shanghai 137

LIBRARY OF DAVIDSON COLLEGE